BUYING A PROPERTY...

Then contact DFX Interactive

Visit our website for the ULTIMATE in property viewing, with our 360° panoramic viewer, for a virtual tour.

What is a VIRTUAL TOUR?

DFX Interactive virtual tours are full 360° panoramic views of the interior & exterior of the property. They immerse you in a space, giving you the same experience as if you were actually there.

You can look left, right, up, down & even zoom in & out, all without leaving the comfort of your chair.

Order your VIRTUAL TOUR Today!

Modern estate agencies have the facility to Email clients immediately

Franchise opportunities exist, for the right people, in a number of departments in France.

DFX INTERACTIVE FRANCE

Le Bourg, 17150 St. Thomas de Conac France

Tel: 00 33 5 46 700 888

Email: david@dfxfrance.com

www.dfxfrance.com

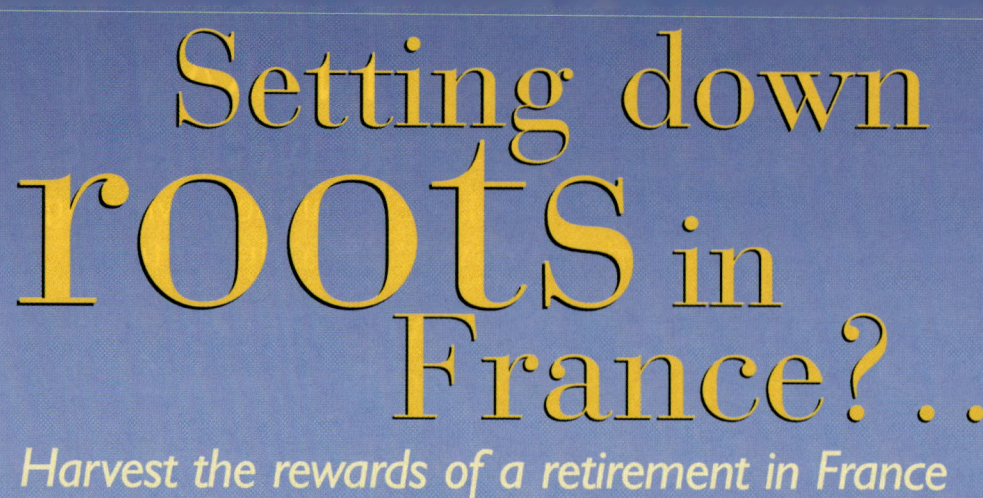

Setting down roots in France?...

Harvest the rewards of a retirement in France with Siddalls to nurture your financial affairs.

How can I pay less tax?... and protect my family from French inheritance laws?
How will my pension be treated in France?

We provide the solutions to give you peace of mind for a secure retirement.

For more information and our free booklet 'Help with Living in France', please contact us…

Siddalls
…all you need to know

INDEPENDENT FINANCIAL
ADVISERS & INVESTMENT BROKERS

Lothian House, 22 High Street, Fareham, Hampshire PO16 7AE
Telephone 01329 288641 Facsimile 01329 281157
france@johnsiddalls.co.uk www.siddalls.net

French Property
buying guide 2003

Châteaux & Belles Demeures

Southern France

Established 14 years

DORDOGNE (24)
Elegant XIXth C. Directoire Logis on edge of very pretty village. C.H. 2nd Dwelling. 2 courtyards, Pigeonnier, Caretaker's Hse. Barns. 16 Ha of park, meadow & woodland. 80 nut trees. Poplar Grove. Very beautiful ensemble.
Ref: E6-4061   **Price: 954,000€**

AUDE (11)
Superb XV/XVIth C. listed Medieval Château. 35 mins Toulouse. 45 Mins Carcassonne. 12 Ha grounds, woods, cultivated land. 4 Receps. 9 Beds. 5 Baths Original features. High Ceilings. 3 houses & outbuildings. Pigeonnier. Pyreneen views.
Ref: B5-6390   **Price; 1,850,000€**

GERS (32)
Charming renovated XVIIIth C. Manoir 100 kms from Toulouse, 5 kms to village with shops. 4 Receps, 7 Beds, 4 Baths. Farmhouse to restore. 2 Gites. Store House. Many original features. Large Pool. Terraces, 11 Ha. Suitable for B & B or Gites. Peaceful position.
Ref: C9-407   **Price: 857,000€**

GARD (30)
Magnificent XVIth C. Château, lake and pool on a hillside with views. 3.2 Ha. Restored. C.H. 1000m² habitable space. 5 Receps. 15 Beds. 9 Baths. Original Features. Listed in part. 15 chalets concealed from Château in grounds.
Ref: H8-1931   **Price: 7,000,000€**

Specialising in Châteaux throughout France
Châteaux, Manoirs, Vineyards, Country Houses, Mas, Bastides & Villas in Southern France
(South West, Midi Pyrénées, Languedoc Roussillon and Provence/Côte d'Azur)

Tel: **+44(0)20 7384 1200**   Fax: **+44(0)20 7384 2001**

Email: **french@sifex.co.uk**

www.sifex.co.uk

The ultimate guide to buying a French property

French Property buying guide 2003

EDITOR
ROWENA MEDLOW

French Property Buying Guide 2003

Compiled, edited and designed by
Merricks Media Ltd
Charlotte House
12 Charlotte Street
Bath BA1 2NE
Tel: 01225 786800
m.guides@merricksmedia.co.uk

Managing Director **Lisa Doerr**
Editor **Rowena Medlow**
Production Editor **Casey Nolan**
Researcher **Helen Binns**
Art Director **Jon Billington**
Advertisement Designer **Steve Mallinson**

Sales Director **Keith Burnell**
Sales Executive **Greg Martin**

All rights reserved. No part of this work may be reproduced or used in any form or by any means, electronic or mechanical, including photocopying, recording or any information storage and retrieval system, without the prior written permission of the publishers.

While every care has been exercised in the compilation of this guide, neither the authors, editors nor publishers accept any liability for any factual inaccuracies or for any financial or other loss incurred by reliance placed on the information contained in *French Property Buying Guide 2003*.

The exchange rate used when the sterling price equivalent was calculated was 1.6 euros to the pound, and has been rounded to the nearest five pounds.

m guide is a trademark of Merricks Media Ltd

Cover image © E Brenckle/V.M
Contents image thanks to Simply Travel
Price Guide Contents and Regions Contents images thanks to Something Special
Directory Contents image © Wallis Photothèque
Touring Map © Bartholomew Ltd 2002
Reproduced by permission of HarperCollins Publishers
Administrative Map © Merricks Media Ltd

Printed and bound in Croatia by Zrinski d.d
First published in the United Kingdom in 2002 by Merricks Media Ltd

Copyright © 2002 Merricks Media Ltd
(excepting Buying Guide and The Regions © 2002 Rowena Medlow)

ISBN 0-9543523-0-0
British Library Cataloguing in Publication Data
A catalogue record for this book is available from the British Library

ABOUT THE EDITOR

Rowena Medlow has been passionate about France since the first time she sampled rural French life at its best as a child in Dordogne – sleepy hamlets, fragrant markets, milk and eggs fresh from the local farmer.... Since then, she has travelled widely in the country, from the Provençal Alps to the beaches of Vendée, and also spent a year in Paris while studying modern languages at university. Rowena has edited *French Magazine* since its launch in 2001, and writes and talks regularly about the French property market and buying homes in France, as well as about the country's food and wine.

EDITOR'S ACKNOWLEDGEMENTS

Throughout my research for this book, I was captivated by the vivid tales of so many of the British who are now living either full- or part-time in France today. I have much to thank those who have so willingly shared their experiences and passed on their tips.

I would also like to offer particular thanks to the following individuals and companies for their invaluable assistance in the preparation of the guide:

Delphine Arker of Sifex

Phillippa Bowman of Live France Group

Andrew Burrows of Burrows-Hutchinson

Peter Collins of Burgundy Property Specialists

John Deeley of Siddalls

Sébastien Duquesne of Abbey National

David Howard of Devon International

Mike Johnson of London & European Title Insurance Services

Lisa McGee

Ian Morris

Graham Platt of Fox Hayes

Russell-Cooke Solicitors

Elisabeth Toffaloni of Magellan

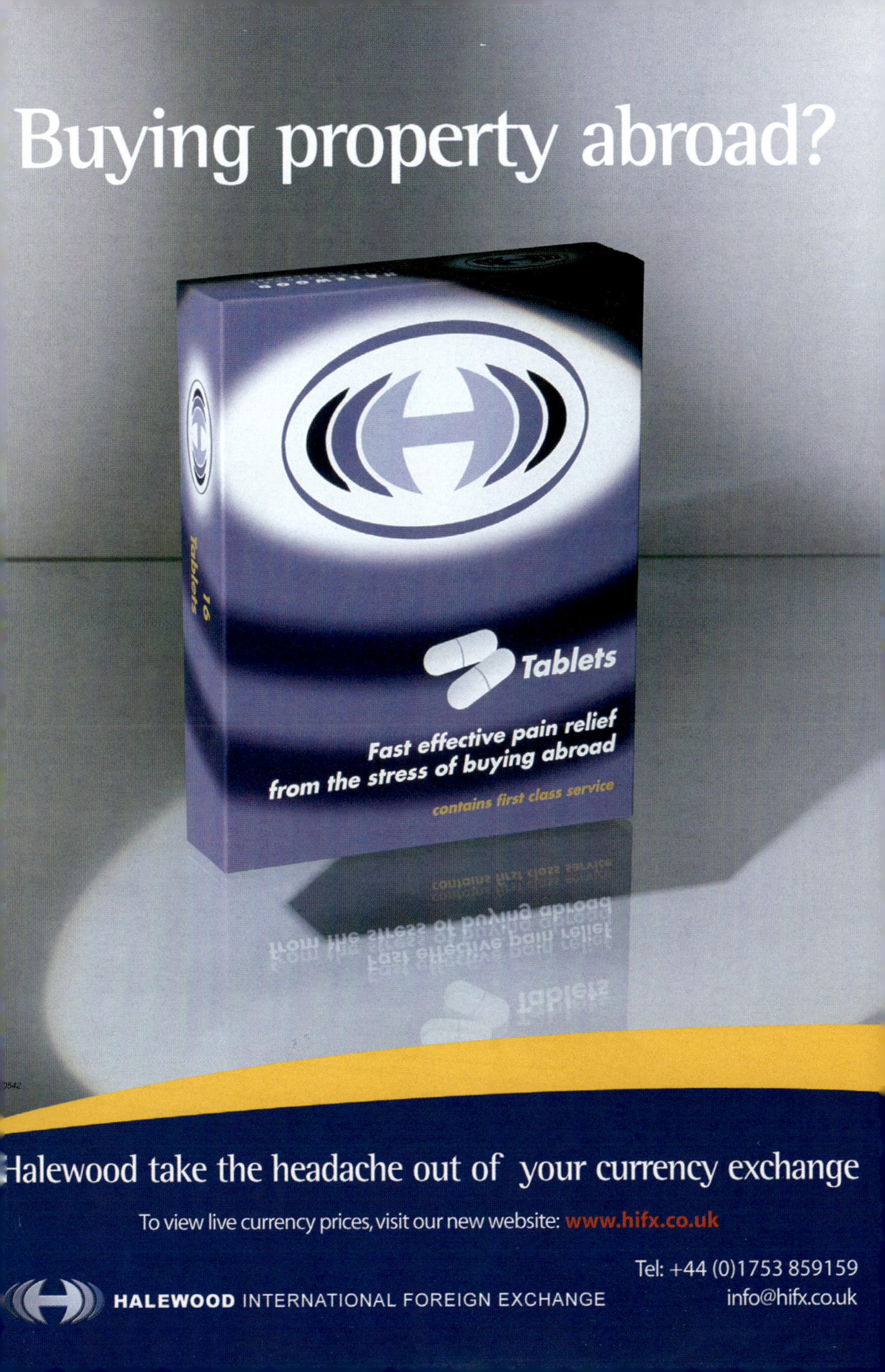

Buying property abroad?

Halewood take the headache out of your currency exchange

To view live currency prices, visit our new website: **www.hifx.co.uk**

Tel: +44 (0)1753 859159
info@hifx.co.uk

 **HALEWOOD** INTERNATIONAL FOREIGN EXCHANGE

CONTENTS

Introduction   15

Buying Guide   16

The Regions   40

Price Guide   106

Directory   368

afeelingforfrance

Buy and own a property in France with complete peace of mind. With the experience, knowledge and skills, we are the company to help you.

London office
All properties on-line
VEF offices in France
Qualified legal team to secure your purchase

www.vefuk.com
e: info@vefuk.com
t: 020 7515 8660

Think France. Think vef

INTRODUCTION

Dreaming about owning a home in the sun has become a national pastime and, of all the favourite places we dream about, France is a firm favourite. But what draws so many of us to the other side of the Channel for a second home or a place to retire to? Is it the promise of clement weather, good food and wine? Or is it the idea of a lifestyle that can really allow us to get away from it all? Or maybe it's the beautiful country itself…?

France provides such a diversity of landscapes that in some places it is not inconceivable to go skiing in the morning and end the day swimming in the sea. But as well as snow and sand, there are mountainous forested massifs, undulating hills and valleys, lakes, meandering rivers and canals, wide estuaries, rocky cliffs and acres of meadowland.

Most foreign buyers concentrate on the resorts with access to world-class skiing or sun-drenched Mediterranean beaches, but many of us crave the simplicity of a quiet village hidden away from the hustle and bustle of the glamourous holiday spots. These rural options offer a friendly welcome in the village, tranquillity, a slow pace of life and local markets offering the freshest of produce.

To make finding your ideal region a little simpler, there is a series of regional profiles in this guide (see pages 40 to 105). When you read them, take the opportunity to discover new parts of France you may not have considered before. These areas are increasingly easily accessible – often thanks to new direct budget flight routes to regional towns. Areas that once would have taken a packed car 12 hours on the road to access, can now be reached from various UK airports in an hour and a half, meaning you can realistically commute to and from your French home. Deep in the heart of France is where the best value is to be found, and this really sets French property apart from the British. For the price of a one-bedroom flat in London, a large country house with unspoilt views and even its own lake can be yours.

If you're looking for a home with a sense of history and character, whether an 18th-century château or a run-down farmhouse, these rural enclaves are rich in period properties. Countrywide there's a plethora of traditional styles to choose from – be it a modest, granite-built Breton cottage or Provençal stone *mas*. And houses often come with outbuildings that are ideal for transforming into guest accommodation, so owners can make a little money from their property.

All the plus points about buying a home in France have obviously made French properties extremely popular of late, and when you talk to agents you may get swept up in the fast turnover of properties and feel you must make a hasty decision, maybe at the end of a whistle-stop house-hunting tour. But bear in mind that after buying in haste you may be left repenting at leisure, so choose carefully and take time to contemplate this life-changing decision. You will then find you have plenty of time to relax, enjoy freshly-baked bread and regional cheeses and sip the local wine, revelling in the knowledge that you made the right decision when buying your dream French home.

Rowena Medlow

Rowena Medlow, Editor

HOW TO USE THE GUIDE

French Property Buying Guide 2003 contains a guide to the buying process (Buying Guide, page 16), profiles of the French regions (The Regions, page 40) and an illustrated guide to property prices in France (Price Guide, page 106), as well as a useful directory of companies who offer services to those buying French property (page 368). In The Regions and Price Guide you will see we have divided France into 15 regions. Some, like Brittany, are complete administrative areas; others are groupings of neighbouring administrative regions that we have combined because they are often considered together, like Centre and Pays de la Loire, or because of their size or current appeal to British buyers. Where there is a common English version of a name, we have used it rather than the French one. The regions appear as they do on the French map – from west to east, north to south. So, if a particular part of France interests you, it's easy to see where you can extend your search by looking at the sections either side of the one that has captured your imagination.

BUYING GUIDE

How to buy property in France, tales from those who have bought a dream French home and a glossary of terms

STEPS TO BUYING
Finding the Right Property — 18
Judging the Real Price — 20
The Survey — 21
Financing the Purchase — 22
The Legal Process — 23
Taxation — 25
Moving In — 27
Living and Working in France — 28
Renovations — 30
Maintaining and Renting Out Your Property — 31

GLOSSARY — 32

CASE STUDIES — 34

Buying Guide

STEPS TO BUYING

Buying a property abroad is not a decision to be taken lightly, nor is it a decision that should be made on impulse, even when the turnover of properties in the area you choose is swift. Buying a house you fall in love with at the end of a holiday, for example, can be a recipe for disaster. There are legal, cost and other practical issues that should be taken into consideration before anyone leaps into a house purchase, especially in a foreign country.

One of the first questions you should ask yourself is how much can you really afford to spend. When you know how much you can raise, consider the purchasing costs and then set yourself a realistic price limit. Once you have set your budget, you will know whether you should be looking for a stone *fermette* (a small farmhouse), a town house or a much grander *manoir* (a manor house). In some regions, a manor house can cost the same as a farmhouse does in another, so by taking a look at property in areas you may never have considered before, simply because your travels have not taken you there yet, or it is not an area that people tend to talk about, you can open up your options. This is especially crucial today, as budget flight routes and high-speed train links have made areas that were once inconceivable to visit for a long weekend, for example, easily accessible from the UK.

A house in a village or town can be a more practical choice than one in the middle of the countryside with no neighbours or amenities nearby

JUSTIN POSTLETHWAITE/MERRICKS MEDIA

FINDING THE RIGHT PROPERTY

Buying a home abroad can be an emotive business, but it is crucial that buyers are practical when choosing a property. An isolated farmhouse can be all very well for escaping the hustle and bustle of city life, but if you need medical assistance close at hand, or would like neighbours to look after your property when you are away, you should probably think of buying somewhere within easy reach of other households and village amenities. You should also spend time getting to know the locality properly, seeing it in winter as well as summer if possible.

There are several different routes buyers can follow to find their dream French home today. You can simply trail around the region of your choice, hunting out '*à vendre*' (for sale) signs and looking in the windows of *agents immobiliers* (estate agents). But you don't have to rely on this method to track down your dream home. A good way to start is by searching through specialist magazines and websites, as

Steps to Buying

Even in areas like the Alpes-Maritimes (left) and Provence (below), where properties can change hands fast, buyers should consider their purchase carefully

well as attending the growing number of overseas property fairs held in the UK.

There is an increasing number of UK-based agents specialising in French properties who have a network of French agents providing them with local knowledge and property details. British buyers often choose these agents because they both understand the foreign buyers' needs, and, of course, offer an English-speaking service.

If you decide to use an estate agent based in France, whether they are a French or British national, it is a good idea to check they have a *carte professionelle*. This licence proves they have the correct professional qualifications, are backed by a financial guarantee and professional liability insurance and also that they are members of a regulatory body such as the Fédération Nationale des Agents Immobiliers et Mandataires, or FNAIM for short. Their fees are normally included in the sale price, so buyers usually don't have to worry about raising extra money to pay them. Mortgage providers usually lend only a percentage of the actual sale price and do not take additional costs into consideration.

Much of the property sold in France is still sold through *notaires*, however. *Notaires* are highly trained lawyers who oversee the purchase, and their sales commission will not normally be included in the price. Property sold through *notaires* can be more reasonably priced than those sold through estate agents, who are usually more aware of market trends.

You should also consider private sales or buying at auction. Private sales are advertised in specialist magazines and on a variety of websites, while auction details will appear in local papers. At an auction, or *vente aux enchères*, a *notaire* must usually bid on behalf of the buyer. Auctions can be the source of real bargains, because properties are often sold at one as a result of inheritance disputes or mortgage defaults, and are subsequently priced keenly for a swift sale.

It may be more convenient, however, to work with a property search agent, or 'homefinder'. Based in France or even the UK, they can cut the legwork out of finding your dream home and present a select range of properties for you to view. These could be on the books of local estate

19

Buying Guide

VAT

VAT (TVA) on most goods and services is currently set at 19.6 percent in France.

agents, from forthcoming auctions, or even private sales.

Whichever intermediary you choose, at some point you will have to arrange a trip to France for a viewing of your short list of properties. Narrow the final list down as much as you can before you go. The details intermediaries provide on French properties are not usually as exhaustive as the particulars that agents provide in the UK. Quite often, for example, details like room measurements or fixtures and fittings won't be included unless you ask, so make sure you get extensive details and see as many pictures as you can before taking time out to visit them.

Be careful when looking for an older property. With age comes problems. An older property may have been left for years without proper maintenance, for example, perhaps because it was part of an inheritance and not subsequently lived in. Others may never have been connected to mains electricity or had proper sewerage. The cost of renovating and connecting utilities can be onerous, and should be borne in mind when thinking about buying an old French building.

You may not have considered buying a recently built property, but they are often easier to look after, which is an especially important consideration if it is to be let out, and they are usually much less expensive to buy. For this reason, they can also make a sensible holiday rental investment.

The major disadvantage of buying a property under five years old, which is being sold for the first time, is that VAT, or TVA as it is known in France, is normally charged on the property. There is a way of avoiding this, however. A new freehold property that is leased back immediately to the developers, who then rent the property to holidaymakers over a period of about nine years, is usually exempt from VAT. Owners can expect to earn a net return of around six percent, as well as save on the initial cost of their purchase.

Buying properties leasehold, under a *bail*, is not at all common, however. They are usually bought freehold, or *en propriété libre*. Even owners of apartments normally have a share of the freehold.

These 'co-owners' must usually pay '*charges de copropriété*' (maintenance and service charges), which are usually set in proportion to the size of the individual apartment. The question of whether to buy leasehold or freehold is, therefore, rarely raised in the search for a French home.

Buying a 'bargain' wreck in a field and turning it into a comfortable home is often costlier than buyers imagine

JUDGING THE REAL PRICE

As a rule of thumb, to roughly calculate the total cost of buying a French property, add another 10 percent on top of the actual purchase price. In reality, however, the total can be much higher than this. One of the main costs is the sales commission. This is normally about five to six percent, but, particularly in the case of less expensive properties, it can be up to 20 percent. It is, therefore, important to check whether or not the fee is included in the advertised price, and also whether VAT has been added. Phrases like '*toutes taxes comprises*' or '*TVA comprise*' should indicate that it has.

Although it is sometimes the vendor who pays the agents' commission, the buyer is always responsible for paying the conveyancing fees to the *notaire*. The *notaire's* fees are fixed by law, and are a percentage based on a sliding scale depending on the age and purchase price of property. The fees can range between around 10

Steps to Buying

percent for a property over five years old, and three to four percent for one under five years old, exclusive of VAT. If two *notaires* are appointed, one by the buyer and one by the vendor, the fee will be split between them.

On top of the *notaire*'s own fee, they will collect various duties and fees, including stamp and transfer duties, land registry fees, taxes and disbursements, all of which depend on the location, type, age and value of the property. When a mortgage is taken out on a property, there will also be a charge payable to the *notaire* of usually between one and three percent of the mortgage value for registering the charge of the lender with the relevant land registry, or *conservation des hypothèques*.

Exchange rate fluctuations can potentially increase the cost of financing if a borrower is converting sterling to make payments on a euro mortgage. Fixing the exchange rate through a currency specialist over a long period can give the borrower peace of mind, however. If the property is being bought for cash, it can also be a good idea to fix the exchange rate at the beginning of the purchase process, so the actual price of the property will not increase unexpectedly due to exchange rate fluctuations before the completion date.

One of the biggest costs of buying an older property is often the cost of renovation work. This is not something that all buyers tend to bare in mind from the outset, however. Many people who spot a ruin in a field, for instance, will think it is a bargain and won't consider how much it will actually cost to restore. This cost can be at least as much as the price of the building itself, so to prevent a dream home turning into a renovation project that was never completed, you should calculate all the potential outlays before proceeding with a sale.

THE SURVEY

Foreign buyers are not always aware of the local market prices of property, and can risk paying inflated prices. A valuation by a local valuer, an *expert immobilier*, can help avoid this. They can also help gauge the cost of any renovation work to make the property habitable or to simply improve the living space.

Even an *expert immobilier* will not, however, provide a full structural survey. The survey, or *expertise*, that they carry out is, in effect, more like a valuation. The closest equivalent to a British structural survey is an *evaluation structurale*. The French do not have a professional equivalent to the British chartered building surveyor. They usually either turn to an *architecte* (an architect), who will normally provide only a very brief report on the condition of a building, or they rely on testimonies from local tradesmen, or *artisans*, to gauge a property's state of repair. One of the best ways to obtain a structural survey can be to instruct one of the growing number of properly qualified British building surveyors or architects who now live in France or who will travel across the Channel to carry out such surveys.

British buyers should also note that there are details that should be checked when buying a French property that would not necessarily need checking in the UK. If a property is made up of a collection of buildings, for example, it should be determined whether or not all the buildings are, in fact, included in the sale. Boundaries can often be blurred too, especially if land has been split up into several small plots, known as *parcelles*, or if a wood obscures part of one. They can be checked against a *plan cadastral*, the official record of site boundaries,

BORROWER BEWARE!

■ Your home is at risk if you do not keep up repayments on a mortgage or other loan secured on it.

■ The sterling equivalent of your liability under a foreign currency mortgage may be increased by exchange rate movements.

JUSTIN POSTLETHWAITE/MERRICKS MEDIA

Make sure that you get the right survey for any building you buy in France, especially if it is an older-style property

Buying Guide

Mortgages can often be raised to cover the cost of any renovation works to be carried out on a French property

although this can sometimes be out of date. A land surveyor, a *géomètre*, can help verify such details.

FINANCING THE PURCHASE

Although a high percentage of foreign buyers pay for French property with cash, it has become much easier for non-residents to raise a mortgage, or *prêt immobilier*, on a home in France. There are two basic ways to do this: either by remortgaging a current UK property in sterling or by taking out a new mortgage against a French property in euros. Although there can be a substantial initial exchange rate fee to pay when money is raised in a currency other than the euro, remortgaging in sterling can protect the British buyer against the effect of future exchange rate fluctuations on their repayments. Taking out a mortgage in euros on a French property will always, on the other hand, reflect the true euro value of the property, and the bank will have the first legal charge on the actual property being financed. The cost of the mortgage can also potentially be offset against any income received from letting the property.

Since British and French banks cannot take first legal charge on a property outside their own countries, they do not offer mortgages on properties in any country apart from their own. There are many French lenders for overseas buyers to choose between if a mortgage is to be raised on a property in France, but one of the most interesting propositions today is offered by the French branches of UK banks. All the paperwork can be supplied in English, for instance, and although the mortgage will be in euros, the monthly payments can be made in sterling, straight from a British bank account.

Repayment mortgages, or *prêts immobiliers sans capital différé*, are most commonly offered by French banks to foreign buyers because they have been historically favoured above interest-only mortgages and endowment policies by the French. British buyers are usually lent money by a French lender for between five and 20 years. Rates can be fixed, *à taux fixe*, or variable, *à taux variable*. There are likely to be early redemption charges payable on the former, but not on the latter.

Steps to Buying

French variable rates are linked to the EURIBOR (Euro Interbank Offered Rate) and for foreign buyers this is usually fixed for a period of 12 months, mainly for convenience. One main difference between UK and French variable interest rates is that, whereas in the UK the monthly payments are likely to fluctuate regularly, in France the rates tend to stay stable, and it is only the term of the loan that changes according to the EURIBOR rate change.

A deposit of at least 20 percent is usually required, and it is generally true that the higher the deposit, the better the interest rate. A French lender is obliged to prove that the borrower can afford the repayments, so they usually insist that the monthly payments for all the buyer's mortgages and other fixed outgoings should not exceed 30 to 35 percent of their income.

Even if properties financed by a residential mortgage are to be let out for part of the year, lenders will not usually take into consideration the potential rental income when assessing the loan request. Neither will they lend money to cover the costs of buying a property. Subject to the approval of relevant estimates from builders or developers, mortgages can, however, cover the cost of renovation or construction work.

Note that once a mortgage offer is received, the borrower must wait at least 10 days, but no longer than 30, before signing and accepting it. This is in order to comply with French financial legislation. On the acceptance of a French mortgage offer, an arrangement fee of between one and two percent of the loan value will usually be payable. Borrowers are also obliged to take out a life insurance policy so that, in the event of death or disability, the outstanding loan value will be repaid.

French banks pay the sum of money being lent directly to the *notaire*. The portion covering renovation or construction costs, however, is paid direct to the contractor on presentation of invoices (duly authorised for payment by the customer), and after the customer's personal contribution has been paid. As a general rule, you should allow two months between the receipt of a complete mortgage application and the completion date.

> French homes can be bought by individuals in single, joint or multiple names, or through a property-holding company

THE LEGAL PROCESS

The French legal system can be a minefield for foreign buyers. Never does the expression 'take independent advice' ring more true than in the case of buying a property abroad. A French property can either be purchased by individuals – in single, joint or multiple names – or through a French property-holding company, a *société civile d'immobilière* (SCI), whose shares are held by the buyers. There are different tax implications for each method of buying, and advice is best sought before a decision is made which way to proceed.

THE POINT OF NO RETURN

In France you buy a property subject to contract. A contract, known as a '*compromis de vente*', a '*promesse de vente*' or a '*sous-seing privé*', is entered into early on in the process, and this commits the vendor and buyer to a deal they will conclude with a deed of sale, or conveyance. This can be a private agreement between the parties concerned, or it can be signed in front of the *notaire* who will oversee the completion of the sale. The buyer and vendor can both appoint their own *notaire*. Any *chambre de notaires* can provide details of *notaires* in their area to buyers who want to instruct their own.

ROWENA MEDLOW

Buying Guide

JEREMY POUND/MERRICKS MEDIA

The French legal process can be a minefield for the foreign buyer, so you would do best to seek independent advice

To elaborate, the contract is an agreement between the buyer and vendor to buy and sell at an agreed price by an agreed date, and will include details of the *notaire* or *notaires* overseeing the transaction and of where the deed that completes the conveyancing, the *acte de vente*, which is also sometimes referred to as the '*acte authentique*' or even the '*acte authentique de vente*', will be signed. At this stage, a deposit of 10 percent of the purchase price is paid by the buyer to the *notaire* or the estate agent, if they are backed by a financial guarantee and a professional liability insurance. Under no circumstances should money be paid directly to the vendor at this or any other point in the process.

There is a seven-day 'cooling-off' period from the day the buyer receives a copy of the contract countersigned by the vendor. During this period the buyer can withdraw from the sale and not be liable for any penalties. If the buyer withdraws from the purchase after this cooling-off period, however, they will probably lose their deposit and may be liable for penalties. If a penalty clause is included in the contract, it will stipulate the amount payable in case of withdrawal. If it is the vendor who withdraws, the deposit should normally be refunded, and the vendor must pay any damages stipulated in the contract.

If the contract contains what are called '*clauses suspensives*' (get-out clauses), which lay out conditions to be met during the sale process, the buyer may, in some circumstances, be able to withdraw from the purchase without the risk of losing their deposit and having to pay penalties. The sale can be made conditional to a number of factors, such as the offer of a mortgage, or the absence of rights of way across the property, planning restrictions affecting potential future development or a *droit de préemption* (right of pre-emption) that gives a local authority, land commission or another third party the right to buy the property or its land.

In the case of properties that have not yet been constructed, a *contrat de réservation* precedes the conveyance. On execution of the deed, ownership of the land passes to the buyer, but proprietorship of the building is only transferred as works proceed.

COMPLETING THE SALE

By the completion date, the balance of the purchase price must be paid into the *notaire*'s bank account. It can take a matter of days for a transfer to reach a *notaire*'s account from a UK bank account, so to be sure that the funds arrive in time, it is a good idea to initiate the transfer at least two weeks before the agreed completion date.

It can also take over three months for a *notaire* to complete a sale, as they must carry out the necessary land registry and local authority searches, make arrangements for collection of the balance and their costs and execute the conveyance. The contract usually includes a date for completion, but it cannot always be relied upon. If a buyer is based abroad they do not necessarily have to travel to France to complete the sale. Through a power of attorney, a third party, usually the *notaire*'s clerk, can sign the conveyance in the presence of the *notaire*.

After completion, the notaire will stamp and register the title deed, or *titre*, at the land registry, which can take about six months. A certified copy, or *copie authentique*, is then sent to the buyer, and the original document is filed in the *notaire*'s archives. An *attestation d'acquisition*, which proves ownership of the property, can, however, also be provided on the day of completion.

Steps to Buying

EXPECTING THE UNEXPECTED

The main concern of the *notaire* who oversees the sale of a property is to 'note' the sale, to ensure that the conveyancing is carried out according to the law and to collect the relevant taxes on behalf of the government. Although they are perfectly qualified to provide legal advice, they are not acting on behalf of either side so, to make sure that you are bound by favourable terms, it can be best to instruct a solicitor who specialises in the purchase of French property from the very start of the legal process. There are many solicitors who specialise in the buying and selling of French property now based in the UK.

Not only can a solicitor working on behalf of the buyer draw up any necessary get-out clauses in the contract, they can also advise on the best way to structure the purchase according to their personal circumstances and recommend ways of minimising the effect of French inheritance law. The latter should be considered well before the conveyance is signed.

Special '*assur'titre*' insurance policies can be taken out that insure the title of a property against unknown title defects, like unforeseen claims by third parties and the violation of planning regulations by former owners, as well as mistakes on behalf of the *notaire*. With a policy covering these eventualities, the buyer will have an extra level of security and will be protected against many of the costs that any attacks on the title of a property may incur. These policies are increasingly being offered by estate agents as part of their service, and are a good complement to the advice of an independent solicitor.

TAXATION

A foreign homeowner only usually becomes a resident of France when they spend over 183 days in the country, or their permanent home is there. Even if they are not a tax resident, apart from the taxes paid to

---

TAX RATES*

INCOME TAX
FROM 7.05% TO 49.58%
(Taxable from 4,191 euros (£2,619))

RENTAL INCOME TAX
2.5%

SOCIAL CHARGES
(On income derived from a professional activity)
CSG   7.5%
CRDS   0.5%

WEALTH TAX
FROM 0.55% TO 1.80%
(Taxable from 720,000 euros (£450,000))

CAPITAL GAINS TAX
Non-residents
33$^1/_3$%

INHERITANCE TAX
FROM 5% TO 60%

*correct at time of going to press

Buyers should consider the ways of minimising the effect of French inheritance law before they complete their purchase

Buying Guide

the *notaire* at the time of the property purchase, owners of French homes may also be liable at some time or another to pay a range of other taxes.

Both the tax offices of France and the country in which a foreign national resides will be interested in their annual income from activities in France, which could simply be the interest from a French bank account or the rental income from a French property. If this is above an official threshold, they must make an annual declaration of income in France. A tax resident of France may, in theory, also be liable for both French and UK taxes.

Fortunately for tax residents of both countries, there is a double tax treaty between France and the UK, which protects most British nationals with property in France from paying tax twice. Anyone planning to move permanently from the UK to France should notify the British tax authorities before leaving, providing them with proof of new employment and property details.

It is also important to note that direct taxes are not deducted by means of a PAYE system in France. Instead, they are paid in the year following the tax year in question, which runs from January 1 to December 31. This is done either in three or 10 instalments, and taxation is always on a self-assessment basis. Residents' taxes are collected by the Direction Générale des Impôts, which is organised on a national and a regional level, while non-residents deal with the Centre des Impôts des Non-Résidents in Paris. A tax return form, a *déclaration des revenues*, can be obtained from the local tax office, the *centre des impôts*, which can also help the uninitiated fill out their forms.

PROPERTY TAXES

Based on the average rental value of a property, there are two types of local tax payable by individuals. The *taxe foncière*, a property ownership tax, is paid by the owner, whether a resident in France or not, while the *taxe d'habitation*, a residential tax, is paid by the occupiers, who may or may not be the owners. Both are paid in the year following the rental period. The retired may be exempt from paying these taxes, as can owners of new or uninhabitable properties.

INCOME TAX

Income tax, or *impôt sur le revenu des personnes physiques* (IRPP), is levied on 'earned' income, and depends on the level of income. There are, however, a number of allowances. A tax on investment or 'unearned' income tax, the *impôt sur les revenus de capitaux*, is payable on property and investment income, as well as interest paid on bank accounts. There is also a separate rental income tax called the *contribution sur les revenus locatifs*, which is levied on gross rental income.

WEALTH TAX

A wealth tax called the *impôt de solidarité sur la fortune*, is levied on net assets held in France valued over a certain threshold. The assets can include a property, a car and bank balances.

CAPITAL GAINS TAX

There is no tax on any gain made from the sale of a principal home, but capital gains tax, or *impôt sur les plus-values*, is levied on the profits of the sale of other property, as well as shares, subject to certain allowances.

Steps to Buying

SOCIAL CHARGES
All income and capital gains are subject to social contributions or charges such as the CSG (generalised social contribution) and the CRDS (repayment of the social debt contribution).

INHERITANCE TAX
French inheritance law, which governs inheritance tax and both death and estate duties, and decides who inherits a person's assets, is quite unlike anything that a British buyer will have probably come across before. In theory, inheritance tax is paid on the global assets of a French tax resident. The beneficiaries pay a percentage of their inheritance depending on the value of the estate and how closely they are related. Inheritance tax will also be due on any French property owned by a non-resident.

There are several ways to minimise an inheritance tax bill, however, and careful planning at the time of the house purchase is crucial. In certain circumstances, for example, changes to a marriage contract can help, as can buying through a property-holding company called a *société civile immobilière*, of which the owners are the shareholders. The latter generally only benefits buyers who are going to take up residency in France. To benefit the surviving spouse, provisions can also be made in the French will of an owner to the effect that their husband or wife receives a lifetime interest in the property, or '*usufruit*', on their death. One of the most popular methods that couples opt for, however, is to put a clause called a '*clause tontine*' in the conveyance, which, in effect, suspends the ownership of the entire property until one or other of them dies. This does not, however, necessarily make the property exempt from taxation.

Homeowners in France are obliged by law to take out insurance as soon as they purchase

MOVING IN
The new owners of a French property are officially only allowed to take possession of a property when the sale has been completed by the *notaire*. If the property is vacant, however, vendors sometimes let the next owner in a bit earlier to prepare for moving in. Whenever the moving in date is set, it can require nearly as much planning as the purchase itself.

After completion, the buyer will need to start paying for utilities that are connected, as well as for local services like rubbish collection. A *notaire* or estate agent will often help with this. Water is supplied by a range of private companies in France. When a property is not connected, an application should be made to the local supplier. New owners also have to contact the Electricité de France (EDF) and Gaz de France (GDF) to read the electricity and gas meters and to change the name on the relevant accounts. A connection charge is usually payable, as is a deposit if the owner is a non-resident. Mains gas is not always provided in rural areas, whose habitants usually rely, instead, on cylinder gas.

Homeowners are also legally obliged to take out a third-party liability insurance policy on their property. A *notaire* will ask to see proof that the buyer has adequate insurance cover from the day they take ownership of the property. The vendor's insurance can simply be transferred into the new owner's name. This can be part of a multi-risk household insurance policy, an *assurance multirisques habitation*, which includes contents and buildings insurance. Contents and buildings insurance policies specifically for holiday homes can be best for those who only intend to visit the property from time to time.

IN CASE OF EMERGENCY

Dial the following numbers from any French phone for the relevant emergency services:

Police	17
SAMU (medical services)	15
Fire	18

SOS Médecins
(doctors, Paris)
01 47 07 77 77
or 0820 332424

SOS Dentistes
(dentists, Paris)
01 43 37 51 00

Although it is possible to pay utility bills and insurance premiums from across the Channel, if the French home is not going to be used as a main residence, it can be more convenient to pay by direct debit, or *prélèvement automatique*, from a French bank account. Not only does it make it simpler, but it also means that supplies will not be cut off just because letters and cheques never got to their destination.

Opening a French bank account is easier now than it has ever been. Help is usually on hand from people involved in the purchase – estate agents, homefinders and even solicitors often offer help opening bank accounts as part of their service – and there are even English-speaking branches of French banks in France today. Non-resident as well as resident bank accounts are available. The main difference between the two is that non-resident bank accounts offer no overdraft facilities.

Taking a car into France can involve a little paperwork and the payment of taxes. If a car is to remain in France for over six months each year, it will have to be re-registered. A new registration document, a *carte grise*, can be obtained from a *préfecture* (the administrative offices of the local state representative). Although road tax is still payable if a car registered in France is owned by a business, road tax on cars owned by private individuals was abolished in 2000. There is still a tax levied on cars moved permanently to France, however, if they are less than six months old. Cars over five years old that have been imported will have to pass the French equivalent of an MOT, a *contrôle technique*.

There are no restrictions on the importing of most furniture and other household goods into France by an EU citizen if for personal use. The movement of antiques in and out of the UK can be more complicated than other items, however, and proof of their origin should be kept, ready to be produced when they are moved between countries. Thanks to a new 'pet passport' scheme, pets are much freer to move between the UK and other EU countries these days, without the need for quarantine periods. To enter France, they must have a current Anti-Rabies Vaccination Certificate, and to get back into the UK they will need a pet passport and a microchip.

LIVING AND WORKING IN FRANCE

Although members of the EU can live and work anywhere within the European Union, those moving from another EU country to take up permanent residency in France, or even simply stay there for periods of three consecutive months or more, will need a *carte de séjour*. To obtain a *carte de séjour*, applicants will have to prove that they will not be a burden on the state – they must have a permanent home and have a job, own a business or have independent means of support, as well as medical insurance that will cover them until they join the state health insurance scheme. A *carte de séjour* can usually be obtained from a *mairie*, *gendarmerie* (police station) or *préfecture*. Documentation requirements vary from area to area.

Anyone working in France, either as an employee or self-employed, must be registered with the social security organisations, or *caisses*, that cover their particular occupation and pay contributions called *cotisations* to the relevant *caisses*. Employers should automatically register anyone working for them and arrange for both employer and employee contributions to be paid to the *caisses*. The self-employed must organise the payment of their own contributions into the correct *caisse* for their profession.

Steps to Buying

MEDICAL SERVICES

Anyone working in France is obliged to pay insurance contributions to a *caisse d'assurance maladie* (health insurance fund), whereby they join the state health insurance scheme and much of the cost of their future medical treatment will be covered. For people not working in France, it can be a little more complicated. If you are living but not working in France, you may be entitled to the same treatment and benefits as French nationals, up to a certain time limit. After this period, you may be able to start contributing voluntarily to the state health insurance scheme, otherwise you will have to take out private medical insurance.

If you are a British resident and visit your French home solely for short periods, you will only usually be covered for state-provided emergency medical treatment when you are in France. You will need to present a valid E111 form, which can be obtained from a UK post office, to receive free or reduced-cost emergency treatment.

Even when someone is living in France and has joined the sate health insurance scheme, unless they fall into the 'low income' bracket, or are suffering from a serious illness, the full cost of any consultation or medical treatment is not usually borne by the state health service. This is one of the major differences between the British and French state health services. Another dissimilarity is that consultations, treatments and prescriptions must usually be paid for upfront, before being reimbursed, in full or in part, by the relevant health insurance *caisse*. To help cover all expenses, a complementary private health insurance policy can be taken out through a *mutuelle*.

Additionally, unlike in the UK, patients do not have to be registered with a particular GP and can, in theory, visit any GP, specialist or dentist of their choice. What may help limit the choice is the fact that some medical professionals and hospitals charge rates within the state health service's limits, while others do not, and can charge much more. Contact details of local doctors, dentists and hospitals can be obtained from a *gendarmerie* or by dialling 15 from any French phone.

EDUCATION

Any foreign child living in France has the right to join the French educational system. They can attend either a local state school, a private school, or one of the many bilingual schools – both state run and private – depending on which establishment best suits their needs. Between the ages of three and five, children can join an *école*

There are no restrictions on British buyers moving furniture into their home in France if it is purely for personal use and not antique

Buying Guide

The demand from holidaymakers for traditional French properties to rent out is strong today

maternelle (a nursery). All six to sixteen-year-olds must first attend an *école primaire* (a primary school) then a *collège* (a secondary school). The last two years are spent at a *lycée*, where students either study for a baccalauréat or for vocational qualifications.

The French state education system has a very good reputation, but, if children do not have a very good command of the French language when they arrive in the country, they may be better off at a bilingual school rather than at a local state school. Each region has one or sometimes two *académies* (education districts), managed by a *rectorat* (local education authority), which can provide details of all the different schools and universities based in their locality.

RENOVATIONS

A *plan d'occupation des sols* is the local authority plan that outlines what can or cannot be built on a plot of land, as well as the surrounding terrain. A certificate showing planning permission, a *certificat d'urbanisme*, will provide precise details of the rules regarding the potential development of an individual property. Each area has an official maximum planning 'density', and some have no-build zones. This affects parts of the Alps in particular. Planning restrictions should ideally be reviewed before the purchase of a property.

Some minor works require no formalities, but even before building a swimming pool, you may need to fill in a form called a *déclaration des travaux* at your local *mairie*. In the case of more extensive alterations to a French property, both planning permission and a building permit, called a *permis de construire*, should be obtained through the local *mairie*.

Once the application has been considered by the *mairie*, it is then forwarded on to the local planning office, and once it has been approved, it is then passed back to the *mairie* for a final sign-off. The whole process usually takes about two months. Applications can be made by the owners themselves or through either a *notaire* or a surveyor, unless the net surface area to be built upon exceeds 170 square metres. Then it should be made by an architect who is a member of the Ordre des Architectes. In the case of a building that is, or is situated near, a listed historical building, it will also need to be reviewed by an *architecte des bâtiments de France*.

It may be tempting to try to carry out building work without recourse to builders or architects, but anyone renovating or adding to a historic building must be competent using the local wood and stone and understand the regulations governing the use of building material in the area. French builders are not renowned for their punctuality, but they are known to do a good job. The local *chambre de métiers* (chamber of trade) can supply details of builders registered in the area.

Some British homeowners are more comfortable employing British nationals, however, even though they will probably not be as knowledgeable about the local materials and planning regulations. There are plenty of British builders who either live in France or will travel to France to work. It is essential, however, to check that the work of British builders, electricians, plumbers and other tradesmen complies with French standards.

When the owner cannot be on site to watch over the project, it can be best simply to employ an architect or surveyor, either French or British, to see the project through. They can end up saving money as well as time. However the project is managed, when work has been completed, the owner will need to obtain a certificate, a *certificat de conformité*, proving that it complied with the planning permission. A nationwide organisation called the Conseil d'Architecture d'Urbanisme et de l'Environnement (CAUE), which has local branches in all of France's regions, can offer advice on renovating or extending traditional buildings.

It is also well worth checking with a *mairie* to discover if the local council provides grants for restoring buildings in the area. Some offer particular help to anyone converting buildings into holiday accommodation, as part of a drive to attract tourism into the region. Major gîte-rental companies are also known to offer money for this purpose, under the proviso that the agency will have the right to let out the property.

MAINTAINING AND RENTING OUT YOUR PROPERTY

When owners are away, they often turn to neighbours to help look after their property. Having someone clean the property and tend the garden in their absence makes visiting even more enjoyable. Specialist companies can also offer property checks. They send someone around regularly to the property to see if there has been any damage to it and to check if any pipes are leaking, for example.

If, like many owners of French homes, you plan to rent your property out to holidaymakers, you should make sure that it is well maintained, in good decorative order and well furnished. There is a strong demand for well-appointed French properties, especially those within easy reach of tourist attractions, local stores and restaurants.

To attract business, advertisements can be placed in specialist magazines and on websites. Homeowners can also place the responsibility of their property letting in the hands of experienced letting agents, who will maintain and market the property and manage the handovers for them.

As well as short-term holiday rentals, which are principally during the summer months, owners can also rent their property quite successfully off-season as a long-term let. The weekly rent paid will be much lower, but this way the property is occupied for more of the year, and it will also be more likely to be making money during sluggish periods.

If renting out your property for any period of time, you should check that your insurance policy covers damage caused by tenants and injuries caused to tenants on the premises. To make the letting as tax efficient as possible, advice should be sought from specialists.

Some local councils provide grants to help people convert older buildings into suitable accommodation for tourists

GLOSSARY

A

acompte nm	deposit
acte nm	deed
* **acte authentique**	deed; conveyance
* **acte authentique de vente**	conveyance
* **acte de vente**	conveyance
agent immobilier nm	estate agent
architecte nmf	architect
artisan nm	builder; skilled craftsman
assurance multirisques habitation nf	comprehensive household insurance

B

bail nm	lease
bastide nf	Provençal country house
bâtiment nm	building

C

caisse nf	office; fund
* **caisse primaire d'assurance maladie**	state health insurance centre
carte nf	card; permit
* **carte de séjour**	residence permit
* **carte grise**	car registration document
* **carte professionnelle**	professional licence
cave nf	cellar
caveau nm	small cellar
centre des impôts nm	local tax office
certificat nm	certificate
* **certificat de conformité**	certificate of compliance
* **certificat d'urbanisme**	planning permission certificate
chambre nf	bedroom; chamber
* **chambre des notaires**	chamber of notaries
* **chambre de(s) métiers**	chamber of trade
* **chambres d'hôte**	bed and breakfast; bed and breakfast rooms
chauffage nm	heating
clause nf	clause
* **clause pénale**	penalty clause
* **clause suspensive**	get-out clause
* **clause tontine**	survivorship clause
colombage nm	half-timbering
compromis de vente nm	sales contract
conservation des hypothèques nf	land registry
contrat nm	contract
* **contrat de réservation**	reservation contract for a property still to be constructed
cotisation nf	contributions
contribution sociale nf	social charge
copie authentique nf	certified copy
copropriété nf	co-ownership
* **charges de copropriété**	maintenance and service charges for a block of flats
* **immeuble en copropriété**	block of flats
cuisine nf	kitchen

D

demande de prêt nf	loan application
département nm	administrative area
dépendance nf	outbuilding
dépôt de garantie nm	deposit
domicile nm	place of residence; home
droit nm	right; duty; law
* **droit de préemption**	right of first refusal
* **droits de succession**	inheritance tax
* **droit de timbre**	stamp duty
duplex nm	maisonette

E

eau de la ville nf	mains water
en propriété libre adv	freehold
expert immobilier nm	valuer
expertise nf	valuation; survey

F

ferme nf	farm; farmhouse
fermette nf	small farmhouse
fosse septique nf	septic tank

G

gendarmerie nf	police station
géomètre nm	land surveyor
grange nf	barn
grenier nm	attic

H

hypothèque nf	mortgage; remortgage

I

immobilier nm	property
impôt nm	tax
* **impôt sur les plus-values**	capital gains tax
* **impôt sur le revenu des personnes physiques (IRPP)**	income tax

Glossary

indivision nf	joint ownership

L

location nf	letting; rented accommodation
longère nf	longhouse or long barn

M

mairie nf	town hall
maison nf	house
* **maison bourgeoise**	upmarket period house
* **maison de campagne**	country cottage
* **maison individuelle**	detached house
* **maison jumelée**	semi-detached house
* **maison de maître**	classic mansion-style house
mandat nm	power of attorney
manoir nm	country manor
mas nm	stone farmhouse

N

notaire nm	notary (the lawyer who oversees the conveyancing)

O

occupant nmf	occupier
offre nf	offer; bid

P

parcelle de terre nf	plot of land
pavillon nm	typical modern house
permis de construire nm	planning permission
pierre nf	stone
* **en pierre**	built of stone
* **pierre de taille**	sandstone; limestone
pigeonnier nm	dovecote
plan nm	plan; outline
* **plan cadastral**	official record of site boundaries
* **plan d'occupation des sols**	local authority plan outlining the area's planning restrictions
préfecture nf	administrative offices of the local state representative
prélèvement automatique nm	direct debit
prêt nm	loan
* **prêt immobilier**	mortgage
* **prêt immobilier à taux fixe**	fixed-rate mortgage
* **prêt immobilier à taux variable**	variable-rate mortgage
* **prêt immobilier sans capital différé**	repayment mortgage
promesse de vente nf	sales agreement

R

rectorat nm	local education authority

S

salle nf	room
* **salle à manger**	dining room
* **salle de bain**	bathroom
* **salle d'eau**	shower room
salon nm	sitting room
séjour nm	living room
société civile immobilière (SCI) nf	property-holding company
sous-seing privé nm	private agreement
surface habitable nf	living space
système d'écoulement des eaux nm	drainage

T

taxe nf	tax
* **taxe d'habitation**	residential tax
* **taxe foncière**	property ownership tax
* **taxe sur la valeur ajoutée (TVA)**	VAT
* **toutes taxes comprises (TTC)**	VAT included
titre nm	title deed
toit nm	roof
toiture nf	roofing
tout-à-l'égout nm	mains drainage
type (T) nm	(followed by a number) a property with a given number of main rooms
* **T4**	four-room flat

U

usufruit nm	lifetime interest

V

villa nf	detached modern house
vendre v	to sell
* **à vendre**	for sale
vendeur nm	seller
vente nf	sale
* **vente aux enchères**	auction
versement nm	payment
volet nm	shutter

Buying Guide

POITOU-CHARENTES CHATEAU
PHILIPPA AND NICK FREELAND

Philippa and Nick Freeland moved to Poitou-Charentes from the Cotswolds just over 10 years ago, and after much hard work and determination are now the proud owners of a splendidly restored medieval manor house, Château de Tennessus. It has been a labour of love, but their constant attention to detail has brought the château back to its former glory, as well as turning it into a successful bed-and-breakfast business.

Surrounded by farmland and untouched for years, Château de Tennessus was just what the Freelands were looking for

One of the key stages in turning their dream of moving into a historic French home into reality was the initial search. When the couple started looking for their dream French home – and it was going to be their actual home, not just for holidays – their main criteria was to find something that was easy to get to from across the Channel. The Northwest seemed the obvious place to aim for. The couple looked from Normandy in the north down to Poitou-Charentes, which benefited from a new TGV (high-speed train) connection at Poitiers.

The selection of properties that the Freelands could view was strictly limited to the number of days they had spare to travel to France from their Cotswolds farmhouse. They only had two weekends, so had to strictly narrow their viewing list down to 20, which was a manageable number.

Having chosen quite a wide area, this meant they had to use other criteria to refine the list of possible properties to view. Firstly, while the area within the northwest corner of France didn't matter too much, the position in that area had to be just right. A village location would not do, nor would a site next to another dominating building or a busy road. Then, the property had to be of a certain age. 'We were looking for something built earlier than the 19th century,' recalls Philippa, 'Although we weren't specifically looking for medieval properties at the time.' It also had to have adjoining land – 'We wanted at least five hectares,' she notes – and had to be unspoilt, untouched for years, if necessary.

These may seem quite sensible criteria to set when looking for a full-blown château, but it proved very difficult to find one that had everything right. 'We were sent particulars by every estate agent we could get hold of, and had whittled them down to 60 possibles,' remembers Philippa. 'Fifteen out of the 60 had to be written off simply because they overlooked a motorway or a housing estate, usually because the previous

WWW.TENNESSUS.COM

owners had sold off some of their land.' The château that was to become the Freelands' French residence luckily had ticks in all the right boxes, and the position could not be more idyllic, as Château de Tennessus is surrounded on all sides by farms.

Although Philippa adores the château now, she actually wasn't overkeen on the property when she first saw it. It wasn't the fairy-tale structure that she was hoping for; it was built of granite, with walls almost two metres thick. It was her husband who fell in love with it at first. 'It's a man's place, a real castle,' she laughs.

Fortunately, the buying process was relatively swift and painless for the Freelands, and the only surprise they had was discovering that, after they had put down their deposit of 10 percent of the sale price in advance, they could not go back to the vendors with complaints about the structure of any of the buildings. They were lucky that, in their case, the château was solidly built, so they didn't have to worry about its structure.

Renovating the château, admits Philippa, has cost more than the initial outlay (it cost just £160,000 to buy a decade ago). Owing to the style of the château, the Freelands renovation project was more complicated and expensive than it would have been to renovate, say, a simpler farmhouse. They have had to hire special cranes, scaffolding and winches to help carry out some of the renovation and rebuilding work, and have also had to carve into surrounding granite rock for some of the fittings.

The costliest projects have been the restoration of the top floor of the keep, which created a new suite and cost around £80,000, and the installation of a kitchen, which came to £40,000. Other improvements and decoration have added up to nearly £100,000.

The Freelands' experience has proved that when buying and restoring a sizable older property, money must be set aside for unforeseen projects and setbacks. Fortunately for the couple, it has not been as costly as it could have been. Because their home is a monument of the state, they have found it relatively simple to obtain a substantial amount of state funding for the works. And, of course, renting out rooms from £70 a night on a bed-and-breakfast basis has also helped towards covering some of the costs.

Philippa and Nick feel very fortunate that they chose the area in which they now live. The children have been to the local schools where they have quickly picked up French. They have also been lucky with their neighbours, who have been very welcoming to the family. In fact, they have become quite a part of the local community. The Freelands regularly organise

Above and opposite page, top: the Freelands renovated their entire château, and even added a new floor to its keep

workshops for schools, teaching the children about the history of the château, for example, hire it out as a venue for medieval music concerts and allow the local town hall officials who helped them find materials they needed for their renovations use rooms for functions.

Specialist scaffolding had to be hired for the château renovation project

Buying Guide

LIMOUSIN VILLAGE HOUSE
MARK AND GEORGINA RUSSELL

In spring 2002, Mark and Georgina Russell bought a house and barn in a small village in Limousin. It was in a lovely area and was a bargain, at £15,000 for the lot. There was a catch, however, quite a big one, in fact. The house did not even have sanitation services connected, meaning the Russells couldn't move straight in and would have to live in rented accommodation until they had renovated it.

Like many Brits who move to France, Mark and Georgina thought that buying a place 'with potential', that needed quite a bit of work, would save them money and also allow them to put their own stamp on it. Mark had worked as a builder, after all, and they knew they could renovate it at a steady pace by themselves. Luckily, they had made sure they had not bought a wreck, so the house was in a pretty good condition before they started work on it. Unusually for a small hamlet, they were also fortunate that there was mains drainage available, so even putting a new loo in was not going to cause too many problems.

When they took possession, Mark and Georgina set about restructuring the internal layout of their village house. 'One of the first things we did was to knock most of the walls down,' recalls Mark. 'We just liked the idea of having more space.'

Then, up in the roof, work started on converting the attic into two bedrooms. They needed more space and so they came to a small dilemma: should they lower the ceiling of the rooms below or raise the roof? There was enough head height in what was to become the living room to feasibly lower the ceiling by the six inches that they needed to gain in the attic, and the roof was sound and only 10 years old, so the option of lowering the ceiling won.

For such a big project, and with most of the work being undertaken by Mark, it helped

Above and top: Although both the house and barn were paid for in cash, a mortgage was raised to pay for the planned renovation works

Case Studies

greatly that the couple were renting in the neighbourhood when they started working on their dream home in the making. Apart from the fact that they found themselves in the position of paying rent on one property and a mortgage on another, and having two gardens to look after, it has proved quite convenient.

The couple had chosen to live in Limousin because they were determined to benefit from the great climate of southern France without having to pay the high prices that properties in the South can command. Mark explains: 'We went far enough south to be below the Loire line, for the weather – we get a similar climate here to what you would get 200 miles further south – but the prices are much lower here, and you don't get the winter storms that you would nearer the Mediterranean. People have a lot more time for you here than in the tourist areas too, although it can take you 20 minutes to buy a *pain au raisin* at the local bakers, because people do seem to talk a lot!'

The day Georgina and Mark went house hunting, they drove 140 miles to see five properties, and, in the end, plumped for one that was less than a mile from where they lived! They could have saved themselves all the driving around, but they hadn't thought the house was for them until they finally saw it. 'When we saw a picture of the place, we didn't think we would like it,' recalls Mark, 'But at the end of our house hunting, we hadn't found anything we were interested in and thought we would take a look at it. We had seen a town house that we thought was beautiful, but it needed £60,000 thrown at it, and me to do a lot more work on it than I wanted to.'

The house they finally went for had the added advantage of having a separate barn and a garden, although the garden was on the other side of the barn. This isn't as bad as it might sound, however, as Mark explains: 'We thought that the house not having an attached garden would be a problem, but, in fact, you simply have to cross a lane that is only used by farmers driving their tractors and by ducks.'

The house and the barn were paid for in cash, but the couple had to raise extra money for the renovation costs. This was to cover not only the restoration of the main house, but also the conversion of the barn into a small house. This is because Mark and Georgina intend to live in the barn with its attached garden and rent out the main residence one day.

They applied for a 15-year mortgage of £16,000 – more than the cost of the property – which had to be offered before the conveyance was signed, much to the annoyance of the vendor. Georgina had been lucky enough to find a job locally – not an easy thing in the heart of rural France – with the Vienne offices of the British estate agents VEF, and a bank

Restructuring the layout of the main house to create a sense of space was one of the first jobs of this Limousin renovation

offered to lend them the money to cover the estimated costs. The couple are confident that they will earn back money from the property to pay off some or all of this loan quite quickly, as they feel that in this particular part of France there are not enough gîtes to fulfil the increased demand that budget flights into Limoges and Poitiers are now generating. And, of course, aside from the financial aspect, they are looking forward to settling into their French home life.

The barn is being converted so that one day the Russells can live in it while they are renting the main residence out to holidaymakers

37

Buying Guide

COTE D'AZUR VILLA
LESLIE AND CAROL MUELLER

Having spent each January for many years pouring over holiday brochures trying to find where to spend their annual two-week summer break in the sun, in early 2002 Leslie and Carol Mueller decided it was time to invest in a place of their own. They cast the brochures aside in favour of French property magazines and started their search for their dream home in France.

Top: the Muellers had a new pool built in front of their villa, which their family and guests now enjoy and relax beside in the summer
Above: a view of the garden before the pool was built

The first crucial decision for the Muellers when starting their search was what area they should be looking in. They were after somewhere that was easy to get to from the UK, preferably via one of the many budget flights, with a reliable, warm climate and near to a beach. They also wanted to achieve a rental income that would equal the interest the amount of money they were looking to invest would earn had it been in a bank account.

Having thought about the areas around Perpignan and Carcassonne in Languedoc-Roussillon, which had the beaches, the climate and the budget flight routes, they turned to the Côte d'Azur. The couple realised that here, not only would they be near an airport well-serviced by budget airlines, but they would also be able to earn a higher rental income from the property, this being a more popular destination. This meant they wouldn't have to rent the property out for so long each year, so they could enjoy it themselves for longer periods, and it would have less wear and tear.

The Muellers didn't want to be too near Nice or Cannes, though, as the towns can get quite busy in the summer. The Muellers considered areas further north, but they felt that being too far up in the hills would limit their enjoyment of the property to the summer months. Eventually, they homed in on Grasse, France's perfume capital, only 25 minutes from Nice airport along a toll-free two-lane motorway.

Like most British buyers looking for a home in France to spend their holidays and to rent out to holidaymakers, Leslie Mueller and his wife were initially thinking about an older-style property. But when they realised they wouldn't find one in this part of the country within their budget, they warmed to the idea of buying one of the modern villas that the French build for their holidays. They knew they would rent it out easily and that it would suit their holiday needs. So now they had narrowed down the destination and the style of house, all they had to find was a property with at least three bedrooms – enough for their family and friends to use when

Case Studies

they visited – and a pool, within their budget of £250,000.

The Muellers initially thought that finding their dream home would be quite simple. There were, after all, so many on the market that seemed to fit their criteria. But it was a complex job. Using the internet, specialist magazines and property fairs, they had looked through the particulars of around 600 homes before whittling the list down to around 100. At this point, Leslie visited France to view as many properties as he could.

'I saw about 30 out of the 100 on our short list over four days,' recounts Leslie. 'I whizzed around from one to the next – you know as soon as you get there whether you like it or not. Most of the properties had been built in the 1960s or 1970s, so many had outdated pools and some needed things like the paving redone. One house even had a breeze-block wall built along the boundary so close to the pool that you could no longer walk alongside it.'

The Muellers weren't looking for a refurbishment opportunity, they were simply after a holiday home ready to move in to. So, still without their dream home after all their searching, they took up the offer of a local search agent who had been recommended to them. The agent first picked two properties for the Muellers to view, but then a call came through about a villa in Saint-Jacques, a pretty suburb southwest of Grasse, and this was added to the viewing list.

Leslie looked at them all in his last morning, and there was only one for him, the one in Saint-Jacques. 'It didn't have a pool, but I didn't worry because I had seen so many pools that needed rebuilding again from scratch,' he recalls. 'This one, at the end of my four-day visit, just jumped out at me. I didn't want to go home and start again, but as I was spending nearly £300,000, I also didn't want to make a rash decision.'

While it may not have had a pool, the villa had been specially commissioned by the previous owner, who had paid a lot of attention to detail. It featured curved windows and shutters, reclaimed antique pantiles on the roof and hand-forged steel bars on the windows. There were hand-made tiles everywhere inside, in all the traditional Provençal colours – lavender, bright yellows and aqua – while

When Leslie viewed his French home to be, he was impressed with the quality of its features

the outside walls had a pinky cream render, in a typically Mediterranean style.

'I told my wife, who was stuck in England, that it didn't have a pool, it needed entrance gates, the garden was a mess, there was no proper fencing and there was still building material left all over the place, but we agreed to buy it,' remembers Leslie. Within a week, the preliminary contract had been signed, and the sale went through without a hitch.

Since then, the all-important swimming pool has been built. This was actually no mean feat because, as there was very little topsoil, the pool had to be dug mainly out of rock and some of the boulders that were removed weighed over a ton. They had help gaining planning permission, however, from the search agent who helped them find the villa in the first place. Now, when they are not there enjoying their new home and pool, the couple rent out the villa, which sleeps six to eight, plus a baby, for between £595 and £1,795 a week.

Provençal colour schemes helped attract Leslie to this villa in Grasse

THE REGIONS

Profiles of France's highly individual regions, the styles of property they offer and where to find the best value

MAPS OF FRANCE 42

REGION GUIDES

Brittany	46
Normandy	50
Nord-Pas-de-Calais & Picardy	54
Ile-de-France	58
Champagne-Ardenne	62
Alsace, Lorraine & Franche-Comté	66
The Loire	70
Burgundy	74
Poitou-Charentes	78
Limousin & Auvergne	82
The Rhône-Alps	86
Aquitaine	90
The Midi-Pyrénées	94
Languedoc-Roussillon	98
Provence, Côte d'Azur & Corsica	102

The Regions

Touring Map

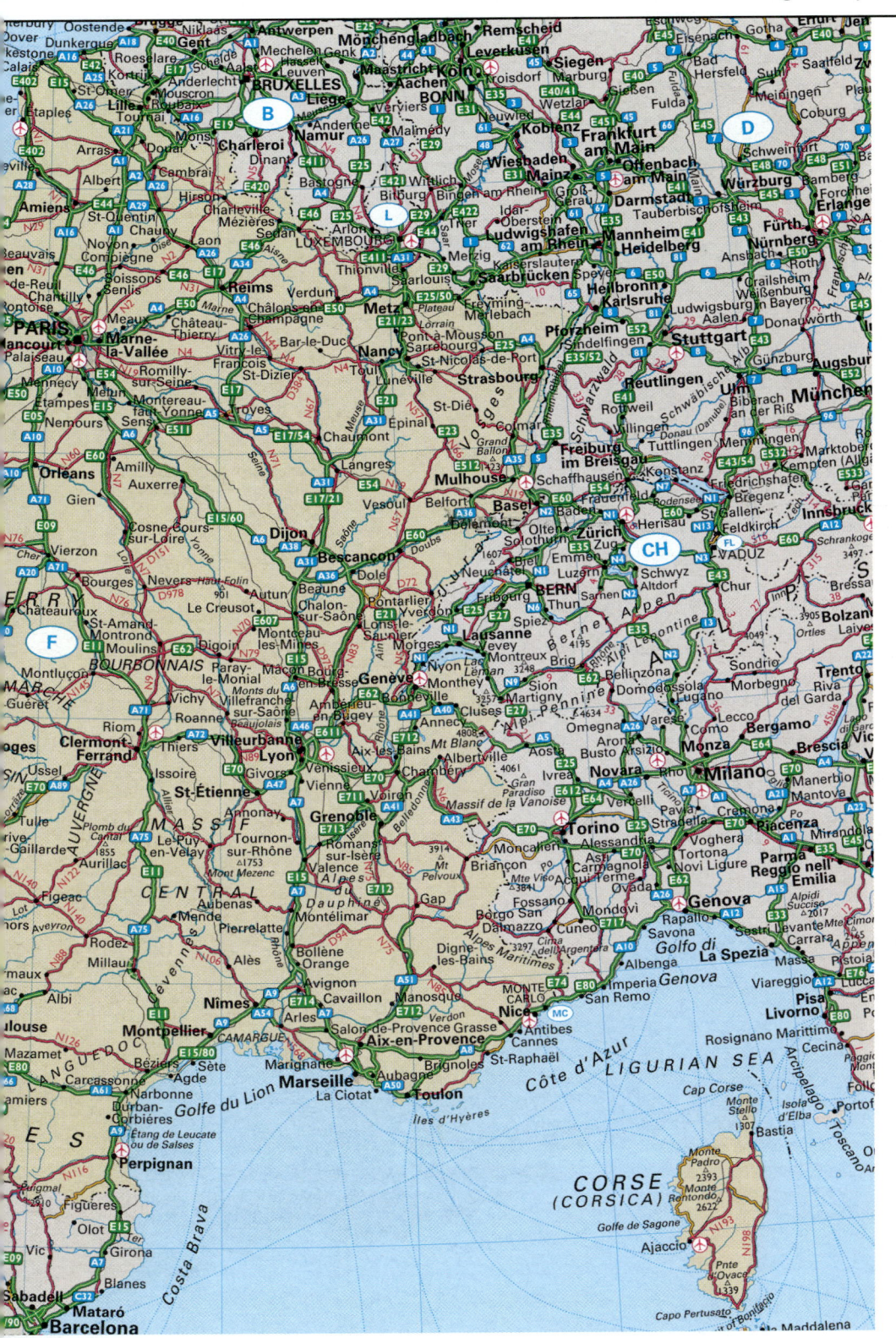

The Regions

THE FRENCH REGIONS

France is officially divided into nearly 100 *départements*, which are local administrative areas quite similar to the British counties. They, in turn, make up the official French regions. This guide has grouped the French regions and their *départements* into 15 sections under the headings and in the order outlined on the opposite page (the names in brackets are the official French versions).

Administrative Map

BRITTANY (BRETAGNE)
Côtes-d'Armor (22), Finistère (29), Ille-et-Vilaine (35), Morbihan (56)

NORMANDY (BASSE-NORMANDIE, HAUTE-NORMANDIE)
Calvados (14), Manche (50), Orne (61) (Basse-Normandie); Eure (27), Seine-Maritime (76) (Haute-Normandie)

NORD-PAS-DE-CALAIS & PICARDY (PICARDIE)
Nord (59), Pas-de-Calais (62) (Nord-Pas-de-Calais); Aisne (02), Oise (60), Somme (80) (Picardie)

ILE-DE-FRANCE
Ville de Paris (75), Seine-et-Marne (77), Yvelines (78), Essonne (91), Hauts-de-Seine (92), Seine-Saint-Denis (93), Val-de-Marne (94), Val-d'Oise (95)

CHAMPAGNE-ARDENNE
Ardennes (08), Aube (10), Marne (51), Haute-Marne (52)

ALSACE, LORRAINE & FRANCHE-COMTE
Bas-Rhin (67), Haut-Rhin (68) (Alsace); Meurthe-et-Moselle (54), Meuse (55), Moselle (57), Vosges (88) (Lorraine); Doubs (25), Jura (39), Haute-Saône (70), Territoire de Belfort (90) (Franche-Comté)

THE LOIRE (CENTRE, PAYS DE LA LOIRE)
Cher (18), Eure-et-Loir (28), Indre (36), Indre-et-Loire (37), Loir-et-Cher (41), Loiret (45) (Centre); Loire-Atlantique (44), Maine-et-Loire (49), Mayenne (53), Sarthe (72), Vendée (85) (Pays de la Loire)

BURGUNDY (BOURGOGNE)
Côte-d'Or (21), Nièvre (58), Saône-et-Loire (71), Yonne (89)

POITOU-CHARENTES
Charente (16), Charente-Maritime (17), Deux-Sèvres (79), Vienne (86)

LIMOUSIN & AUVERGNE
Corrèze (19), Creuse (23), Haute-Vienne (87) (Limousin); Allier (03), Cantal (15), Haute-Loire (43), Puy-de-Dôme (63) (Auvergne)

THE RHONE-ALPS (RHONE-ALPES)
Ain (01), Ardèche (07), Drôme (26), Isère (38), Loire (42), Rhône (69), Savoie (73), Haute-Savoie (74)

AQUITAINE
Dordogne (24), Gironde (33), Landes (40), Lot-et-Garonne (47), Pyrénées-Atlantiques (64)

THE MIDI-PYRENEES
Ariège (09), Aveyron (12), Haute-Garonne (31), Gers (32), Lot (46), Hautes-Pyrénées (65), Tarn (81), Tarn-et-Garonne (82)

LANGUEDOC-ROUSSILLON
Aude (11), Gard (30), Hérault (34), Lozère (48), Pyrénées-Orientales (66)

PROVENCE, COTE D'AZUR & CORSICA (PROVENCE-ALPES-COTE D'AZUR, CORSE)
Alpes-de-Haute-Provence (04), Hautes-Alpes (05), Alpes-Maritimes (06), Bouches-du-Rhône (13), Var (83), Vaucluse (84) (Provence-Alpes-Côte d'Azur); Corse-du-Sud (2A), Haute-Corse (2B) (Corse)

The Regions

BRITTANY

The Breton climate might not be as clement as that of the Côte d'Azur at the opposite end of the country, but the craggy coastline, old-world appeal and relaxed pace of life more than makes up for this in Brittany, which occupies the northwestern tip of France. With its rocky inlets, sandy beaches and diminutive fishing villages, quite reminiscent of the southwest coast of England, Brittany's littoral has a timeless appeal a million miles from the glitzy Mediterranean coast.

Some of France's most dramatic seascapes are found along the northern Breton coast. The beaches of this rugged granite coast, lined with wave-pounded boulders, are some of the most awe-inspiring. Popular with sailors from France and further afield, Brittany's western littoral is a favourite spot for French holidaymakers, and the coastal towns are bustling during the summer months. Inland, villages have an all-year-round charm, with streets lined with traditional stone houses dripping with brightly coloured flowers.

As well as being a haven for sailors and other sea lovers, Brittany is also something of a golfer's

Top: the craggy coastline of northern Brittany is the site of some of France's most dramatic seascapes
Above: Brittany is quite a golfer's paradise, with courses sometimes butting up to a cliff edge

Brittany

Brittany's littoral, quite similar to that of southwest England, is a popular haunt of keen sailors

paradise. Rounds can take the putter perilously close to cliff edges, while it is not unusual for a club house to take the form of a 16th-century château. For non-golfers, the numerous spa centres that have been springing up in the region can provide equal rest and relaxation.

This is the place to get away from it all, to enjoy good food and rediscover a more sedate pace of life. And with ultra-speedy sea crossings taking only four-and-a-half hours and the shortest of short-haul flights available direct into the region, escaping to this northwestern enclave can be as stress-free as the lifestyle that it offers.

BUYING IN BRITTANY
In the past, many Channel-crossers would have chosen the northern French regions because their

GETTING THERE
AIR Dinard receives direct **Ryanair** (0871 246 0000; www.ryanair.com) flights from Stansted, while **Aurigny Air Services** (01481 822886; www.aurigny.com) flies to Dinard from East Midlands, Manchester and Stansted via Guernsey. **Air France** (0845 084 5111; www.airfrance.co.uk) flies from Gatwick to Rennes and Brest, while **buzz** (0870 240 7070; www.buzzaway.com) flies to Brest from Stansted.
SEA Brittany Ferries (0870 536 0360; www.brittany-ferries.com) sails between Portsmouth and Saint-Malo and between Plymouth and Roscoff, while **Condor Ferries** (0845 345 2000; www.condorferries.co.uk) sails from both Poole and Weymouth to Saint-Malo.
ROAD From Calais, take the A16/A28 to Rouen, then the A13/A84 to Rennes via Caen. Take the A11 from Paris to Le Mans, then the A81 on to Rennes.
RAIL TGV services operate between Gare Montparnasse in Paris and Rennes, Brest and Quimper. For rail enquiries, contact **Rail Europe** (0870 584 8848; www.raileurope.co.uk).

AVERAGE DAILY TEMPERATURE (CELSIUS) °C

Brittany											
9.3	8.6	11.1	17.1	16.0	22.7	25.1	24.1	21.2	16.5	12.1	9.3
London											
6	7	10	13	17	20	22	21	19	14	10	7
JAN	FEB	MAR	APR	MAY	JUNE	JULY	AUG	SEPT	OCT	NOV	DEC

The Regions

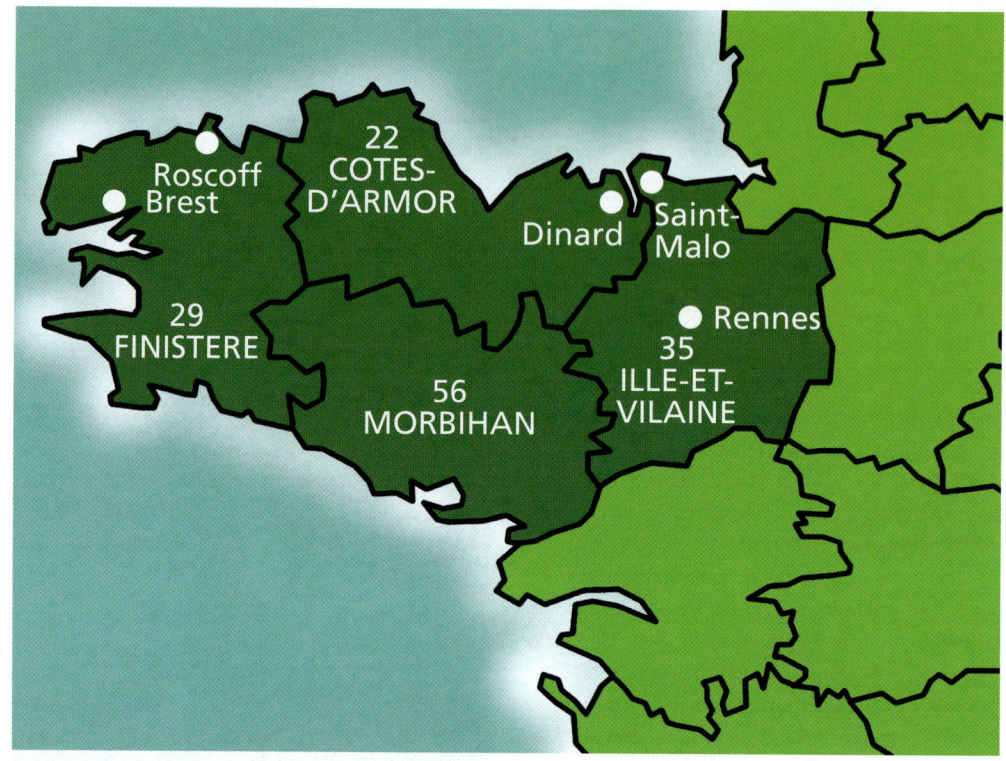

southern counterparts were just too difficult or expensive to get to. However, even though cheap flights are drawing some to the South of France, Brittany is as popular as ever with British buyers. Land and seclusion are still easy to come by – people are buying here to relax.

One of the main attractions of this region has to be its great value. Despite the fact that there have been noticeable price hikes in the area, fully renovated cottages can still be found for under £30,000. There are not, however, many old wrecks to buy for £5,000 and do up over the holidays, as buyers have been doing this here for some years already.

The Gulf of Morbihan on Brittany's southern coast is almost as desirable a location with French people looking for a holiday home as the Mediterranean. Newly-built seaside apartments are more popular than they have ever been with overseas buyers who are looking for something easy to maintain and to leave empty with the minimum of worry. But substantial, traditional properties by the coast or on the numerous Breton islands don't come cheap. Head inland, however, and some of the most keenly-priced properties in France can be found, from a £10,000 village renovation project to a £60,000 long, thin *longère* under a sleek, grey slate roof. Traditional properties – typically built out of Breton granite – in areas like these turn up on agents' books for between £20,000 and £70,000, a price band within which it is becoming increasingly difficult to find properties in France.

Inland Brittany can provide the best of both worlds for would-be second home owners. Not only does it offer tranquil rural settings dotted with traditional stone buildings, some with charming thatched roofs, that have a timeless charm and are often set in a good plot of land, but it also offers easy access to a beautiful coastline and to the western Channel ports – all at a fairly reasonable price.

For a guide to property prices in Brittany, turn to page 111.

USEFUL CONTACTS

PREFECTURE
Préfecture de la Région Bretagne
3 rue Martenot, CS 26517
35065 Rennes Cedex
Tel: +33 2 99 02 10 35
Fax: +33 2 99 02 10 15

LEGAL
Chambre des Notaires
d'Ille-et-Vilaine
2 mail Anne-Catherine
CS 54337
35043 Rennes Cedex
Tel: +33 2 99 65 23 24
Fax: +33 2 99 65 23 20

FINANCE
Direction Régionale des
Impôts de l'Ouest
6 rue Jean Guéhenno
CS 14208
35042 Rennes Cedex
Tel: +33 2 99 87 18 30
Fax: +33 2 99 63 28 90

BUILDING & PLANNING
Chambre Régionale
de Métiers de Bretagne
2 cours des Alliés
35029
Rennes Cedex
Tel: +33 2 99 65 32 00
Fax: +33 2 99 65 32 59

CAUE du Morbihan
13 bis rue Olivier de Clisson
56000 Vannes
Tel: +33 2 97 54 17 35
Fax: +33 2 97 47 89 52

EDUCATION
Rectorat de l'Académie
de Rennes
96 rue d'Antrain
35044 Rennes Cedex
Tel: +33 2 99 28 78 78
Fax: +33 2 99 28 77 72

HEALTH
Caisse Primaire d'Assurance
Maladie d'Ille-et-Vilaine
7 cours Alliés
35000 Rennes
Tel: +33 2 99 29 44 44
Fax: +33 2 99 29 45 74

Brittany offers the buyer a huge range of traditional buildings with a timeless charm

NORMANDY

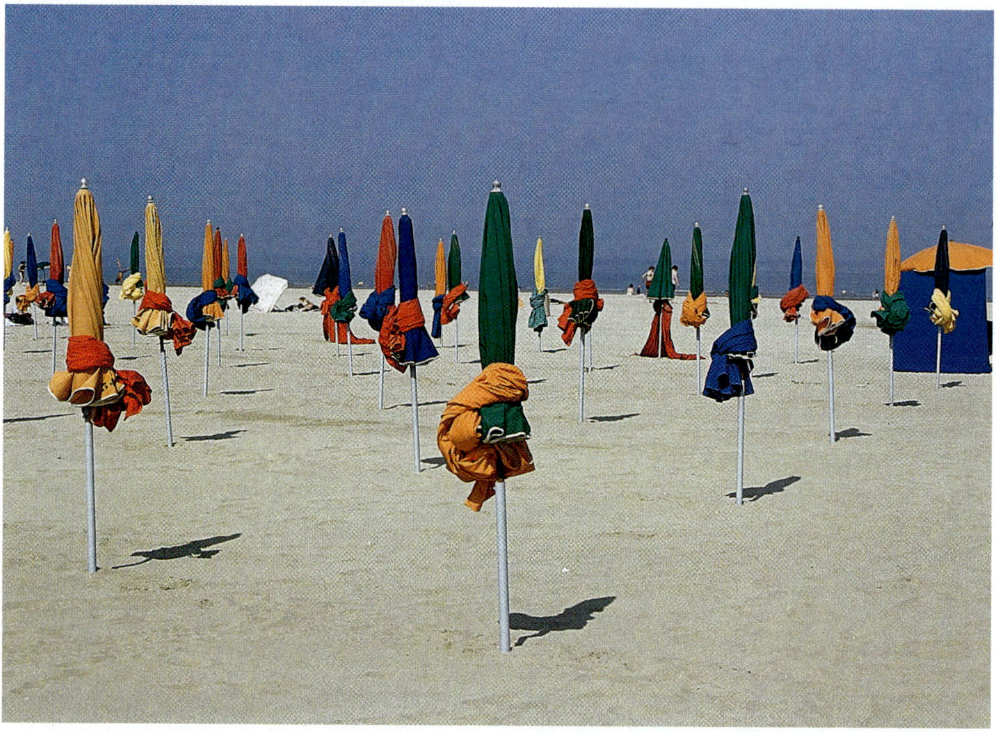

JUSTIN POSTLETHWAITE/MERRICKS MEDIA

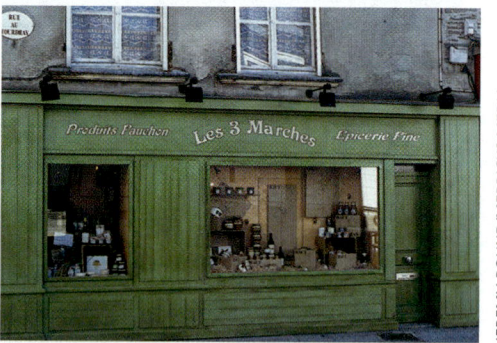

Lush countryside, wide sandy beaches, orchards and cheese… these are the key elements of the allure of the northern coastal region of Normandy. It is as much a family beach holiday destination as it is a foodie's retreat, and so easy to reach from our British shores.

Rural Normandy has a timeless, relaxed appeal with small farms fringed with ancient hedgerows. Today, drivers or cyclists travelling along the long empty lanes are more likely to find themselves slowing down because there is a tractor in front of them rather than because they have found themselves in a traffic jam.

The verdant countryside of the Pays d'Auge, which straddles the three *départements* of Calvados, Orne and Eure, offers a classic taste of Normandy. In its sleepy valleys dotted with black and white half-timbered farm buildings, cows graze peacefully in pastures and apples weigh heavily on the branches of the trees in its many orchards. This is the home of two of Normandy's most prized

JEREMY POUND/MERRICKS MEDIA

Top: Deauville's pristine fashionable beach on the Côte Fleurie

Above: the shops in Cherbourg can provide a diversion from lazing on the sandy beaches of Normandy's Contenin Peninsula

Normandy

Market day in the bustling port of Cherbourg

produce – the soft, creamy cheese Camembert and Calvados, *the* apple brandy.

To the north, along the coast, are found pretty ports such as Honfleur and smart resorts like Deauville and Trouville. Here, wooden promenades, designer boutiques and casinos bring a touch of the Côte d'Azur to the Côte Fleurie, the name given to this fashionable stretch of sand.

The Cotenin Peninsula, which juts out into the Channel just to the west and has the bustling port of Cherbourg on its northern tip, offers a lively and typically French holiday experience. Modern resorts lined with *crêperies* and holiday villas are dotted along the littoral, wherever you are it seems that beaches are never far away. But the shops and markets of Cherbourg, visits to medieval castles and war memorials – poignant reminders of the crucial battles that were fought here during World War II – can provide diversions from lazing about in the sun.

GETTING THERE

AIR Air France (0845 084 5111; www.airfrance.co.uk) flies from Heathrow to Caen, while **buzz** (0870 240 7070; www.buzzaway.com) operates services between Stansted, Caen and Rouen.
SEA Brittany Ferries (0870 536 0360; www.brittany-ferries.com) sails from Portsmouth to Caen-Ouistreham, and Poole to Cherbourg, **P&O Ferries** (0870 242 4999; www.poportsmouth.com) from Portsmouth to Le Havre and Cherbourg, and **Transmanche Ferries** (0800 917 1201; www.transmancheferries.com) from Newhaven to Dieppe. **Hoverspeed** (0870 524 0241; www.hoverspeed.co.uk) operates services between Newhaven and Dieppe and between Portsmouth and Le Havre.
ROAD Take the A16 from Calais to Rouen, then the A13 for Caen.
RAIL From the **Eurostar** (0870 518 6186; www.eurostar.co.uk) at Lille Europe change for the TGV service to Rouen. For rail enquiries, contact **Rail Europe** (0870 584 8848; www.raileurope.co.uk).

AVERAGE DAILY TEMPERATURE (CELSIUS) °C

Normandy												
7.6	6.4	8.4	13.0	14.0	20.0	21.6	22.0	18.2	14.5	10.8	7.9
London												
6	7	10	13	17	20	22	21	19	14	10	7
JAN	FEB	MAR	APR	MAY	JUNE	JULY	AUG	SEPT	OCT	NOV	DEC

The Regions

BUYING IN NORMANDY

Normandy has been a favourite with British buyers for years, and it is as popular as ever today, especially with those who do not want their French home too far from the UK. This is one of the spots to plump for if you want to visit at the weekends and really want to drive, rather than hop on an aeroplane. Londoners who weekend in their own Normandy country home can be heard boasting that it is easier to get to this part of France than many second-home hotspots in the English countryside. Road links from the Channel Tunnel and all the Channel ports are second to none, and cheap flights into the area are on the increase – for those who want to get there fast, or from less convenient locations on British soil.

The charm of a traditional Normandy home can easily fulfil the dreams of foreign buyers. Stone built and sturdy or long, low and half-timbered in black and white, picture-postcard looks are almost guaranteed here. Low price levels are also pretty much assured. At the lower end those who are modest of budget and strong of will can purchase a cottage with 'work required' for around £15,000.

Further up the property ladder, a *longère* (a longhouse), often a converted farm building with or without some half-timbering in that quintessential Normandy black and white colouring, with four bedrooms, outbuildings and a couple or more hectares could be bought for under £100,000, as could a *maison de maître*, a smart period house with three bedrooms and a sizeable garden. For an extra few dozen thousand pounds – or euros – the property could be a farmhouse with numerous outbuildings and acres of land to enjoy.

For a guide to property prices in Normandy, turn to page 133.

USEFUL CONTACTS

PREFECTURE

Préfecture de la Région
Basse-Normandie
rue Saint-Laurent
14038 Caen Cedex
Tel: +33 2 31 30 64 00
Fax: +33 2 31 30 64 90

Préfecture de la Région
Haute-Normandie
7 place de la Madeleine
76036 Rouen Cedex
Tel: +33 2 32 76 50 00
Fax: +33 2 35 98 10 50

LEGAL

Chambre des Notaires
du Calvados
6 place Louis Guillouard
14000 Caen
Tel: +33 2 31 85 42 21
Fax: +33 2 31 85 82 62

Chambre des Notaires
de la Seine-Maritime
39 rue du Champ des Oiseaux
BP 248
76000 Rouen
Tel: +33 2 35 88 63 88
Fax: +33 2 35 98 70 61

FINANCE

Direction des Impôts du Nord
13–15 boulevard de la Liberté
59800 Lille
Tel: +33 3 20 17 64 90
Fax: +33 3 20 17 64 99

Direction des Impôts de l'Ouest
6 rue Jean Guéhenno, CS 14208
35042 Rennes Cedex
Tel: +33 2 99 87 18 30
Fax: +33 2 99 63 28 90

BUILDING & PLANNING

Chambre Régionale de Métiers
de Basse-Normandie
BP 5205
14074 Caen 5 Cedex
Tel: +33 2 31 95 42 00
Fax: +33 2 31 95 99 30

Chambre Régionale de Métiers
de Haute-Normandie
5–9 avenue de Caen
BP 1154
76176 Rouen Cedex
Tel: +33 2 32 18 06 40
Fax: +33 2 32 18 06 49

CAUE du Calvados
28 rue Jean Eudes
14000 Caen
Tel: +33 2 31 15 59 60
Fax: +33 2 31 15 59 65

CAUE de Seine-Maritime
5 rue Louis Blanc
BP 1283
76178 Rouen
Tel: +33 2 35 72 94 50
Fax: +33 2 35 72 09 72

EDUCATION

Rectorat de l'Académie
de Caen
168 rue Caponière
BP 6184
14061 Caen Cedex
Tel: +33 2 31 30 15 00
Fax: +33 2 31 30 15 92

Rectorat de l'Académie
de Rouen
25 rue de Fontenelle
76037 Rouen
Cedex
Tel: +33 2 35 14 75 00
Fax: +33 2 35 71 56 38

HEALTH

Caisse Primaire d'Assurance
Maladie du Calvados
boulevard Général Weygand
BP 6048
14031 Caen Cedex 4
Tel: +33 2 31 45 79 00
Fax: +33 2 31 45 79 80

Caisse Primaire d'Assurance
Maladie de Rouen
50 avenue Bretagne
76039 Rouen
Tel: +33 2 35 03 63 63
Fax: +33 2 35 03 63 03

A monument to one of France's great leaders in Cherbourg

The Regions

NORD-PAS-DE-CALAIS & PICARDY

Lille, a cosmopolitan shopping centre and venue of a vibrant market each September that takes over its streets

The most northern of French territories, Nord-Pas-de-Calais and Picardy, are also the easiest to get to by car from the British side of the Channel. With the mouth of the Channel Tunnel opening up on its northern tip, and regular speedy ferries scurrying between here and British soils, this is a destination for lovers of France who prefer to keep their journeys short.

Many pass this most northern region of France in haste, either in a hurry to reach more southern climes or in high-speed trains connecting with services heading to all corners of France. Those who take time to get to know this often somewhat disregarded area, however, take advantage of its expansive sandy beaches – some quite exclusive – dense forests and many lakes. Then there are the unspoilt villages that are often lined with gargantuan displays of flowers, and quiet country lanes of the sort that seem to be fewer and farther between in Britain today.

The shopping opportunities offered up by historic towns such as Lille, Boulogne and Calais, combined with their easy access from the UK by boat, car or train, make this the ideal destination for shopaholics, and not just those on a 12-hour booze cruise. Lille is very much a cosmopolitan shopping centre, but each September its streets are the setting for a rather more charming and parochial shopping experience. This is its famous *braderie*, in which miles of stalls selling cut-price goods line the cobbled streets and *moules-frites* are sold in large quantity. The coastal towns of Boulogne and Calais are perfect all year round for picking up regional produce and even well-priced antiques.

Further down the coast, the Somme Canal joins the Channel where the Opal Coast becomes the

Nord-Pas-de-Calais & Picardy

Historic Nord-Pas-de-Calais is just a short trip away by car or Eurostar

Picardy coast, and brightly coloured sailboards dart through the water in the summer. Modest fishing villages and great expanses of beaches with rolling sand dunes characterise this part of the northern French coast. Inland, the flat countryside, a cyclist's dream, is criss-crossed with waterways and dotted with lakes.

The climate in this part of France is very similar to that of southern England, but this is probably the only similarity between the two regions. The long open roads are generally traffic-free and the pretty villages are mostly empty in the summer months.

BUYING IN NORD-PAS-DE-CALAIS AND PICARDY
France's northern *départements* have traditionally been popular with British buyers, as they have been with close neighbours looking for holiday homes like the Belgians and Dutch, and with holidaying Parisians. Any buyer considering this area should not think they have come across an area neglected by other house hunters just because the region's

GETTING THERE
AIR Ryanair (0871 246 0000; www.ryanair.com) flies from Dublin and Glasgow to Beauvais; **Air France** (0845 084 5111; www.airfrance.co.uk) from Heathrow to Lille-Lequin; and **Lyddair** (01797 320000; www.lyddair.co.uk) from Lydd to Le Touquet.
SEA P&O (0870 242 4999; www.posl.com) and **SeaFrance** (0870 571 1711; www.seafrance.com) sail from Dover to Calais, while **Norfolkline** (0870 870 1020; www.norfolkline.com) sails between Dover and Dunkirk. **Hoverspeed** (0870 524 0241; www.hoverspeed.com) operates services between Dover and Calais.
ROAD From the Channel Tunnel or Calais's ferry port, take the A26 through both Pas-de-Calais and Picardy. Take the A1 from Arras for central Picardy. Follow the A16 out of Calais for the coastal towns of Pas-de-Calais and Picardy, as well as Amiens and Beauvais. For Lille, take the A1 from Arras or the A25 from Dunkirk.
RAIL Direct **Eurostar** (0870 518 6186; www.eurostar.co.uk) services operate between Waterloo and Lille. Change at Lille for SNCF services to other towns. For rail enquiries, contact **Rail Europe** (0870 584 8848; www.raileurope.co.uk).

AVERAGE DAILY TEMPERATURE (CELSIUS) °C

Nord-Pas-de-Calais & Picardy
6.6	5.6	8.3	13.7	14.9	21.5	22.7	24.0	19.3	15.3	8.3	6.9

London
6	7	10	13	17	20	22	21	19	14	10	7
JAN	FEB	MAR	APR	MAY	JUNE	JULY	AUG	SEPT	OCT	NOV	DEC

The Regions

nomenclatures do not have the romantic connotations of, say, Provence or Dordogne.

There has been a substantial increase in the value of properties in this part of France in recent years, mainly thanks to the improvement in transport links, including the construction of the Channel Tunnel. Price rises have been gradual, but one noticeable knock-on effect of rising interest from foreign buyers is that there are fewer properties for renovation to be found here.

Anyone looking for a private lake, either for regular personal use or to provide fishing opportunities for holidaying Brits, may find just what they are looking for here. Extra-large coarse fish and tranquil countryside make northern France a popular spot with British anglers. Picardy is of particular interest to anglers because it has many acres of lakes, of both private and commercial proportions, and it is only an hour or two's drive from Calais. Expect to pay a sizable premium for the privilege of fishing on private land, though, even when private fishing lakes seem in abundance. While modest country houses can be found in Picardy for between £50,000 and £100,000, a simple detached house with a three-acre lake can cost in the region of £150,000.

Proximity to the coast and, in particular, to the fashionable coastal town of Le Touquet, whose beach is nicknamed 'Paris-Plage' because it is so popular with Parisians fleeing the city in the summer months, also has an upward effect on prices. The forested area is the most sought-after of spots. Travel half an hour or so inland from the coast, however, and properties dip in price noticeably, and it's not too difficult to find a detached house with a sizeable plot of land.

For a guide to property prices in Nord-Pas-de-Calais and Picardy, turn to page 157.

Nord-Pas-de-Calais & Picardy

USEFUL CONTACTS

PREFECTURE

Préfecture de la Région
Nord-Pas-de-Calais
Place de la République
2 rue Jacquemars-Giélée
59039 Lille Cedex
Tel: +33 3 20 30 59 59
Fax: +33 3 20 30 52 58

Préfecture de la Région Picardie
51 rue de la République
80020 Amiens Cedex 1
Tel: +33 3 22 97 80 80
Fax: +33 3 22 92 13 98

LEGAL

Chambre des Notaires
du Pas-de-Calais
1 rue du Collège
62000 Arras
Tel: +33 3 21 51 81 91
Fax: +33 3 21 71 42 20

Chambre des Notaires
de la Somme
11 place d'Aguesseau
BP 331
80003 Amiens Cedex 1
Tel: +33 3 22 82 08 92
Fax: +33 3 22 82 08 97

FINANCE

Direction des Impôts du Nord
13–15 boulevard de la Liberté
59800 Lille
Tel: +33 3 20 17 64 90
Fax: +33 3 20 17 64 99

BUILDING & PLANNING

Chambre Régionale de Métiers
du Nord-Pas-de-Calais
9 rue Léon Trulin, BP 114
59001 Lille Cedex
Tel: +33 3 20 14 96 14
Fax: +33 3 20 55 51 92

Chambre Régionale de Métiers
de Picardie
Cité des Métiers
80440 Boves
Tel: +33 3 22 50 40 55
Fax: +33 3 22 50 40 59

CAUE du Nord
148 rue Nationale
59800 Lille
Tel: +33 3 20 57 67 67
Fax: +33 3 20 30 93 40

CAUE de la Somme
5 rue Vincent Auriol
80000 Amiens
Tel: +33 3 22 91 11 65
Fax: +33 3 22 92 29 11

EDUCATION

Rectorat de l'Académie d'Amiens
(Aisne, Oise, Somme)
20 boulevard d'Alsace-Lorraine
BP 2609
80026 Amiens Cedex 1
Tel: +33 3 22 82 38 23
Fax: +33 3 22 92 82 12

Rectorat de l'Académie de Lille
(Nord, Pas-de-Calais)
20 rue Saint-Jacques
BP 709
59033 Lille Cedex
Tel: +33 3 20 15 60 00
Fax: +33 3 20 15 65 90

HEALTH

Caisse Primaire d'Assurance
Maladie du Nord
2 rue d'Iéna, BP 01
59895 Lille Cedex 9
Tel: +33 3 20 42 34 00
Fax: +33 3 20 54 33 64

Caisse Primaire d'Assurance
Maladie de la Somme
8 place Louis Sellier
80021 Amiens Cedex 1
Tel: +33 3 22 97 50 00
Fax: +33 3 22 97 50 01

Above and left: largely thanks to great transport links with the UK, Calais's shopping opportunities and Lille's splendour can be readily enjoyed today

The Regions

ILE-DE-FRANCE

FELIX STENSSON/ALAMY

The focus of much emotive and philosophical writing, France's political, economic and cultural centre, Paris, has a tough image to live up to. But its tree-lined boulevards, cafés and quiet river walkways easily help maintain its romantic reputation.

One of the best ways to explore this vibrant city is to follow in the footsteps of famous artists and writers who would stroll along the pavements in search of inspiration. The streets come alive in the day with colourful markets selling fresh produce from around the country, antiques or brightly coloured material, while at night it's the bustling restaurant and bar scene that livens up the avenues. Paris is, after all, a hub for all that is best to cook and eat in the whole country, as it is for the best theatre, art and shopping.

The jewel in the crown of the Ile-de-France region is undoubtedly Paris, but the land spreading out from it in all directions is dotted with other, more modestly sized, gems. This countryside, comprising contrasting wide open fields and dense forests, was once the chosen site for the outdoor pursuits of many past kings and noblemen, and this led to the building of elegant châteaux and the emergence of 'royal towns' within about 50 miles of the capital. The most significant royal town is Versailles, to the southwest of Paris. Home to the eponymous château built by the 'Sun King' Louis XIV, it was the seat of the royal court from the late 17th century to the Revolution in 1789. Others include the former favourite of hunting royals, Fontainebleau, with its vast deciduous woodland and Renaissance château, as well as Rambouillet,

Ile-de-France

Opposite: a view of Montmartre, a good area for tourist lets
Right: the Louvre, one of Paris's great art centres

ROWENA MEDLOW

whose palace, built by Louis XIV's son, was once the scene of Marie-Antoinette's escapist milkmaid role-playing.

BUYING IN ILE-DE-FRANCE

While the environs of Paris provide plenty of opportunities for those looking for larger houses, perhaps even châteaux, close to the country's epicentre and its excellent communication network, the city itself is an ideal place for a pied-à-terre in France. The thriving metropolis is within easy reach of the UK – only a three-hour train ride from its centre to London, and serviced by many budget and regular airlines – with connections to the rest of France and Europe beyond (high-speed train services to the Mediterranean within three hours). More and more foreign house hunters are choosing Paris, either so that they would never have to book another hotel in the capital again, or so that their French base would have easy access to the UK and the rest of Europe.

GETTING THERE

AIR Air France (0845 084 5111; www.airfrance.co.uk), **British Airways** (0845 773 3377; www.britishairways.com) and **British Midland** (0870 607 0555; www.britishmidland.com) between them fly to Paris's Charles de Gaulle airport from Heathrow, Gatwick, London City, Aberdeen, Belfast, Birmingham, Bristol, Cardiff, Edinburgh, Glasgow, Humberside, Leeds/Bradford, Manchester, Newcastle, Plymouth, Southampton and Teesside. **Ryanair** (0871 246 0000; www.ryanair.com) and **buzz** (0870 240 7070; www.buzzaway.com) offer low-cost alternative flights from Stansted, as does **easyJet** (0870 600 0000; www.easyjet.com) from Luton and Liverpool. **British Airways** also operates services to Orly.
ROAD From the Channel Tunnel or Calais's ferry port, take the A26 to Arras, then join the A1 south, which leads straight to Paris. Travelling from Dieppe, take the D915 to the northwestern outskirts of the city. From Le Havre, head out on the A131, then join the A13, which continues on to the western suburbs. The N13 runs from Cherbourg directly to the city.
RAIL Eurostar (0870 518 6186; www.eurostar.co.uk) services run from London, Waterloo to Paris's Gare de Nord. Take SNCF trains on to other Ile-de-France towns. Contact **Rail Europe** (0870 584 8848; www.raileurope.co.uk).

AVERAGE DAILY TEMPERATURE (CELSIUS) °C

Ile-de-France											
7.5	7.1	10.2	15.7	16.6	23.4	25.1	25.6	20.9	16.5	11.7	7.8
London											
6	7	10	13	17	20	22	21	19	14	10	7
JAN	FEB	MAR	APR	MAY	JUNE	JULY	AUG	SEPT	OCT	NOV	DEC

The Regions

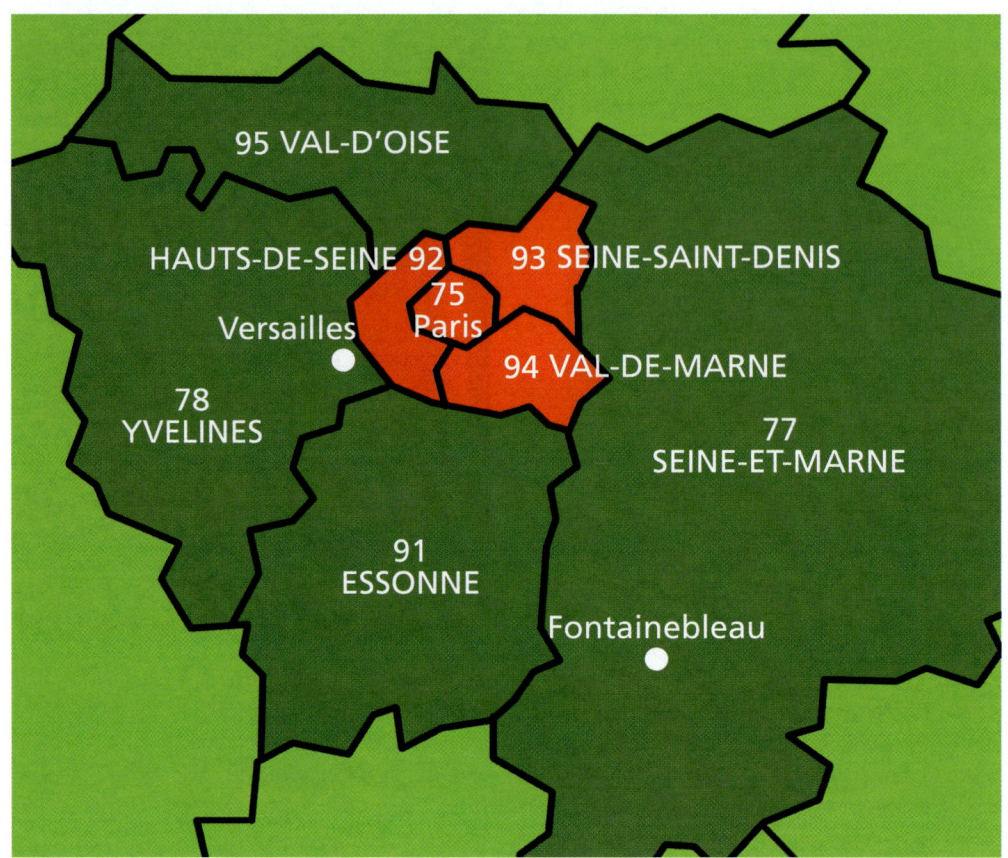

Each area, or *arrondissement*, of Paris has its own particular look, but there is one architectural style that is most prevalent in the capital. This is the neo-classicism made so popular by Georges-Eugène Haussmann. Under Haussmann's instructions, much of Paris was demolished in the 19th century so that the city could be both modernised and beautified. The resulting wide boulevards lined with trees and elegant pale stone apartment buildings provide much of Paris's charm today. There is usually a steady stream of apartments on the market in this style of building, as well as behind more modern façades, from budget studios that were once maids' quarters on the top of 19th-century residences to split-level duplexes that would provide adequate entertaining space for the busiest of socialites.

Prices vary quite dramatically between *arrondissements*, with the most exclusive addresses to be found in the 17th and 16th, and in the streets spreading out from the Eiffel Tower. More up-and-coming areas like the Bastille, whose streets are dotted with fashionable boutiques and bars today, are places where those in search of a good value pied-à-terre, either for personal use or to rent out, could look.

There is always a strong demand for rental properties in Paris, and owners tend to have a wide choice of prospective tenants. Apartments rarely stand empty, and gross rental yields are currently between five and eight percent, so buying to let out in Paris can be a sound investment. To attract tourists, the Latin Quarter and Montmartre are good areas to buy in, but to interest professional tenants, it can be better to buy near the Champs-Elysées or in one of the business districts like the 8th *arrondissement*.

For a guide to property prices in Ile-de-France, turn to page 169.

Ile-de-France

USEFUL CONTACTS

PREFECTURE

Préfecture de la Région
d'Ile-de-France
29 rue Barbet de Jouy
75007 Paris
Tel: +33 1 44 42 62 87
Fax: +33 1 44 42 63 37

LEGAL

Chambre des Notaires de Paris
12 avenue Victoria
75001 Paris
Tel: +33 1 44 82 24 00
Fax: +33 1 44 82 24 20

Chambre Interdépartementale
des Notaires de Versailles
40 avenue de Paris
78000 Versailles
Tel: +33 1 39 50 01 75
Fax: +33 1 39 02 38 44

FINANCE

Direction des Impôts
d'Ile-de-France
33 avenue de l'Opéra
75002 Paris
Tel: +33 1 44 77 99 59
Fax: +33 1 44 77 99 79

Centre des Impôts des
Non-Résidents
9 rue d'Uzès
75094 Paris Cedex 02
Tel: +33 1 44 76 18 00
Fax: +33 1 42 21 45 04

BUILDING & PLANNING

Chambre Régionale de Métiers
d'Ile-de-France
72 rue de Reuilly
75592 Paris Cedex 12
Tel: +33 1 53 33 53 07
Fax: +33 1 43 43 71 74

Union Régionale des CAUE
d'Ile-de-France
37 rue du Chemin Vert
93000 Bobigny
Tel: +33 1 48 32 25 93
Fax: +33 1 48 31 15 36

EDUCATION

Rectorat de l'Académie
de Crétail
(Seine-et-Marne, Seine-
Saint-Denis, Val-de-Marne)
4 rue Georges-Enesco
94010 Crétail
Tel: +33 1 49 81 60 60
Fax: +33 1 49 81 65 90

Rectorat de l'Académie
de Paris
47 rue des Ecoles
75230 Paris Cedex 5
Tel: +33 1 40 46 22 11
Fax: +33 1 40 46 20 10

Rectorat de l'Académie
de Versailles
(Essonne, Hauts-de-Seine,
Val-d'Oise, Yvelines)
3 boulevard de Lesseps
78017 Versailles Cedex
Tel: +33 1 30 83 44 44
Fax: +33 1 39 50 02 47

HEALTH

Caisse Primaire d'Assurance
Maladie de Paris
21 rue Georges Auric
75948 Paris Cedex 19
Tel: +33 1 53 38 70 00
Fax: +33 1 53 38 73 47

Caisse Primaire d'Assurance
Maladie des Yvelines
92 avenue de Paris
78014 Versailles
Tel: +33 1 39 20 30 00
Fax: +33 1 39 49 58 31

Caisse Primaire d'Assurance
Maladie du Val de Marne
9 avenue Général de Gaulle
94031 Crétail
Tel: +33 1 43 99 33 33
Fax: +33 1 43 99 11 07

Colourful markets and lively
bars bring Paris's streets alive

CHAMPAGNE-ARDENNE

One of the easiest French regions to reach from the northern ports and the Channel Tunnel, Champagne-Ardenne is a land of lush meadows and vast woodlands, with a few illustrious vineyards thrown in for good measure, it would appear. This is a land that has plenty to offer both the nature lover and the foodie in search of a taste of the good life.

Highlights for anyone travelling to the region must be the Champagne 'houses', the name given to larger producers of the celebrated fizz, centred on the town of Reims and Epernay, the latter having over 70 miles of underground chalk cellars primed with bottles of bubbly. Following the Champagne route out of these towns opens up even more opportunities to taste and discover new styles and names.

At the southern end of the wine route, in the Aube, the rolling hills are dotted with tiny villages and vestiges of the area's monastic past, and vineyards start giving way to forests. Here sits the town of Troyes, its roads lined with multicoloured, half-timbered buildings, aptly formed in the shape of a Champagne cork.

To the north of this green and pleasant region is Ardennes, which is steeped in history, mostly of the warring variety. The fortification of everything from a village church to an entire town is a reminder of Ardennes's chequered past, having been a border territory. The Ardennes town of Sedan is, in fact, the site of Europe's largest fortified castle, Château de Sedan, which grew even stronger after every attack, as the inhabitants would reinforce it a little more each time.

The turbulent past of this northern outpost can be completely left behind, however, in the vast forested area that covers a third of Ardennes. The mountain biking and hiking trails are extensive, with those in the Meuse Valley offering some of the most spectacular scenes such as panoramic views of the meandering River Meuse itself.

Not only does the Champagne-Ardenne region have breathtaking scenery, a rich heritage and first-class wines, but it also benefits from a very

Champagne-Ardenne

Opposite, left and right: the elegant town of Reims; half-timbered houses in Troyes; a sleepy Champagne village

pleasant climate. It is said that Champagne-Ardenne is milder and sunnier than both Brittany and Normandy.

BUYING IN CHAMPAGNE-ARDENNE

It is generally considered that the British, once off the ferry or out of the tunnel and travelling south, stay on the road after Reims and don't stop until they get to Burgundy. Although the Belgians, Dutch and members of Luxembourg's cosmopolitan population have warmed to the charms of Champagne-Ardenne, our equally close nation across the Channel does not seem to have quite discovered it yet.

This is a good thing, perhaps, for those looking for a property that has not witnessed the same

GETTING THERE

AIR Fly to Paris, Charles de Gaulle with **Air France** (0845 084 5111; www.airfrance.co.uk), **British Airways** (0845 773 3377; www.britishairways.com), British Midland (0870 607 0555; www.britishmidland.com), **Ryanair** (0871 246 0000; www.ryanair.com), **buzz** (0870 240 7070; www.buzzaway.com) or **easyJet** (0870 600 0000; www.easyjet.com) from London and regional UK airports. Flights to Brussels-South Charleroi can be convenient for northern Champagne-Ardenne, while flying to Dijon is good for the south. **Ryanair** flies to Charleroi from Glasgow, Liverpool and Stansted and **buzz** flies to Dijon from Stansted.
ROAD Take the A26 from Calais straight to Reims or Troyes, or change on to the N43 at Arras for Charleville-Mézières. From Paris, take the A4 straight to Reims.
RAIL SNCF services operate between Gare de l'Est in Paris and Reims, Châlons-en-Champagne, Troyes and Charleville-Mézières. Alternatively, take the **Eurostar** (0870 518 6186; www.eurostar.co.uk) to Lille-Europe and change there for SNCF services. For rail enquiries, contact **Rail Europe** (0870 584 8848; www.raileurope.co.uk).

AVERAGE DAILY TEMPERATURE (CELSIUS) °C

Champagne-Ardenne

6.2	5.6	8.9	13.8	15.1	22.5	23.8	24.9	19.3	15.0	9.6	6.2

London

6	7	10	13	17	20	22	21	19	14	10	7
JAN	FEB	MAR	APR	MAY	JUNE	JULY	AUG	SEPT	OCT	NOV	DEC

The Regions

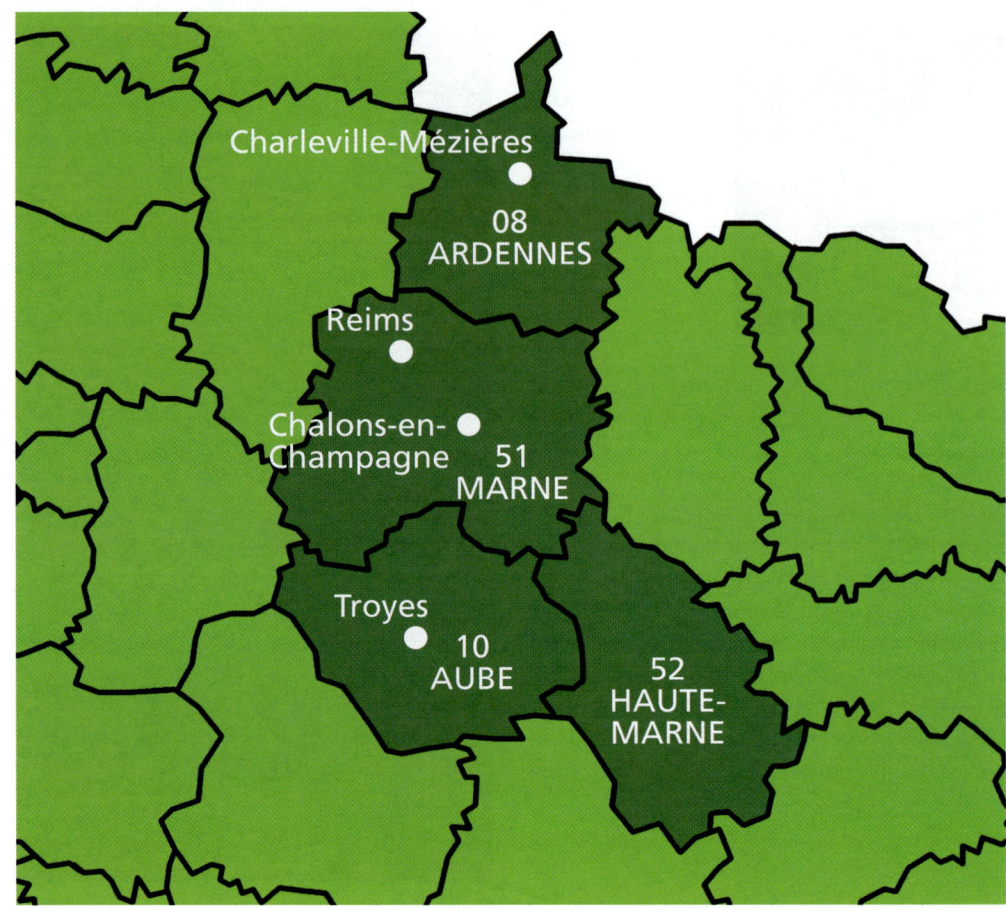

price hikes as those in spots favoured by the British in the past two to three years. In the northern enclave of Ardennes, for example, an entire hamlet can sometimes be picked up for £350,000. Wood panelling and wooden floors give traditional Ardennes properties their unique character. In the towns of Reims and Epernay, elegant three-storey houses with tall windows are typical, and in the town of Troyes, brightly hued half-timbered buildings are commonly found.

While the Champagne towns like Reims offer up smart town houses and spacious apartments, Champagne country has a wealth of both elegant châteaux with lofty slate roofs and more modest stone-built village homes. These occasionally have vaulted cellars dug out of the local chalky ground, just like the grand Champagne houses have for storing their prized sparkling wine.

Apart from relatively modest property prices, people moving into this area also benefit from both being surrounded by beautiful countryside and being close to sophisticated cities like Luxembourg, Brussels and Paris. There are also first-rate transport links to the UK, which is invaluable if frequent travel between a home in France and the UK is likely. Flights out of Charleroi just over the Belgian border are fast, frequent and cheap, and the drive up to the Channel Tunnel is swift. It can take just two hours, in fact, to reach Calais from this region by car.

For a guide to property prices in Champagne-Ardenne, turn to page 175.

USEFUL CONTACTS

PREFECTURE
Préfecture de la Région
Champagne-Ardenne
38 rue Carnot
51036 Châlons-en-Champagne
Cedex
Tel: +33 3 26 26 10 10
Fax: +33 3 26 26 12 63

LEGAL
Chambre des Notaires
44 cours Jean-Baptiste Langlet
BP 1181
51100 Reims Cedex
Tel: +33 3 26 86 72 10
Fax: +33 3 26 86 72 11

FINANCE
Direction des Impôts de l'Est
2 rue du Cardinal Tisserant
BP 70307
54006 Nancy Cedex
Tel: +33 3 83 36 32 80
Fax: +33 3 83 36 32 89

BUILDING & PLANNING
Chambre Régionale de Métiers
de Champagne-Ardenne
42 rue Titon
51000 Chalons-en-Champagne
Tel: +33 3 29 68 10 55
Fax: +33 3 26 66 88 06

CAUE de Haute-Marne
Maison de l'Habitat
BP 178
16 rue des Abbés Durand
52006
Chaumont Cedex
Tel: +33 3 25 32 52 62
Fax: +33 3 25 02 37 16

EDUCATION
Rectorat de l'Académie
de Reims
1 rue Navier
51082 Reims Cedex
Tel: +33 3 26 05 69 69
Fax: +33 3 26 05 69 42

HEALTH
Caisse Primaire d'Assurance
Maladie de la Marne
14 rue Ruisselet
51100 Reims Cedex
Tel: +33 3 26 84 40 40
Fax: +33 3 26 84 41 10

Champagne country offers up modest stone-built houses that can have chalk cellars just like the grand Champagne houses

ALSACE, LORRAINE & FRANCHE-COMTE

Lake Gérardmer nestling on the lower contours of the Vosges

The three regions of Alsace, Lorraine and Franche-Comté are highly individual, but are linked by one geological formation. This is the great forested massif of the Vosges. This thickly wooded, mountainous zone divides Lorraine from Alsace, and its southern peaks dominate the northern reaches of Franche-Comté.

To the west, in Lorraine, expansive lakes appear in the middle of dense forests. The 'Valley of the Lakes', comprising lakes Gérardmer, Longemer and Retournemer, during the summer months is a windsurfer's paradise and a joy for hikers who follow the trails along fir tree-lined forest paths. In the winter, cross-country skiers flock to the region. The round summits – rising to just under 1,500m in places – are found in the south, and the nature reserve they are part of forms the northern reaches of Franche-Comté's Territoire de Belfort *département*. Here, the same combination of woods and hidden lakes characterises the terrain.

The Vosges provide plenty of opportunities for climbing, mountain biking and skiing. On the eastern side in Alsace, however, life can be enjoyed at a much slower pace. The countryside is much less wild here, and vineyards stretch for miles along the lower contours of the massif. Here, some of France's best whites are produced. Both the wines and residents benefit from a particularly sunny and warm climate, being sheltered from strong winds and excessive rain by the mountainous terrain to the west.

There is a wine road here that starts at Marlenheim, near Strasbourg, and passes through an array of pretty villages with Germanic-sounding names lined with half-timbered houses, finally ending at Thann, a small town not far from Mulhouse. In contrast to these dormant villages, Strasbourg, with its European connections, is very much a cosmopolitan city. Only a part of France since the 17th century, its centre features a network of waterways and its streets are bordered by tall, colourful half-timbered buildings.

Lorraine, once an important industrial centre, has cities rich in architectural and cultural heritage. Metz and Nancy are both dramatic sights, with

Alsace, Lorraine & Franche-Comté

imposing gothic architecture in the former and squares surrounded by pillared buildings built by the Polish king Stanislas in the latter. The region has lost much of its industry now, but this has to some extent helped the countryside stay green and pleasant in this northeastern corner of France.

BUYING IN ALSACE, LORRAINE AND FRANCHE-COMTE

Despite being popular holiday destinations for the French and other neighbouring nations, Alsace, Lorraine and Franche-Comté do not seem to have caught on with British buyers keen to set up home in France. In fact, those British who are scouring the rolling hills and forested mountainsides of these eastern French regions for a second home or more permanent residence can appear like intrepid explorers.

Having a low rate of British expats may, itself, be quite appealing for house hunters, as the better-known areas of Dordogne and Provence become more and more anglicised. Traditionalists are also

Rural Franche-Comté

likely to be lured here by the abundance of period building styles. Alsace is dotted with both colourful half-timbered and Alpine chalet-style houses, while more rugged white-rendered granite-built houses with small square windows are perched on the slopes of the Lorraine Vosges. Sturdy, typically creamy-beige-rendered farmhouses with steep-pitched roofs housing attic rooms ripe for conversion and large arched doorways are plentiful in the Franche-Comté's Jura.

One of the most appealing things about

GETTING THERE

AIR Air France (0845 084 5111; www.airfrance.co.uk) flies direct to Strasbourg from Gatwick. Fly to Brussels-South Charleroi for northern Lorraine, or Dijon for Franche-Comté. **Ryanair** (0871 246 0000; www.ryanair.com) flies to Charleroi from Glasgow, Liverpool and Stansted, while **buzz** (0870 240 7070; www.buzzaway.com) flies to Dijon from Stansted.
ROAD Take the A26 from Calais straight to Reims, then the A4 on to Metz or Strasbourg. Nancy is on the A31 south of Metz. From Paris, follow the same route, taking the A4 to Reims. For Besançon, follow the A26 from the Channel ports, or the A5 from Paris to Troyes, then continue on the A5 then the A31 to Dijon, changing to the A39 and then the A36.
RAIL TGV services operate between Gare de l'Est in Paris and Nancy, Metz and Strasbourg, and Gare de Lyon and Besançon. Alternatively, take the **Eurostar** (0870 518 6186; www.eurostar.com) to Lille Europe and take a TGV service on to Besançon, or transfer to Lille Flanders for direct services to Metz. For rail enquiries, contact **Rail Europe** (0870 584 8848; www.raileurope.co.uk).

AVERAGE DAILY TEMPERATURE (CELSIUS) °C

Alsace, Lorraine & Franche-Comté

JAN	FEB	MAR	APR	MAY	JUNE	JULY	AUG	SEPT	OCT	NOV	DEC
5.5	5.1	9.5	14.0	15.7	23.0	24.4	26.4	21.4	15.0	8.3	5

London

JAN	FEB	MAR	APR	MAY	JUNE	JULY	AUG	SEPT	OCT	NOV	DEC
6	7	10	13	17	20	22	21	19	14	10	7

The Regions

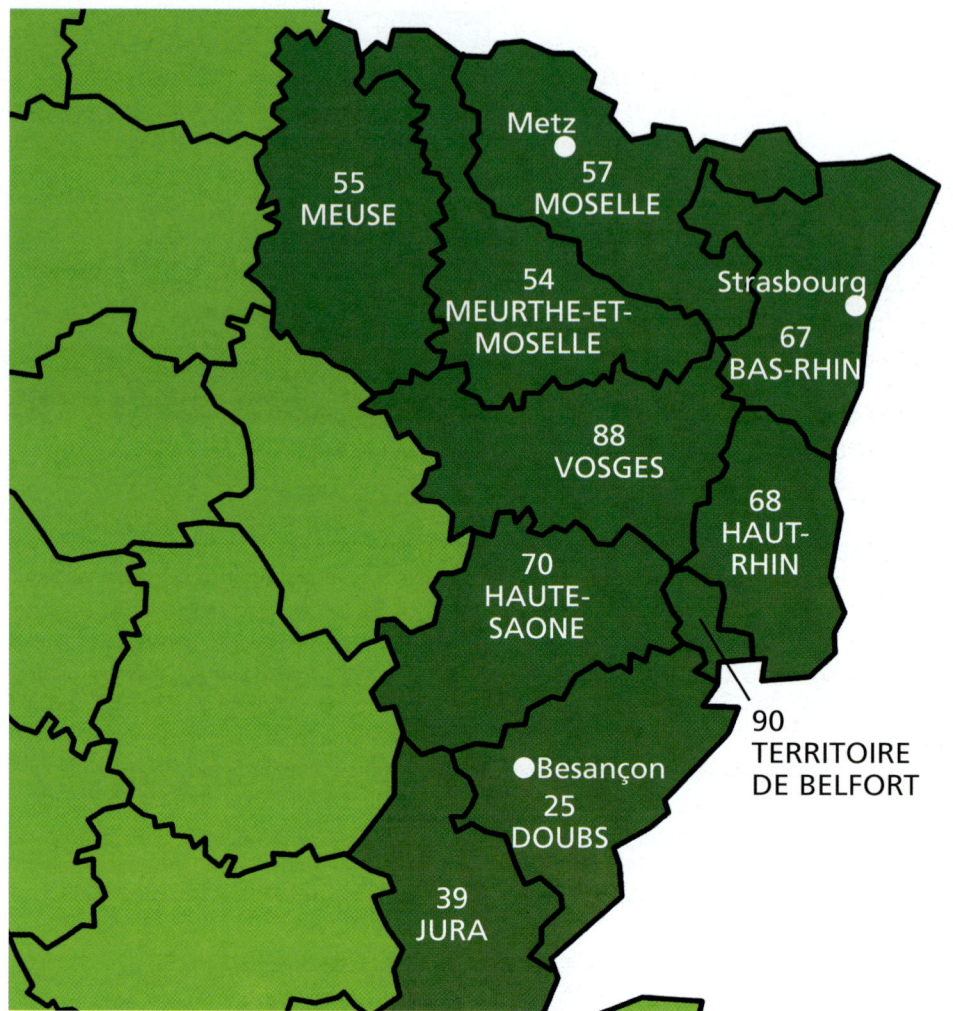

properties in these adjoining territories, however, must be that the buyer gets a lot for their money. When price levels in a number of French enclaves are climbing heights beyond the reach of most budgets, simple yet perfectly presentable properties can still be found here with an asking price under £30,000.

It is not just a matter of low prices, but also the amount of living space that houses have here that can make them such good value for money. Traditionally, there has been no scrimping on space, even in the most modest properties. In the Meuse *département* of Lorraine, for example, houses are typically exceptionally deep from front to back. Multiple-bedroomed houses appear quite affordable too.

Properties with as many as eight bedrooms can be found in the valleys between Colmar and Mulhouse in Alsace, for example, with a price tag under £120,000.

In some parts, government funds are available for modernising houses and converting buildings into apartments for rent, making larger properties even more attractive in eastern France. With opportunities like these and such a wealth of good value properties to hand, it just shows how rewarding it can be to look outside the areas that so many British buyers have turned their attention to before.

For a guide to property prices in Alsace, Lorraine and Franche-Comté, turn to page 185.

USEFUL CONTACTS

PRÉFECTURES

Préfecture de la Région Alsace
Petit Broglie
67073 Strasbourg Cedex
Tel: +33 3 88 21 67 68
Fax: +33 3 88 21 60 56

Préfecture de la Région Lorraine
place de la Préfecture
57034 Metz Cedex 1
Tel: +33 3 87 34 87 34
Fax: +33 3 87 32 57 39

Préfecture de la Région
Franche-Comté
8 bis rue Charles-Nodier
25035 Besançon Cedex
Tel: +33 3 81 25 10 00
Fax: +33 3 81 83 21 82

LEGAL

Chambre des Notaires du Doubs
22a rue de Trey
25000 Besançon
Tel: +33 3 81 50 40 52
Fax: +33 3 81 50 77 79

Chambre des Notaires
du Bas-Rhin
2 rue des Juifs
67000 Strasbourg
Tel: +33 3 88 32 10 55
Fax: +33 3 88 23 40 39

Chambre des Notaires
de la Moselle
1 rue de la Pierre Hardie
57000 Metz
Tel: +33 3 87 75 27 93
Fax: +33 3 87 74 08 20

FINANCE

Direction des Impôts de l'Est
2 rue du Cardinal Tisserant
BP 70307
54006 Nancy Cedex
Tel: +33 3 83 36 32 80
Fax: +33 3 83 36 32 89

BUILDING & PLANNING

Chambre Régionale de Métiers
d'Alsace
Espace Européen de l'Entreprise
avenue de l'Europe
67300 Schiltigheim
Tel: +33 3 88 19 60 65
Fax: +33 3 88 19 79 79

Chambre Régionale de Métiers
de Franche-Comté Valparc
Espace Valentin Est
25048 Besançon Cedex
Tel: +33 3 81 47 45 50
Fax: +33 3 81 53 45 31

Chambre Régionale de Métiers
de Lorraine
2 rue Augustin Fresnel
57082 Metz Cedex 3
Tel: +33 3 87 20 36 80
Fax: +33 3 87 75 41 79

CAUE du Bas-Rhin
5 rue Hannong
67000 Strasbourg
Tel: +33 3 88 15 02 30
Fax: +33 3 88 21 02 75

CAUE du Doubs
8 rue de la Vieille Monnaie
25000 Besançon
Tel: +33 3 81 82 19 22
Fax: +33 3 81 82 34 24

CAUE du Jura
9 avenue Jean Moulin, BP 48
39002 Lons le Saunier Cedex
Tel: +33 3 84 24 30 36
Fax: +33 3 84 24 63 89

EDUCATION

Rectorat de l'Académie
de Nancy-Metz
2 rue Philippe-de-Gueldres
BP 13
54035 Nancy Cedex
Tel: +33 3 83 86 20 20
Fax: +33 3 83 86 23 01

Rectorat de l'Académie
de Strasbourg
6 rue de la Toussaint
67081 Strasbourg
Cedex 9
Tel: +33 3 88 23 37 23
Fax: +33 3 88 23 39 99

Rectorat de l'Académie
de Besançon
10 rue de la Convention
25030 Besançon Cedex
Tel: +33 3 81 65 47 00
Fax: +33 3 81 65 47 60

HEALTH

Caisse Primaire d'Assurance
Maladie du Doubs
2 rue Denis Papin
25000 Besançon
Tel: +33 3 81 47 53 00
Fax: +33 3 81 47 53 40

Caisse Primaire d'Assurance
Maladie de la Moselle
18 rue Haute Seille
57000 Metz
Tel: +33 3 87 39 36 36
Fax: +33 3 87 76 15 71

Caisse Primaire d'Assurance
Maladie du Bas-Rhin
16 rue Lausanne
67000 Strasbourg
Tel: +33 8 20 90 41 50
Fax: +33 3 88 76 88 99

THE LOIRE

The 16th-century château in the village of Sillé-le-Guillaume is one of many to be found in the Loire

The River Loire starts its life high up in the Rhône-Alps of southeastern France and ends its course at Nantes on the Atlantic coast, some 350 miles to the northwest. But it is in the two administrative regions of Pays de la Loire and Centre where it is at its widest and most prominent, and it is for this reason that this part of France is referred to as the Loire.

Along the meandering river, around the town of Tours, fairy-tale castles line the banks. These are the most famous sites of the valley and are the vestiges of the privileged position this part of France held as the seat of the French court during the Renaissance. Chenonceau is probably the most photographed of all, with its commanding arched bridge leading to the main residence across the River Cher, in which the reflection of the château is picture perfect. During the summer months, these châteaux make dramatic backdrops to *son et lumière* shows.

Having always been a bearable drive away from the Channel ports, a new budget flight route from the UK to Tours has made this destination more accessible than ever. One can feasibly leave the UK after work on a Friday evening and be enjoying the excellent local wines like the reds of Chinon or whites of Vouvray and goat's cheese at lunchtime on Saturday.

The Loire

Above: much of the Loire's skyline is dominated by grand châteaux **Right:** seafood is abundant in Vendée

Follow the Loire as it winds its way through the 'Garden of France', so called because of its fertile rolling hills lined with vineyards, orchards and flowers. Along the Atlantic coast, from Nantes down through Vendée, seafood is gathered in abundance. This coastline also offers up seemingly endless sandy beaches and plenty of choice for the water sports enthusiast. This section of the coast is well loved by yachtsmen from around the world, and is well known for being the home of the Golden Globe, the first challenging single-handed, non-stop yacht race around the world, which starts off and finishes in the Vendée port of

GETTING THERE

AIR Air France (0845 084 5111; www.airfrance.co.uk) flies from Gatwick to Nantes, while **buzz** (0870 240 7070; www.buzzaway.com) operates services between Stansted and Tours and La Rochelle, just to the south of Vendée.
ROAD From the Channel ports, head to western Loire along the N138 via Rouen or the A84, N12, and N137 via Caen. Take the A10 from Paris to Orléans and on to Tours.
RAIL TGV services leave from Gare Montparnasse in Paris for Angers, Le Mans, Nantes and La Rochelle. Contact **Rail Europe** (0870 584 8848; www.raileurope.co.uk) for details.

AVERAGE DAILY TEMPERATURE (CELSIUS) °C

The Loire											
8.85	7.7	10.8	16.9	16.6	23.5	25.8	24.6	21.5	16.6	11.8	8.3
London											
6	7	10	13	17	20	22	21	19	14	10	7
JAN	FEB	MAR	APR	MAY	JUNE	JULY	AUG	SEPT	OCT	NOV	DEC

The Regions

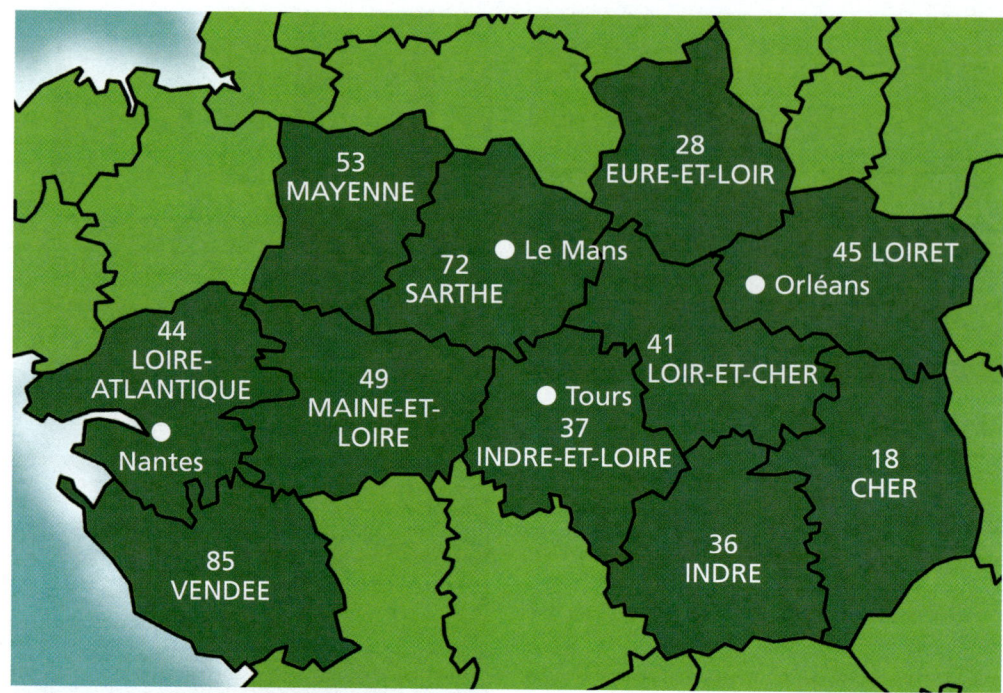

Les Sables-d'Olonne. Getting to this spot is anything but a challenge for most conventional travellers today, however, as direct budget flight routes between Stansted and nearby La Rochelle are making flying between here and the UK both easy and affordable.

BUYING IN THE LOIRE

The Loire has been popular with the British looking for a slice of rural French life for decades. The Touraine and Saumur, which are centred on the towns of Tours and Saumur respectively, have always been particular favourites. Their appeal shows no sign of waning, especially as the addition of a budget airline route to Tours is helping fuel interest in the area, and property prices reflect this.

Anyone buying in this area can, however, potentially reap the rewards of owning a home in a popular tourist centre through rental income. The Loire has proven to be one of the best areas to let out a home to holidaying families and couples. In high season, a two-bedroom attached gîte can be rented out for £400 a week, while renting out a detached country house sleeping six for a week can bring in £800.

Within an hour's drive of Tours, traditional slate-roofed village houses – built out of the mellow, cream-coloured local limestone called *tuffeau* – reflect the style of the riverside châteaux, and with that all-important cellar to store the local wine, can be found for under £50,000.

Further outside this catchment area still, but only four-and-a-half hours away from the nearest Channel ports (thanks, in particular, to the recent opening up of the A20 motorway) and easily reachable from the international airport at Tours, the southern Loire is home to some of the best value homes in the whole of the Loire. In this area, small period houses ready to move in to can still be found for around £20,000. This is the kind of price tag that can help turn the dream of owning an idyllic French retreat into a reality.

For a guide to property prices in the Loire, turn to page 195.

USEFUL CONTACTS

PREFECTURES

Préfecture de la Région Centre
181 rue de Bourgogne
45042 Orléans
Cedex 1
Tel: +33 821 80 30 45
Fax: +33 2 38 53 32 48

Préfecture de la Région
Pays-de-la-Loire
6 quai Ceineray
BP 33515
44035 Nantes
Cedex 1
Tel: +33 2 40 41 20 20
Fax: +33 2 40 41 20 25

LEGAL

Chambre des Notaires
de Loire-Atlantique
119 rue Coulmiers
44000 Nantes
Tel: +33 2 40 74 37 16
Fax: +33 2 40 29 21 29

Chambre des Notaires du Loiret
4 rue d'Escures
45000 Orléans
Tel: +33 2 38 24 04 24
Fax: +33 2 38 81 10 48

FINANCE

Direction des Impôts
du Centre
70 rue de la Bretonnerie
BP 2457
45032 Orléans Cedex 1
Tel: +33 2 38 74 55 25
Fax: +33 2 38 74 55 62

Direction des Impôts de l'Ouest
6 rue Jean Guéhenno
CS 14208
35042 Rennes Cedex
Tel: +33 2 99 87 18 30
Fax: +33 2 99 63 28 90

BUILDING & PLANNING

Chambre Régionale
de Métiers du Centre
30 faubourg de Bourgogne
BP 24 45015
Orléans
Cedex 1
Tel: +33 2 38 68 03 32
Fax: +33 2 38 68 01 37

Chambre Régionale de Métiers
des Pays de la Loire
6 boulevard des Pâtureaux
44980 Sainte-Luce-Sur-Loire
Tel: +33 2 51 13 31 31
Fax: +33 2 51 13 31 30

Union Régionale des CAUE
des Pays de la Loire
Le Tertre au Jau
49100 Angers
Tel: +33 4 41 22 99 99
Fax: +33 4 41 22 99 00

EDUCATION

Rectorat de l'Académie
de Nantes
La Houssinière
BP 72616
44326 Nantes Cedex 3
Tel: +33 2 40 37 37 37
Fax: +33 2 40 37 37 00

Rectorat de l'Académie
d'Orléans-Tours
21 rue Saint-Etienne
45043 Orléans
Cedex 1
Tel: +33 2 38 79 38 79
Fax: +33 2 38 62 41 79

HEALTH

Caisse Primaire d'Assurance
Maladie de Loire-Atlantique
9 rue Gaétan Rondeau
44200 Nantes
Tel: +33 2 51 88 88 88
Fax: +33 2 51 88 87 87

Caisse Primaire d'Assurance
Maladie du Loiret
9 place Général de Gaulle
45000 Orléans
Tel: +33 2 38 79 47 00
Fax: +33 2 38 42 24 70

Mélusine Tower in the pretty village of Vouvant is a fine example of Vendée's exceptional cultural heritage

BURGUNDY

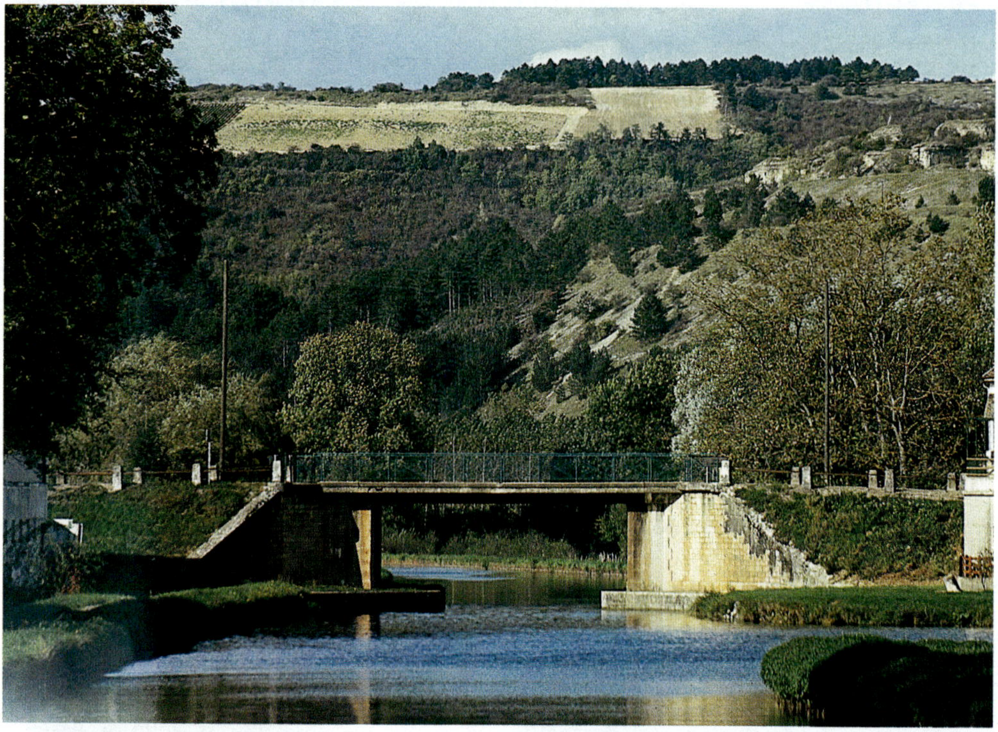

JEREMY POUND/MERRICKS MEDIA

The Eastern French region of Burgundy is well known around the world for its wines, but its picture-postcard terrain does not just simply offer a perfect habitat for growing first-class grapes. This is rural French life at its most beautiful and tranquil, with an outstanding natural backdrop.

It is the *départements* of Yonne, Côte-d'Or and Saône-et-Loire that are the wine regions par excellence. Yonne, in the north, is home to France's possibly most famous whites, Chablis, while the Côte-d'Or offers up elegant whites and high-brow reds, and in the south the Saône-et-Loire produces well-travelled whites like Pouilly-Fuissé.

The regions may have the same prized produce in common, but they are in their own way very different. The Côte-d'Or is dominated by a ridge that has vines growing on its sunny slopes and apparently on every spare inch right up to the roadside. It is quite a contrast to the gently rolling landscape of the Mâconnais in the Saône-et-Loire, which is punctuated by the occasional rocky outcrop.

JEREMY POUND/MERRICKS MEDIA

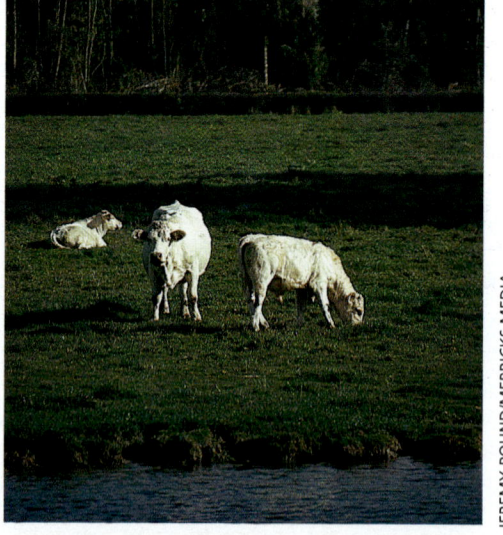

Top and above: the rugged, wooded and pleasantly unspoilt Yonne Valley in rural northwest Burgundy, where the Nivernais Canal starts its course and fertile pastures and a quieter pace of life can be enjoyed

Burgundy

The gently rolling landscape of the Mâconnais is covered with vines and punctuated by rocky outcrops

A strong gastronomic tradition complements the production of these great wines, with the number of Michelin-starred restaurants to be found here a testimony to this. Quintessential rustic French fare like snails in garlic butter feature among the local specialities.

Great expanses of unspoilt land such as the extensive Morvan Regional Park, a land of forests, rolling hills, lakes and waterways, deep in the heart of Burgundy, prove that the region is not just about eating and drinking. An area of great beauty and calm, it is an excellent spot in which to unwind and enjoy a quieter pace of life, and can perhaps provide the perfect foil to the gastronomic overload of a trip to one of the wine zones.

To the west of the Morvan Mountains flows the Nivernais Canal, which starts its course in the rugged, wooded Yonne Valley. Then, by means of a series of locks, it reaches the lakes of Vaux and Baye, the highest part of its course, before gently descending towards the River Loire. Crossing unspoilt countryside along its course, it is almost entirely the preserve of pleasure boats today. Gentle countryside and wide open spaces, ideal for cycling

GETTING THERE
AIR buzz (0870 240 7070; www.buzzaway.com) flies from Stansted direct to Dijon.
ROAD From the northern ports, head to the A26, changing at Troyes to the A5 eastbound or westbound for east or west Burgundy respectively. The A6 from Paris leads straight to the heart of Burgundy.
RAIL Take the **Eurostar** (0870 518 6186; www.eurostar.co.uk) to Lille Europe, then change to the **TGV** service to Dijon. **TGV** services also operate between Dijon and Gare de Lyon in Paris. For rail enquiries, contact **Rail Europe** (0870 584 8848; www.raileurope.co.uk).

AVERAGE DAILY TEMPERATURE (CELSIUS) °C

Burgundy

JAN	FEB	MAR	APR	MAY	JUNE	JULY	AUG	SEPT	OCT	NOV	DEC
6.1	5.9	10.3	15.3	15.8	23.8	25.8	26.1	21.2	15.5	9.1	6.2

London

JAN	FEB	MAR	APR	MAY	JUNE	JULY	AUG	SEPT	OCT	NOV	DEC
6	7	10	13	17	20	22	21	19	14	10	7

The Regions

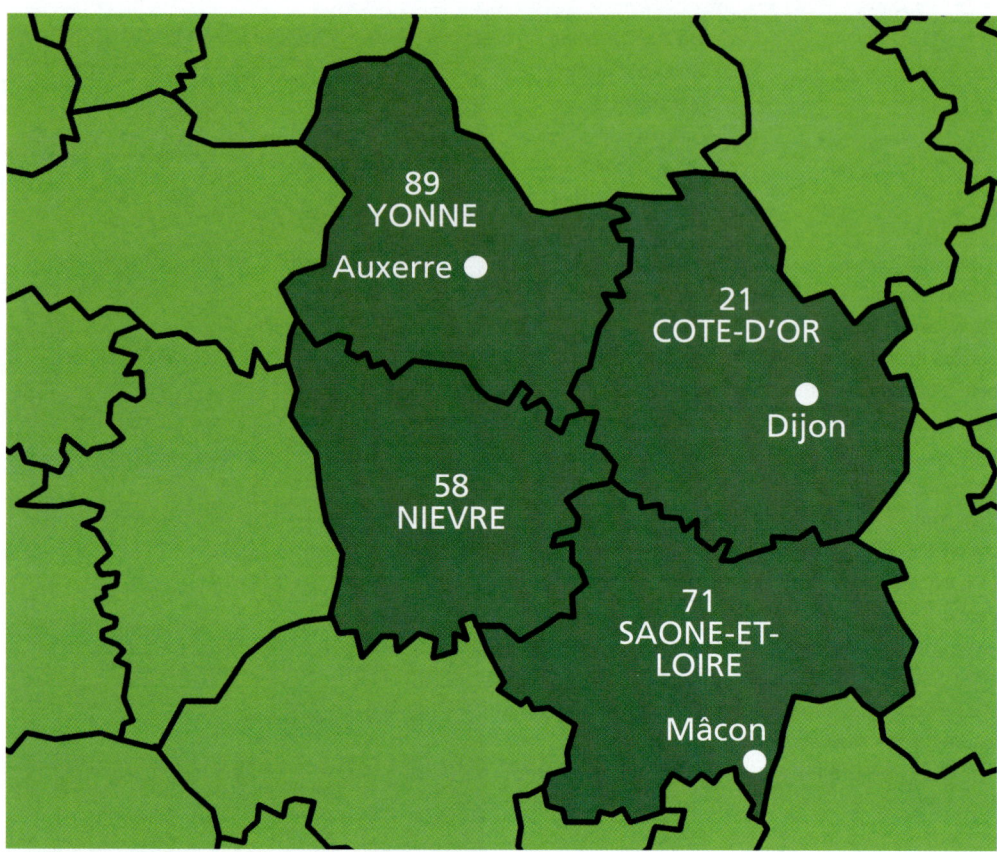

or riding through, are found in the Châtillonnais to the north of Dijon.

Throughout the region, quiet villages and hamlets break up the landscape. Grand manors punctuate the landscape from time to time too, some displaying the same multi-coloured roof tiles that characterise the architecture of the historic city of Beaune. Along with Dijon, this was once a seat of the Dukes of Burgundy, and the style and decoration of some of the most important buildings, with their idiosyncratic multi-coloured roof tiles, are the vestiges of Flemish artists who made this their home when the dukedom extended as far afield as Flanders and the Netherlands.

BUYING IN BURGUNDY

Burgundy is far from inundated with overseas buyers at the moment, and this can be an attractive prospect for buyers looking for an authentic French setting. Those who are buying into the area are doing so for the quality of life. The air here is very clean, thanks largely to the abundance of parkland, and life can be very peaceful. The traditional styles of properties that the region abounds in are also very attractive. There is also the occasional opportunity to realise the dream of owning a few rows of vines in one of France's finest winemaking areas.

Besides being accessible using the new direct budget flights to Dijon, Burgundy is a fairly swift drive from the Channel ports and is only six hours from central London by Eurostar. Despite its easy access, scenery and gastronomy, even the smallest budget seems to go a long way in Burgundy at present. Stone barns to convert can be found priced £15,000, while £50,000 can buy a village house or modest farmhouse that just needs a little work. At the other end of the market, a substantial *maison bourgeoise* with six bedrooms or more, various reception rooms and a reasonably sized

USEFUL CONTACTS

PREFECTURE
Préfecture de la Région
Bourgogne
53 rue de la Préfecture
21041 Dijon Cedex
Tel: +33 3 80 44 64 00
Fax: +33 3 80 30 65 72

LEGAL
Chambre des Notaires
de la Côte-d'Or
3 rue du Lycée
21000 Dijon
Tel: +33 3 80 67 12 21
Fax: +33 3 80 66 80 74

FINANCE
Direction Régionale des Impôts
Rhône-Alpes Bourgogne
41 cours de la Liberté
69422 Lyon
Cedex 3
Tel: +33 4 78 63 54 10
Fax: +33 4 78 63 53 93

BUILDING & PLANNING
Chambre Régionale de Métiers
de Bourgogne
46 boulevard de la Marne
BP 56721
21067 Dijon Cedex
Tel: +33 3 80 28 81 00
Fax: +33 3 80 28 81 01

CAUE de la Côte-d'Or
24 rue de la Préfecture
21000 Dijon
Tel: +33 3 80 30 02 38
Fax: +33 3 80 30 06 40

EDUCATION
Rectorat de l'Académie
de Dijon
51 rue Monge
BP 1516
21033 Dijon
Cedex
Tel: +33 3 80 44 84 00
Fax: +33 3 80 44 84 88

HEALTH
Caisse Primaire d'Assurance
Maladie de la Côte-d'Or
8 rue du Docteur Maret
BP 1548
21045 Dijon
Cedex
Tel: +33 3 80 59 37 59
Fax: +33 3 80 59 37 77

plot of land can be bought for around £250,000. A budget of just over £400,000 could finance a classic 18th-century château in a few acres of parkland, complete with guardian's house and useful outbuildings.

Sitting midway between the northern Channel coast and the South of France, and under two hours by car from Paris, Burgundy is quite a convenient place to be based. And, because the 12-hour drive from Calais to the Côte d'Azur can be split comfortably by an overnight stay in this central French region, anyone looking to set up a bed and breakfast establishment in the country may find this just the right spot to start searching for a suitable property.

Burgundy abounds in attractive traditional property styles like this half-timbered town house in Yonne

For a guide to property prices in Burgundy, turn to page 215.

POITOU-CHARENTES

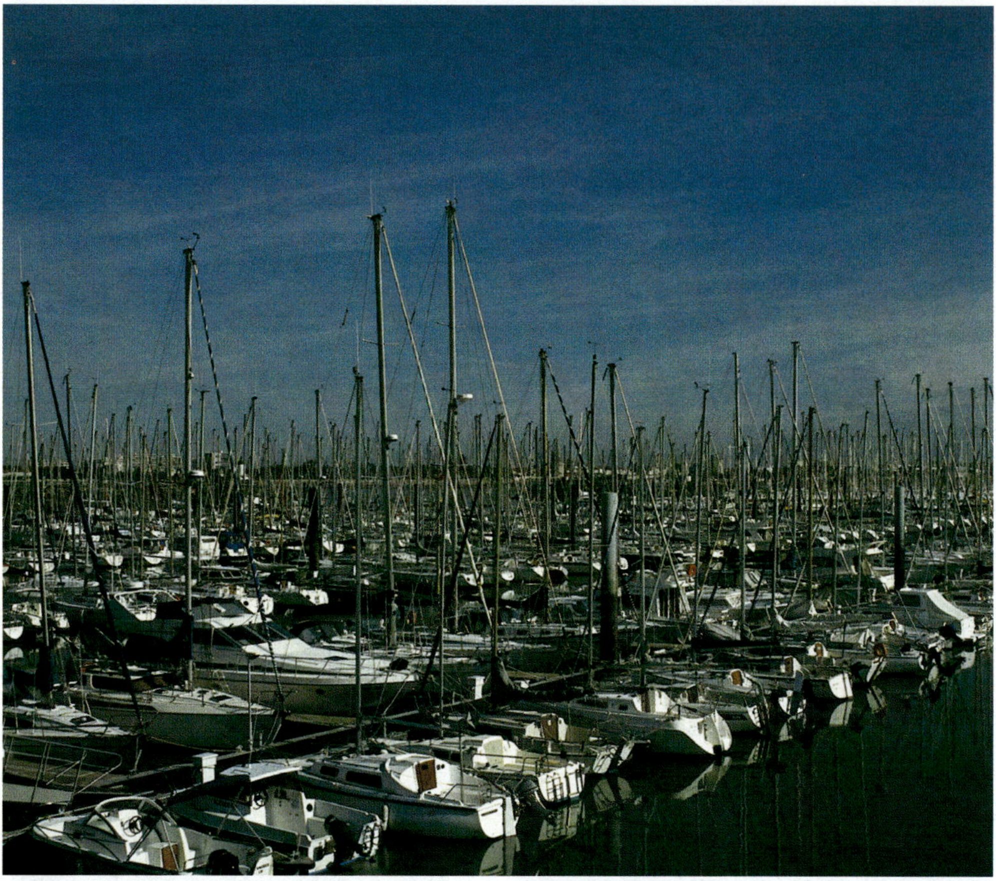

PHOTOGRAPHY: JUSTIN POSTLETHWAITE/MERRICKS MEDIA

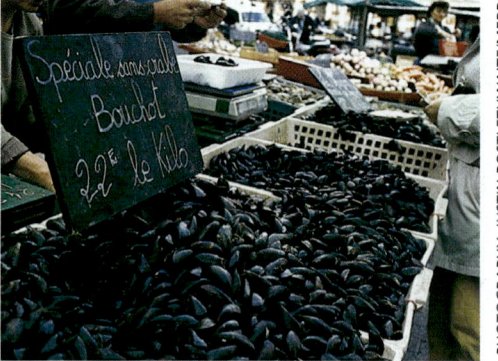

Reputedly the second sunniest part of France after the Mediterranean, and opening onto the Atlantic Ocean, Poitou-Charentes has a lot to offer the sun and surf seeker. As well as benefiting from warmer weather and easier access to the coast than most of the neighbouring Loire Valley, it is also easily reached by budget airlines, as both La Rochelle on the coast and the inland city of Poitiers are now cheap flight destinations.

The coast here is fringed with over 150 miles of sandy beaches and dotted with fishing ports, whose markets are the source of freshly landed Atlantic fish and seafood. Regimented rows of high-masted yachts line the marina of the port of La Rochelle, revealing its perennial attraction to sailors. Just off the coast here, more picturesque ports and sandy

Top: La Rochelle is popular with sailors, as its marina lined with yachts reveals **Above:** seafood fresh from the Atlantic is sold in the lively markets of fishing ports along the Poitou-Charentes coastline

Poitou-Charentes

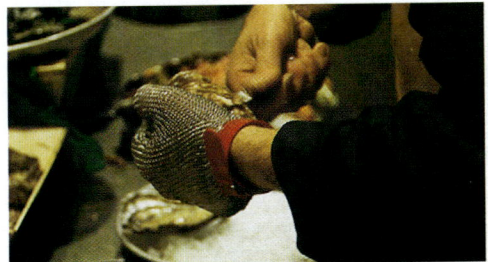

Above: preparing seafood, a staple of the local diet, in a popular La Rochelle restaurant **Right:** the backstreets of the historic fishing port of La Rochelle

coves perfect for picnics are dotted along the coast of the Ile-de-Ré, a favourite destination for chic holidaying Parisian families.

Inland is Cognac country. Vineyards blend into woodlands along the River Charente, and along this meandering waterway you can retrace the routes of flat-bottomed boats that would once have transported cereals and prized brandy to the Atlantic and then returned with salt and fish fresh from the sea. Here, villages glowing white in the sun rise up on gentle slopes from the banks of a veritable network of rivers and streams where fishermen patiently wait for a pike, a bream, a large carp or maybe a rainbow trout to bite.

In the northeast Poitou-Charentes *département* of Vienne, the pretty spa town of La Roche-Posay is popular in the summer, when people come here to take 'the cure'. Vienne is also home to one of

GETTING THERE

AIR buzz (0870 240 7070; www.buzzaway.com) operates direct flights between Stansted and both La Rochelle and Poitiers.
ROAD The A10 links Poitiers and Saintes with Paris. Take the N11 west from the A10 to La Rochelle, or the N10 south to Angoulême.
RAIL TGV services to Angoulême, Poitiers and La Rochelle leave from Gare Montparnasse in Paris. For rail enquiries, contact **Rail Europe** (0870 584 8848; www.raileurope.co.uk).

AVERAGE DAILY TEMPERATURE (CELSIUS) °C

Poitou-Charentes											
10	8.7	11.7	18.2	16.4	22.4	25.3	24.6	22.0	18.4	14.0	9.8
London											
6	7	10	13	17	20	22	21	19	14	10	7
JAN	FEB	MAR	APR	MAY	JUNE	JULY	AUG	SEPT	OCT	NOV	DEC

The Regions

France's leading theme parks, Futuroscope. Here visitors can experience journeys through time and space and enter discovery zones ranging from a tasting room to a special effects studio. A futuristic thinking person's theme park, it can be a perfect foil, if one is needed, to the restful inland countryside that offers a perfect slice of French country life.

BUYING IN POITOU-CHARENTES

Poitou-Charentes has started to attract the attention of buyers looking to avoid the high prices of popular enclaves of the Loire and Dordogne and who are equally charmed by the good weather, food, wine and tranquillity that these regions offer. The southern *département* of Charente is just to the west of northern Dordogne, while Deux-Sèvres and Vienne are only a short distance to the south of Saumur, a Loire Valley favourite with second home owners. Four-bedroom hamlet houses are available around the £60,000 mark, while it is possible to find village houses with outbuildings ripe for conversion for about £30,000.

Properties in this region have their own unique appeal. The old town of La Rochelle is lined with black and white half-timbered houses with a unique slate detail, while inland, in Vienne traditional styles are typically rendered in cream or pale blue, with doors and window surrounds in a faced limestone called *tuffeau*. A typical house in Charente is the *charentaise*, a long, often white-rendered house with painted shutters and a low-pitched roof.

New budget flight routes to the area mean that it is likely to become increasingly popular with buyers and visitors alike who might not have thought of coming here before good value direct flights were available. Buyers are therefore likely to have stronger competition than ever, therefore, but a great advantage is that the holiday rental value of any property that is an easy drive from the airport is equally likely to increase, as more and more fly into this relatively undiscovered part of France.

It is good to be near tourist attractions and good transport links if rental income is an important consideration, but being too close to

Poitou-Charentes

USEFUL CONTACTS

PREFECTURE
Préfecture de la Région
Poitou-Charentes
place Aristide-Briand
86021 Poitiers Cedex
Tel: +33 5 49 55 70 00
Fax: +33 5 49 88 25 34

LEGAL
Chambre des Notaires
de la Vienne
avenue Thomas Edison
86360 Chasseneuil-du-Poitou
Tel: +33 5 49 49 42 60
Fax: +33 5 49 49 42 63

FINANCE
Direction des Impôts
du Sud-Ouest
2 rue des Piliers de Tutelle
BP 45
33025 Bordeaux Cedex
Tel: +33 5 57 14 21 00
Fax: +33 5 57 14 21 09

BUILDING & PLANNING
Chambre Régionale de Métiers
de Poitou-Charentes
13 place Charles de Gaulle
86000 Poitiers Cedex
Tel: +33 5 49 88 70 52
Fax: +33 5 49 60 72 80

CAUE de Charente-Maritime
85 boulevard de la République
Les Minimes
17076 La Rochelle Cedex 9
Tel: +33 5 46 31 71 90
Fax: +33 5 46 31 71 91

EDUCATION
Rectorat de l'Académie
de Poitiers
5 cité de la Traverse
BP 625
86022 Poitiers
Cedex
Tel: +33 5 49 54 70 00
Fax: +33 5 49 54 70 01

HEALTH
Caisse Primaire d'Assurance
Maladie de la Vienne
41 rue Touffenet
86000 Poitiers
Cedex
Tel: +33 5 49 44 59 97
Fax: +33 5 49 44 54 20

---

tourist hotspots and transport routes may not be ideal for a holiday home. Buyers should watch out, for instance, for the Châtellerault-Poitiers corridor, which has both the Aquitaine motorway, the A10, and TGV tracks running through it.

The sleepier countryside of southern Vienne is a good part of Poitou-Charentes to find larger buildings, parts of which can be turned into gîtes, at a modest cost, as the land here is relatively poor. Budding gîte owners should, however, make sure that the market in the area they pick has not already been saturated by other owners who have had the same idea.

The old town of La Rochelle houses a unique style of half-timbered building with slate details

For a guide to property prices in Poitou-Charentes, turn to page 231.

LIMOUSIN & AUVERGNE

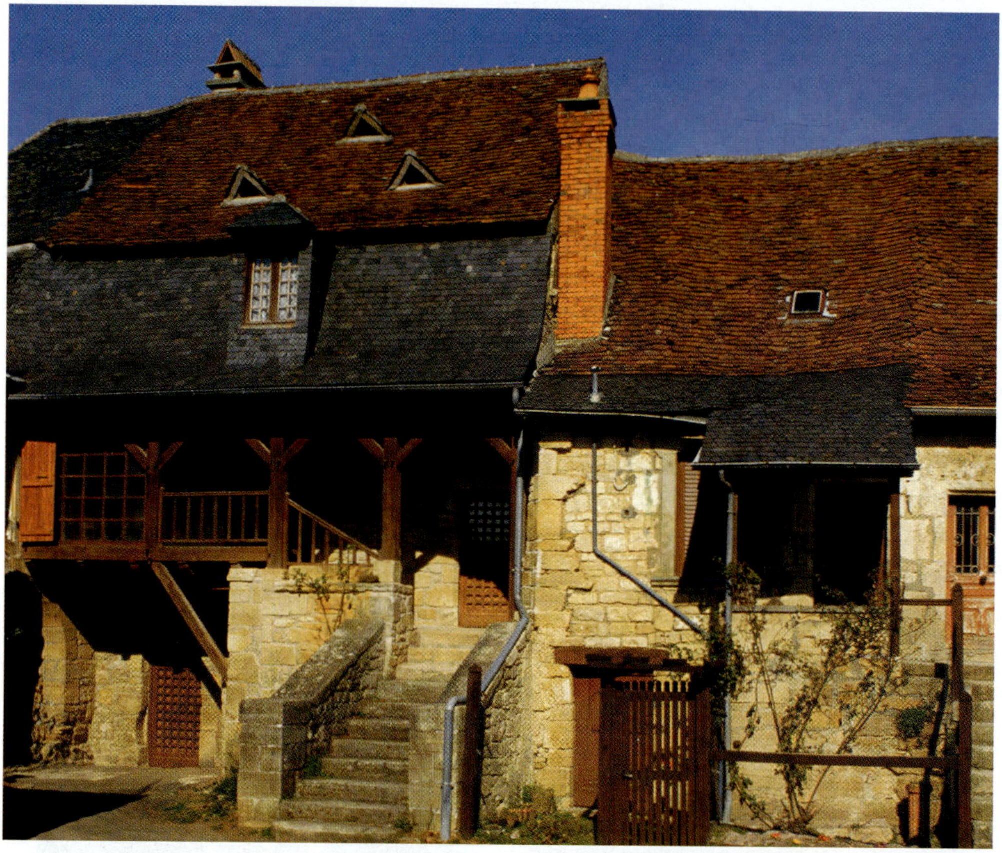

ROBERT HARDING WORLD IMAGERY/ALAMY

At the very heart of France, Limousin and Auvergne are just starting to be recognised as the places to go to get away from it all, as these are two of the most isolated and rural of French regions. Offering countryside as unspoilt as it gets in France today, they are not, however, difficult to reach from outside France.

There can be few better sites where one can escape the modern rat race than the sparsely populated Auvergne region. This land of volcanic mountains and lakes must be the ultimate spot in which to relax, unwind and be good to one's health. Pure air and water and great walking countryside are the vital ingredients to any healthy regime, and this region has all three.

As town names like Volvic, Vichy and Evian reveal, Auvergne is the source of many of France's

OT VOLVIC

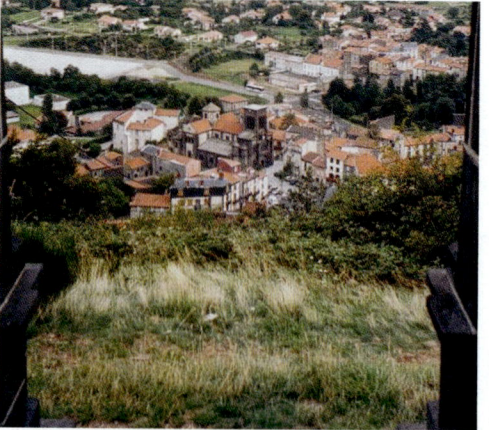

Top: simple Limousin houses offer some of the best value in France **Above:** sparsely populated Auvergne is an ideal place to get away from it all and unwind

Limousin & Auvergne

On the site of the town of Volvic's spring, a fountain spouting some of Auvergne's famously pure water

most popular mineral waters, all naturally filtered by the local volcanic rock. It is also home to nearly a dozen spa towns, which offer treatment facilities in a beautiful natural environment.

Not mountainous like its neighbour, Limousin is, however, equally dotted with lakes and waterfalls and cut through by rivers. The lakes more than make up for the distance from the coast, and watersports can feature heavily on the itinerary of any visit. This is a lush, agricultural region, understandably nicknamed the 'Green Heart of France', and is the place for peace and calm, as this is one of the most unspoilt of all French regions.

All corners of these regions may seem a million miles from anywhere, but they are easily reached by plane, train or car, thanks to recent improvements in transport links. Limoges's airport is now receiving direct budget flights from the UK, as is Saint-Etienne, just to the west of Auvergne, while the A20 and A75 cut through Limousin and Auvergne

GETTING THERE
AIR Air France (0845 084 5111; www.airfrance.co.uk) flies from London City to Clermont-Ferrand, while **buzz** (0870 240 7070; www.buzzaway.com) operates services between Limoges and Stansted.
ROAD Take the A10 from Paris then the A71 and A20 to Limoges. For Clermont-Ferrand and the rest of Auvergne, follow the A10 from Paris to Orléans, then carry on on the N71.
RAIL TGV services operate between Gare d'Austerlitz in Paris and Limoges. A fast, direct rail route links Gare de Lyon with Clermont-Ferrand. For more details, contact **Rail Europe** (0870 584 8848; www.raileurope.co.uk).

AVERGE DAILY TEMPERATURE (CELSIUS) °C
Limousin & Auvergne

7.1	6.3	9.9	16	16	23.2	25.9	24.1	22.2	16.7	11.9	8.4

London

6	7	10	13	17	20	22	21	19	14	10	7
JAN	FEB	MAR	APR	MAY	JUNE	JULY	AUG	SEPT	OCT	NOV	DEC

The Regions

respectively. Thanks to new flight routes, weekending is now very much a possibility in this, the rural heart of France.

BUYING IN LIMOUSIN AND AUVERGNE

Limousin and Auvergne are very much in the ascendant as far as the property market is concerned. Although there are increasing numbers of buyers on the lookout for their ideal rural French retreat in this agricultural land, properties here still represent great value for money.

A burgeoning interest in properties in both Limousin and Auvergne has been generated to a large extent by the value that they both offer to buyers when their prices are compared with those for homes in the more popular regions. But it is also, in part, due to ever-improving access to these regions in the heart of France, as well as the rural idyll they provide, with tranquil, gently rolling countryside dotted with sleepy villages reached by long, peaceful country lanes.

Limousin offers some of the best value in France for house buyers today. It is still relatively easy to find bargain renovations – from barns to cottages and farmhouses, as well as village houses – ready to move in to for around the £10,000 mark. With some local residents leaving for the more frenetic lifestyle offered by the cities, there are plenty of properties available, many with a lot of land. Since these were usually built for agricultural workers, properties in this area usually have a harsh simplicity about them, built in modest styles, often from either sandstone or granite. There is still reportedly a lack of rental accommodation in the area, so anyone interested in creating gîtes should consider looking here.

Auvergne is getting serious attention from buyers from neighbouring countries and the UK who are looking for a warmer climate than the northern *départements* offer, but with none of the traffic and noise of the South of France. Bargains can still be unearthed, though, and there are no signs of British ghettos forming.

Houses here can be highly characterful, often built of dark grey granite, schist or black basalt, with some use of grey stone and the local *pisé* pebbles.

USEFUL CONTACTS

PREFECTURES
Préfecture de la Région Auvergne
18 boulevard Desaix
63033 Clermont-Ferrand Cedex
Tel: +33 4 73 98 63 63
Fax: +33 4 73 98 61 00

Préfecture de la Région Limousin
place Stalingrad
87031 Limoges Cedex
Tel: +33 5 55 44 18 00
Fax: +33 5 55 44 17 54

LEGAL
Chambre des Notaires du
Puy-de-Dôme
10 rue du Maréchal Foch
63000 Clermont-Ferrand
Tel: +33 4 73 29 16 66
Fax: +33 4 73 29 16 63

Chambre des Notaires
de la Corrèze
3 place Winston-Churchill
87000 Limoges
Tel: +33 5 55 77 15 91
Fax: +33 5 55 79 28 33

FINANCE
Direction des Impôts du Centre
70 rue de la Bretonnerie
BP 2457
45032 Orléans Cedex 1
Tel: +33 2 38 74 55 25
Fax: +33 2 38 74 55 62

Direction des Impôts
du Sud-Ouest
2 rue des Piliers de Tutelle
BP 45
33025 Bordeaux Cedex
Tel: +33 5 57 14 21 00
Fax: +33 5 57 14 21 09

BUILDING & PLANNING
Chambre Régionale de Métiers
d'Auvergne
Centre Victoire
1 avenue de Cottages
BP 358
63010 Clermont-Ferrand
Cedex 1
Tel: +33 4 73 29 42 00
Fax: +33 4 73 29 42 09

Chambre Régionale de Métiers
du Limousin
14 rue de Belfort
87100 Limoges
Tel: +33 5 55 79 45 02
Fax: +33 5 55 79 30 29

CAUE de Haute-Vienne
1 rue des Allois
87000 Limoges
Tel: +33 5 55 32 32 40
Fax: +33 5 55 32 23 25

CAUE du Puy-de-Dôme
Hôtel du Département
30 rue Saint Esprit
63000 Clermont-Ferrand
Tel: +33 4 73 42 21 20
Fax: +33 4 73 93 27 64

EDUCATION
Rectorat de l'Académie
de Clermont-Ferrand
3 avenue Vercingétorix
63033 Clermont-Ferrand
Cedex 1
Tel: +33 4 73 99 30 00
Fax: +33 4 73 99 30 01

Rectorat de l'Académie
de Limoges
13 rue François-Chénieux
87031 Limoges Cedex
Tel: +33 5 55 11 40 40
Fax: +33 5 55 79 82 21

HEALTH
Caisse Primaire d'Assurance
Maladie de la Haute-Vienne
22 avenue Jean Gagnant
87037 Limoges
Tel: +33 820 90 41 31
Fax: +33 5 55 45 88 29

Caisse Primaire d'Assurance
Maladie du Puy-de-Dôme
rue Pélissier
63000 Clermont-Ferrand
Cedex 9
Tel: +33 4 73 42 81 00
Fax: +33 4 73 42 81 59

Flat-roofed houses with wooden verandas are typical, as are the two-storey barn-cum-stables *auvergnats*, often constructed against the slope of a hill, which are dream conversions in the making.

For a guide to property prices in Limousin and Auvergne, turn to page 249.

THE RHONE-ALPS

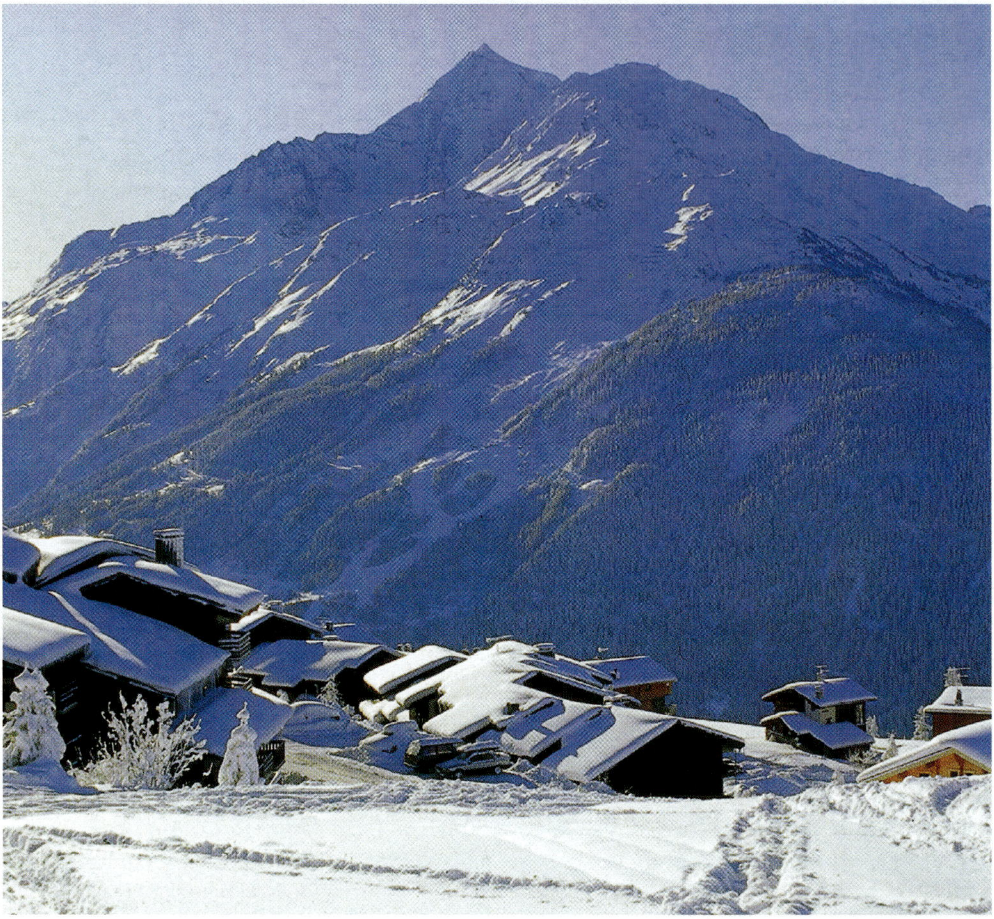

ROGER GAIDE/OT LA ROSIERE

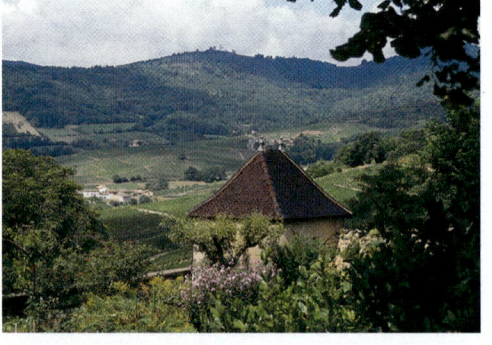

The Rhône-Alps is one of the largest French regions, and is home to some of France's most spectacular mountain ranges. Its boundaries encompass the highest peaks in the French Alps – including every mountaineer's challenge, Mont-Blanc – as well as boasting the biggest skiing area in the world, the Trois Vallées. What the French have known for many years, and what the rest of us are only just beginning to realise, is that there can be wonderful ski stations 'off the beaten' track like La Rosière and that the French Alps are not just a winter holiday destination. The region also offers a wide range of activities for both the nature lover and the adventurer during the summer months. Opportunities for white-water

ROWENA MEDLOW

Top: La Rosière, one of the quieter resorts of the French Alps, which is home to some of the country's most spectacular mountain ranges **Above:** the Beaujolais wine route, just to the north of Lyon

The Rhône-Alps

The Alps is not just a winter destination – its mountain passes are the setting for many outdoor pursuits in the summer, too

rafting, mountain biking and sailing on the expansive lakes that dot this part of France are at least as prevalent as the skiing possibilities at high-altitude stations during the winter season.

This is not just a region for those who love the great outdoors, though. The cities, from Lyon in the west, to Saint-Etienne and Chambéry on the border with Switzerland in the east, while dripping in rich cultural heritage, are an eclectic group of lively cosmopolitan cities. Lyon is well known as a gastronomic centre and is also an innovative centre for the arts, while Saint-Etienne houses the largest collection of modern art in France outside Paris.

This is also a region with a rich wine heritage. The Beaujolais wine route follows the contours of hills just to the north of Lyon, while to the south the Rhône Valley is the origin of deeply coloured, robust reds like Hermitage and Côte-Rôtie.

GETTING THERE

AIR From Stansted, **buzz** (0870 240 7070; www.buzzaway.com) flies to Lyon, Grenoble and Chambéry and **go** (0845 605 4321; www.gofly.com) to Lyon, while **easyJet** (0870 600 0000) flies between Luton and Geneva. **Air France** (0845 084 5111; www.airfrance.co.uk) operates services from Heathrow to Lyon.
ROAD Take the A6 from Paris to Lyon, then the A43 to Chambéry and Grenoble.
RAIL During the ski season, a direct **Eurostar** (0870 518 6186; www.eurostar.co.uk) service takes skiers from Waterloo or Ashford to Bourg-Saint-Maurice, which is ideal for resorts such as Val d'Isère, Courchevel and Les Arcs. TGV services operate throughout the year from between Gare de Lyon in Paris to Lyon and Grenoble. For rail enquiries, contact **Rail Europe** (0870 584 8848; www.raileurope.co.uk).

AVERAGE DAILY TEMPERATURE (CELSIUS) °C

The Rhône-Alps

JAN	FEB	MAR	APR	MAY	JUNE	JULY	AUG	SEPT	OCT	NOV	DEC
5.3	5.2	9.4	14.8	16.5	24	27.2	26.7	23.1	16.2	10.6	7.1

London

JAN	FEB	MAR	APR	MAY	JUNE	JULY	AUG	SEPT	OCT	NOV	DEC
6	7	10	13	17	20	22	21	19	14	10	7

The Regions

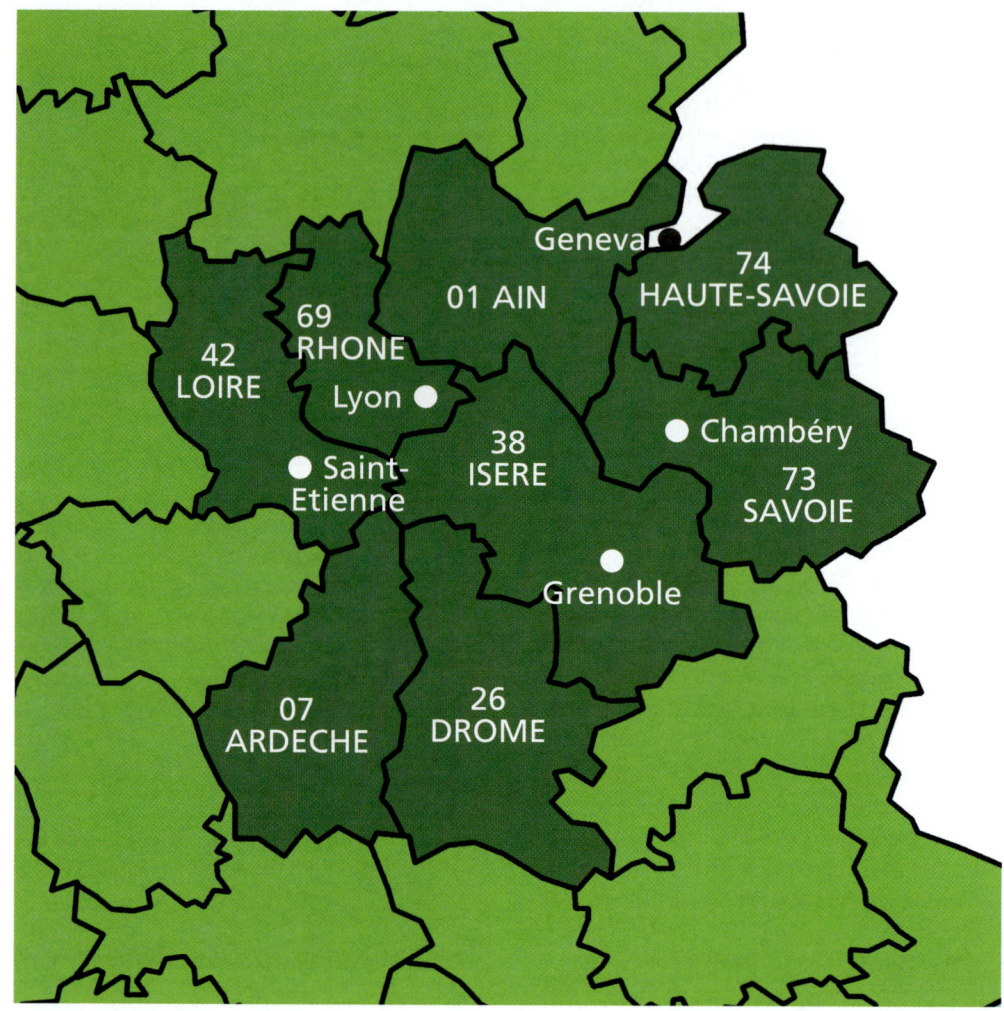

BUYING IN THE RHONE-ALPS

While the diverse architectural styles of the region, from loft-style apartments in former silk workers' buildings in Lyon, to lakeside châteaux and Ardèchois stone farmhouses, offer something for pretty much all tastes, the properties of the moment in the Rhône-Alps have to be those sited in the famous ski stations, from Courchevel in Savoie to Megève in Haute-Savoie, providing immediate access to some of Europe's best pistes and some of the most glamorous off-piste entertainment. The kudos of staying in a 'ski-in, ski-out' residence in one of these world-class resorts is more attractive than ever, and property prices here have shot up dramatically over the past year or two, with land prices almost trebling. Chalets in resorts offering direct access to the pistes are rare, and, when they do become available, cost in the millions, while apartment developments are usually sold before construction even starts, such is the intense interest. There is, however, a continual supply of small, older-style apartments, either studios or with a separate bedroom, in the major ski stations that range from modern complexes to more traditionally styled resort towns.

If you are looking for a true French village atmosphere, however, hunt outside the big-name resorts, slightly down the mountainside, in old farming communities. Here, a wealth of properties is always available, from newly built chalets to

USEFUL CONTACTS

PREFECTURE
Préfecture de la Région Rhône-Alpes, 106 rue Pierre-Corneille
69419 Lyon Cedex 03
Tel: +33 4 72 61 60 60
Fax: +33 4 78 60 49 38

LEGAL
Chambre des Notaires du Rhône
58 boulevard des Belges
BP 6079, 69412 Lyon Cedex 06
Tel: +33 4 78 93 32 49
Fax: +33 4 72 44 05 47

FINANCE
Direction Régionale des Impôts Rhône-Alpes Bourgogne
41 cours de la Liberté
69422 Lyon Cedex 3
Tel: +33 4 78 63 54 10
Fax: +33 4 78 63 53 93

BUILDING & PLANNING
Chambre Régionale de Métiers de Rhône-Alpes
Central Parc 1
119 boulevard Stalingrad
69100 Villeurbanne
Tel: +33 4 72 44 13 30
Fax: +33 4 78 89 93 73

CAUE du Rhône
6 bis quai Saint Vincent
69283 Lyon Cedex 01
Tel: +33 4 72 07 44 55
Fax: +33 4 72 07 44 59

EDUCATION
Rectorat de l'Académie de Grenoble
(Ardèche, Drôme, Isère, Savoie, Haute-Savoie)
7 place Bir-Hakeim
BP 1065
38021 Grenoble Cedex
Tel: +33 4 76 74 70 00
Fax: +33 4 76 74 75 00

Rectorat de l'Académie de Lyon
(Loire, Rhône, Ain)
92 rue de Marseille
BP 7227
69365 Lyon Cedex 07
Tel: +33 4 72 73 54 54
Fax: +33 4 78 58 54 78

HEALTH
Caisse Primaire d'Assurance Maladie de Lyon
102 rue Masséna
69471 Lyon Cedex 6
Tel: +33 820 90 41 15
Fax: +33 4 72 75 82 30

traditional Savoyard farmhouses, which are built partly in stone, partly in wood, and can still be found in a state ripe for renovation. If buyers look in the lower villages, away from the resort centres, they will find the properties are all at a much reduced cost compared with those in the major resort centres, but within easy reach of the pistes. And these properties can also provide that increasingly important 'dual-season' status because the lower slopes are far more picturesque in the summer months and residents have more of a feeling of being in a traditional French village. This means extended letting periods for those looking to rent out to help towards the upkeep of the property as well as providing a home 'for all seasons'.

The wide range of building styles available in the Rhône-Alps provides something for every taste

For a guide to property prices in the Rhône-Alps, turn to page 267.

The Regions

AQUITAINE

MEON VILLAS

The 'Alternative South' is the tag given to this southwestern region, and it definitely offers a very different holiday experience for those used to the Mediterranean coast. Here, for example, the beaches are endless and sandy, and pounded by some of the finest surf France can lay claim to, while inland a rural scene of rolling hills, vineyards, forests and sleepy villages greets the visitor.

The vineyards spreading out from the city of Bordeaux have long been renowned for being the source of some of the world's finest, and also most expensive wines like Saint-Emilion, Margaux and Pomerol. So many great estates are packed into such a small area around the Gironde Estuary. Fortunately for those who find these bottlings just a little too exclusive, wineries throughout the region make affordable wines in a similar vein.

Upstream in the heart of the Dordogne, the bustling markets of Bergerac and Sarlat make for lively, highly scented and colourful outings. The quiet *bastide* towns typical of the area, which were built with an encircling wall to help protect the townsfolk, offer a taste of simple French life. Dordogne is divided into four colour-coded regions – Green, White, Black and Purple Périgord – after the forests, rocks, oak trees, truffles and vineyards that characterise these areas respectively.

Further south, an even more unspoilt rural landscape is offered by the Lot-et-Garonne. Its agricultural success has earnt the *département* the nickname 'the Granary of France', and has meant that it is has been almost oblivious to the tourist trade until very recently. Its historic towns like Nérac, for instance, have only just woken up to the idea of encouraging visitors to enjoy their period architecture and riverside walks. Having been the political and cultural hub of France in the 16th century, Nérac in particular has a fair amount of interest to offer visitors. The former bath house of Queen Margot, wife of Henri IV, is just one of the vestiges of the intriguing past of this rather undiscovered gem of rural France.

Aquitaine

Opposite: a typical sturdy stone-built *maison périgordine*
Right: an idyllic, quiet way of life is enjoyed in Périgord

ELIZABETH DISNEY

Together with the Basque Country on the Spanish border, with its bullfights and colourful festivals, and the sparsely populated pine forest- and dune-strewn Landes, these varied territories comprise one of France's most diverse regions.

BUYING IN AQUITAINE

Aquitaine's Dordogne *département* has been a British favourite for decades as a retirement location or a spot for a second home. With the arrival of a new direct flight route to Bergerac from Stansted, the area is hotter than ever. Foreign buyers are choosing this well-known spot to buy homes for their own holidays or as an investment to let out to the increasing number of holidaymakers who are coming to the region.

Prices in this British stronghold had been rising dramatically even before the announcement of new budget flight services, however. Over the past two years, for example, house prices have reportedly risen by almost 50 percent. This represents a far greater increase than most other regions in France have witnessed over the same period.

Some parts of Périgord, the historical name of the region, are so popular with overseas buyers that

GETTING THERE

AIR Bordeaux-Mérignac receives **British Airways** (0845 773 3377; www.britishairways.com) flights from UK regional airports and **buzz** (0870 240 7070; www.buzzaway.com) flights from Stansted. **Buzz** and **Ryanair** (0871 246 0000; www.ryanair.com) also now fly direct from Stansted to Bergerac and Biarritz respectively.
ROAD The A10 from Paris leads right to Bordeaux. Take the A63 on to Bayonne and Biarritz. For Dordogne, take the A10 from Paris, then the A71 and A20 after Orléans, and join the N21 at Limoges.
RAIL The **TGV** Atlantique runs from Gare Montparnasse in Paris to Bordeaux. **TGV** services to Bayonne and Biarritz leave from Gare d'Austerlitz. Contact **Rail Europe** (0870 584 8848; www.raileurope.co.uk) for details.

AVERAGE DAILY TEMPERATURE (CELSIUS) °C

Aquitaine

JAN	FEB	MAR	APR	MAY	JUNE	JULY	AUG	SEPT	OCT	NOV	DEC
10.0	9.4	12.2	19.5	18	23.7	27.2	25.7	24.2	19.7	15.4	11.0

London

JAN	FEB	MAR	APR	MAY	JUNE	JULY	AUG	SEPT	OCT	NOV	DEC
6	7	10	13	17	20	22	21	19	14	10	7

The Regions

some villages here even boast their own cricket team. Of course, this will not please everyone who is looking to immerse themselves in the culture of the country in which they set up home or in which they have a second home, but it does deserve bearing in mind that it can be both a comfort and a convenience having fellow expats within easy reach.

Aquitaine is a highly diverse region, not just in its countryside, but also in the styles of property it offers. The half-timbered, exposed-brick Basque Country farmhouse, for example, is a stark contrast to the typically sturdy *maisons périgordines* of Dordogne with their high four-sided roofs. The more classical proportions of Gironde's houses are worth considering too, especially now cheap flights have been added to the long-established direct services from the UK to Bordeaux.

The wine lover could do much worse than find an old detached stone house to convert in the middle of the vineyards of the extensive Bordeaux wine region. A budget of £30,000 should cover the purchase. At a higher price, properties with wine cellars and a plot scored with vines do come on to the market quite regularly. Although this may not be the makings of a *grand cru* business, it could provide a vital component of the French lifestyle.

Right: Aquitaine is a charming southern French location in which to buy a dream home in the sun and by the sea

For a guide to property prices in Aquitaine, turn to page 275.

Aquitaine

USEFUL CONTACTS

PREFECTURE
Préfecture de la Région
Aquitaine, 4 bis Esplanade
Charles-de-Gaulle
33077 Bordeaux Cedex
Tel: +33 5 56 90 60 60
Fax: +33 5 56 24 08 03

LEGAL
Chambre des Notaires
de la Gironde
6 rue Mably
33000 Bordeaux
Tel: +33 5 56 48 00 75
Fax: +33 5 56 81 34 75

FINANCE
Direction des Impôts
du Sud-Ouest
2 rue des Piliers de Tutelle
BP 45
33025 Bordeaux Cedex
Tel: +33 5 57 14 21 00
Fax: +33 5 57 14 21 09

BUILDING & PLANNING
Chambre Régionale de Métiers
d'Aquitaine
353 boulevard du
Président Wilson
33200 Bordeaux
Tel: +33 5 57 22 57 22
Fax: +33 5 57 22 57 20

Union Régionale des CAUE
d'Aquitaine
Maison des Maires
rue Etienne Dolet
47000 Agen
Tel: +33 5 53 69 42 42
Fax: +33 5 53 69 42 41

EDUCATION
Rectorat de l'Académie
de Bordeaux
5 rue Joseph de Carayon Latour
BP 935
33060 Bordeaux
Cedex
Tel: +33 5 57 57 38 00
Fax: +33 5 56 96 29 42

HEALTH
Caisse Primaire d'Assurance
Maladie de la Gironde
148 cours Médoc
33000 Bordeaux
Tel: +33 820 90 41 40
Fax: +33 5 56 11 54 55

WWW.FRENCHLIFE.CO.UK

THE MIDI-PYRENEES

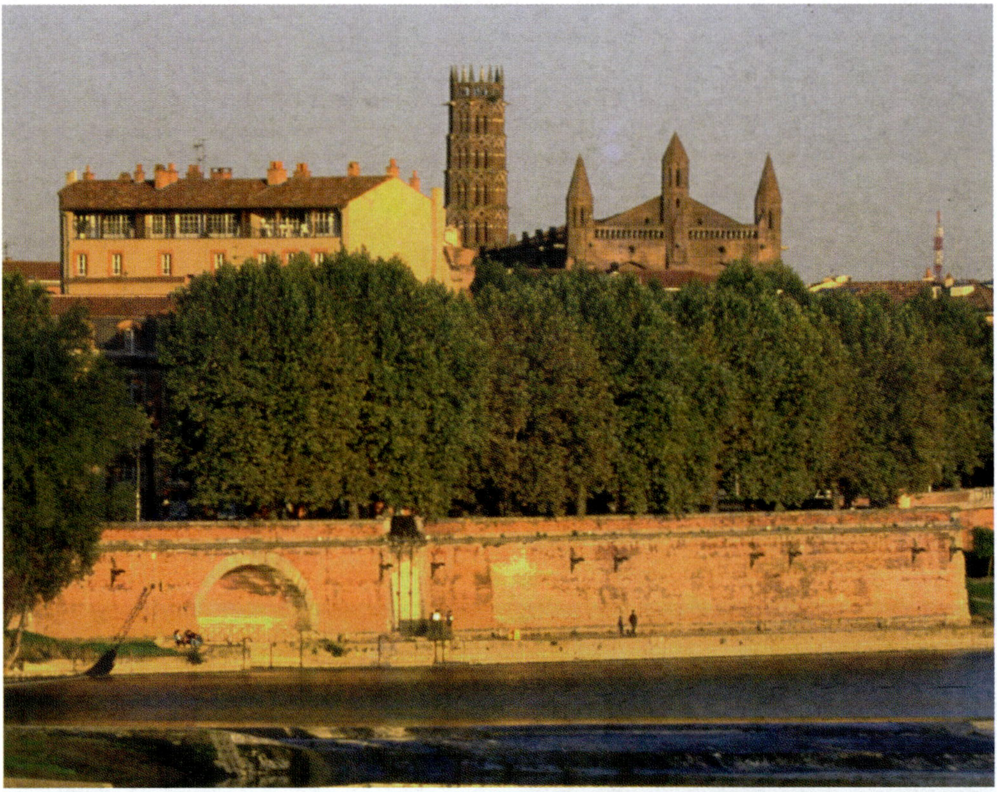

D VIET/CRT TOULOUSE MIDI-PYRENEES

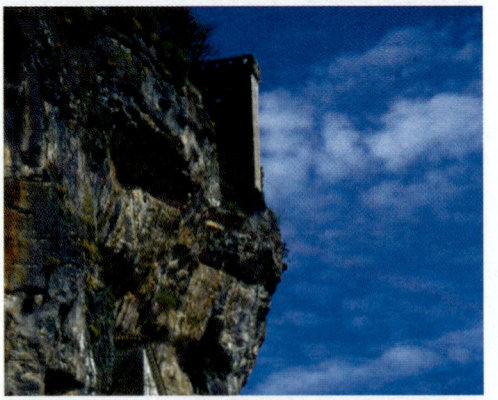

The strong southern sun, quintessential rustic French food and wine and sleepy villages gives the Midi-Pyrénées its unique blend of charm. At its heart is the region of Gascony, which is frequented quite famously by high-profile British politicians and media heavyweights during the summer months.

The name of the pre-revolutionary Duchy of Gascony is still used today when referring to the *département* of Gers, which more or less replaced the duchy after the Revolution. It is a name that conjures up images of a romantic rural idyll, a dream that is actually relatively easy to turn into a reality in this sunny, peaceful corner of southwest France. Simple pleasures – good food (duck ruling most menus), taking time to enjoy the day, being greeted in the street, the antithesis of the rushed modern

ELIZABETH DISNEY

Top: the River Garonne running through the city of Toulouse, which glows pink as a result of the hue of the local brick **Above:** buildings cling to the cliffs above the medieval village of Rocamadour

The Midi-Pyrénées

The town of Albi, with its famous connection with artist Toulouse-Lautrec, offers cultural diversions from the quiet rural life in the Midi-Pyrénées

cosmopolitan existence – are at the heart of everyday life in this southern enclave. Although popular with the discerning traveller, and the home of the elegant brandy Armagnac, it has, thankfully, managed to avoid being overrun with tourists and the usual ensuing developments. The lush, sunflower-strewn rolling hills, dotted with statuesque Gascon dovecotes, are populated almost as sparsely as they were in the Middle Ages.

Tarn and Aveyron to the northeast are truly unspoilt lands of gorges and dense forest. To the east lies the second most visited site in France, the cliff-hugging medieval village of Rocamadour. In the south, the foothills of the Pyrenees rise up. This southern mountainous border between France and Spain offers miles of ski runs in the winter and mountain biking and hiking tracks in the summer.

GETTING THERE

AIR British Airways (0845 773 3377; www.britishairways.com) and **Air France** (0845 084 5111; www.airfrance.co.uk) fly to Toulouse from Gatwick and Heathrow respectively, while **buzz** (0870 240 7070; www.buzzaway.com) operates services between Stansted and Toulouse. **British European** (0870 567 6676; www.flybe.com) flies between Birmingham and Toulouse.
ROAD From Paris, take the A10 to Orléans, then the A71 and the A20 to Toulouse. From the Channel ports, travel to Le Mans, then take the N138 followed by the N143 to the A20 at Châteauroux, which carries on south to Toulouse.
RAIL TGV services leave Gare d'Austerlitz in Paris for Toulouse. Contact **Rail Europe** (0870 584 8848; www.raileurope.co.uk) for details.

AVERAGE DAILY TEMPERATURE (CELSIUS) °C

The Midi-Pyrénées

JAN	FEB	MAR	APR	MAY	JUNE	JULY	AUG	SEPT	OCT	NOV	DEC
10.0	9.0	12.3	18.3	19.1	26.4	27.6	27.2	25.0	19.3	15.5	9.8

London

JAN	FEB	MAR	APR	MAY	JUNE	JULY	AUG	SEPT	OCT	NOV	DEC
6	7	10	13	17	20	22	21	19	14	10	7

The Regions

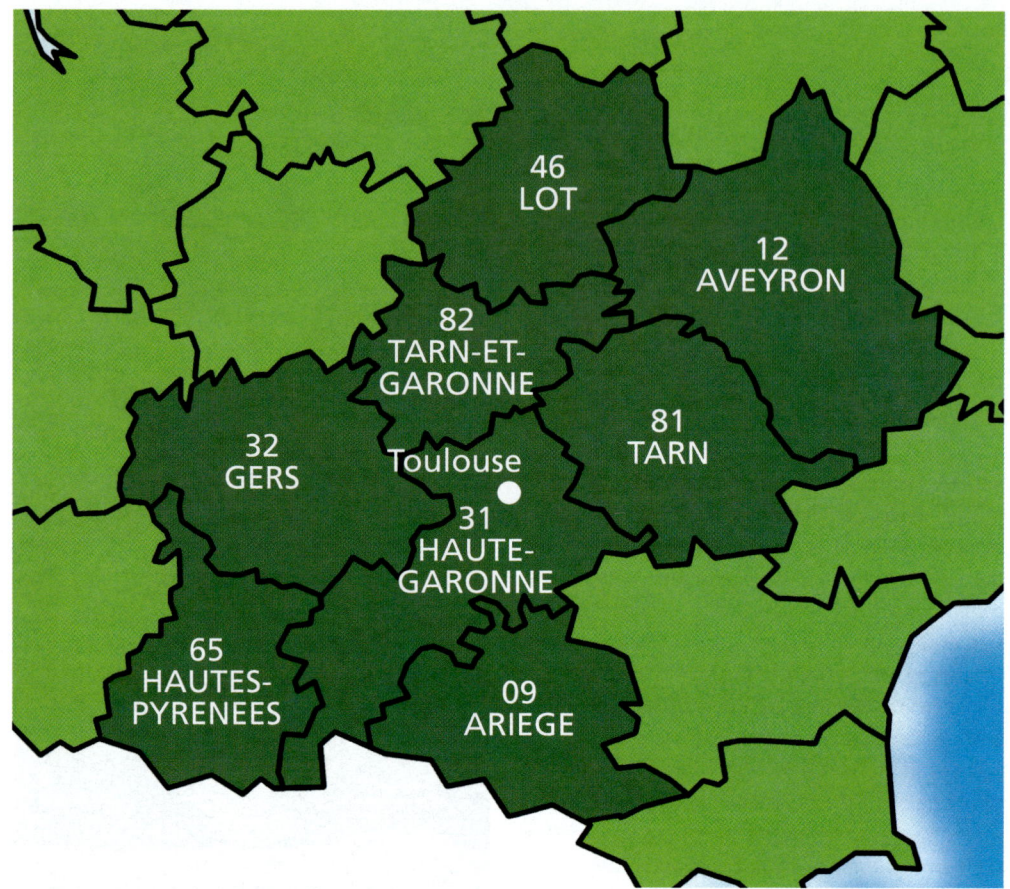

The spa town of Cauterets is the hub of winter sports activity in this ski centre, which is rather a hidden gem of France's ski scene compared with the bustling Alpine resorts.

The famously pink city of Toulouse, its hue the product of the local pink brick, and towns like Albi, equally pink, but better known for its connection with the artist Toulouse-Lautrec, are at hand to provide cultural diversions. Right at the heart of the region, Toulouse has recently become the destination of cheap flights from the UK, so the city and a wide range of rural Midi-Pyrénées destinations are now only a short flight away.

BUYING IN THE MIDI-PYRENEES

Of all this sunny, peaceful area, the focus of most foreign buying attention is Gers. Interest has picked up here in the past two years, partly due to the media coverage of the movers and shakers who have bought a home or holiday here. And whereas many French regions still offer a large number of cheap properties ripe for conversion, the market in Gascony is what is described by estate agents as 'mature'. That is, most houses being sold here are fully converted, quite comfortable to live in from the start. There may always be outbuildings included in the sale, however, for those who want to turn their hand to a spot of restoration.

Luckily for those still looking, good value is a term that can still be used when describing the varied property styles available in this region. From simple dovecotes in a field, which can reap staggeringly high rental yields when converted into a studio or one-bedroom dwelling, through golden stone-built farmhouses, to grander manor houses, buyers get much more for their money here than they would in the fashionable parts of Provence, for example. Here, £200,000 can secure a habitable

The Midi-Pyrénées

USEFUL CONTACTS

PREFECTURE
Préfecture de la Région
Midi-Pyrénées
1 place Saint-Etienne
31038 Toulouse Cedex 09
Tel: +33 5 34 45 34 45
Fax: +33 5 34 45 37 38

LEGAL
Chambre des Notaires
de Haute-Garonne
51 rue Raymond IV
31000 Toulouse
Tel: +33 5 62 73 58 68
Fax: +33 5 62 73 00 91

FINANCE
Direction des Impôts
Sud-Pyrénées
Immeuble Le Sully
1 place Occitane
BP 7164
31072 Toulouse
Cedex 7
Tel: +33 5 34 45 29 41
Fax: +33 5 34 45 29 59

BUILDING & PLANNING
Chambre Régionale de Métiers
de Midi-Pyrénées
59 terrace Chemin Verdale
31240 Saint-Jean
Tel: +33 5 62 22 94 22
Fax: +33 5 62 22 94 30

Union Régionale des CAUE
de Midi-Pyrénées
39 rue de la Concorde
31000 Toulouse
Tel: +33 5 34 41 39 59
Fax: +33 5 34 41 39 51

EDUCATION
Rectorat de Rectorat de
l'Académie de Toulouse
place Saint-Jacques
31073 Toulouse
Cedex
Tel: +33 5 61 36 40 00
Fax: +33 5 61 52 80 27

HEALTH
Caisse Primaire d'Assurance
Maladie de Haute-Garonne
3 boulevard Professeur
Léopold Escande
31000 Toulouse
Tel: +33 5 62 73 80 00
Fax: +33 5 62 73 85 93

character property with a handful of bedrooms and a sizeable plot of land. Head to the north and east, to Tarn and Aveyron, and this will buy a pretty stone-built house with more bedrooms still. Up the budget by an extra £100,000, and a turreted medieval fortified castle could well be within reach.

The whole of the Midi-Pyrénées is more accessible today than it was even two years ago. Thanks to budget airlines setting up direct flights from regional UK airports, getting to this southern region could not be simpler. Though house prices are some way off the level of those in many of France's regions, ease of access will make this area more popular with both British house hunters and gîte renters, and an upward pressure on prices is very likely to follow.

The town of Auch, the capital of Gers, which is attracting a lot of attention from foreign buyers

For a guide to property prices in the Midi-Pyrénées, turn to page 297.

The Regions

LANGUEDOC-ROUSSILLON

The Pont du Gard aqueduct in the Gard *département*, one of the vestiges of the Roman Empire still visible today in northern Languedoc-Roussillon

For some time, Languedoc-Roussillon has been known as 'the poor man's Provence', but this moniker does not do justice to the region's very own attractions. Yes, it does have the characteristic purple swathes of lavender fields, vine-clad hills and access to the Mediterranean, with its sun-baked beaches, and is still very much a good value destination, but the region has its own very particular style. It is much calmer and less crowded in the summer months than its neighbour to the east, and has defining cultural influences that give it a charming identity all of its own.

Just over the Rhône from Provence, the *département* of the Gard has a much more laid-back, peaceful ambience than its Provençal neighbours with which it shares much in common. It, like Provence, is the site of prominent vestiges of the Roman Empire, the Pont du Gard aqueduct being the most famous. To the south, in Aude, which is famous for its hearty *cassoulets*, lies Carcassonne. A majestic, fully-restored fortified medieval town rises up above the city, lending Carcassonne a fairy-tale-like quality.

Further down the coast towards the Spanish border lies Roussillon, which has a thriving Catalan culture. The traditional Catalan dance, the *sardane*, for example, is still an important community activity – and definitely not merely a show for the tourists. Colourful striped espadrilles are donned and groups gather in town and village squares alike, even when there is no special occasion to mark, to carry on the tradition of this dance, with hands held high, and to pass it down to future generations.

Languedoc-Roussillon

The Languedoc's charm is drawing buyers and holidaymakers alike across the Rhône from Provence

This sunny enclave is peppered with hidden treasures ripe for discovery. Take the tiny creeks that dot the Côte Vermeille on the border with Spain. These are generally quite secluded, and perfect for impromptu picnics or barbecues by the sea. Then there are the unique inland towns to explore, like Céret, which holds cherry festivals and houses important pieces by modern artists in its art museum.

BUYING IN LANGUEDOC-ROUSSILLON

The Languedoc-Roussillon region is increasingly being recognised by overseas buyers looking for a second home as an all-year-round holiday destination. There are seemingly limitless sun and sea activities in the summer, while in winter the region offers a warmer climate than other parts of France, and, if a property is within easy driving distance of the mountains, winter sports facilities too. Both distinct sectors of this region – the Languedoc to the northeast and Roussillon to the southwest – are getting more and more attention for those seeking their own place in the sun.

Buyers who once may have been lured by the charms of Provence, for instance, are now acknowledging the tranquillity afforded by the

ROWENA MEDLOW

GETTING THERE

AIR Ryanair (0871 246 0000; www.ryanair.com) flies direct from Stansted to Carcassonne, Nîmes and Perpignan, while **British Airways** (0845 773 3377; www.britishairways.com) operates services via Paris to Montpellier.
ROAD Take the A10 from Paris, then the A20 from Orléans on to Toulouse. Here the A61 leads to the A9, which carries on south to Perpignan and north to Montpellier and Nîmes.
RAIL TGV services run between Paris, Gare de Lyon and Nîmes, Montpellier and Perpignan. Services also operate between Lille Europe and Perpignan. For details, contact **Rail Europe** (0870 584 8848; www.raileurope.co.uk).

AVERAGE DAILY TEMPERATURE (CELSIUS) °C

Languedoc-Roussillon

12.4	11.5	12.5	17.6	20.1	26.5	28.4	28.1	26.1	21.1	15.8	13.5

London

6	7	10	13	17	20	22	21	19	14	10	7
JAN	FEB	MAR	APR	MAY	JUNE	JULY	AUG	SEPT	OCT	NOV	DEC

The Regions

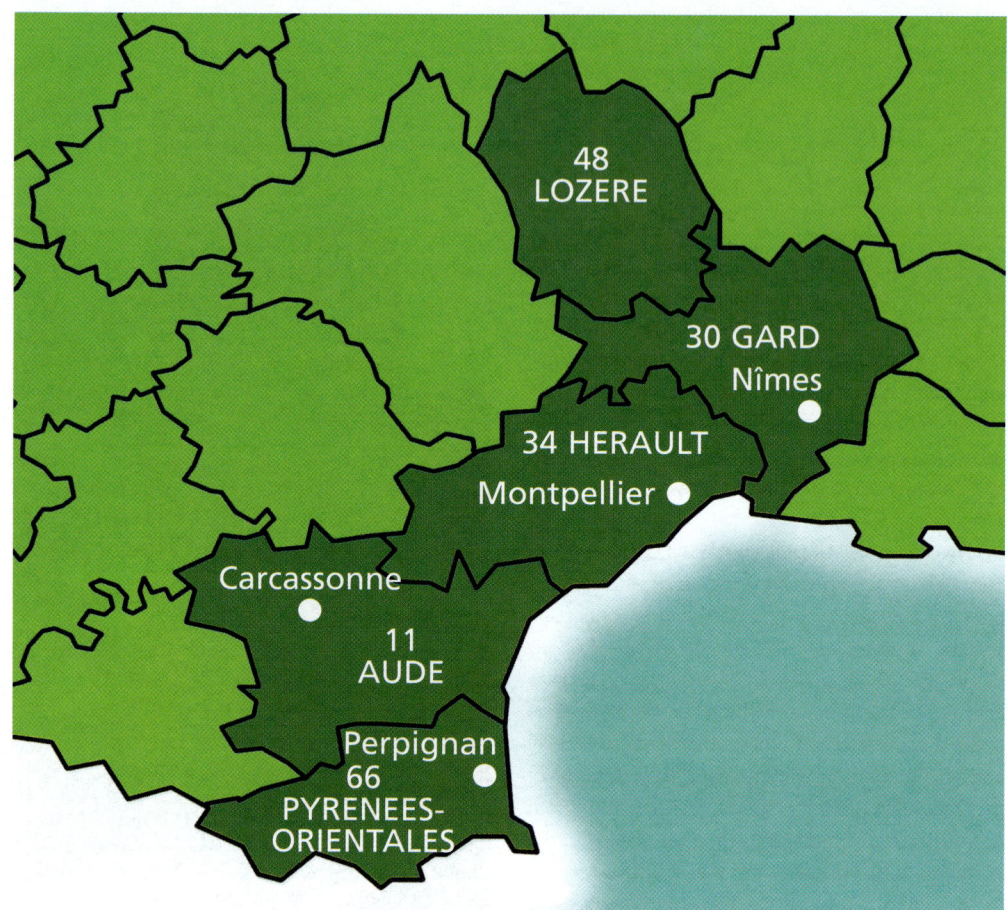

Languedoc *département*s, with property styles in a similar vein, such as old *mas* built around a courtyard or stone-built village houses perched on the top of rocky outcrops. This has become a more popular spot also, in part, because cheap flights direct from the UK are available to both Nîmes and Carcassonne, at the heart of this area. Price hikes have, unsurprisingly, been considerable, with properties near the major towns such as Nîmes, in particular, gaining substantially on their Provençal counterparts.

There has also been considerably increased interest in Roussillon, the southern half of Languedoc-Roussillon, which butts up against the border with Spain. It is an area that once would have seemed to many people a location far too troublesome to get to from the UK – it is a good 14-hour journey by car from the Channel ports – even for a long summer break. Mainly thanks to the budget flights available direct to Perpignan, however, it is now being considered by many as a weekend getaway with pretty much guaranteed sunshine.

Roussillon is not the place to expect to find cheap properties for renovation. Prices for older-style houses have gone up noticeably because there are very few offered for sale. But for those looking for relaxation instead of renovation during their time in France, there are plenty of new apartments and villas that will provide good value – apartments with sea views are commonly priced around £25,000 – and require little maintenance, either between visits or changeover days if the property is let out.

For a guide to property prices in Languedoc-Roussillon, turn to page 319.

Languedoc-Roussillon

USEFUL CONTACTS

PREFECTURE
Préfecture de la Région
Languedoc-Roussillon
place des Martyrs-de-
la-Résistance
34062 Montpellier Cedex
Tel: +33 4 67 61 61 61
Fax: +33 4 67 02 25 38

LEGAL
Chambre des Notaires
de l'Hérault
565 avenue des Apothicaires
34000 Montpellier
Tel: +33 4 67 04 10 52
Fax: +33 4 67 52 60 31

Chambre des Notaires
des Pyrénées-Orientales
21 boulevard Clémenceau
66000 Perpignan
Tel: +33 4 68 35 14 79
Fax: +33 4 68 35 02 15

FINANCE
Direction des Impôts
Sud-Pyrénées
Immeuble Le Sully
1 place Occitane
BP 7164
31072 Toulouse Cedex 7
Tel: +33 5 34 45 29 41
Fax: +33 5 34 45 29 59

BUILDING & PLANNING
Chambre Régionale de Métiers
du Languedoc-Roussillon
L'Orangerie
44 avenue Saint-Lazare
34965 Montpellier Cedex 2
Tel: +33 4 67 02 68 40
Fax: +33 4 67 79 50 08

CAUE des Pyrénées-Orientales
11 rue du Bastion
Saint-Dominique
66000 Perpignan
Tel: +33 4 68 34 12 37
Fax: +33 4 68 34 80 90

EDUCATION
Rectorat de l'Académie
de Montpellier
31 rue de l'Université
34064 Montpellier
Cedex 02
Tel: +33 4 67 91 49 99
Fax: +33 4 67 91 50 51

HEALTH
Caisse Primaire d'Assurance
Maladie de l'Hérault
29 Cours Gambetta
34934 Montpellier
Cedex 9
Tel: +33 4 99 52 53 54
Fax: +33 4 99 52 55 09

Caisse Primaire d'Assurance
des Pyrénées-Orientales
2 rue des Remparts
Saint-Mathieu
66013 Perpignan Cedex
Tel: +33 4 68 35 95 95
Fax: +33 4 68 35 96 96

The fortified medieval town rising up above Carcassonne lends a fairy-tale quality to the budget flight destination

PROVENCE, COTE D'AZUR & CORSICA

Perhaps the most glamourous of all French regions, Provence and the Côte d'Azur encompasses some of France's most fashionable holiday destinations. The legendary old fishing village of Saint-Tropez, the chic cities of Cannes and Nice, and rural Provence, made so popular by the writing of Peter Mayle, are all found in this region, which makes up the country's southeastern corner. Off the coast, tranquil Corsica, an island of beaches and wild scrubland, couldn't be more of a contrast to the often crowded mainland region.

With the almost intoxicating combination of designer boutiques, sandy beaches, Michelin-starred restaurants and casinos, the Côte d'Azur may be a playground for the rich and famous, but it is more accessible than ever for those who are looking for a simple lifestyle in a clement climate and with the enviable diet the Mediterranean provides. Now that cheap flights from both UK regional and London airports to Nice are a regular fixture throughout the year, even weekending along this smart coastline is no longer the preserve of the jet set.

It is also easier now to travel between other parts of the region and the UK too. A new fast TGV service takes the traveller from London straight to the heart of Provence in under seven hours during the summer months, while budget airlines have set up direct routes to nearby Nîmes, as well as Marseille, and these operate throughout the year.

A gentler pace of life can be enjoyed among the rolling hills and lavender fields of inland Provence. Towns here show the signs of their former Roman occupation, with grand amphitheatres and the remains of aqueducts and bath houses. The northwest enclave near Avignon is also home to big, spicy red wines like Châteauneuf-du-Pape. To the

Provence, Côte d'Azur & Corsica

Opposite: Menton, on the ever-alluring Côte d'Azur **Right:** Nice's colourful old town, a source of good value pied-à-terres

south is the quite magical Camargue, a delta comprising lagoons, marshes and dunes formed where the River Rhône divides and joins the Mediterranean. Here, white horses run wild and pink flamingos gather en masse in the marshy lands creating a striking display.

BUYING IN PROVENCE, THE COTE D'AZUR AND CORSICA

The Riviera is undoubtedly one of France's hottest property spots. The popularity of Nice as the place for a home from home is nothing new. At the turn of the 19th century, the Riviera was one of the most desirable locations for a spot of winter sun worship. Today, the mix is a lot more cosmopolitan. Russians and Americans are joining members of Britain's A-list, and are helping keep prices for the best homes in the millions.

Those looking for a simpler, more moderately priced modern villa with the kudos of a Côte d'Azur

GETTING THERE

AIR From Stansted, **buzz** (0870 240 7070; www.buzzaway.com) flies to Toulon-Saint-Tropez and Marseille. **go** (0845 605 4321; www.go-fly.com) flies to Nice from Bristol and Stansted, **easyJet** (0870 600 0000; www.easyjet.com) to Nice from Stansted and Liverpool and **bmibaby** (0870 607 0555; www.bmibaby.com) from East Midlands to Nice. **Air France** (0845 084 5111; www.airfrance.co.uk) flies to Ajaccio from Heathrow, while **British Airways** (0845 773 3377; www.britishairways.com) flies to Marseille and Nice from Heathrow.
ROAD Take the A6 from Paris to Lyon, then the A7 on to Orange and Avignon.
SEA Southern Ferries/SNCM (020 7491 4968; www.sncm.fr) sails from Nice and Marseille to Ajaccio, Bastia, Calvi and Propriano in Corsica.
RAIL TGV services run from Paris, Gare de Lyon and Lille to Avignon, Aix-en-Provence and Marseille. Direct **Eurostar** (0870 518 6186; www.eurostar.co.uk) services operate between Waterloo and Avignon in the summer. For rail enquiries, contact **Rail Europe** (0870 584 8848; www.raileurope.co.uk).

AVERAGE DAILY TEMPERATURE (CELSIUS) °C
Provence, Côte d'Azur & Corsica

JAN	FEB	MAR	APR	MAY	JUNE	JULY	AUG	SEPT	OCT	NOV	DEC
12.4	12	14.2	17.8	20.9	26.2	28.1	28.2	25.4	21.9	17.2	14.2

London

JAN	FEB	MAR	APR	MAY	JUNE	JULY	AUG	SEPT	OCT	NOV	DEC
6	7	10	13	17	20	22	21	19	14	10	7

The Regions

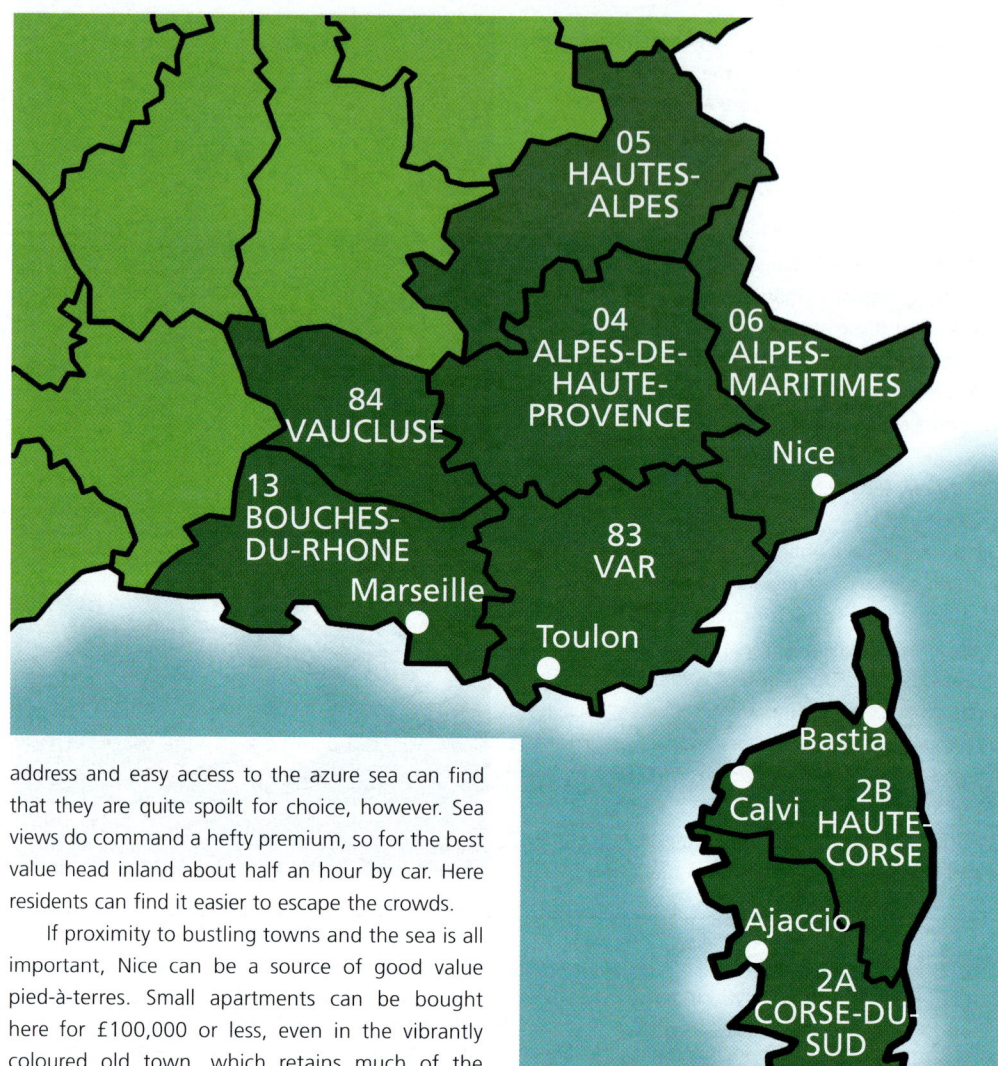

address and easy access to the azure sea can find that they are quite spoilt for choice, however. Sea views do command a hefty premium, so for the best value head inland about half an hour by car. Here residents can find it easier to escape the crowds.

If proximity to bustling towns and the sea is all important, Nice can be a source of good value pied-à-terres. Small apartments can be bought here for £100,000 or less, even in the vibrantly coloured old town, which retains much of the architecture and charm that made it so popular in the early 1900s.

In Provence, the 'Peter Mayle effect' still has a strong influence on prices, and estate agents are still thanking him for having made this corner of France so popular with the UK buyer. Provençal *mas*, farmhouses traditionally built around a courtyard with adjoining stables, barns and other outbuildings, have been particularly popular with people looking to create holiday accommodation to let out. In an area like Provence, potential clients are not hard to come by. *Mas* like this ripe for conversion are increasingly difficult to come across though, as are any well-sized farmhouses in a good state of repair for under £500,000. Stone-built village houses are a more affordable alternative, with a budget of £100,000 being still quite realistic for a simple house with two to three bedrooms.

For a guide to property prices in Provence, the Côte d'Azur and Corsica, turn to page 339.

USEFUL CONTACTS

PRÉFECTURES
Préfecture de la Région
Provence-Alpes-Côte d'Azur
2 boulevard Paul-Peytral
13282 Marseille
Cedex 20
Tel: +33 4 91 15 60 00
Fax: +33 4 91 15 61 90

Préfecture de Corse
9 parc Belvédère
BP 229
20179 Ajaccio Cedex
Tel: +33 4 95 29 99 29
Fax: +33 4 95 21 32 70

LEGAL
Chambre des Notaires
des Bouches-du-Rhône
77 boulevard Périer
13008 Marseille
Tel: +33 4 91 53 49 67
Fax: +33 4 91 81 24 84

Chambre des Notaires
des Alpes-Maritimes
18 rue du Congrès
06000 Nice
Tel: +33 4 93 87 94 30
Fax: +33 4 93 87 76 51

Chambre des Notaires
de la Corse du Sud
2 cours Grandval
20000 Ajaccio
Tel: +33 4 95 51 31 36
Fax: +33 4 95 21 04 24

FINANCE
Direction des Impôts
Sud-Est Réunion
23 rue Roux de Brignoles
13281 Marseille Cedex 6
Tel: +33 4 91 13 82 01
Fax: +33 4 91 37 92 69

BUILDING & PLANNING
Chambre Régionale de Métiers
Provence-Alpes-Côte d'Azur
L'Orangerie
44 avenue Saint-Lazare
34965 Montpellier cedex 2
Tel: +33 4 67 02 68 40
Fax: +33 4 67 79 50 08

Chambre Régionale de Métiers
de Corse
Chemin de la Sposata
20090 Ajaccio
Tel: +33 4 95 23 53 00
Fax: +33 4 95 23 53 03

CAUE des Bouches-du-Rhône
35 rue Montgrand
13006 Marseille
Tel: +33 4 91 33 02 02
Fax: +33 4 91 33 42 49

CAUE de Haute-Corse
2 bis rue de l'Annonciade
20200 Bastia
Tel: +33 4 95 31 80 90
Fax: +33 4 95 31 54 80

EDUCATION
Rectorat de l'Académie
d'Aix-Marseille
(Bouches-du-Rhône, Vaucluse,
Alpes-Haute-de-Provence,
Hautes-Alpes)
place Lucien-Paye
13621 Aix-en-Provence
Cedex 1
Tel: +33 4 42 24 88 88
Fax: +33 4 42 26 68 03

Rectorat de l'Académie de Nice
(Alpes-Maritimes, Var)
53 avenue Cap-de-Croix
06181 Nice Cedex
Tel: +33 4 93 53 70 70
Fax: +33 4 93 53 72 44

Rectorat de l'Académie de Corse
(Corse-du-Sud, Haute-Corse)
boulevard Rossini
BP 808
20192 Ajaccio Cedex
Tel: +33 4 95 50 34 08
Fax: +33 4 95 51 27 06

HEALTH
Caisse Primaire d'Assurance
Maladie des Alpes-Maritimes
48 rue Roi Robert Comte
de Provence
06100 Nice
Tel: +33 4 92 09 40 00
Fax: +33 4 92 09 43 43

Caisse Primaire d'Assurance
Maladie d'Ajaccio
boulevard Abbé Recco
Quartier Les Padules
BP 910
20702 Ajaccio Cedex 9
Tel: +33 4 95 23 52 00
Fax: +33 4 95 20 64 74

The Côte d'Azur is as charming today as it was in the early 1900s

JUSTIN POSTLETHWAITE

PRICE GUIDE

A guide to the prices of the wide range of properties available throughout France today

HOW TO USE THIS GUIDE 108

REGIONAL PRICE GUIDES

Brittany	111
Normandy	133
Nord-Pas-de-Calais & Picardy	157
Ile-de-France	169
Champagne-Ardenne	175
Alsace, Lorraine & Franche-Comté	185
The Loire	195
Burgundy	215
Poitou-Charentes	231
Limousin & Auvergne	249
The Rhône-Alps	267
Aquitaine	275
The Midi-Pyrénées	297
Languedoc-Roussillon	319
Provence, Côte d'Azur & Corsica	339

INDEX OF AGENTS 358

Price Guide

HOW TO USE THIS GUIDE

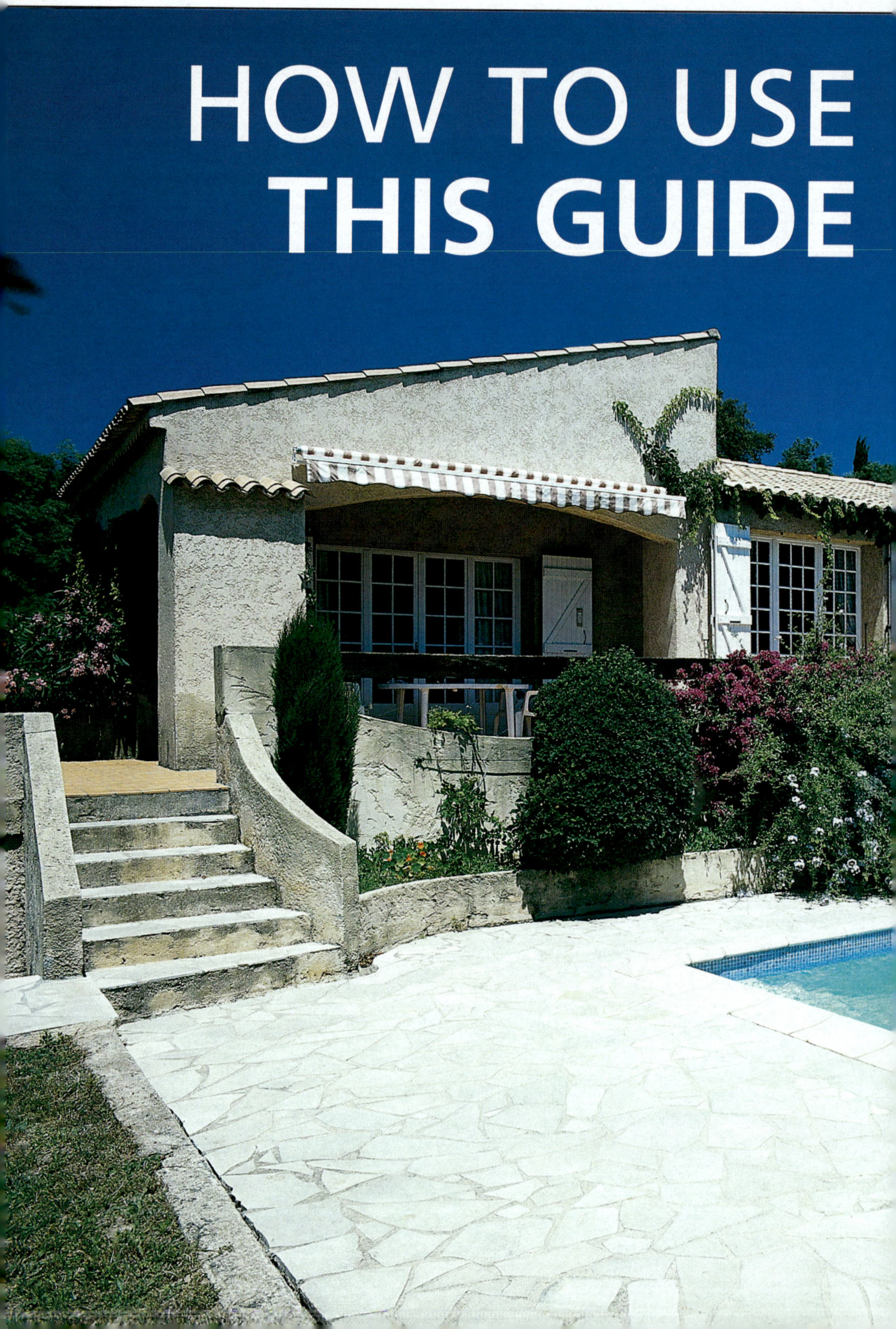

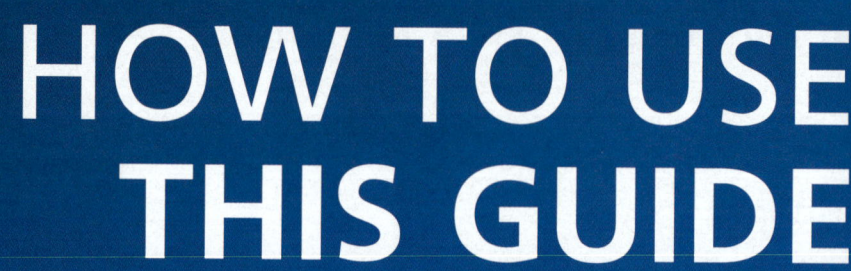

How to Use This Guide

The Price Guide has been compiled to give you as much detail as possible to help make searching for your dream home in your ideal area – and within your budget – as easy as possible. Over the next 250 pages you will find example properties from all of France's official regions. These have been grouped into 15 sections and appear in this guide as they do on a map of France, from north to south, west to east.

The properties have all been on the market in the past six to 12 months. With prices given in euros and pounds sterling, they have been selected to suit all budgets and have a detailed description showing you what to expect from a property at that price in the same region.

In some cases, the price given is the actual price the property was sold for (these are marked 'S'); in others, it was the guide price (these are marked 'GP'). To contact an agent whose properties appear in this section, turn to page 358 and check against the corresponding agent code.

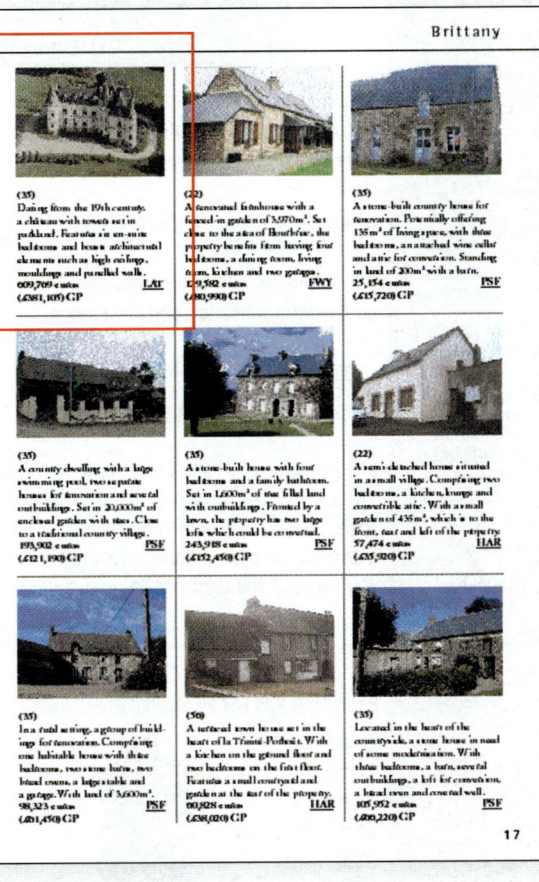

DEPARTEMENT CODE
Each entry has the number of the *département* (the administrative area) in which the property is situated. The map on pages 44 and 45 shows the location of each of France's *départements*.

PRICE
The price, given in both euros and sterling, shows either the guide price (GP) at which the property was marketed or the price at which it was sold (S).

PARTICULARS
A description of the example property including information such as the number of bedrooms, size of land and state of repair.

(35)
Dating from the 19th century, a château with towers set in parkland. Features six en-suite bedrooms and original architectural details such as high ceilings, mouldings and panelled walls.
609,769 euros   LAT
(£381,105) GP

AGENT CODE
With each listing there is a three-letter code that indicates the agent who marketed the property. This code can be cross-referenced against the list of agents that appears in the Index of Agents, starting on page 358.

FrenchWays ©

Search
- 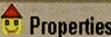 **Properties**
- 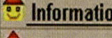 **Information**
- 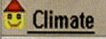 **Climate**

SearchClub
- Advanced Previews
- Newsletters
- Appointments
- Complete Itineraries
- **Join Us**

Services
- French Mortgages
- Currency Exchange
- French Language
- Accommodation
- Removals
- Ferries
- Flights
- **Services**

Purchasing
- Starting Out
- The French System
- The Notaire
- The Contracts
- **Purchasing**

Restoring
Restoration projects by D-I-Y or using Artisans

Restoration

Converting
A host of useful conversions to make the differences easier.
Conversions

Mortgages

---

www.frenchways.com

FrenchWays ©

The **French Property Exhibition** on the Internet.

Welcome to **www.frenchways.com**.

This is the most comprehensive website on the Internet for property in France.

Click here now to visit our on-line Exhibition Centre *New*

At any given time, you'll find more than **750 up to date** properties listed in our search engine and with **thousands more** on our agents books, we're sure you can find the right one for you.

FrenchWays for Property in

Brittany
Normandy
Mayenne
Loire-Atlantique
Loire
Charente
Charente-Maritime

Limousin - Gironde - Dordogne
Pyrenees-Atlantiques - Aude - Herault
Pyrenees-Orientales - Lot-et-Garonne
Tarn - Haute-Garonne - Provence

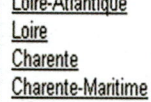

FrenchWays for Property throughout France

Looking for a **gite to rent**, *New*
simply click **Gite Rentals**

For French property and much, much more visit

www.frenchways.com

e-mail:- property@frenchways.com

Bienvenue

Send someone a French postcard from our "virtual" post office.
La Poste

Give yourself a daily boost with one of our screensavers.
ScreenSavers

Have you tried the French Life Forums yet?
Join in, share your experiences and have some fun at
Le Bar

Got some questions?
Don't bother with Jeeves.
Ask René at Le Bar

Join our **SearchClub**.

- If you know what you want!
  - we'll match your requirements.
- If you're just looking!
  - we'll keep you informed.
- ready to view with us!
  - we'll organise your trip.

Our success rate is high because we try harder.

Golf
Golf courses listed by Region.
GolfCentre

Wine
Everything you need to know about French wine.
WineCentre

Recipes
A different French recipe for each day of the week.
Meat - Fish - Vegetarian.
RecipeCentre

Gardening
Your gardening encyclopaedia for flowers, fruit and vegetables.
inc monthly jobs list.
GardenCentre

Learn French the easy way with an offer you can't refuse

Contact
Contact us

BRITTANY

Price Guide

(56)
A semi-detached house located in Josselin. With superb views to the rear of the property over a well-known canal and a famous château. Comprises a kitchen, four bedrooms and side courtyard.
320,122 euros   **JOS**
(£200,075) GP

(56)
A detached stone *longère* with a kitchen, lounge, three bedrooms and several rooms in need of total renovation. Outbuildings include a storeroom and a bread oven. Set in over 1,310m² of rural land.
57,474 euros   **JOS**
(£35,920) GP

(56)
A detached *longère* surrounded by 1,240m² of land, set in peaceful countryside. The property features a lounge with fireplace, kitchen, three bedrooms, bathroom and garage at the rear of the house.
128,972 euros   **JOS**
(£80,610) GP

(22)
In a village setting, a traditional stone house in need of decoration. Comprises two bedrooms, a large living room and a kitchen with fireplace. Features a woodburning stove and a large rear courtyard.
50,308 euros   **FWY**
(£31,445) GP

(56)
This detached house is arranged over two floors. Comprising a fitted kitchen, four bedrooms, a convertible attic and a living room with granite fireplace. Set in a small garden with a pretty terrace.
142,723 euros   **PSF**
(£89,200) GP

(56)
A terraced house in need of some modernisation. With a barn for conversion and set in the centre of a pretty village. The main house comprises one large room, two bedrooms and a store room.
53,506 euros   **HAR**
(£33,440) GP

(56)
Close to Locminé, this renovated mill stands in grounds of 1,000m² with a lake and stream. Benefiting from a tranquil environment, the mill features three bedrooms, one bathroom and a corner-kitchen.
161,748 euros   **PSF**
(£101,095) GP

(56)
A renovated country cottage built from stone. Situated between two villages. The ground floor features one large room with a fireplace and corner-kitchen. A wooden staircase leads to three bedrooms.
125,000 euros   **FWY**
(£78,125) GP

(22)
This renovated *longère* is set in a secluded and enclosed garden of 15,000m² with three stone-built stables. Featuring two spacious bedrooms, a mezzanine sitting room and fully-fitted kitchen.
238,583 euros   **PSF**
(£149,115) GP

KBM CONSULTANCY

KBM Consultancy (France) Ltd
Tawny Barn, Downs Mill, Frampton Mansell
Stroud, Gloucestershire, GL6 8JX

· BRITTANY · NORMANDY ·
· PAS DE CALAIS · LOT · TARN ·
· VENDEE · LOIRE · DORDOGNE ·
· AUDE · HERAULT ·
· POITOU-CHARENTES ·

And now introducing in 2003
IMMOTOURS
Guided mini tours of Normandy and Brittany with visits to local Immobiliers, tours of the area, including coach travel and accommodation.

We are a family run business specialising in helping families find their 'home from home'

FOR FURTHER DETAILS AND AN APPLICATION FORM PLEASE:

Tel: 08700 11 31 41
Fax: 08700 11 32 42
or register online at
Web: www.kbmconsultancy.com

COMPLETE SERVICE OFFERED

Alioth Properties
• HOUSES • HOMES • GITES • INVESTMENTS •

Looking for a property to buy in France?
Look no more.

Alioth Properties have what you are looking for.

A COMPLETE SERVICE

Visit our web site:
www.french-property.com/alioth/index.htm

Telephone (English speaking):
00 33 2 96 24 61 72

Telephone (French speaking):
00 33 2 98 93 30 36

Josselin Immobilier

19 Rue Oliver de Clisson, 56120 JOSSELIN, France
Tel: 00 33 2 97 75 64 78   Fax: 00 33 2 97 75 64 78
Email: josselin.immobilier@free.fr
www.frenchpropertysales.com

Ref: 284 - HELLEAN (56) Group of stone buildings surrounded by 41,880m² of land. Comprising of a restored cottage, two gites and a mill in ruins. Situated in a country setting close to the river.

PRICE: 320,122€ inc. agency fees

Ref: 296 - CAMPENEAC Detached stone longere in a small hamlet close to Campeneac. Comprises of a lounge with fireplace, kitchen, study/bedroom, WC, bathroom, 2 bedrooms & garage and an attic for conversion. All services connected. 1240m² of land.

PRICE: 128,972€ inc. agency fees

Price Guide

(56)
Two stone cottages for renovation. Set in the village of Lanouée at the end of a quiet country lane. With 3,956m² of land, which is to the front and rear of the property. Benefits from a secluded spot.
41,711 euros   **HAR**
(£26,070) GP

(22)
Set in the beautiful countryside of Côtes d'Armor, this little 18th-century cottage needs nothing more. Inside has been finished to a high standard and boasts some fabulous original features.
116,000 euros   **FDC**
(£72,500) GP

(22)
Close to town and the beach, a newly built house set in an elevated position with sea views. The property offers three bedrooms and 1,308m² of land and is located in a residential area.
224,862 euros   **FWY**
(£140,540) GP

(22)
In a village setting, a detached Breton-style house. Comprising a kitchen, one bedroom, newly fitted conservatory, dining area and garage. The house comes with a small field and vegetable plot.
49,700 euros   **LIN**
(£31,065) GP

(22)
This semi-detached stone-built house has two bedrooms and is set in a garden of 2,400m² with a small lake. Offers a dining room, corner-kitchen and a sitting room opening up on to a large veranda.
137,375 euros   **PSF**
(£85,860) GP

(22)
In the centre of a town, close to the beach, a character house with a walled garden. The property offers four rooms with two being arranged as bedrooms. Recently restored and boasting sea views.
209,160 euros   **FWY**
(£130,725) GP

(22)
Originally a restaurant, this large property benefits from having five bedrooms, two shower rooms, a kitchen and bar area. In need of some internal renovation, it is set a short distance from a lake.
83,847 euros   **LIN**
(£52,405) GP

(22)
A modern house built in 1988. Close to a small town, the property features an open kitchen, large dining room and five bedrooms. Outside is a lawned garden, terrace, utility room and single garage.
117,386 euros   **LIN**
(£73,365) GP

(22)
This *longère* was completely restored to a high standard in 2001. Set in enclosed parkland of 8,000m². With four bedrooms, a mezzanine, a separate building for renovation and two gîtes.
400,179 euros   **PSF**
(£250,110) GP

French Discoveries

Brittany Office

Telephone our office in Brittany for less than 10p/minute on 0871 717 4163
or e-mail: Brittany@french-discoveries.com

The *French Discoveries* offices are run by English couples who have been helping people to purchase property in France for more than 10 years.

Supported by our dedicated French and English teams, we offer a friendly, professional service, including translation and legal advice.

We invite you to visit our website on:

www.french-discoveries.com

which is up-dated weekly, or to chat *in English* with the people who have actually visited the properties.

Associate offices in Normandy and Charente.
Offices opening soon in Burgundy, Languedoc and Loire.

10521

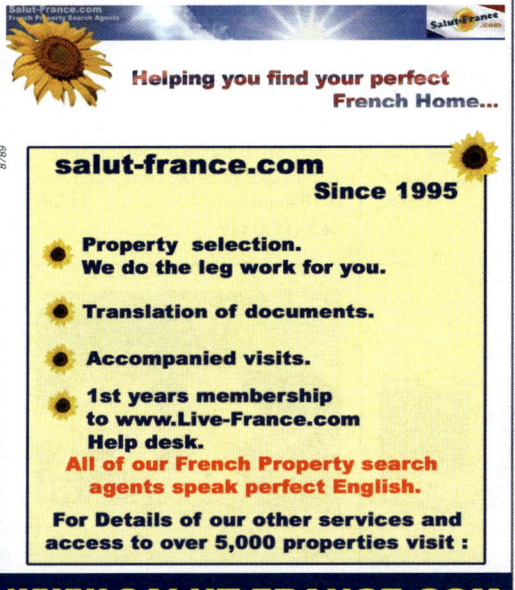

Helping you find your perfect French Home...

salut-france.com
Since 1995

- **Property selection.**
  We do the leg work for you.
- **Translation of documents.**
- **Accompanied visits.**
- **1st years membership to www.Live-France.com Help desk.**

All of our French Property search agents speak perfect English.

For Details of our other services and access to over 5,000 properties visit:

WWW.SALUT-FRANCE.COM
TEL UK: 0871 717 4295
TEL: 0033 2.99.90.25.75
FAX: 0033 2.99.90.25.83
EMAIL: sales@salut-france.com

Cheapest Property in France!

CHEAP-IN-FRANCE.COM

Properties from £5,000 to Maximum of £35,000

WWW.CHEAP-IN-FRANCE.COM
TEL UK: 0871 717 4295
TEL FRANCE: 0033 2.99.90.25.75
FAX: 0033 2.99.90.25.83
EMAIL: info@cheap-in-france.com

Price Guide

(22)
Close to the beach and boasting sea views, this detached residence has three bedrooms, a living room, kitchen and back-kitchen. Featuring a large stone fireplace and set in a garden of 400m².
257,639 euros   **PSF**
(£161,025) GP

(22)
A large house in need of some interior work. Featuring a garage and several bedrooms, the property is reached via a long drive. Benefits from an enclosed garden with outbuildings and pool.
548,328 euros   **HEX**
(£342,705) GP

(22)
Entirely renovated, a traditional house standing in land of 1,800m² planted with trees. Featuring five bedrooms, a living room, kitchen and open fireplace. Approached via a long private driveway.
192,086 euros   **PSF**
(£120,055) GP

(22)
A short walk from the coast, this peacefully situated house is set in 950m² of land. On the ground floor is a kitchen, living room and two bedrooms. Upstairs are two further spacious bedrooms.
145,589 euros   **PSF**
(£90,995) GP

(56)
A semi-detached house with one large room with two fireplaces. On the outskirts of a rural village in rugged countryside. Boasting uninterrupted views, the property comes with a small field.
25,764 euros   **HAR**
(£16,105) GP

(56)
Situated close to the village of Le Cambout. In need of complete renovation, the property offers a kitchen, two other rooms and a store room. There is a small garden of 240m² at the front and rear.
37,046 euros   **HAR**
(£23,155) GP

(22)
A stone-built house to finish. Located close to the sea and with land of 2,500m². Comprises a kitchen, three bedrooms, loft and outbuildings in need of some work. A short walk from a village.
144,604 euros   **PSF**
(£90,380) GP

(22)
This small house is situated a short distance from the sea and near Cap Fréhel. Standing in 500m² of land, the building features two panelled bedrooms and a large veranda. Enjoys a quiet setting.
74,000 euros   **PSF**
(£46,250) GP

(22)
On the coast, a stone house set in an enclosed tree-filled garden of 600m². On the ground floor is a living room, kitchen, bathroom and one bedroom. Upstairs are a further three bedrooms and a loft.
135,600 euros   **PSF**
(£84,750) GP

Brittany

(56)
Between Vannes and Nantes, this large manor house sits in 2,500m² of landscaped grounds featuring a pool, stables and woodland. There are 11 bedrooms, a billiard room, sitting room and fitted kitchen.
953,416 euros   **DEE**
(£595,885) GP

(22)
This modern Breton house has been completely renovated and is situated a short distance from the coast. Featuring a veranda, garage and several outbuildings. Set in a tree-filled garden of 1,800m².
145,427 euros   **PSF**
(£90,890) GP

(22)
A stone house with a rustic slate roof. Surrounded by parkland of 6,000m². Features marble floors, an open fireplace and large living room. Benefits from a tranquil setting and a secluded location.
320,143 euros   **PSF**
(£200,090) GP

(22)
Minutes from the coast, a restored house with four main rooms. Set in land of 620m², the house offers two spacious bedrooms and boasts a living area of 80m². With open views, stretching as far as the sea.
109,762 euros   **FWY**
(£68,600) GP

(22)
Enclosed in land of 2,800m², this *longère* is in need of complete restoration. With four bedrooms, the property features a large living room with a granite fireplace, a mezzanine and fitted kitchen.
112,812 euros   **PSF**
(£70,510) GP

(56)
A mid-terrace stone cottage in need of renovation. Set in a small hamlet close to the village of Lanouée. The building comprises one room and a lean-to on the ground floor. Features a garden.
12,958 euros   **HAR**
(£8,100) GP

(22)
A stone house with an enclosed garden planted with trees. On the ground floor is a living room, kitchenette and bathroom. On the first floor are two bedrooms to renovate and two studio flats.
51,832 euros   **PSF**
(£32,395) GP

(22)
In the countryside, but close to a village and the coast. This large stone-built house sits in land of 1,600m² in an elevated position. With habitable space of 125m² and featuring four main rooms.
177,603 euros   **FWY**
(£111,000) GP

(22)
A renovated *longère* set in land of 2,600m². The property stands alone and offers three large bedrooms. Situated in a secluded spot on the edge of a small village with shops and all facilities.
192,085 euros   **PSF**
(£120,055) GP

Price Guide

(22)
A detached house situated in a quiet village. Set in a garden with trees and shrubs. Benefiting from the use of a garage, the property features five bedrooms and boasts unrestricted views of the country.
105,100 euros   **VEF**
(£65,690) GP

(56)
Set on the outskirts of a village, this 150-year-old stone cottage was formerly a farmer's home. Completely restored, it has two bedrooms and a huge barn and garden at the back of the property.
68,000 euros   **LAR**
(£42,500) GP

(29)
An ensemble of thatched cottages close to the sea. Standing in land of 6,500m^2, the property features four bedrooms, a dining room and kitchen. Electrically heated, there is also a mezzanine and garage.
272,884 euros   **PSF**
(£170,555) GP

(29)
A stone-built house standing in 40,000m^2 of land with a small creek and near a town. Boasting parquet floors, large rooms with high ceilings and seven bedrooms. The property enjoys coastal views.
399,569 euros   **PSF**
(£249,730) GP

(22)
This rural 15th-century Cistercian convent has three bedrooms, a large living room, exposed stone walls, wood beams and a staircase made out of quarter tree trunks. Set in a hamlet with open views.
168,800 euros   **VEF**
(£105,500) GP

(29)
A thatched house with 4,000m^2 of wooded parkland and a covered swimming pool. Surrounded by agricultural land, the house offers five bedrooms, two bathrooms, a billiards room, cellar and office.
399,569 euros   **PSF**
(£249,730) GP

(29)
Bordering the River Aven and not far from the coast, a stone-built house with one bedroom, dining room, corner-kitchen and cellar. Set in a small garden of 200m^2, a short distance from a village.
106,028 euros   **PSF**
(£66,270) GP

(29)
A renovated stone *longère* in a quiet country location. Standing in land of 5,300m^2 with its own stream. The building features two large bedrooms on the first floor. Outside is a small stone building.
114,032 euros   **PSF**
(£71,270) GP

(22)
With eight bedrooms and set in over 40,000m^2 of open land. In an isolated location, this property enjoys a tranquil environment and is ready to move in to. Approached by a long driveway.
602,134 euros   **VEF**
(£376,335) GP

Brittany

(29)
An ensemble of stone buildings with one habitable house, plus a *longère* for renovation. In a quiet country hamlet setting with open views. Offers two bedrooms, a large kitchen and living room.
106,028 euros   **PSF**
(£66,270) **GP**

(29)
A six-bedroom property set in wooded parkland of 1,300m² above Pont-Aven. Entered via a huge reception room, the house has a billiard room, stained-glass windows and five large bedrooms.
403,990 euros   **PSF**
(£252,495) **GP**

(56)
A detached stone building for renovation. Comprising one large room with an open fireplace. There is a garden of 400m² to the rear and left-hand side of the property. Boasts open views.
6,098 euros   **HAR**
(£3,810) **GP**

(29)
A thatched cottage moments from the coast. Features exposed beams, a stone fireplace and mezzanine. Currently there is one bedroom, but plenty of room in the loft to create more. Set in a 300m² garden.
152,450 euros   **PSF**
(£95,280) **GP**

(22)
A stone-built residence situated on the outskirts of Lanvollon. In a tranquil location, the property has been recently renovated. Offering four bedrooms and two bathrooms. Set in 2,200m² of open land.
193,610 euros   **FWY**
(£121,005) **GP**

(29)
A renovated stone *longère* in a village. Comprising a living room with fireplace, kitchen, two bedrooms and a bathroom. The property comes with a single garage and a small, pretty garden.
96,970 euros   **PSF**
(£60,605) **GP**

(56)
This semi-detached house is set in the heart of a small town. Split over three storeys, the house features five bedrooms, kitchen, bathroom and a conservatory. To the rear of the house is a garden.
112,050 euros   **PSF**
(£70,030) **GP**

(22)
Set in a quiet hamlet with all amenities, a rustic property in need of some work. Features a patio and two bedrooms. Boasts open views over the surrounding countryside. Ready to move in to.
53,650 euros   **VEF**
(£33,530) **GP**

(35)
In a town near Saint-Malo, a large stone house arranged over three storeys. Close to the coast. Features a spacious kitchen with a fireplace, living room and five bedrooms. Set in a pretty garden.
107,000 euros   **PSF**
(£66,875) **GP**

Price Guide

(29)
A fully-renovated farmhouse with four bedrooms, two bathrooms, and several scattered outbuildings including a barn. Set in an enclosed private garden on an island off the coast of Brittany.
324,726 euros   **PSF**
(£202,955) GP

(22)
Set in a village close to Dinan and near the River Rance, an old farmhouse in need of total renovation. Features a bread oven and 1,060m² of tree-filled garden. Rooms have yet to be created.
41,400 euros   **PSF**
(£25,875) GP

(35)
Dating from the 19th century, a hunting inn between Redon and Châteaubriant. Comprises a main residence, two smaller houses and large outbuildings. Set in a vast garden bordered by a river.
289,653 euros   **DEE**
(£181,035) GP

(56)
A two-bedroom cottage set in 2,000m² of land. Partially renovated, the property features an open fireplace, kitchen, lounge and bathroom. In a village location, a short distance from the coast.
43,500 euros   **JBF**
(£27,190) GP

(22)
Two detached stone-built houses situated in 20,000m² of grounds. In a quiet hamlet setting, a short drive from the coast. Both houses require renovation and new septic tanks. Fronted by a courtyard.
73,224 euros   **LAT**
(£45,765) GP

(35)
A thatched cottage set in a calm location overlooking a river. Totally renovated, the building features a granite fireplace and beamed ceilings. Offers five large bedrooms and three bathrooms.
523,000 euros   **PSF**
(£326,875) GP

(22)
A terraced cottage situated at the end of a quiet country lane. Set on the outskirts of a small hamlet, it boasts two large bedrooms and sits in a secluded garden. Close to beaches and a picturesque village.
104,000 euros   **PRV**
(£65,000) GP

(22)
Dating from the 18th century, this stone-built house is currently arranged as five studio flats. On the ground floor there are old beamed ceilings and an open fireplace. Features a small garden.
114,337 euros   **LAT**
(£71,460) GP

(35)
This semi-detached thatched cottage benefits from tranquil surroundings and looks out across the River Rance. Benefits from four bedrooms, a wine cellar and kitchen. Set in a large garden.
251,000 euros   **PSF**
(£156,875) GP

Brittany

(22)
Dating from the 19th century, a house with a garage. Situated in a village, close to Dinan. Offering four bedrooms, the house requires some finishing-off work. Comes with a garage and basement.
131,400 euros   LAT
(£82,125) GP

(22)
A detached cottage in need of renovation. Set in 1,700m² of land. Accommodation comprises a kitchen, shower room and bedroom. Situated in the country, close to the village of Plumieux.
33,539 euros   HAR
(£20,960) GP

(35)
This stone house is located on the edge of a village, 10 minutes from the coast. Features three bedrooms on the first floor and two more on the second floor. Comes with various outbuildings.
225,000 euros   LAT
(£140,625) GP

(22)
A one-bedroom apartment with a balcony. Situated close to Saint-Malo and the beach. The property is detached and set in a residential area. Boasting unrestricted views and a peaceful environment.
98,000 euros   PSF
(£61,250) GP

(35)
Dating from 1890, a listed house with four bedrooms. Located in a historic area close to the Rance Estuary. Boasts its own mooring buoy, accessed by a rowing boat. Features four spacious bedrooms.
719,000 euros   PSF
(£449,375) GP

(35)
A totally renovated stone-built residence. Enclosed by a walled garden, this light-filled, spacious house features a south-facing terrace, three bedrooms and a mezzanine. Boasts open views.
227,000 euros   PSF
(£141,875) GP

(35)
Situated close to a village with all amenities, an ancient *longère* for complete renovation. Boasts a possible 250m² of living space and features a stone fireplace. In a rural setting with 8,000m² of land.
17,500 euros   PSF
(£10,940) GP

(56)
Set in hilly countryside, with a lake and stunning views, this large renovated *longère* is entered via a hall with marble flooring. Offers four bedrooms, a reception room and south-facing terrace.
434,000 euros   PSF
(£271,250) GP

(56)
A semi-detached house built in the 1960s. Featuring a kitchen, living room, three bedrooms and a terrace. Set in a garden, which surrounds the house. Situated in a quiet village, just west of Pontivy.
72,413 euros   FPP
(£45,260) GP

Price Guide

(22)
Situated between Loudéac and Josselin, a cottage in need of total renovation. Comprises a kitchen, two large bedrooms and a bathroom. Set beside the road in a quiet village with all amenities.
22,868 euros   **LIN**
(£14,290) GP

(35)
A renovated stone-built house in a rural location at the end of a country lane. Set in 4,000m² of land and boasting five bedrooms, the property enjoys a cellar, garage and south-facing courtyard.
195,150 euros   **PSF**
(£121,970) GP

(56)
A renovated four-bedroom house, set in a picturesque village. The ground floor features a kitchen, living room and utility room. On the first floor is a master bedroom and two en-suite bedrooms.
193,458 euros   **PSF**
(£120,910) GP

(56)
A granite *longère* for renovation. Set in 2,500m² of land on the outskirts of a quiet village. This building stands in an isolated area in rugged countryside. There are no services connected at present.
74,014 euros   **PSF**
(£46,260) GP

(56)
This renovated *longère*, within a short walk of a nearby village, is set in over 4,000m² of grounds. Boasting unrestricted views, the property features four bedrooms, a double garage and chicken house.
190,287 euros   **PSF**
(£118,930) GP

(56)
A country cottage set close to a golf course and river. With three bedrooms, the property boasts a garden of 1,500m² with country views. Offers a large living room, shower room and corner-kitchen.
59,608 euros   **PSF**
(£37,255) GP

(22)
Dating from the 15th century, this manor house has three bedrooms and is surrounded by countryside. Located in wooded grounds of 5,000m². Outside is a three-storey outbuilding in need of renovation.
221,932 euros   **LIN**
(£138,710) GP

(56)
This stone *longère* comprises four bedrooms, a living room, one bathroom, an open-plan kitchen and mezzanine. Situated in a pretty hamlet close to the coast, with a large garden and a barn.
209,313 euros   **PSF**
(£130,820) GP

(22)
A stone-built house in a village setting. Comprising a kitchen with fireplace, a veranda and four bedrooms. The property comes with a second attached house in need of some finishing-off work.
105,647 euros   **LIN**
(£66,030) GP

Brittany

(35)
Close to Dinan, this three-storey house with two stone outbuildings sits in a 400m² garden. Located in a quiet hamlet, the house benefits from an entrance hall, kitchen, two bedrooms and a large living room.
190,800 euros   **LAT**
(£119,250) GP

(22)
A traditional farm building for conversion. The ground floor offers a large room with beamed ceilings and a fireplace. On the first floor is a large attic. Located in pleasant rural surroundings.
35,489 euros   **LIN**
(£22,180) GP

(56)
A large granite property consisting of three houses and several barns in 6,850m² of land. The first house needs complete renovation, the second offers three bedrooms and the third has a spacious attic.
117,470 euros   **PSF**
(£73,420) GP

(56)
A stone-built *longère* situated close to the village of Melrand. Comprising a living room with fireplace, kitchen, cellar and three bedrooms. Set in 3,000m² of rural landscape with a double garage.
149,400 euros   **PSF**
(£93,375) GP

(56)
With views over a river, this three-bedroom stone house is arranged over two floors. Offering an open-plan kitchen and dining room with a stone fireplace. The property features a large scullery.
78,816 euros   **PSF**
(£49,260) GP

(22)
This large farm building is a short drive from a busy market town. In need of total renovation, accommodation has yet to be created or services connected. Set in a generous 12,000m² of land.
42,686 euros   **LIN**
(£26,680) GP

(56)
A detached *longère* in need of renovation. Partly habitable, the buildings comprise three large bedrooms, a kitchen-diner and a bathroom. Set in 3,000m² of land with a garage and outbuilding.
106,028 euros   **PSF**
(£66,270) GP

(22)
In a rural village close to Saint-Brieuc, this ensemble of three buildings and a ruined house is set in over 1,000m² of rural land. Boasts open views and a private location. In need of renovation.
30,490 euros   **LIN**
(£19,055) GP

(56)
In the town of Plouay, this *longère* features an open-plan kitchen, two bedrooms and a mezzanine. Set in a secluded area, with a well-maintained garden laid to lawn, and a large double garage.
130,039 euros   **PSF**
(£81,275) GP

Price Guide

(56)
Set in 16,000m² of grounds at the edge of a quiet village. The house has a kitchen with a dining area, living room, five bedrooms and two bathrooms. With numerous outbuildings, stables and a shed.
225,000 euros   **LAT**
(£140,625) GP

(56)
A stone cottage comprising a living room with a fireplace and an open-plan kitchen. On the first floor are two bedrooms, a shower room and WC. Standing in land of 9,000m² with country views.
114,032 euros   **PSF**
(£71,270) GP

(22)
Dating from the 18th century, this manor house comprises an old chapel, bread oven and annexe building. Set in enclosed land, the house features six bedrooms and original parquet and stone floors.
329,290 euros   **LAT**
(£205,805) GP

(56)
A granite *longère* divided into two houses. In a country location, the first home comprises a kitchen, living room and three bedrooms. The second home is in need of renovation. Set in a large garden.
161,748 euros   **PSF**
(£101,095) GP

(56)
In need of complete renovation. A granite *longère* set in an ancient meadow. Accommodation has yet to be created and no services are connected. Benefits from open views and a tranquil environment.
32,014 euros   **PSF**
(£20,010) GP

(35)
This three-bedroom stone house and separate studio apartment are set around a courtyard with an ornamental pool and a well-stocked lake. The house enjoys a conservatory and open views.
412,684 euros   **LAT**
(£257,930) GP

(35)
A stone-built house in need of restoration with two bedrooms and a convertible loft. The house is situated close to the ferry port of Saint-Malo and is set in land of 750m² with unrestricted views.
30,185 euros   **PSF**
(£18,865) GP

(35)
Nestling in the Bay of Mont-Saint-Michel, this large house has nine en-suite bedrooms and two outbuildings that have been converted into studio apartments. Set in 2,000m² of mature garden.
480,214 euros   **PSF**
(£300,135) GP

(35)
An ensemble of two stone houses standing in a garden with a small lake and toolshed. Set in a country location, the property has a total of nine bedrooms and has been recently renovated.
457,347 euros   **PSF**
(£285,840) GP

Brittany

(35)
A house of modern construction, a short drive from the old town of Dinan. Set in rural landscape of 1,700m², the house has three bedrooms, two bathrooms and boasts spacious, light-filled rooms.
205,044 euros PSF
(**£128,155**) GP

(35)
A traditional bakery in need of total restoration. Set in 645m² of land in rugged countryside. At the moment the property offers one bedroom. Services have yet to be connected. Close to a quiet village.
8,385 euros PSF
(**£5,215**) GP

(22)
A renovated house with a double garage. Set in 10,000m² of land with a small lake. Features one en-suite bedroom, two further bedrooms, an open-plan living/dining room and kitchen.
429,750 euros LAT
(**£268,595**) GP

(35)
A tidy house set in a small garden. Comprising three bedrooms, a kitchen, living room, bathroom and utility room. In a quiet village location with all amenities, and close to Mont-Saint-Michel.
58,723 euros PSF
(**£36,700**) GP

(35)
A group of two buildings for renovation. At present the property has one functional bedroom, but has the potential for up to 12 main rooms. Standing in land of 520m² with assorted outbuildings.
41,920 euros PSF
(**£26,200**) GP

(35)
A stone-built property in need of complete renovation. Currently featuring five bedrooms and three bathrooms. This semi-detached house is situated in a small village and faces a quiet country road.
126,533 euros PSF
(**£79,085**) GP

(35)
A stone-built house in a village setting. Standing in 600m² of garden, the property offers three bedrooms and is in need of partial renovation. Comes with a further small building for restoration.
98,330 euros PSF
(**£61,455**) GP

(35)
This large house is set in wooded land of over 4,000m². Featuring a rustic fitted kitchen, nine en-suite bedrooms and four bathrooms. It is approached via a long driveway and boasts a swimming pool.
1,131,097 euros PSF
(**£706,935**) GP

(35)
A stone-built house in need of some work. In a rural setting close to Dol-de-Bretagne. On the ground floor a corridor leads to two rooms. Upstairs are five bedrooms arranged over two floors.
25,154 euros PSF
(**£15,720**) GP

Price Guide

(56)
Set in almost 800m² of wooded grounds, this large residence has six bedrooms over three storeys. Offering a study, living room and adjoining garage. Close to Vannes, the house enjoys stunning views.
1,152,515 euros   **LAT**
(£720,320) GP

(35)
A stone house of character for renovation. Located in a quiet country hamlet close to Dol-de-Bretagne. Approached via a long drive, the property features five bedrooms and is set in a garden.
161,596 euros   **PSF**
(£101,000) GP

(35)
A stone-built house standing in 10,000m² of land, a short distance from Dol-de-Bretagne. Offering three bedrooms and outbuildings, the property boasts open views and benefits from a quiet location.
320,095 euros   **PSF**
(£200,060) GP

(35)
Situated with views over the Bay of Mont-Saint-Michel, this stone house offers three bedrooms and a convertible loft. Set in an enclosed garden of 4,000m² with various trees and a working well.
98,323 euros   **PSF**
(£61,450) GP

(35)
A large stone house with eight en-suite bedrooms, situated close to the port of Saint-Malo. Set in a pretty garden, the property is fully furnished and is in need of some interior modernisation.
130,344 euros   **PSF**
(£81,465) GP

(35)
Enjoying sea views, this large house boasts a covered pool, boat house and sauna. South-facing, with a sunny patio and well-maintained garden. The property features seven bedrooms.
600,000 euros   **LAT**
(£375,000) GP

(35)
Built in 1978, a rural residence set in a manicured garden of nearly 5,000m² with trees and shrubs. Comprising five bedrooms, two bathrooms and a fitted kitchen. Enjoys a secluded, quiet location.
161,585 euros   **PSF**
(£100,990) GP

(56)
A traditional mill house and guest cottage dating from the 18th century. Entered via a tower, the property features a study, library and lounge. Standing in 5,200m² of woodland, bordered by a river.
296,361 euros   **LAT**
(£185,225) GP

(35)
A detached five-bedroom house in a peaceful rural setting. Standing in a small, well-kept garden, the house enjoys a secluded location and features a veranda. Approached via a private drive.
145,580 euros   **PSF**
(£90,990) GP

Brittany

(35)
Dating from the 19th century, a château with towers set in parkland. Features six en-suite bedrooms and boasts architectural elements such as high ceilings, mouldings and panelled walls.
609,769 euros **LAT**
(£381,105) GP

(22)
A renovated farmhouse with a fenced-in garden of 3,970m². Set close to the area of Bourbriac, the property benefits from having four bedrooms, a dining room, living room, kitchen and two garages.
129,582 euros **FWY**
(£80,990) GP

(35)
A stone-built country house for renovation. Potentially offering 135m² of living space, with three bedrooms, an attached wine cellar and attic for conversion. Standing in land of 200m² with a barn.
25,154 euros **PSF**
(£15,720) GP

(35)
A country dwelling with a large swimming pool, two separate houses for renovation and several outbuildings. Set in 20,000m² of enclosed garden with trees. Close to a traditional country village.
193,902 euros **PSF**
(£121,190) GP

(35)
A stone-built house with four bedrooms and a family bathroom. Set in 1,600m² of tree-filled land with outbuildings. Fronted by a lawn, the property has two large lofts which could be converted.
243,918 euros **PSF**
(£152,450) GP

(22)
A semi-detached house situated in a small village. Comprising two bedrooms, a kitchen, lounge and convertible attic. With a small garden of 435m², which is to the front, rear and left of the property.
57,474 euros **HAR**
(£35,920) GP

(35)
In a rural setting, a group of buildings for renovation. Comprising one habitable house with three bedrooms, two stone barns, two bread ovens, a large stable and a garage. With land of 3,600m².
98,323 euros **PSF**
(£61,450) GP

(56)
A terraced town house set in the heart of La Trinité-Porhoët. With a kitchen on the ground floor and two bedrooms on the first floor. Features a small courtyard and garden at the rear of the property.
60,828 euros **HAR**
(£38,020) GP

(35)
Located in the heart of the countryside, a stone house in need of some modernisation. With three bedrooms, a barn, several outbuildings, a loft for conversion, a bread oven and covered well.
105,952 euros **PSF**
(£66,220) GP

Price Guide

(35)
In a hamlet not far from the sea, a stone house with outbuildings. Set on 2,000m² of land with two bedrooms, one bathroom, living room and dining room. Features a south-facing veranda with views.
137,966 euros   **PSF**
(£86,230) GP

(56)
Built in 1850 and situated in the pretty village of Bohal, a mill house set in 1,000m² of land with ornamental and fruit trees. In a peaceful spot, bordered by a river. The property benefits from a large annexe.
238,000 euros   **LAT**
(£148,750) GP

(35)
Set in a hamlet, a partly renovated *longère*, currently with a loft for conversion and two bedrooms. With 50,000m² of tree-filled land, the property is situated a short distance from Dol-de-Bretagne.
98,329 euros   **PSF**
(£61,455) GP

(35)
This little stone-built house is in need of total renovation. Close to shops and a school, the house is semi-detached and facing a road. Accommodation has yet to be created. Set in a tranquil area.
9,909 euros   **PSF**
(£6,195) GP

(35)
A two-storey stone-built house with a barn. Both are in need of total renovation and accommodation has not yet been created. Semi-detached, the property offers 780m² of land with views.
25,164 euros   **PSF**
(£15,730) GP

(35)
This two-bedroom stone house comes with a loft for conversion, two bedrooms and one bathroom. Set in a private garden of 700m². With plenty of room for parking, a patio area and stunning views.
114,336 euros   **PSF**
(£71,460) GP

(35)
In the countryside near Laval, a building for complete renovation. 2,400m² of land, within easy reach of a village. Boasting a living area of 150m² and one large bedroom. Enjoys a quiet, rural location.
42,000 euros   **PSF**
(£26,250) GP

(35)
A stone house in a picturesque hamlet setting. Comprises four bedrooms with open fireplaces and a loft for conversion. Set in 1,400m² of enclosed land, with outbuildings in need of renovation.
98,329 euros   **PSF**
(£61,455) GP

(56)
Near the small town of Guer, a detached house with five bedrooms arranged over two floors. Adjoining the property is a double garage and store room. Set in a garden of 27,700m² with a cellar.
209,876 euros   **HIF**
(£131,170) GP

Brittany

(56)
A terraced town house with a courtyard and garden of 525m² with outbuildings. Features two attic bedrooms, two bedrooms on the first floor, a large living room, corner-kitchen and lounge.
107,324 euros   **HIF**
(£67,080) GP

(35)
Nestling in the Bay of Mont-Saint-Michel, a stone-built *longère* to renovate. Benefiting from five bedrooms and habitable space of 215m² with open fireplaces, plus a garden with one outbuilding.
67,139 euros   **PSF**
(£41,960) GP

(35)
Entirely renovated, a stone-built house just south of a market town. Features three bedrooms and an attic for conversion. Stands in a well-maintained garden boasting a terrace with views.
146,000 euros   **SIN**
(£91,250) GP

(35)
An ensemble of two houses for renovation, with the possibility of creating 16 main rooms. Set in 1,500m² of rural land in a calm spot with south-facing exposure and open views. Village location.
66,468 euros   **PSF**
(£41,545) GP

(35)
Close to Saint-Malo, this stone-built house is in need of total renovation. Set in a tranquil position with southern exposure. Accommodation has yet to been created or services connected.
50,370 euros   **PSF**
(£31,480) GP

(35)
Located in the heart of an old village, a château dating from the 18th century. Boasts five spacious bedrooms and many original features. Standing in 10,000m² of land with one large outbuilding.
295,500 euros   **PSF**
(£184,690) GP

(35)
Within easy reach of Laval, this renovated country house features four bedrooms, one bathroom and outbuildings. Standing in land of 5,000m² with trees, a pond and a greenhouse. Boasts open views.
106,028 euros   **PSF**
(£66,270) GP

(35)
Situated in a hamlet close to the town of Dol-de-Bretagne, a stone house for renovation. Comprises three bedrooms, convertible loft and outbuildings. All services are connected. Set in 1,800m² of land.
41,923 euros   **PSF**
(£26,200) GP

(35)
In the countryside, a farmhouse in an isolated area. With five main rooms and several outbuildings, including a stable. The building is in need of major interior work and stands in 1,000m² of land.
295,000 euros   **PSF**
(£184,375) GP

Price Guide

(22)
An apartment in a large house with a sea view. Featuring two large bedrooms, living room, bathroom and a fitted kitchen. Set close to the coast and within easy reach of a small village.
163,722 euros   **HEX**
(£102,325) GP

(35)
An ancient stable, fully renovated and offering 210m² of habitable space. Set in 10,000m² of land with numerous outbuildings and a converted house. The main house features two spacious bedrooms.
540,000 euros   **PSF**
(£337,500) GP

(56)
Situated in the small hamlet of Radenac, this stone *longère* is just one-room deep. Comprises four bedrooms, several outbuildings, garage and an open-plan kitchen with an old woodburning stove.
193,458 euros   **LAR**
(£120,910) GP

(22)
A detached cottage within a short walk of a medieval market town and close to the ferry port of Saint-Malo. Comprises a large bedroom, living room with a corner-kitchen and open fireplace.
69,641 euros   **HEX**
(£43,525) GP

(35)
A stone-built house set in a small village on the Normandy border. Features two spacious bedrooms, a kitchen, dining room and sitting room. Close to the town of Combourg. Comes with a cellar.
104,374 euros   **HEX**
(£65,235) GP

(22)
Dating from the 17th century, a renovated presbytery. Situated in the countryside on the outskirts of a medieval village. Comprises four en-suite bedrooms, four bathrooms and an artist's studio.
428,609 euros   **HEX**
(£267,880) GP

(22)
A large manor house dating from the 17th century comprising three separate houses with numerous bedrooms. Close to Dinan, the property benefits from a heated swimming pool and pretty gardens.
548,328 euros   **HEX**
(£342,705) GP

(22)
In a village setting, a stone house with a large living room, kitchen and four bedrooms. Features an open fireplace and a garden of 2,000m². Semi-detached, the house has been partially renovated.
66,315 euros   **PSF**
(£41,445) GP

(35)
A stone-built house in a village setting within easy reach of Dinan. Features three bedrooms, a kitchen, living room with log fire and two bathrooms. Offering a garden with a double garage.
119,650 euros   **HEX**
(£74,780) GP

Brittany

(56)
A five-bedroom detached house. Featuring a fully-fitted kitchen, large living room, hallway and a convertible attic. Below the house there is a basement and garage. Set in a lawned garden of 840m².
146,350 euros   **HIF**
(£91,470) GP

(22)
In a country setting, a small stone residence. Featuring two spacious attic bedrooms, one bedroom on the first floor, a living room and fitted kitchen. Standing in ground of over 1,000m² with open views.
89,945 euros   **PSF**
(£56,215) GP

(35)
A stone stable in need of total renovation. Set in 15,000m² of land, in an isolated position. The stable is surrounded by countryside and boasts unrestricted views. There are no services connected.
153,211 euros   **PSF**
(£95,755) GP

(35)
Currently being run as a licensed bar, this stone-built house is a short drive from Dinan. Set in a lively village, this semi-detached property offers four bedrooms, and one large family bathroom.
99,000 euros   **PSF**
(£61,875) GP

(56)
A renovated 17th-century thatched cottage offering a total of 420m² of living space, six bedrooms and extensive gardens of 5,800m². The property is 10 minutes from a golf course.
899,451 euros   **MER**
(£562,155) GP

(29)
For renovation, a *longère* built from stone. Set in a quiet country location and approached via a long, open drive. Accommodation has yet to be created or services connected. Close to a village.
32,014 euros   **PSF**
(£20,010) GP

(35)
Situated a short drive from the busy town of Laval, a group of buildings for renovation and a house ready for occupation. Standing in 26,000m² of quiet rural land featuring two lakes.
327,000 euros   **PSF**
(£204,375) GP

(35)
Between Rennes and Saint-Malo. A house with two bedrooms and a second house for renovation. Set in 36,000m² of land with stone-built barns and a pigsty. Within easy reach of the beach and a village.
87,406 euros   **HEX**
(£54,630) GP

(56)
On the Arradon headland, close to the town of Vannes, a house with a large landscaped garden. Built in the 20th century. Features a wooden staircase, five bedrooms and a cellar. In a village setting.
1,295,816 euros   **DEE**
(£809,885) S

No.1 FOR TRAVEL | FOOD | WINE | HOMES | PROPERTY

french
magazine

Published six times a year, *French magazine* has a fantastic selection of up to date properties to buy and rent, so whether you are planning your next holiday or looking to buy, we have 1000s to choose from.

No.1 FOR BUYING AND LETTING OVER 100 PAGES OF PROPERTY INSIDE

Available in WH Smith and all good newsagents. If you wish to subscribe, call:

01225 786844

NORMANDY

Price Guide

(76)
Close to the coast, a brick-built house set in 300m² of land. With gas heating, the property features three bedrooms, a living room with fireplace, bathroom, dining room and a fully-fitted kitchen.
79,273 euros   LAT
(£49,545) GP

(50)
A detached south-facing cottage located in a hamlet near the coast. Recent new roof, but requiring internal renovation. Offers 4,000m² of land, including an orchard and meadow, plus a barn.
54,500 euros   FDC
(£34,060) GP

(14)
Close to the small town of Pont-d'Ouilly. This detached house stands in grounds of 5,000m² with outbuildings and stables. Features four bedrooms, an open fireplace and convertible attic.
175,600 euros   LAR
(£109,750) GP

(27)
An imposing home surrounded by gorges, valleys, pine forests and cultivated fields. Set in 2,300m² of land with a small lake, stables, barn and dovecote. Offers three bedrooms, kitchen and bathroom.
210,379 euros   LAR
(£131,485) GP

(50)
In the town of Percy, a house with business potential. Benefits from sweeping lawns to the front and an attractive garden to the rear. A stream runs through mature trees at the boundary of the property.
218,510 euros   AIM
(£136,570) GP

(61)
A detached stone-built property in its own courtyard with access via a drive. In need of some work, the house offers three bedrooms and original features including open fires and exposed beams.
54,147 euros   AIM
(£33,840) GP

(61)
This half-timbered house is set in a small town close to Flers and is ready for habitation. With three bedrooms and a convertible loft. Centrally heated, the property is set in a garden and faces the road.
106,028 euros   PSF
(£66,270) GP

(50)
A stone house with a garage and 3,135m² of gardens. The sitting room features terracotta tiles, an open fireplace and beams. Offers three bedrooms, cellar and fitted kitchen. Renovation work needed.
99,091 euros   LAT
(£61,930) GP

(50)
A stone-built *maison de maitre* with a new garage and gardens of 4,815m². Comprising a stone outbuilding, four bedrooms, an open-plan kitchen and large bathroom. In a countryside location.
121,000 euros   LAT
(£75,625) GP

French Discoveries

Normandy Office

Telephone our office in Normandy for less than 10p/minute on 0871 717 4162 or e-mail: Normandy@french-discoveries.com

The *French Discoveries* offices are run by English couples who have been helping people to purchase property in France for more than 10 years.

Supported by our dedicated French and English teams, we offer a friendly, professional service, including translation and legal advice.

We invite you to visit our website on:

www.french-discoveries.com

which is up-dated weekly, or to chat in English with the people who have actually visited the properties.

Associate offices in Brittany and Charente.

Offices opening soon in Burgundy, Languedoc and Loire.

AIMS INTERNATIONAL
FRENCH PROPERTY CONSULTANTS

Ref: 766 - Normandy, Orne. A rare opportunity to buy a large country home with the added attraction of a 2nd property, plus large outbuildings workshops and stables. Position: A large stone built property under a slate roof, with gardens to the front and rear, situated in its own grounds, not far from the town of Alencon and access to the motorway system. Paris 2 hours drive. Channel Port of Caen, 1.5 hours, and the Port of Calais 3.5 hours. Panoramic views over the surrounding countryside.
Price: 529,595€ inclusive of all fees (approx £350,000)

For further details about any of the properties we have to offer phone:
00 33 2 43 04 26 99

or email: aimsinternational2000@yahoo.com

Or view our web site: **www.aimsinternational.com**

You can buy the property above or the property below in NORMANDY. Either way, the perfect contact is:
Immobilier Saint Michel
10, rue Saint Michel CAEN
(Calvados) 10 mins from Ouistreham
00.33.2.31.34.55.55
www.immostmichel-caen.fr
Email: immostmichel.caen@wanadoo.fr

LA MANCHE IMMOBILIER
3 agencies at your service
www.mancheimmobilier.fr

Agence Centre Manche	Agence Nord Cotentin	Agence Suisse Normande
25, rue de Villedieu	10, rue du Calvaire	Rue de la Libération
50000 SAINT-LÔ	50250 LA HAYE-DU-PUITS	14690 PONT-D'OUILLY
Tel: 00 33 2 33 05 14 07	Tel: 00 33 2 33 07 49 82	Tel: 00 33 2 31 69 31 11
or: 00 33 2 33 72 05 10	or: 00 33 2 33 07 96 86	Fax: 00 33 2 31 69 91 47
Fax: 00 33 2 33 05 05 00	Fax: 00 33 2 33 07 50 38	
lamanche-immobilier@wanadoo.fr	manche-immobilier@wanadoo.fr	manche-immo@wanadoo.fr

Price Guide

(27)
Beside a trout river, this thatched property comprises two cottages set in peaceful mature grounds. The first offers a balcony and one bedroom. The second has up to six bedrooms and a garage.
665,600 euros   **WAT**
(£416,000) GP

(61)
A stone-built house with a fitted kitchen and five bedrooms. There is a loft in need of finishing off and a large living room featuring a granite fireplace. Set in 5,658m² of enclosed land with open views.
145,436 euros   **PSF**
(£90,900) GP

(76)
A large brick-built house with a garage and 1,000m² of gardens surrounding the house. Featuring spacious rooms, this half-timbered property has exposed wooden beams and three large bedrooms.
114,337 euros   **LAT**
(£71,460) GP

(76)
A two-bedroom country home with a garage set in 685m² of gardens. Benefits from a quiet location. In need of finishing off work. Features a large living room and fully-fitted kitchen.
83,085 euros   **LAT**
(£51,930) GP

(76)
A traditional Normandy-style house set in a garden of 700m². Features a kitchen, utility room, three bedrooms and a bathroom. In need of some modernisation and set in the heart of a village.
121,654 euros   **LAT**
(£76,035) GP

(76)
A brick-built *maison de maître* with four bedrooms. Set in over 20,000m² of land, featuring a spacious barn, cellar and guest house with three bedrooms for renovation. Offers idyllic views.
151,687 euros   **LAR**
(£94,805) GP

(61)
A large stone house comprising four bedrooms, a fitted kitchen and a three-car garage. Standing in a garden of 2,500m² featuring a well, patio area, fish pond and outbuilding. Surrounded by trees.
136,899 euros   **PSF**
(£85,560) GP

(61)
This large house is set in a garden of 10,000m² with trees and a large outbuilding. Fronted by a lawn, the property comprises of five bedrooms, two bathrooms, and two fully-fitted kitchens.
250,510 euros   **PSF**
(£156,570) GP

(61)
Set in the countryside, close to the medieval town of Domfront. This cottage is on a slight hill at the edge of a regional park. Offers a double bedroom and mezzanine. Features exposed stone walls.
68,000 euros   **LAR**
(£42,500) GP

Buy your own place on the North West Coast

The most beautiful properties are in George V Normandy-Brittany

Deauville-St-Arnoult

Cabourg

Dinard

Le Havre

Trouville

Honfleur

NEXT

Just released!
- Deauville - St Arnoult. Between the golf course and the racecourse, buy your own 1 bedroom apartment with underground parking and garden in a private residence.
105 217 €*
☎ : 00 33 (0)2 31 87 50 10

New! In Cabourg.
On the beach. Buy your 1 bedroom apartment with parking and garden in a wooded residence.
69 370 €*
☎ : 00 33 (0)2 31 91 64 41

- Seize the opportunity now in Dinard. Take advantage & buy your own 2 bedroom apartment with garage. Near the beach and town center.
125 290 €*
☎ : 00 33 (0)2 99 46 69 20

New! In Trouville.
Exceptional! 2 bedroom apartment with balcony, parking and basement. 350 m from the quayside.
87 640 €*
☎ : 00 33 (0)2 31 88 30 07

Just released!
In Le Havre. In one of the most popular parts of Le Havre, take advantage of this exceptional location and buy your 1 bedroom apartment with loggia. South facing Residence.
77 899 €*
☎ : 00 33 (0)2 35 21 20 45

Unique in Trouville!
Take advantage & buy your own 2 bedroom house with a garden shed and parking in a private estate with tennis court. Fabulous sea views.
131 057 €*
☎ : 00 33 (0)2 31 88 30 07

Yes I am interested in one (or more) of your properties. Please send me a brochure.

Specify : ....
....
Mr/Mrs/Ms ....
Address ....
....
Country ....
Telephone number ....
Email address ....

Please return this coupon to:
George V Normandie - Chemin des Salines
14800 Saint-Arnoult - FRANCE

*Prices from ... extras included, dependent on availability from 27th September 2002.

GV GEORGE V Normandie

Chemin des Salines
14800 Saint-Arnoult - FRANCE

Buying your own place couldn't be easier!

www.georgev.net
Immobilier-Fiscalité-Finance

FBPG 10/02

Price Guide

(14)
Located at the end of a lane, deep in the Bocage countryside. South-facing, the house is set in 4,000m² of grassland. Access to the second floor is via a ladder. Offers a kitchen and large sitting room.
66,000 euros   **LAR**
(£41,250) GP

(76)
Dating from the 15th century, an old house with outbuildings set in over 2,455m² of grounds. A short journey from the coast, the house features a large kitchen, lounge, four bedrooms and a vaulted cellar.
215,000 euros   **LAT**
(£134,375) GP

(61)
On the outskirts of Flers, a manor house with six bedrooms. Enjoys a tennis court, golf driving range and large outbuildings. Set in 16,000m² of mature gardens, with an independent caretaker's house.
475,641 euros   **PSF**
(£297,275) GP

(76)
A half-timbered cottage with a thatched roof and a garden. Comprising four bedrooms and situated in a small village. The cottage features 200m² of living space and a fitted kitchen.
224,100 euros   **LAT**
(£140,065) GP

(76)
Located on a quiet road, this half-timbered house is set in a garden of 750m² with a small outbuilding and garage. Featuring two bedrooms, a sitting room, shower room, study and kitchen.
121,959 euros   **LAR**
(£76,225) GP

(61)
Two town houses for renovation offering a living area of 150m². Accommodation has to be created and services connected. With a garden of 880m², the property is semi-detached and faces the road.
41,542 euros   **PSF**
(£25,965) GP

(61)
A character stone house in need of some modernisation. Currently there are two bedrooms and one outbuilding. Set in a quiet rural location with unrestricted views over the surrounding countryside.
58,235 euros   **PSF**
(£36,395) GP

(50)
This modern house with a large balcony is situated in a dominant position with open sea views. Comprises three bedrooms, a large garden and double garage. Set in a resort, close to a beach.
381,123 euros   **LAT**
(£238,200) GP

(27)
South of the River Seine and located a short distance from the busy market town of Brionne. This pretty, renovated cottage has a swimming pool, two bedrooms and landscaped gardens.
121,197 euros   **LAR**
(£75,750) GP

Normandy

(61)
A detached stone *longère* with open south-facing views and 4,500m² of land. Offers a kitchen, cellar, two bedrooms and an outbuilding. The property features exposed beams and tiled floors.
118,500 euros   **LAT**
(£74,065) GP

(61)
Enjoying a secluded location, this detached stone-built property features two bedrooms and one bathroom. With a new roof and in need of partial renovation, the house is set in a garden of 130m².
46,496 euros   **PSF**
(£29,060) GP

(61)
A south-facing house offering two bedrooms with fireplaces and parquet floors. Set in 1,500m² of land featuring a terrace and outbuildings including a garage, barn, two toolsheds and a well.
66,500 euros   **LAT**
(£41,565) GP

(61)
Dating from the 18th century, this former vicarage enjoys a heated swimming pool set in a 1,700m² tree-filled garden with plenty of room for parking. Features five bedrooms and two bathrooms.
225,167 euros   **PSF**
(£140,730) GP

(61)
For complete renovation, a stone-built barn set in 2,000m² of land. With two bedrooms and plenty of room for further accommodation, the building is set in an open field enjoying unrestricted views.
10,122 euros   **PSF**
(£6,325) GP

(61)
In a village location, a south-facing detached house with a garage and barn set in over 1,500m² of land. Comprises a kitchen, living room and four bedrooms. Oil-fired heating and open fireplaces.
63,500 euros   **LAT**
(£39,690) GP

(61)
A short drive from Vassy, this four-bedroom property boasts an enclosed garden of 5,000m² with trees and outbuildings. Features a living room with a fireplace, fitted kitchen and a room for renovation.
320,142 euros   **PSF**
(£200,090) GP

(61)
A semi-detached, south-facing house in need of interior modernisation. The property offers three bedrooms, one bathroom and a garden of 900m². Located near a village with all amenities.
30,441 euros   **PSF**
(£19,025) GP

(76)
Set in 1,400m² of grounds, an ensemble of two half-timbered houses. Located close to the port of Dieppe, the property offers three bedrooms, a study, living room with fireplace and kitchen.
198,00 euros   **LAT**
(£123,750) GP

Price Guide

(76)
This farmhouse is set in over 12,150m² of land with a stable block, garage and vaulted cellars. Features exterior staircases at both ends of the property, an enclosed veranda and three large bedrooms.
146,350 euros   **LAT**
(£91,470) GP

(50)
Down a quiet country lane, this farmhouse is in need of renovation. With 28,000m² of grounds, an orchard and fields. Offers three bedrooms with beamed ceilings and features a spiral staircase.
126,000 euros   **LAR**
(£78,750) GP

(14)
A colourful stone house in an elevated position. Comprising four bedrooms, two bathrooms and two outbuildings. The house is surrounded by a large garden and approached via a long drive.
212,075 euros   **PSF**
(£132,545) GP

(76)
A traditional half-timbered Normandy house with a garage. Offers an enclosed garden of 970m² and three bedrooms. Located in the heart of a small village near the town of Aumale.
106,714 euros   **LAT**
(£66,700) GP

(50)
This 15th-century manor house is set in over 10,000m² of land in a rural location. Recently renovated, the property offers five bedrooms and four bathrooms, with two further rooms in need of completion.
320,121 euros   **PSF**
(£200,075) GP

(50)
A short drive from Brécey, this stone property dates from the 17th century and has been fully renovated. Features an open fireplace and two bedrooms. Set on the edge of a large forest.
112,812 euros   **PSF**
(£70,510) GP

(50)
In the heart of a quiet village, a period three-bedroom stone-built house with a garden of 9,000m² and a courtyard. The property features a living room with open fireplace and many original details.
57,927 euros   **PSF**
(£36,205) GP

(50)
An ensemble of three buildings in need of renovation. Set in a quiet rural location in 4,050m² of gardens. Comprising three bedrooms, the property is detached and a short walk from a nearby village.
53,357 euros   **PSF**
(£33,350) GP

(76)
A traditional Normandy house with outbuildings and 500m² of grounds. Features a spacious living room with a fireplace, a master bedroom and two further bedrooms. In a quiet village location.
105,190 euros   **LAT**
(£65,745) GP

Normandy

(76)
A thatched house set in 12,000m² of land with outbuildings and a pond. Comprises a living room, dining room, three bedrooms, dressing room and mezzanine. In a hamlet near Ourville-en-Caux.
271,969 euros   LAT
(£196,980) GP

(50)
Two stone properties with new roofs but in need of renovation. Offers three bedrooms and open views. Sitting in 4,000m² of land in a remote rural location, with water and electricity connected.
70,127 euros   PSF
(£43,830) GP

(50)
In need of complete renovation and with the potential for three bedrooms, a *longère* set in 3,100m² of land in an isolated rural area. Accommodation has not been created nor services connected.
44,210 euros   PSF
(£27,630) GP

(61)
A detached, south-facing stone house with a well. Recently restored and offering two bedrooms with parquet floors. Features a terrace, tiled floors, wood beams and an outbuilding.
87,000 euros   LAT
(£54,375) GP

(50)
Located between two villages, this period stone house is set in a garden of 300m² with a large outbuilding. Comprises a kitchen, living room, veranda and three bedrooms. Features two fireplaces.
92,994 euros   PSF
(£58,120) GP

(76)
A traditional Normandy house in almost 3,000m² of secluded grounds. Located in a small hamlet, the property features a fitted kitchen, four bedrooms, a double garage and woodstore.
205,000 euros   LAT
(£128,125) GP

(50)
An attractive stone house with a garage and 1,900m² of gardens. Set in a small village and offering four bedrooms with washbasins. Features a kitchen with fireplace, shower room and a dining room.
91,470 euros   LAT
(£57,170) GP

(50)
Located in a small village with all amenities, this stone-built two-bedroom detached house is in need of modernisation. Set in an enclosed garden of 500m² to the front and rear of the house.
41,200 euros   PSF
(£25,750) GP

(50)
This three-bedroom semi-detached house is situated in a small, friendly village just a few metres from the beach. With light, spacious rooms arranged over three floors and a small garden.
58,000 euros   PSF
(£36,250) GP

Price Guide

(50)
On 500m² of land in a small town, this house with an extension offers four bedrooms, a fitted kitchen, living room and lounge. Benefits from a double garage, a shed and large greenhouse.
125,009 euros   **LAT**
(£78,130) GP

(50)
A former mill divided into two dwellings offering five bedrooms. Set in woodland of over 6,000m² with a stream and stunning rural views. Completely renovated, the property features one outbuilding.
167,682 euros   **PSF**
(£104,800) GP

(50)
Set in a large garden, a detached stone residence with open views. Offering two bedrooms, the property is centrally heated and features a living room, bathroom, fitted kitchen and laundry room.
91,470 euros   **LAT**
(£57,170) GP

(14)
In a quiet location and surrounded by countryside, a renovated stone house close to Vire. Offers two bedrooms, one bathroom and 1,000m² of garden. Within a short drive of shops and a village.
89,945 euros   **PSF**
(£56,215) GP

(50)
A massive property set in over 130,000m² of land with outbuildings. Currently being renovated, the main house provides 400m² of living space including five bedrooms and three bathrooms.
472,560 euros   **PSF**
(£295,350) GP

(50)
This detached family home has been renovated recently and offers three spacious bedrooms. The property enjoys 5,000m² of well-maintained gardens with an outbuilding. Close to amenities.
228,300 euros   **PSF**
(£142,690) GP

(50)
A stone house for renovation. On 1,000m² of land in an elevated position, the property offers two bedrooms with potential for more. In a remote area with open views of the surrounding countryside.
21,343 euros   **PSF**
(£13,340) GP

(76)
In a small coastal village, this L-shaped house is set in 1,800m² of land. Close to the sea, the property features a kitchen with dining area, study, lounge, three bedrooms, a veranda and garage.
157,785 euros   **LAT**
(£98,615) GP

(50)
A grand stone-built property featuring four bedrooms and two bathrooms. Approached via a long, open driveway and situated on land of 22,500m². In need of some minor interior decoration.
140,253 euros   **PSF**
(£87,660) GP

Normandy

(50)
Set in a village, a town house in need of partial renovation. With six light-filled bedrooms, this colourful house offers 3,000m² of land at the rear of the property. Features a renovated outbuilding.
126,533 euros   **PSF**
(£79,085) GP

(76)
Dating from the 17th century, a half-timbered single-storey house. Featuring a fully-fitted kitchen and two bedrooms, the property is located in a small rural village within easy reach of the beach.
176,231 euros   **LAT**
(£110,145) GP

(50)
A renovated stone house with a large living room of 50m² featuring a granite fireplace. Offers three bedrooms, two bathrooms and one outbuilding. Standing in open land of over 1,720m².
114,337 euros   **PSF**
(£71,460) GP

(50)
Just 10km from Avranches, a large stone house comprising five bedrooms and two bathrooms. Set in 4,660m² of fenced-in land with two verandas, a barn and shed. Located in a quiet village setting.
167,694 euros   **PSF**
(£104,810) GP

(50)
Set in a tranquil hamlet a short drive from Brécey, this detached stone-built cottage offers two bedrooms with the possibility of converting a third. The property features a small mezzanine.
42,682 euros   **PSF**
(£26,675) GP

(50)
This rustic half-timbered house with a barn is in need of renovation. The property is set on a generous 30,000m² of land and currently offers two bedrooms. All services are ready for connection.
45,700 euros   **PSF**
(£28,565) GP

(76)
A half-timbered cottage with a thatched roof. Set in a garden of 2,600m², it features two bedrooms, a study, fitted kitchen and living room with fireplace. With electric and solid-fuel heating throughout.
170,000 euros   **LAT**
(£106,250) GP

(50)
A large stone-built *longère* in need of some minor work. This traditional dwelling is set in 50,000m² of land with a lake. The property benefits from assorted outbuildings including six horse boxes.
148,000 euros   **PSF**
(£92,500) GP

(76)
Set in over 1,410m² of gardens, a three-bedroom house offering a sitting room with fireplace, shower room and fitted kitchen. Features a balcony with open views over rolling countryside.
163,120 euros   **LAT**
(£101,950) GP

Price Guide

(14)
Dating from the 17th century, a traditional half-timbered farmhouse offering four bedrooms and two bathrooms. Situated in rural land of over 164,000m² with six stables and two outbuildings.
488,142 euros   **PSF**
(£305,090) GP

(76)
Built in 1903, this vine-covered residence is set in gardens of 2,500m². The property features a marble fireplace, parquet flooring and four bedrooms. Located in the heart of a small rural village.
163,120 euros   **LAT**
(£101,950) GP

(50)
Arranged over two floors, a large detached residence covered with vines. Set in a secluded woodland park of 4,640m², the house boasts five bedrooms, two bathrooms, cellar, a porch and a large garage.
284,697 euros   **PSF**
(£177,935) GP

(50)
This detached house is situated in 1,700m² of open land. Comprises four bedrooms, two bathrooms and a kitchen. Newly built, the house features a sunny patio area and plenty of space for parking.
330,000 euros   **PSF**
(£206,250) GP

(76)
A traditional farmhouse with a garage and outbuildings. Offering three good-sized bedrooms and set in 12,000m² of land with outbuildings, the property features a large study and fitted kitchen.
150,925 euros   **LAT**
(£94,330) GP

(50)
A four-bedroom stone-built house bordered by a river and set in tree-filled land of over 5,000m². Features open views, large windows and plenty of room for an extension. Set close to a village.
212,000 euros   **PSF**
(£132,500) GP

(50)
A sizeable detached country home set in 6,000m² of land with one large outbuilding. Comprises three bedrooms, kitchen, back-kitchen, sitting room and a large cellar. In need of some renovation.
131,000 euros   **PSF**
(£81,875) GP

(76)
This contemporary three-bedroom dwelling with a garage and outbuildings sits in grounds of almost 4,000m². The house features a half-timbered living room with open beams and a log fire.
144,980 euros   **LAT**
(£90,615) GP

(50)
A large stone-built property set in 100m² of garden with two garages and an outbuilding. Comprises one en-suite bedroom, four further bedrooms, four bathrooms, two dressing rooms and a kitchen.
244,528 euros   **PSF**
(£152,830) GP

Normandy

(50)
A large detached house set close to the sea with private moorings. Featuring a tennis court, seven bedrooms, greenhouses and an old stable block. Set in glorious wooded parkland of 40,000m².
533,572 euros   PSF
(£333,485) GP

(14)
A detached three-bedroom house. In a quiet and picturesque setting, this property is arranged over three spacious floors and features a large dining room and comfortable sitting room with fireplace.
365,878 euros   PSF
(£228,675) GP

(50)
Close to the beach, a large stone house with terracotta-tiled floors. This semi-detached house features two bedrooms and a living room, and is set in a pleasant garden with a well, garage and barn.
170,516 euros   LAT
(£106,575) GP

(50)
A stone-built property standing in 30,000m² of agricultural land with one outbuilding and a second house for renovation. The main property comprises four large bedrooms and one bathroom.
187,512 euros   PSF
(£117,195) GP

(50)
This traditional residence is set close to the west coast of Manche. Standing in nearly 58,000m² of land with outbuildings, stables and a small lake, the house offers five bedrooms and two bathrooms.
266,786 euros   PSF
(£166,740) GP

(14)
In a country location near the town of Lisieux, a main house featuring three large bedrooms and a self-contained studio. Ideal for the equestrian, with extensive stabling and two big paddocks.
487,500 euros   SUC
(£304,690) GP

(50)
Fronted by a garden of 400m², a large residence with outbuildings. Comprising four bedrooms and two bathrooms, the property is centrally heated and features a massive monumental fireplace.
487,898 euros   PSF
(£304,935) GP

(50)
Dating from the 19th century, a fully-renovated property with outbuildings converted into letting gîtes. The main residence features five bedrooms and four bathrooms and is set in 5,000m² of land.
731,984 euros   PSF
(£457,490) GP

(50)
An old stone house set in a garden with outbuildings. Totally renovated, the house features exposed beams, a stone fireplace and wood-burning stove. Offers three bedrooms and one bathroom.
126,000 euros   LAT
(£78,750) GP

Price Guide

(50)
Set in landscaped gardens, a five-bedroom detached house with a basement. Located in a quiet village, the building features a large living room, fitted kitchen, laundry room, storeroom and a garage.
132,631 euros   **LAT**
(£82,895) GP

(50)
Dating from the 17th century, a large building with 230m² of living space. With an adjoining outbuilding, the house features four bedrooms and two bathrooms. Situated in grounds of 14,000m².
309,471 euros   **PSF**
(£193,420) GP

(50)
A stone house with seven main rooms and four bedrooms. Dating from the 18th century and in need of some minor interior work, this house features a large hall with a stone staircase and oak panelling.
325,784 euros   **PSF**
(£203,615) GP

(14)
Close to the small town of Livarot but set deep in the countryside. Offering three bedrooms, outbuildings and 33,290m² of rural land, this farmhouse is in need of some interior decoration.
161,000 euros   **SUC**
(£100,625) GP

(50)
In the Cotentin Regional Park and close to a town, this 18th-century house offers five bedrooms and four bathrooms. Set in 15,000m² of grounds full of trees and shrubs featuring a small lake.
407,000 euros   **PSF**
(£254,375) GP

(14)
Dating from the 17th century, this manor house with a tower is set in 25,000m² of wooded parkland. Bordered by a river and accessed via an avenue flanked with trees, the manor offers six bedrooms.
374,415 euros   **PSF**
(£234,010) GP

(14)
Comprising a living room, four bedrooms, study, dining room, fully-fitted kitchen and cellar, this large residence is set in 13,625m² of land with a barn, garage, toolsheds and a stone outhouse.
157,480 euros   **LIN**
(£98,425) GP

(50)
Near the coast, this rural home has been partially restored and is set in 30,000m² of grounds with outbuildings. Centrally heated, the house features two bedrooms and benefits from a secluded spot.
260,000 euros   **PSF**
(£162,500) GP

(14)
Bordered by a river and enjoying open views, this large residence is set in a conservation area close to Caen. South facing, the property is enclosed in a mature garden with a pool. Offers five bedrooms.
472,000 euros   **PSF**
(£295,000) GP

Normandy

(14)
With views overlooking the Calvados countryside, this 17th-century manor house stands alone in land of 20,500m². The property offers three bedrooms, two bathrooms and several outbuildings.
262,000 euros   **PSF**
(£163,750) GP

(50)
In need of complete restoration, an old barn for conversion. With accommodation yet to be laid out, the property is set in 3,000m² of land offering rural views. Close to the town of Truttemer-le-Grand.
18,290 euros   **LIN**
(£11,430) GP

(14)
Comprising two houses, this large property is approached via a long private drive with electric gates. Set in 5,500m² of lawned gardens with outbuildings and mature trees. Features five large bedrooms.
325,900 euros   **PSF**
(£203,690) GP

(50)
Dating from the 16th century, a listed château featuring 16 main rooms plus a library, a tower, six bathrooms and a guest cottage. Set in land of 230,000m² with a dovecote, garage and stable block.
650,000 euros   **PSF**
(£406,250) GP

(50)
Close to a market town, a barn for renovation. Set in a small garden with open views, accommodation has yet to be created or services connected. Benefits from tranquil surroundings in rural countryside.
27,440 euros   **LIN**
(£17,150) GP

(50)
Standing in land of 15,000m², this stone-built château dates from 1860 and is set in a pleasant valley. Centrally heated and in good condition, it features an outbuilding suitable for conversion.
500,000 euros   **PSF**
(£312,500) GP

(50)
An old country home nestling in wooded hills. Offering three large bedrooms, a fitted kitchen and an outside cellar. The house features a small garden and veranda with views out over the countryside.
107,019 euros   **LIN**
(£66,885) GP

(14)
This detached stone house offers two bedrooms and one bathroom. Set in a garden of 600m² laid to lawn, the property is located in a residential area close to a small village and is ready to move in to.
65,800 euros   **PSF**
(£41,125) GP

(14)
Overlooking a beautiful valley, this stone-built residence stands in 12,000m² of land just south of Caen. The property comprises seven main rooms, including five bedrooms, a cellar, loft and bakery.
236,000 euros   **PSF**
(£147,500) GP

Price Guide

(14)
Set in wooded land, a furnished chalet within easy reach of a golf course. Comprising three bedrooms, a kitchen, living room, bathroom and a cellar. The property features a terrace and balcony.
53,662 euros   **LIN**
(£33,540) GP

(14)
An ivy-clad stone-built house set in 14,000m² of lawned garden. Features two sitting rooms, open-plan living room and a fully-equipped kitchen. With a mezzanine and three bedrooms.
276,500 euros   **PSF**
(£172,815) GP

(14)
Dating from the 17th century, a farmhouse located in a peaceful hamlet. Comprises a kitchen with oak units, four bedrooms and a dining room. Set in a sheltered garden with an orchard and barn.
204,000 euros   **PSF**
(£127,500) GP

(50)
An 18th-century château looking out to sea. Offering seven large bedrooms, this country residence is set in 25,000m² of land with outbuildings and an old bakery. Benefits from a quiet location.
1,626,800 euros   **PSF**
(£1,016,750) GP

(50)
This old country house with three bedrooms is set in a small garden. Located on the outskirts of a village with all amenities, this character house features a kitchen, living room and a cellar.
50,770 euros   **LIN**
(£31,730) GP

(50)
Close to a pretty village, this detached property comprises two bedrooms, two bathrooms and sitting room. The house stands in land of nearly 2,500m² with a two-room gîte and outbuilding.
145,500 euros   **PSF**
(£90,940) GP

(50)
Dating from the 18th century, an impressive château with 13 main rooms and five bedroom suites arranged over three storeys. Set in extensive parkland with lakes, a dovecote and mature trees.
838,470 euros   **PSF**
(£524,045) GP

(50)
Two buildings for renovation set in land of 4,000m². Living space has yet to be laid out or services connected. Close to a busy market town, the buildings benefit from a quiet location in a rural area.
27,440 euros   **LIN**
(£17,150) GP

(14)
Near the coast and a listed church, this stone-built presbytery is set in tranquil rural landscape and surrounded by 1,600m² of parkland. Comprises seven main rooms, including four bedrooms.
196,000 euros   **PSF**
(£122,500) GP

Normandy

(50)
A stone-built cottage with exposed beams, featuring a study, living room, two bedrooms and a fitted bathroom. Set in 3,000m² of gardens with an outbuilding, garage and cellar. Great views.
125,130 euros   LIN
(£78,205) GP

(50)
This old stone property with a slate roof is in need of work. On the ground floor is a room with a fireplace, office, shower and kitchen. Upstairs is a bar and washroom. With 10,000m² of land.
139,100 euros   PSF
(£86,940) GP

(50)
A two-storey house in need of renovation. Situated in 1,652m² of land, the accommodation comprises a kitchen, living room, and two bedrooms. Features open views and a secluded location.
42,681 euros   LIN
(£26,675) GP

(61)
A restored four-bedroom farmhouse close to Sourdeval. Featuring a lawned garden with trees and flowerbeds, various barns and outbuildings, a small field, hen house and caravan.
168,000 euros   FFF
(£105,000) GP

(50)
Set in tranquil surroundings, this detached home features a kitchen, living room and veranda. With central heating and two spacious bedrooms, the house stands in 1,965m² of land with an outhouse.
114,700 euros   PSF
(£71,690) GP

(14)
In the Vire Valley, this detached house is arranged over two storeys and offers three bedrooms, a living room, scullery, cellar and garage. Set in 2,500m² of rural land with stunning open views.
98,500 euros   PSF
(£61,565) GP

(14)
This spacious house comprises seven main rooms and features three bedroom suites. Set in 11,000m² of woodland traversed by a freshwater brook, the property enjoys sweeping country views.
221,000 euros   PSF
(£138,125) GP

(14)
Comprising a main house and a *longère* set around a courtyard, this property stands in land of 10,080m² featuring an orchard, two lakes and woodland. The main house offers five bedrooms.
292,900 euros   PSF
(£183,065) GP

(14)
Set in 10,000m² of grounds, a period two-bedroom farmhouse with outbuildings. With many original features, the house offers a living room with fireplace, dining room and two workshops.
105,000 euros   SUC
(£65,625) GP

Price Guide

(50)
Set in 1,000m² of land close to Cherbourg and within a short walk of the coast, this house has open beams, a minstrels' gallery and tiled floors. Centrally heated, with six south-facing bedrooms.
255,057 euros   LAT
(£159,410) GP

(14)
Situated close to Saint-Martin-des-Besaces, an old house with one bedroom, one bathroom, a kitchen, cellar, summer room and loft. Situated in an enclosed garden enjoying country views.
46,880 euros   PSF
(£29,300) GP

(76)
Bordered by a freshwater brook, a cottage with an annexe set in a small garden. Half-timbered, the cottage features a study, two en-suite bedrooms with walk-in wardrobes and a fitted kitchen.
192,848 euros   LAT
(£120,530) GP

(50)
A fully-renovated stone house offering eight main rooms, five bedrooms, two bathrooms and a basement. Within easy reach of local amenities, this detached property has 1,132m² of gardens.
195,876 euros   PSF
(£122,425) GP

(76)
Set in large grounds, a timber- and brick-built property, featuring cathedral-style ceilings, a sitting room floored with *tommette* tiles and a fitted kitchen. The house benefits from a vaulted wine cellar.
216,478 euros   LAT
(£135,300) GP

(50)
An old three-bedroom stone-built house comprising a living room, fitted kitchen, sitting room and a loft suitable for conversion. Centrally heated and set in land of 5,000m² with trees and shrubs.
98,500 euros   PSF
(£61,565) GP

(14)
This château lies in extensive wooded grounds overlooking a port. In need of some work, the building features a stone staircase, a large living room, library, cellars, offices, kitchens and 10 bedrooms.
1,130,000 euros   LAT
(£706,250) GP

(14)
This detached character residence is approached via a long drive and set in 2,500m² of land with an outbuilding. Comprises five bedrooms, a kitchen, scullery, office and a south-facing veranda.
114,600 euros   PFS
(£71,625) GP

(76)
A traditional half-timbered Normandy property. Set in rural surroundings, with a kitchen and seven bedrooms. South facing, the property features a beamed sitting room, a cellar and single garage.
216,478 euros   LAT
(£135,300) GP

Normandy

(14)
A stone-built property with a slate roof, set in pasture of 45,000m² with a stable block, several ponds, an enclosed courtyard and one outbuilding. Recently renovated, the house offers four bedrooms.
325,398 euros   PSF
(£203,375) GP

(76)
A half-timbered bungalow set in grounds of 7,800m² with a garage, outbuildings and pond. Benefits from four bedrooms, kitchen and dining room. Many original features including a bread-oven.
193,610 euros   LAT
(£121,005) GP

(14)
This former farmhouse is set in 3,000m² of land with an outbuilding for renovation. Offers four bedrooms, two bathrooms and plenty of space for extension. Benefits from a quiet environment.
117,843 euros   PSF
(£73,650) GP

(50)
This renovated *longère* stands in stunning countryside in a peaceful and tranquil setting. Close to the Normandy beaches, the house has four bedrooms and 20,500m² of open grounds.
160,060 euros   PSF
(£100,040) GP

(50)
Dating from the 19th century, a spacious four-bedroom house. Set in 15,000m² of land with one outbuilding. Comprises four bedrooms, with the possibility of creating more. Enjoys open views.
244,528 euros   PSF
(£152,830) GP

(76)
A traditional Normandy-style residence set in mature grounds of 1,830m². Bordered by a river, the house faces west and features four bedrooms and a study. Within easy reach of a busy market town.
187,512 euros   LAT
(£117,195) GP

(50)
Located near Villedieu-les-Poêles, a stone cottage for renovation currently offering two bedrooms and 3,000m² of open countryside with an outbuilding. Water and electricity have been connected.
22,900 euros   PSF
(£14,315) GP

(50)
Two 16th-century stone houses set in 5,900m² of grounds in a rural location. Close to the beach and a golf course, the property offers a kitchen, several bedrooms and a heated swimming pool.
579,306 euros   LAT
(£362,065) GP

(50)
This stone cottage is in need of major renovation work and comes with the option to buy a second house. Situated a short drive from the coast and near a village, it currently features two bedrooms.
18,320 euros   PSF
(£11,450) GP

Price Guide

(50)
A detached farmhouse in need of some renovation. Situated close to the coast, the building features four bedrooms and a kitchen. Set in open land of 4,000m² with an outbuilding and sweeping views.
67,175 euros   **PSF**
(£41,985) GP

(50)
A rustic *longère* for renovation. Built from stone and with a new roof, the building features five bedrooms and is set in land of over 3,000m². Situated close to a town with shops and all amenities.
59,000 euros   **PSF**
(£36,875) GP

(61)
This stone house currently offers two bedrooms. In need of total renovation, the property overlooks the countryside of Orne and boasts a secluded location. Water and electricity need installation.
18,599 euros   **PSF**
(£11,625) GP

(61)
A large farmhouse with three stone outbuildings. Standing in 10,000m² of land and approached via a long open drive. The house offers four bedrooms, a fitted kitchen, large garage and a well.
161,595 euros   **PSF**
(£101,000) GP

(50)
A large house with a slate roof, set in land of 6,500m² with a cow shed, cellar, two garages and an old bakery. The property offers three bedrooms and an open-plan fitted kitchen and dining room.
106,562 euros   **PSF**
(£66,600) GP

(61)
This ensemble of stone buildings for renovation is located in the idyllic countryside surrounding Flers. Featuring two bedrooms, services have yet to be connected. Set in open land of over 1,310m².
19,818 euros   **PSF**
(£12,385) GP

(27)
A beautiful country house set outside a village on the banks of the River Seine. In open landscape, enjoying panoramic views over lakes and woodland. Offers five bedrooms and a swimming pool.
228,600 euros   **PRV**
(£142,875) GP

(50)
A country residence arranged over one floor, comprising a kitchen, living room, sitting room and two bedrooms. The property features an open fireplace and beamed ceilings. Set in 1,200m² of land.
73,960 euros   **PSF**
(£46,225) GP

(61)
A detached stone barn for total renovation. Currently comprising three bedrooms, the building offers original stone features and is set in farmland and pasture of over 6,395m². In need of a new roof.
26,678 euros   **PSF**
(£16,675) GP

(27)
A typical country home that has been fully renovated. Features a large fitted kitchen, living room with fireplace and four spacious bedrooms. Set in a secluded and secure lawned garden of 844m^2.
101,308 euros **DEL**
(£63,320) GP

(27)
This rustic cottage offers 70m^2 of living space divided into three rooms. All services are connected, but the property is in need of complete renovation. Situated in an extensive wooded garden.
20,000 euros **JBF**
(£12,500) GP

(27)
This renovated water mill is surrounded by mature trees and bordered by a stream. With four spacious bedrooms, two bathrooms and a kitchen, it is set on the edge of a lively old village.
172,500 euros **JBF**
(£107,500) GP

(14)
A large property set among orchards and meadows, offering four bedrooms, stables and land of 20,000m^2. Within easy reach of a village, it features half-timbering, open fires and stunning views.
132,000 euros **LAR**
(£82,500) GP

(14)
This ensemble of buildings boasts a manor house, guest house, barns and several gîtes. In an idyllic location overlooking a large lake and river, the property is set in 6,000m^2 of beautiful countryside.
499,118 euros **HEX**
(£311,950) GP

(14)
Just outside Lisieux, a bungalow featuring a kitchen, a lounge with a fireplace that doubles as a bedroom, a second bedroom and bathroom. Located in 3,675m^2 of well-maintained gardens.
60,522 euros **NON**
(£37,825) GP

(50)
A large thatched cottage with tiled floors, exposed beams, open fireplaces and a huge lounge with a mezzanine. Set in 2,825m^2 of gardens with several outbuildings. Accessed via a long private drive.
213,428 euros **HAM**
(£133,395) GP

(14)
Set in beautiful and extensive wooded grounds, a typical half-timbered Normandy house. The property features a dining room with fireplace, office, kitchen, bathroom and three bedrooms.
95,000 euros **NON**
(£59,375) GP

(27)
Two half-timbered thatched cottages in nearly 2,200m^2 of garden laid to lawn and planted with mature trees. Offering uninterrupted rural views, the property has recently been fully renovated.
195,420 euros **FRA**
(£122,140) GP

Price Guide

(14)
A traditional half-timbered Normandy-style house. Fully furnished and in good condition, the property stands in 6,800m² of grounds near a peaceful village just a short drive from the coast.
170,992 euros   SUC
(£106,870) GP

(14)
Located in an isolated spot in rural surroundings, a half-timbered two-bedroom home standing in 1,000m² of land featuring a massive outbuilding and garage. Close to the busy town of Lisieux.
65,000 euros   SUC
(£40,625) GP

(14)
Approached via a long driveway, this detached house stands in a garden of 1,200m² containing a large garage. Features a dining room with fireplace, kitchen, six bedrooms and four shower rooms.
392,366 euros   SUC
(£245,230) GP

(14)
Ready to move in to and a short drive from the town of Honfleur, a detached bungalow standing in land of 750m² in a village setting. Centrally heated and comprising three bedrooms and a kitchen.
135,878 euros   SUC
(£84,925) GP

(14)
At the edge of the town of Pont-l'Evêque, this traditional detached house sits in shaded grounds of nearly 59,000m². The property features a dining room, three bedrooms, bathroom and garage.
147,328 euros   SUC
(£92,080) GP

(14)
A traditional Normandy house in Pont-l'Evêque. Surrounded by a colourful garden of 660m² in a very peaceful location. Comprises three bedrooms, a large fitted kitchen, dining room and lounge.
155,725 euros   SUC
(£97,330) GP

(14)
Near a village in the heart of the countryside, two traditional half-timbered cottages with thatched roofs. Set in 4,800m² of gardens planted with mature trees, the main house offers three bedrooms.
244,275 euros   SUC
(£152,670) GP

(14)
Dating from the 18th century, a traditional house offering three en-suite bedrooms and many original details. Located in a small town on the coast, close to the beach and set in a private garden.
244,275 euros   SUC
(£152,670) GP

(14)
Only 20 metres from the beach, a large detached residence with a tree-filled garden. Renovated to a high standard 25 years ago, the house offers a dining room, sitting room and three large bedrooms.
195,420 euros   SUC
(£122,140) GP

Normandy

(14)
In a small village close to a forest, a traditional half-timbered house with two bedrooms, sitting room, kitchen, terrace and massive underground cellars. Set in a very peaceful location with rural views.
259,542 euros   **SUC**
(£162,215) GP

(14)
Nestling in wooded land and set in a quiet location bordered by a stream, this large family residence with bright interiors features a kitchen, back-kitchen, dining room and eight bedrooms.
340,000 euros   **SUC**
(£212,500) GP

(14)
In a quiet rural area close to Lisieux, a traditional Normandy house with half-timbering. Approached via a country lane, the property offers four bedrooms, outbuildings and a double garage.
290,076 euros   **SUC**
(£181,300) GP

(14)
Near a busy market town but in a tranquil location, a 19th-century castle set in 40,000m² of parkland with mature trees and a long gravel drive. This large property is in need of some renovation.
610,687 euros   **SUC**
(£381,680) GP

(14)
Close to Deauville, this vast estate is privately situated and has been totally renovated. The main house comprises four bedrooms and boasts a swimming pool. Features a small cottage and outbuildings.
577,099 euros   **SUC**
(£360,685) GP

(14)
A 17th-century home retaining many original features including an oak staircase. Comprises a kitchen, corner-kitchen, dining room and four bedrooms. Comes with a two-bedroom guest house.
374,046 euros   **SUC**
(£233,780) GP

(14)
Centrally heated, this secluded detached property sits in woodland of 8,000m² with several outbuildings. Set in a quiet village and close to a town, it offers five bedrooms and two bathrooms.
274,809 euros   **SUC**
(£171,755) GP

(14)
A 15th-century manor house set on the outskirts of a village. In the process of restoration, the house boasts many features including an ancient tower with a spiral staircase and exposed stone walls.
320,143 euros   **SUC**
(£200,090) GP

(61)
In need of some finishing off and situated close to a large town, a detached property hidden away in wooded land. In a rural setting, the residence comprises five bedrooms, kitchen and large cellar.
442,102 euros   **SUC**
(£276,315) GP

155

Price Guide

(61)
Dating from 1850, a country house set on the edge of a village. Featuring five bedrooms, a fitted kitchen, study, dining room and mezzanine, and offering stunning panoramic views of the region.
305,245 euros   **SUC**
(£190,780) GP

(61)
This stone-built property is set in an elevated position with views over the local countryside. At the end of lane on the edge of a village and arranged over three levels, it offers two bedrooms and a studio.
175,000 euros   **SUC**
(£109,375) GP

(61)
Dating from the 18th century, a large house situated in the heart of the countryside. Comprises two wings, six bedrooms, kitchen and dining room with fireplace. The house sits in 6,000m² of gardens.
163,121 euros   **SUC**
(£101,950) GP

(61)
A half-timbered manor house located on the edge of a quiet village. The property features a fitted kitchen, sitting room, three bedrooms and timber carport. Offers a large garden and two fields.
140,458 euros   **SUC**
(£87,785) GP

(14)
Located just outside Honfleur in a typical Normandy village, a traditional thatched house dating from the 17th century and set in a garden of 4,115m² planted with trees and bordered by two springs.
163,359 euros   **SUC**
(£102,100) GP

(14)
A recently-built home close to Pont-l'Evêque, set in a garden with 710m² of lawns and a terrace affording open views. With four bedrooms, kitchen, living room and an underground garage.
212,214 euros   **SUC**
(£132,635) GP

(14)
A short drive from a busy town but set deep in the country, this traditional home comprises four bedrooms, kitchen, dining room with fireplace and cellar. Comes with a two-storey barn and garage.
141,985 euros   **SUC**
(£88,740) GP

(14)
A traditional Normandy house set in isolated countryside close to Lisieux. With 13,000m² of grounds featuring pasture and fields, the property offers a number of outbuildings and a garage.
244,275 euros   **SUC**
(£152,670) GP

(14)
Completely secluded in a small private valley, a large farmhouse dating from the 15th century. Close to a busy market town and offering three bedrooms, a living room and several outbuildings.
295,000 euros   **SUC**
(£184,375) GP

NORD-PAS-DE-CALAIS & PICARDY

Price Guide

(62)
A pretty *fermette* and a separate guest house set in 2,580m² of gardens with five brick outbuildings. This property was renovated in 1955 and retains many original features including exposed beams.
91,500 euros   LAT
(£57,190) GP

(62)
Located between Montreuil and Fruges and set in almost 850m² of gardens, this traditional half-timbered house has been fully renovated and offers a farmhouse-style kitchen and two large bedrooms.
105,190 euros   LAT
(£67,745) GP

(62)
Set in 2,000m² of grounds close to the town of Hesdin, a *fermette* with several small outbuildings. The property features exposed beams throughout, spacious rooms, a log fire and bread oven.
105,000 euros   LAT
(£65,625) GP

(62)
In the style of the region, a typical three-bedroom *fermette*. Just a short drive from the coast, this charming property is set in 3,000m² of mature gardens complete with several outbuildings.
129,582 euros   LAT
(£80,990) GP

(62)
This detached, singe-storey house with a double garage features three bedrooms and a living room. Near the coast, the house enjoys 1,800m² of gardens with mature trees and a south-facing terrace.
176,841 euros   LAT
(£110,525) GP

(62)
Located in the Authie Valley, this half-timbered *fermette* is set in over 1,200m² of grounds. The property is mainly renovated but is in need of some finishing-off work. Offers three bedrooms.
105,200 euros   LAT
(£65,750) GP

(62)
This three-bedroom house features an enclosed courtyard and is set in lawned gardens of 1,000m². With exposed beams throughout, the property is offered complete with three barns.
144,827 euros   LAT
(£90,520) GP

(60)
This character house, just a short drive from Paris, benefits from a secluded location. With 1,300m² of landscaped gardens, the property offers a living room, two bedrooms and a small veranda.
160,000 euros   FPL
(£100,000) GP

(80)
A traditional Picardy-style house with outbuildings. Set in gardens of 1,400m² in the centre of a large village, the property comprises two bedrooms, a sitting room with fireplace and a fitted kitchen.
111,989 euros   LAT
(£69,995) GP

THE FIRST CHOICE FOR A SECOND PROPERTY

Souillac Country Club is proud to announce that La Valee and Les Geneviers, the fourth and fifth phase of this quality development, are available for purchase. The houses are on individual plots bordered on one side by an established 9 hole golf course (18 in 2003) and countryside on the other. They provide the ideal location from which to enjoy the peace and tranquillity of the picturesque Dordogne Valley and the facilities of he club.

- 9 Hole Golf Course
- Swimming Pools
- Tennis
- Bar and Restaurant
- Full Property Management
- Good Rental Return

Please call for an information pack on this excellent investment opportunity
Email: **sales@souillac-countryclub.com**

Come and see us on stands P82 & P84 at the French Property Exhibition, Olympia, London, W14 from the 17th-19th January 2003

www.souillaccountryclub.com

SUCCESS IMMOBILIER
PAS-DE-CALAIS
LES 7 VALLEES

BILINGUAL STAFF
AFTER SALES SERVICE

PROPERTIES URGENTLY WANTED, ANY CONDITION, BUYERS WAITING

VISIT OUR WEBSITE.
LARGE CHOICE OF PROPERTIES WITHIN 80KM REGION

WWW.SUCCESSIMMOBILIER.COM
EMAIL: INFO@SUCCESSIMMOBILIER.COM

28, Rue d'Hesdin
62130 SAINT POL SUR TERNOISE

Tel: **00 33 6 09 62 91 92**
00 33 3 21 04 58 46
Fax: **00 33 3 21 04 58 49**

---

hexagone france limited

The Northern France Specialists

Webster House · 24 Jesmond Street · Folkestone · Kent · CT19 5QW
Tel: (01303) 221077 · Fax: (01303) 244409 · Email: sales@hexagonefrance.com

www.hexagonefrance.com

Price Guide

(80)
Dating from the 18th-century, this château is approached along an avenue of lime trees. With a heated pool and terrace, the property offers 21 bedrooms and sits in mature parkland of 140,000m².
2,591,633 euros   **SIF**
(£1,619,770) GP

(60)
In a village setting, these two houses stand in 3,000m² of gardens. Dating from 1870, the property has been fully renovated and features an open-plan living area and a central courtyard.
480,900 euros   **LAT**
(£300,620) GP

(60)
This prestigious home, dating from 1850, is set in parkland with mature trees and tennis courts. Architectural features include vaulted cellars and a traditional gatehouse. Offers 10 main rooms.
595,000 euros   **FPL**
(£371,875) GP

(82)
A rural estate consisting of extensive parkland featuring an ornamental temple, fountains and a waterfall. The estate buildings include a bell tower, manor house, two cottages and several barns.
519,000 euros   **FPL**
(£324,375) GP

(62)
With open views and a pleasant garden, this three-storey house is situated in a residential area near the centre of a resort town. Offers four bedrooms, living room, balcony and parking for two cars.
480,214 euros   **LAT**
(£300,135) GP

(62)
A large country house close to the sea. This family home is set in 10,000m² of land, with the option of purchasing more. Offering several bedrooms and bathrooms, the property is located in a village.
490,000 euros   **FPL**
(£306,250) GP

(62)
A thatched cottage with a south-facing terrace and large living room, standing in 2,800m² of garden. This three-bedroom cottage enjoys open fireplaces and sweeping views over the Canche Valley.
185,000 euros   **LAT**
(£115,625) GP

(62)
This 18th-century house has many original features including open fireplaces and tiled floors. Bordered by a river, the property offers a separate guest cottage, enclosed courtyard and a field.
412,000 euros   **LAT**
(£257,500) GP

(62)
Located close to the small town of Hesdin, a large farmhouse with a separate cottage together forming a private courtyard. This character property features oak beams throughout and offers a huge barn.
250,000 euros   **FPL**
(£156,250) GP

Nord-Pas-de-Calais & Picardy

(80)
This traditional farmhouse is located near a forest and comprises a sitting room, dining room and three bedrooms. Standing in fenced-in land of 2,200m² with mature trees and outbuildings.
150,162 euros   **LAR**
(£93,850) GP

(62)
Set on the outskirts of a small town, this rustic cottage is in need of total renovation. Within a small garden and surrounded by rural land, accommodation has yet to be laid out or services connected.
14,504 euros   **SUC**
(£9,065) GP

(62)
Just a short drive from the Channel Tunnel, this renovated farmhouse is ready for occupation. Set in a small garden, it offers three bedrooms, a cellar and an open-plan kitchen and living area.
68,702 euros   **LAR**
(£42,940) GP

(62)
A one-bedroom house close to the town of Frévent. In need of interior renovation, the property features an outbuilding, open fireplace and country views. Services have yet to be connected.
30,534 euros   **SUC**
(£19,085) GP

(62)
Standing in wooded ground, this small house is set at the edge of a village, close to the old town of Saint-Pol-sur-Ternoise. The house offers two bedrooms, an open fireplace and central heating.
38,168 euros   **SUC**
(£23,855) GP

(62)
One hour from the Channel Tunnel, this renovated farmhouse stands in nearly 1,000m² of mature gardens and is situated on the banks of an idyllic river. Benefits from a tranquil location.
179,604 euros   **HEX**
(£112,255) GP

(62)
A traditional farmhouse with a well and over 2,000m² of land set on the edge of a small village in picturesque surroundings. Offers two bedrooms, outbuildings, two garages and a large paddock.
109,645 euros   **HEX**
(£68,530) GP

(62)
This villa offers 14 main rooms and 7,500m² of land planted with trees and shrubs. Secluded and comfortable, the property is approached via a drive and has several outbuildings and a cellar.
1,339,790 euros   **HAM**
(£837,368) GP

(62)
A traditional farmhouse property located close to a fishing village on the Opal Coast. In need of total renovation, it offers three large bedrooms, kitchen and garden overlooking a rural valley.
67,000 euros   **HEX**
(£41,875) GP

Price Guide

(62)
Located in a village and surrounded by picturesque countryside, this traditional farmhouse retains many original features. Offering two large bedrooms with views over the well-maintained garden.
107,200 euros   **HEX**
(£67,000) GP

(62)
A restored farmhouse close to the market town of Hesdin. Features include a heavy pantiled roof, a white stone fireplace and rendered walls. Comprises two double bedrooms, a kitchen and cellar.
91,470 euros   **LAR**
(£57,170) GP

(62)
Currently a small hotel, this cottage is a short distance from the Channel Tunnel. With several spacious bedrooms, garage and a fitted kitchen. Set in a picturesque location with unrestricted views.
193,000 euros   **HEX**
(£120,625) GP

(62)
In a village close to the town of Crécy-en-Ponthieu, this two-bedroom bungalow stands in a garden of 5,000m^2 planted with trees and shrubs. Features a kitchen with woodburning fire and outhouses.
41,221 euros   **SUC**
(£25,765) GP

(62)
A house with a garage in the rural town of Hesdin. The house features three bedrooms with fireplaces and is set in a large garden with an outbuilding. The property is ready to move in to.
42,748 euros   **SUC**
(£26,720) GP

(80)
A two-bedroom cottage close to the fishing port of Saint-Valery-sur-Somme. Renovated and set in 3,000m^2 of land, the cottage enjoys exceptional views over the surrounding country landscape.
100,616 euros   **LAR**
(£62,885) GP

(62)
A small detached one-bedroom *longère* in a village setting a short distance from the town of Montreuil. Standing in 1,000m^2 of garden, the house features many original architectural details.
42,748 euros   **SUC**
(£26,720) GP

(62)
This old stone-built house offers two bedrooms and central heating. Set in a village, the property is in need of renovation as currently there are no mains sewerage facilities or services connected.
48,855 euros   **SUC**
(£30,535) GP

(62)
Located a short distance from the town of Anvin, this two-bedroom residence is arranged over two floors and approached via a private drive. Stands in a small garden with a single garage.
59,542 euros   **SUC**
(£37,215) GP

Nord-Pas-de-Calais & Picardy

(62)
Set in a peaceful village down a quiet country lane, this farmhouse offers three double bedrooms, a separate studio flat and several barns. Features a traditional Picardy fireplace and a garden.
102,500 euros　　　　　　**LAR**
(£64,065) GP

(62)
In need of interior renovation, a large house comprising four bedrooms, a study, a sitting room with open fireplace and a cellar. Standing in land of 1,450m² with a garage and several outbuildings.
122,000 euros　　　　　　**HEX**
(£76,250) GP

(62)
A short walk from a village with all amenities, an unusual *longère* built from wood. Set in the middle of 1,300m² of tree-filled land with several outbuildings, the house has one large bedroom.
74,046 euros　　　　　　**SUC**
(£46,280) GP

(62)
Standing in mature gardens of 1,700m² with a covered terrace and built-in barbecue, this farmhouse-style home has two bedrooms, a woodburning stove and sitting room with exposed beams.
115,800 euros　　　　　　**LAR**
(£72,375) GP

(62)
A large residence featuring seven bedrooms and three bathrooms. Approached via a driveway, the property comes with 4,280m² of land planted with trees, and is complete with several outhouses.
595,420 euros　　　　　　**SUC**
(£372,140) GP

(62)
Just a short distance from a busy town, this character half-timbered *longère* is set in land of over 10,000m². On the edge of a village, the property comprises three bedrooms and one bathroom.
381,679 euros　　　　　　**SUC**
(£238,550) GP

(62)
With six bedrooms, this large residence is approached via a long drive flanked with trees. Near a small town, the property stands in land of 35,000m² surrounded by hilly woodland countryside.
366,412 euros　　　　　　**SUC**
(£229,010) GP

(62)
Enjoying spacious light-filled rooms, this detached residence features eight bedrooms. In a quiet village setting near the town of Saint-Pol-sur-Ternoise, with lovely views of the countryside.
305,344 euros　　　　　　**SUC**
(£190,840) GP

(62)
An imposing house dating from the 19th century offering eight double bedrooms, one large family bathroom and a tower. Situated in rural woodland, with grounds of 10,900m² and one outbuilding.
297,710 euros　　　　　　**SUC**
(£186,070) GP

Price Guide

(62)
On the edge of a bustling village, this property stands in 3,500m² of land with trees and shrubs. Offers five double bedrooms and three bathrooms. Centrally heated, the house is detached and habitable.
256,489 euros   **SUC**
(£160,305) GP

(62)
Featuring five spacious bedrooms and decorative half-timbering, a *longère* in the heart of a small village. The house features three bathrooms and sits in garden of 2,000m² with several outbuildings.
238,168 euros   **SUC**
(£148,855) GP

(62)
A two-storey house comprising four bedrooms, two bathrooms, a fitted kitchen and a double garage. Set in a quiet village a short distance from the coast and a large medieval market town.
213,740 euros   **SUC**
(£133,590) GP

(80)
Close to the busy town of Aumale, this half-timbered property offers two bedrooms, a kitchen and a large sitting room with a fireplace. The house is set in grounds of nearly 2,000m².
93,756 euros   **LAR**
(£58,600) GP

(62)
A stone-built *longère* comprising five spacious bedrooms and two bathrooms. Situated in a large garden of 8,000m² with trees and shrubs. In a village setting close to the seaside town of Berck.
190,840 euros   **SUC**
(£119,275) GP

(62)
This classic five-bedroom *longère* benefits from an enclosed private garden of 12,000m². Set in a friendly village with all amenities, the property features a large outbuilding ideal for conversion.
183,206 euros   **SUC**
(£114,505) GP

(62)
With plenty of space for parking, this two-bedroom L-shaped house is located close to the busy town of Frévent. Situated in a small country village on 4,500m² of land with mature trees and shrubs.
175,573 euros   **SUC**
(£109,735) GP

(62)
Fronted by a lawn, a house with three bedrooms. A short distance from the town of Anvin, this property is set in tree-filled land of 4,000m² with outbuildings. In a secluded spot offering rural views.
167,939 euros   **SUC**
(£104,960) GP

(62)
In a picturesque village setting close to the town of Hesdin, a two-storey property offering three large bedrooms, one bathroom and an outbuilding. Set in land of 2,500m² with a courtyard.
155,727 euros   **SUC**
(£97,330) GP

Nord-Pas-de-Calais & Picardy

(62)
Set in a picturesque valley in a pretty garden of 1,700m², a two-bedroom house featuring a terrace, fitted kitchen and sitting room with log fireplace. In a residential area close to Fruges.
131,288 euros   HEX
(£82,055) GP

(62)
A two-bedroom house located in a busy seaside town. Centrally heated, the property benefits from spacious, light-filled rooms and an enclosed garden of 9,000m² planted with trees and shrubs.
160,305 euros   SUC
(£100,190) GP

(62)
Dating from the 19th century, this six-bedroom château is close to the town of Hesdin. Recently renovated and south facing, the property stands in grounds with a stream, three bridges and stabling.
675,000 euros   CUR
(£421,875) GP

(62)
A classic three-bedroom *longère* in the heart of a quiet village close to the town of Anvin. Detached and standing in land of 2,000m² with outbuildings, the property benefits from a private location.
152,672 euros   SUC
(£95,420) GP

(62)
This four-bedroom manor house stands in a small enclosed garden featuring a courtyard. Offering four bedrooms and one family bathroom, the house is set in a quiet village with all amenities.
148,855 euros   SUC
(£93,035) GP

(62)
This detached house comprises six bedrooms, two bathrooms and a fully-fitted kitchen. In a village setting, the property stands in land of nearly 6,600m² with outbuildings and several barns.
152,672 euros   SUC
(£95,420) GP

(62)
A four-bedroom house close to the town of Crécy-en-Ponthieu. Located in a quiet village with shops and a school, the property stands in 2,500m² of open land with panoramic country views.
145,038 euros   SUC
(£90,650) GP

(62)
A detached house surrounded by 1,500m² of enclosed garden. Set in a quiet village close to the busy town of Montreuil, the property features a large outbuilding and enjoys a secluded location.
145,649 euros   SUC
(£91,030) GP

(62)
A period house set in the heart of the city of Arras. Offering an enclosed courtyard, gardens, cellar and two garages, the property is a short drive from Paris and features five bedrooms and a balcony.
295,774 euros   HEX
(£184,860) GP

Price Guide

(62)
This three-bedroom bungalow is set in 4,500m² of land planted with trees and approached via a drive. In a village setting close to the medieval town of Hesdin, the property is ready to move in to.
145,038 euros   SUC
(£90,650) GP

(62)
An old farmhouse set in a quiet village a short drive from the market town of Hesdin. In a garden of 1,000m² with a garage and several outbuildings, it features two bedrooms and a large cellar.
90,562 euros   HEX
(£56,600) GP

(62)
In a village setting, this L-shaped house offers three bedrooms. Close to the market town of Saint-Pol-sur-Ternoise, it stands in an enclosed garden of 8,000m² with ample room for parking.
131,900 euros   SUC
(£82,440) GP

(62)
Near Saint-Pol-sur-Ternoise, this two-bedroom house stands in land of nearly 5,000m² with a small outbuilding. Situated in a quiet village, the property has central heating and is habitable.
122,137 euros   SUC
(£76,335) GP

(62)
Standing in an enclosed garden of 1,800m², this small house enjoys a secluded location and stunning views. Situated in a quiet village, the property has three good-sized bedrooms and a large bathroom.
123,664 euros   SUC
(£77,290) GP

(62)
Set in 3,000m² of garden with a patio area and outbuildings, this one-bedroom house is located in the centre of a rural village. With oil-fired central heating, the house benefits from a secluded location.
129,771 euros   SUC
(£81,105) GP

(62)
A two-bedroom L-shaped house with one family bathroom. In a village close to the town of Saint-Pol-sur-Ternoise, it stands in lawned gardens of 5,000m² with mature trees, flowers and shrubs.
108,397 euros   SUC
(£67,750) GP

(62)
Situated in hilly woodland this simple cottage offers a number of outbuildings arranged around a courtyard. Comprises a sitting room with an open fireplace, two bedrooms, bathroom and kitchen.
56,400 euros   LAR
(£35,250) GP

(62)
Set in quiet countryside, this old farmhouse features a garage and several outbuildings. Standing in 2,500m² of land with a private drive, the property benefits from two bedrooms and one bathroom.
105,344 euros   SUC
(£65,840) GP

Nord-Pas-de-Calais & Picardy

(62)
An L-shaped *longère* set in rural land of 10,000m². Located near a village, the house has four bedrooms and open fireplaces. In need of some renovation, the property is ready to move in to.
91,603 euros SUC
(£57,250) GP

(62)
In a village setting close to the town of Montreuil, this *longère* features two bedrooms, one large bathroom and a kitchen. The property is set in rural land of 1,500m² with panoramic views.
82,443 euros SUC
(£51,525) GP

(62)
A detached house located in a rural village with all amenities. Close to the town of Hesdin, the property offers two good-sized bedrooms and is set in a private garden of 800m² laid to lawn.
70,229 euros SUC
(£43,895) GP

(62)
A modern three-bedroom house located in a large village with all amenities. Close to the River Canche and near a busy market town, the house offers a good-sized garden with mature trees.
126,400 euros HEX
(£79,000) GP

(62)
Currently comprising one large bedroom, a *longère* in a quiet country setting. Situated close to the town of Fruges, the property features a garage, an outbuilding and is set in over 2,500m² of land.
88,550 euros SUC
(£55,345) GP

(62)
A characterful country residence with two bedrooms located in a quiet village close to a busy town. Featuring many original details including open fireplaces, the property offers two bathrooms.
56,489 euros SUC
(£35,305) GP

(62)
In a busy seaside town, this two-bedroom apartment features a bathroom and a garage. Close to all amenities, the apartment enjoys a balcony with panoramic views and is ready to move in to.
76,336 euros SUC
(£47,710) GP

(62)
Set in idyllic country surroundings, this large *longère* is located in a quiet village close to the town of Hesdin. The property offers three double bedrooms, an open fireplace and a 1,500m² garden.
76,336 euros SUC
(£47,710) GP

(62)
This family home stands in 3,300m² of land and offers five bedrooms and two outbuildings. Surrounded by woodland, meadows and fields, the house enjoys scenic views of the Ternoise Valley.
143,000 euros HAM
(£89,375) GP

Price Guide

(62)
Standing in 8,000m² of land, two picturesque houses draped in vines and fronted by a colourful garden. Boasts uninterrupted views across open countryside. Just a short distance from the Channel Tunnel.
268,114 euros   **HEX**
(£167,570) GP

(62)
Five minutes from a busy town, this small house is set in 1,132m² of tree-filled land. Features three large bedrooms, a living room and two bathrooms. South facing, with a sunny terrace and patio.
186,000 euros   **RAV**
(£116,250) GP

(62)
This colourful five-bedroom villa is approached along a private driveway. Totally renovated, the property is set in 2,000m² of land and features a spacious kitchen, dining room and two bathrooms.
355,800 euros   **RAV**
(£222,375) GP

(02)
A 17th-century château set in 21,000m² of grounds with an aviary, orchard, ornamental lake, guest cottage and woods. The property features 12 bedrooms and an enormous dining room.
274,408 euros   **DEE**
(£171,505) S

(62)
A large house in a peaceful village location. Set in 1,700m² of land, the property is fronted by a lawn and features four bedrooms, a dining room and study, but is in need of complete renovation.
209,615 euros   **RAV**
(£131,010) GP

(62)
This extensive villa stands in land of 2,200m² and offers six large bedrooms. The property features a vast living room, cellar and garage, and is a short distance from a seaside town and golf club.
721,850 euros   **RAV**
(£451,155) GP

(62)
Standing in 2,000m² of gardens, this recently renovated house offers five bedrooms, a living room and mezzanine. The property features a garage and self-contained two-bedroom guest house.
335,000 euros   **RAV**
(£209,375) GP

(62)
Comprising five bedrooms, two bathrooms, a cellar and double garage, this two-storey villa is set in a colourful garden. With light, spacious rooms, the house is located deep in the countryside.
335,000 euros   **RAV**
(£209,375) GP

(62)
This large six-bedroom villa benefits from spectacular views of the sea. Featuring two bathrooms and a cellar, the property offers a small garden and garage, and is located in a quiet neighbourhood.
320,250 euros   **RAV**
(£200,155) GP

ILE-DE-FRANCE

Price Guide

(78)
This vast 18th-century château enjoys views over the Seine Valley. The property has a total of 19 bedrooms and seven bathrooms and features a courtyard. It is set in 50,000m² of mixed parkland.
1,830,000 euros   **SIF**
(£1,143,750) S

(77)
Surrounded by forest and set in 730m² of garden a short drive from Paris. This 18th-century stone-built house comes with five bedrooms, an office, two bathrooms and open fireplaces.
350,632 euros   **FPL**
(£219,145) GP

(95)
Located in the Parisian suburb of Enghien-les-Bains, a small split-level studio flat in a recently renovated building. Offering one large mezzanine bedroom and just a short walk from the city centre.
70,000 euros   **FPL**
(£43,750) GP

(75)
This historic mansion is located in quiet countryside a short distance from the centre of Paris. The property offers 220m² of living space and is set in 1,600m² of parkland with mature trees.
678,272 euros   **PPC**
(£423,920) GP

(75)
Located on a quiet avenue in Saint-Germain close to galleries and shops, this studio apartment is situated on the fourth floor of an impressive building. Offers a total of 29m² of living space.
240,000 euros   **PPC**
(£150,000) GP

(75)
Enjoying light-filled rooms and benefiting from a quiet residential location, a studio set on the sixth floor of an apartment building. The property features two bedrooms, kitchen and living room.
59,800 euros   **ITT**
(£37,375) GP

(75)
In a quiet, well-lit street, this studio apartment offers 21.5m² of living space. Set in a residential area close to amenities, it features a living room, kitchenette, cellar, one bedroom and a large balcony.
103,093 euros   **ITT**
(£64,435) GP

(75)
On the top floor of an apartment building with a balcony enjoying city views. This property offers four bedrooms, two shower rooms and a bathroom. Complete with a parking space and wine store.
942,984 euros   **ITT**
(£589,365) GP

(75)
Set in a quiet residential neighbourhood a short walk from Volontaires métro station. This house has 11 main rooms with 290m² of living space and is currently arranged as four flats.
1,185,000 euros   **ITT**
(£740,625) GP

FONCIA

27 Bd. Montparnasse 75006 Paris
Tel: **00 33 1 49 54 77 78**
Fax: **00 33 1 45 44 83 69**

Between the Musée d'Orsay and the Boulevard Saint Germain, in a 19th century building, a spacious 295m² appartment, consisting of a vast lobby, 3 reception rooms, dining room, 3 bedrooms, study, kitchen, maid's room and 3 cellars. Good view point and south facing.
High ceilings, beautiful rooms, wooden floors and fireplaces. Ideal for professionals.

Exclusively sold by Foncia

Price : 2,451,750€

Email: foncia-montparnasse@wanadoo.fr

Agence CHAUMETTE
TRANSACTION & MANAGEMENT SERVICES

Elysabeth Bergeon-Chaumette
Specialising in Prime Property Since 1948

TRADITIONAL HOUSES
PROPERTIES
VILLAS
FNAIM   LAND
LETTING
MANAGEMENT

39 grande rue, 77630 BARBIZON

Tel: **00 33 1 60 66 40 24**
Fax: **00 33 1 60 66 21 17**

Closed Wednesday
Email: www.agence-chaumette@wanadoo.fr

www.paris-property.com

We are a french real estate company based in Paris and Nice, we market a very wide range of properties in central Paris and on the Riviera most exclusive locations.

You are looking for a home or to invest in properties...
Visit our websites !

www.french-real-estate.com | www.french-investments.com

105, boulevard Haussmann - 75008 Nice
Tel +33 (0) 142.660.088 - Fax +33 (0) 142.651.444

Price Guide

(77)
Located in the heart of a small village, this grand château has 450m² of living space. Featuring six bedrooms, several galleries and vast reception rooms, the property is set in 12,000m² of parkland.
1,365,000 euros   **PPC**
(£853,125) GP

(75)
Close to the 16th *arrondissement*, a spacious two-bedroom apartment with large reception rooms and two bathrooms. Retains many original features including mouldings and monumental fireplaces.
913,170 euros   **PPC**
(£570,730) GP

(95)
Dating from the 19th century this imposing castle has been renovated to a very high standard. Standing in 400,000m² of grounds including a private airfield, vineyard, golf range and fitness centre.
10,500,000 euros   **PPC**
(£6,562,500) GP

(75)
On the fourth floor of a modern building, a spacious, light-filled apartment with seven rooms. The property offers 263m² of living space and features four bedrooms, dining room and two wine stores.
1,406,650 euros   **ITT**
(£879,155) GP

(95)
Located near Auvers-sur-Oise, this character house is draped in vines and surrounded by parkland gardens. The property features a swimming pool, putting green and several spacious bedroom suites.
2,100,000 euros   **PPC**
(£1,312,500) GP

(75)
Close to Victor Hugo métro station, a second-floor apartment featuring a spacious double living room, dining room, four bedrooms and a fireplace. Just a short walk from shops and amenities.
1,269,000 euros   **ITT**
(£793,125) GP

(75)
A studio apartment situated on the fifth floor of an impressive building. With many original details, the property offers a large living room overlooking a courtyard, two bedrooms and a kitchen.
118,600 euros   **ITT**
(£74,125) GP

(77)
Close to Parc Monceau in the 8th *arrondissement*, a spacious three-bedroom apartment on the fourth floor of a large freestone building set around a courtyard. Features wooden floors and open fires.
964,000 euros   **PCC**
(£602,500) GP

(75)
On the second floor of a secure building, a spacious apartment with a light, open-plan living area. Set close to Porte de Versailles métro station, the property offers two bedrooms and a large kitchen.
121,802 euros   **ITT**
(£76,125) GP

Ile-de-France

(75)
Overlooking a small garden, an apartment with a living room, fitted kitchen and bathroom. Set in a quiet residential area, this spacious light-filled studio features a balcony and wine store.
134,021 euros ITT
(£83,765) GP

(75)
This large two-bedroom apartment is located a short distance from all amenities. The property features a mezzanine, spacious open-plan living room, fully-fitted kitchen and two wine stores.
154,000 euros ITT
(£96,250) GP

(77)
Dating from the 18th-century, a farmhouse with a separate guest cottage. Standing in a garden of 1,160m² offering a *boules* pitch, two ornamental fountains, a paved courtyard and conservatory.
290,000 euros HOM
(£181,250) GP

(75)
In a mansion set on a quiet private street, this two-bedroom apartment offers a self-contained studio flat, a study and a balcony. Features marble floors, wood panelling and a garden with a terrace.
1,900,000 euros DEE
(£1,187,500) GP

(75)
On the third floor of a stylish building, a large, one-bedroom apartment with a living room, kitchen and bathroom. Featuring wooden floors and high ceilings, the property is set in a quiet area.
157,000 euros ITT
(£98,125) GP

(75)
Close to a métro station, this studio apartment is on the sixth floor of a building with a lift and caretaker. Dating from the 18th century, the apartment enjoys southeasterly views across the city.
176,800 euros ITT
(£110,500) GP

(75)
On the third floor of a modern building, this apartment features large windows and light-filled rooms. Near a métro station, the flat offers a fitted kitchen, bedroom, bathroom and wine store.
188,600 euros ITT
(£117,875) GP

(75)
A two-bedroom apartment on the fifth floor of a typical Parisian building in a quiet district close to a métro station and shops. The property features a fitted kitchen and light-filled living room.
157,200 euros ITT
(£98,250) GP

(75)
On the ground floor overlooking a courtyard and garden with trees, this spacious one-bedroom apartment offers a big living room, cellar and fully-fitted kitchen. Set in a peaceful part of the city.
188,600 euros ITT
(£117,875) GP

Price Guide

(75)
A two-bedroom apartment in a newly-constructed building. Features a fitted kitchen, living room with wood flooring, dining room and dressing room. On a quiet street overlooking a park.
204,313 euros   <u>ITT</u>
(£127,695) GP

(75)
Close to Balard métro station, a studio apartment on the seventh floor of a building with a lift. Features two rooms with wood floors and a wine store. Set on a tree-lined avenue close to shops.
189,700 euros   <u>ITT</u>
(£118,565) GP

(75)
On the top floor of a modern stone-built building located on a quiet street near a métro station. This light, spacious apartment offers two bedrooms, wood flooring, a wine store and a balcony.
226,805 euros   <u>ITT</u>
(£141,755) GP

(75)
On the ground floor of a well-managed building with gardens and a caretaker. This apartment has two bedrooms, dressing room, kitchen and living room, and features wood flooring throughout.
229,000 euros   <u>ITT</u>
(£143,125) GP

(94)
A three-bedroom cottage located in a quiet residential area of Vincennes. Overlooking a tree-filled garden, the property is a short distance from shops and has recently been entirely renovated.
160,072 euros   <u>ARM</u>
(£100,045) GP

(75)
A modern home with three large bedrooms. Set in a quiet district close to shops, this house enjoys spacious light-filled rooms and a secluded and private garden planted with mature trees and shrubs.
480,214 euros   <u>ARM</u>
(£300,135) GP

(78)
Located near a small town on the River Seine, this traditional house comes with a caretaker's flat. A particular feature is the large garden, which offers external lighting and a circular swimming pool.
1,101,900 euros   <u>CUR</u>
(£688,690) GP

(75)
Close to a métro station, this second-floor apartment offers four principal rooms and features wooden floors, a large ornamental fireplace and bay windows. The property is in need of some work.
550,000 euros   <u>AIB</u>
(£343,750) GP

(78)
A large 19th-century château set close to the Rambouillet Forest and a golf course. This impressive property stands in 50,000m² of landscaped garden with mature trees, a stream and outbuildings.
1,219,592 euros   <u>DEE</u>
(£762,245) GP

CHAMPAGNE-ARDENNE

Price Guide

(52)
Recently renovated, this 18th-century château, now a hotel, boasts 28 bedrooms, 32 bathrooms and a pavilion. Set in parkland of 20,000m² with a trout stream bordering a golf course.
1,000,000 euros   **SIF**
(£625,000) S

(10)
Situated three hours from Calais, this large house comprises four bedrooms, two bathrooms, two lounges and a snooker room. Set in a village, the property features a second independent guest cottage.
259,163 euros   **FPL**
(£161,977) GP

(08)
This listed 16th-century château with vast outbuildings sits in 30,000m² of landscaped grounds. Looks out across a meadow and boasts two towers. Approached via an avenue flanked by old trees.
1,260,000 euros   **DEE**
(£787,500) GP

(52)
An old house for renovation. In a quiet country setting, the building is split over two floors and features a large attic suitable for conversion. Set in a garden with an orchard, barn and terrace.
5,600 euros   **VOL**
(£3,500) GP

(52)
A three-bedroom, stone-built house in need of total renovation. Comprises a living room with a log-burning fire and dining room looking out on to the street. In a village setting with a back yard.
25,100 euros   **VOL**
(£15,690) GP

(10)
In a pleasant village, a house for renovation with adjoining stable and cowshed. Set beside a picturesque stream, the house features three main rooms and a cellar. Ready to move in to.
40,000 euros   **ADL**
(£25,000) GP

(52)
In the area of Chalindrey, a house comprising a hall, living room, kitchen, bathroom, WC and one bedroom. Split over two levels and facing the road. Features a small front yard and rear garden.
88,000 euros   **VOL**
(£55,000) GP

(52)
A traditional country home with three bedrooms. Standing in land of 630m², which is to the side and rear of the property. Set in a quiet village. Features include a cellar, patio and an adjoining garage.
74,000 euros   **VOL**
(£46,250) GP

(52)
In Auberive, a house comprising a shower room, lounge, kitchen and two bedrooms. Boasts a large enclosed garden with outbuildings and stables. Features log fires, a cellar and attached double garage.
89,900 euros   **VOL**
(£56,190) GP

Champagne-Ardenne

(10)
A cottage in need of restoration. Set in an isolated spot in wooded countryside. Comprising three main rooms, the home has a stable, attic suitable for conversion, a barn and a small garden.
52,000 euros **MDF**
(£32,500) GP

(10)
In the heart of a grape-growing village, close to Bar-sur-Seine. A traditional stone-built house with a kitchen, sitting room and two bedrooms. Set in a garden, with a courtyard, garage and small cellar.
54,000 euros **MDF**
(£33,750) GP

(52)
Close to Prauthoy, a detached house with a kitchen, living room and two bedrooms. Standing in a garden backing on to a meadow of 2,238m². With oil fired central heating and set in a small village.
57,800 euros **VOL**
(£36,125) GP

(10)
A traditional house with five principal rooms including three bedrooms. Set in 973m² of gardens to the front and rear of the building. Featuring open beams, large fireplaces and a huge cellar.
96,000 euros **MDF**
(£60,000) GP

(10)
Close to a market town, this small residence boasts an idyllic setting, surrounded by greenery. The house comprises a fitted kitchen opening on to a living room with fireplace and one huge bedroom.
64,000 euros **MDF**
(£40,000) GP

(52)
Three hours from Paris and close to a large lake, a detached house with half-timbering. Boasting a kitchen with an alcove, dining room, bedroom, pantry and cellar. Situated in a garden of 1,790m².
65,600 euros **ADL**
(£41,000) S

(10)
Set in an enclosed garden of over 907m² complete with a wooden veranda, a two-bedroom home featuring a living room, hallway, kitchen and bathroom. Situated just south of Nogent-sur-Seine.
100,000 euros **MDF**
(£62,500) GP

(52)
A house in Auberive with a hall, living room, kitchen and two large bedrooms. Comes with a small bakehouse, large wine cellar and garden. The property features an open fireplace and stucco ceiling.
41,300 euros **MDF**
(£25,815) GP

(52)
A house in Langres looking out across a fishing lake. Boasts two bedrooms and is privately situated. Features a kitchen, living room, summer-kitchen and an annexe. Garden stocked with trees.
114,300 euros **MDF**
(£71,440) GP

Price Guide

(10)
In the heart of Troyes, this vast castle stands in 40,000m² of land surrounded by forest and boasts its own chapel. Retaining many original architectural details, including marble fireplaces and stairs.
2,744,086 euros MER
(£1,715,055) GP

(52)
Fronted by an extensive lawn and approached along a sweeping driveway flanked by mature trees, this huge castle boasts 45 rooms and sits in 20,000m² of wooded grounds with several outbuildings.
2,126,667 euros MER
(£1,329,170) GP

(52)
Just outside Langres, a large period house with original features. Detached and privately situated in a pleasant garden. Comprises a lounge, kitchen, cellars, bathroom and six bedrooms over two floors.
137,200 euros VOL
(£85,750) GP

(10)
On the banks of Lake Amance, a detached house with a swimming pool. Enjoying country views and a secluded situation, the residence features four bedrooms, kitchen, living room, bar and shower room.
190,600 euros ADL
(£119,125) GP

(10)
A rural residence in the heart of the Aube Valley. Comprises a kitchen, lounge, bathroom and four upstairs bedrooms. Features many outbuildings, stables and an artist's workshop. Set in a garden.
180,000 euros MDF
(£112,500) GP

(10)
In a district scattered with lakes and woodland, a house that comprises a living room, kitchen, dining room, five bedrooms and a bathroom. Also boasts a garden and swimming pool.
160,071 euros MDF
(£99,645) GP

(10)
Dating from the 19th century and set beside a river, a large manor house and two-storey hunting lodge. In a secluded situation, the property boasts a courtyard, patio area and 3,000m² of wooded land.
266,800 euros MDF
(£166,750) GP

(10)
This stone-built house is set just off a main road and benefits from an enclosed garden of 1,168m². In a typical village setting, the house features a reception room, four bedrooms, a lounge and study.
192,200 euros ADL
(£120,125) GP

(52)
This 18th-century château stands in nearly 40,000m² of land. In a rural environment, it features six bedrooms, a guest cottage and a vast reception room. Fronted by a courtyard and close to Langres.
600,000 euros MDF
(£375,000) GP

Price Guide

(51)
In Courtisols, a modern house with three bedrooms. Situated in a residential area close to a small village. Features an office and garage. In an enclosed garden of 230m², with trees and lawn.
116,122 euros   **ALI**
(£72,575) GP

(51)
This semi-detached house stands in a small garden planted with trees and shrubs. Features a large basement, kitchen, living room and four bedrooms. In a secluded situation on a peaceful street.
117,386 euros   **ALI**
(£73,365) GP

(51)
Detached and cosy, a residence split over two floors and boasting four light-filled bedrooms. In a residential area, close to a village with all amenities. The house has a terrace and attached garage.
134,155 euros   **ALI**
(£83,845) GP

(51)
A detached residence fronted by a lawn and accessed via a private drive. Set in a secluded spot, the home stands in a garden backing on to a vineyard. Comprises five rooms, terrace and large garage.
121,959 euros   **ALI**
(£76,224) GP

(51)
Close to a school and shops, a small bungalow in need of some work. Situated in the heart of a market town, the property boasts a terrace with views, a small garden and several large bedrooms.
121,197 euros   **ALI**
(£75,750) GP

(51)
In a quiet village setting, this large semi-detached home is in need of total renovation. Comprises a fitted kitchen, three good-sized bedrooms, an office and massive basement under the whole house.
121,959 euros   **ALI**
(£76,225) GP

(51)
Just outside a market town and on the edge of a pretty village, this four-bedroom bungalow sits in a good-sized garden with trees and shrubs. Benefits from being in a quiet and private situation.
129,582 euros   **ALI**
(£80,989) GP

(51)
Located in a quiet neighbourhood and close to shops, this family home offers three bedrooms and a terrace with open views. Boasts a garden to the rear and comes complete with a garage.
128,057 euros   **ALI**
(£80,035) GP

(51)
A three-bedroom residence set in the heart of a village. Featuring a terrace looking out on to a garden to the rear, and offering a garage. Boasts a vast living room, fitted kitchen and dining room.
129,582 euros   **ALI**
(£80,989)GP

Champagne-Ardenne

(51)
Detached and built from stone, a house with traditional shutters. Situated along a quiet country lane, it boasts four bedrooms and a fitted kitchen. Features wooden floors and a small rear garden.
134,155 euros   **ALI**
(£83,845) GP

(51)
Twenty minutes from a market town, a large country house with 10 main rooms and a mezzanine. Set just off a quiet rural road, the property stands in a secluded, well-stocked garden near a quiet village.
320,143 euros   **ALI**
(£200,090) GP

(51)
In a quiet district, a small house fronted by a private, enclosed garden laid to lawn. Split over two floors and offering 220m² of living space. Boasts a terrace with superb views and a huge basement.
301,849 euros   **ALI**
(£188,655) GP

(51)
A large detached house set in a residential area. On the edge of a village, the property stands in a small garden. Benefits from light-filled rooms, a mezzanine and a balcony with stunning views.
268,310 euros   **ALI**
(£167,695) GP

(51)
An old terraced house with nine rooms. Situated in a quiet, well-lit street with easy access to nearby shops and amenities. Vast open views, flower boxes and many original architectural features.
289,653 euros   **ALI**
(£181,035) GP

(51)
A detached house with a garden of 1,700m². Includes three large bedrooms, playroom, kitchen and a terrace looking out to the rear garden. Situated in a residential area close to a picturesque village.
243,918 euros   **ALI**
(£152,450) GP

(51)
In a village setting, this L-shaped house with four bedrooms. Set in a garden laid to lawn, with trees and far-reaching views. Boasts a terrace, extensive basement and dining room with rustic flooring.
201,995 euros   **ALI**
(£126,245) GP

(51)
A five-bedroom house with large bay windows and spacious, airy rooms. Set in the heart of a quiet village in an enclosed tree-filled garden. Features a living room, terrace and two family bathrooms.
210,280 euros   **ALI**
(£131,425) GP

(51)
In a quiet district, five minutes from the centre of a town, this semi-detached house boasts three bedrooms, a fitted kitchen and a garage. Set in a private garden, laid to lawn and filled with trees.
213,429 euros   **ALI**
(£133,395) GP

Price Guide

(51)
A charming bungalow with three rooms. The property features a large basement, attic suitable for conversion and a garage. Set in an extensive, private and secluded garden, with patio and large lawn.
193,610 euros   **ALI**
(£121,005) GP

(51)
Situated in a quiet district, this contemporary house comprises three bedrooms, a fitted kitchen, office, bathroom and living room. Slightly raised, the property offers good views and sits in a garden.
190,561 euros   **ALI**
(£119,100) GP

(51)
This detached house stands in a large garden of 726m^2 bursting with trees and shrubs. Located on the outskirts of Saint-Memmie, it offers eight principal rooms, a large terrace and double garage.
187,512 euros   **ALI**
(£117,195) GP

(51)
Situated in a market town, a character house designed by a contemporary architect. Includes four bedrooms, a terrace, fitted kitchen and dining room. There is also a basement for conversion.
170,743 euros   **ALI**
(£106,715) GP

(51)
A semi-detached house with four bedrooms and a garage. Features a fitted kitchen and a terrace with open views. Set in an enclosed garden in a peaceful residential area close to a busy market town.
163,120 euros   **ALI**
(£101,950) GP

(51)
In Fagnières, a bungalow with a huge basement and large garage. Detached and cosy, the property is centrally heated and is fronted by an attractive lawned garden. Located on the edge of a village.
155,498 euros   **ALI**
(£97,185) GP

(52)
For conversion, an old stable with an attic. Situated on the outskirts of a quiet village, this stone-built building boasts an idyllic and rural setting. Surrounded by greenery, woodland and hilly landscape.
7,500 euros   **VOL**
(£4,690) GP

(52)
A brick-built house in need of total renovation. Just one room deep, the dwelling is set over two storeys. Features low ceilings and open fireplaces. In a large garden with a barn. Rustic and isolated.
5,600 euros   **VOL**
(£3,500) GP

(51)
Set in a fenced garden of 500m^2, this L-shaped home features a fitted kitchen, three bedrooms, a living room, family bathroom and separate WC. Situated in a quiet neighbourhood with all amenities.
150,162 euros   **ALI**
(£93,850) GP

Champagne-Ardenne

(51)
With five principal rooms, a large house and garage. The façade of the property boasts traditional shutters and a porch. Surrounded by an enclosed garden, with an outbuilding and extensive cellar.
137,204 euros   **ALI**
(£85,755) GP

(51)
Just on the outskirts of a pretty village, a four-bedroom house with a fully-fitted kitchen and large terrace. Semi-detached, the building stands in a garden laid to lawn and planted with shrubs.
135,680 euros   **ALI**
(£84,800) GP

(51)
Attractively restored 18th-century farmhouse of stucco construction. Set in the quiet residential village of Clesles, the property features original exposed beams throughout and comes with 1,800m^2 of land.
230,000 euros   **FPL**
(£143,750) GP

(52)
This stone-built house is arranged over two floors and set in a small courtyard garden. Offers three bedrooms, summer-kitchen, fitted kitchen, dining room, living room and cellar. In a village setting.
144,826 euros   **VOL**
(£90,515) GP

(52)
Completely renovated, a detached house with three bedrooms. Set in a rural environment, the house enjoys panoramic views over the surrounding countryside. Features a dining room, kitchen and attic.
86,500 euros   **VOL**
(£54,065) GP

(52)
A semi-detached house in need of complete renovation. On the ground floor is a kitchen, a large room and bathroom. Upstairs is one bedroom. Includes a barn and stables, set in a small courtyard.
19,750 euros   **VOL**
(£12,345) GP

(10)
An old farmhouse for renovation near Chavanges. The property has a kitchen, five further rooms and an attic suitable for conversion. It also features a courtyard, cellars, and comes with 9,329m^2 of land.
33,500 euros   **ADL**
(£21,940) GP

(10)
A traditional small country house for renovation. Three rooms plus an attic and adjoining barn. The property also comes with a separate two-room building, stables and 1,660m^2 of land.
25,000 euros   **ADL**
(£15,625) GP

(10)
Near the village of Piney, this half-timbered, three-bedroom house retains many original features including open fireplaces, a terrace and cellar. Garden of 615m^2 and a traditional courtyard.
68,700 euros   **ADL**
(£42,940)

ALSACE, LORRAINE & FRANCHE-COMTE

Price Guide

(90)
In a quiet village, a fully renovated, half-timbered residence. Features an indoor swimming pool, five bedrooms, a gymnasium and 5,000m² of land featuring an aviary and summer house.
400,000 euros   MOR
(£250,000) GP

(67)
A newly-built residence located 20km west of Strasbourg. Set in 2,500m² of landscaped gardens, it benefits from dominant views across the wooded surroundings. Offers four bedrooms and garage.
602,173 euros   DEE
(£376,360) GP

(90)
This rustic house is fronted by a colourful flower garden and offers six rooms. Features four spacious bedrooms, a tiled drawing room and farmhouse-style kitchen. In a garden of 6,370m² with a garage.
259,500 euros   MOR
(£162,190) GP

(70)
An 18th-century château set in 24,000m² of parkland with assorted stone-built outbuildings. The guest wing offers nine bedroom suites and four reception rooms lie off the grand entrance hall.
650,000 euros   BPS
(£406,250) GP

(90)
An L-shaped house with eight rooms, including three bedrooms, a living room and drawing room. Enjoys south-facing views, some stained-glass windows, a garage for seven cars and a small garden.
289,500 euros   MOR
(£180,940) GP

(88)
This privately situated chalet is located deep in the country and surrounded by farmland and hills. Comprises a kitchen, dining room, bathroom and three large bedrooms split over two floors.
114,336 euros   PYI
(£71,460) GP

(90)
This modern house stands in land of 9,900m² surrounded by forest. Features spacious, light rooms and a large terrace. Comprises a living room, fully-fitted kitchen and four bedrooms split over two floors.
192,000 euros   MOR
(£120,000) GP

(90)
West-facing, a stone-built house with a double living room, four bedrooms, oak parquet floors and a large terrace. On the edge of a quiet village with all amenities. Detached, with a small garden.
212,000 euros   MOR
(£132,500) GP

(90)
This spacious four-bedroom villa stands in 1,900m² of rural land. Comprises a rustic living room, veranda, large kitchen and cellar. Comes with a separate basement flat offering two large rooms.
259,000 euros   MOR
(£161,875) GP

Alsace, Lorraine & Franche-Comté

(90)
Near Belfort, a house with south-facing balcony and a great view. Comprises three bedrooms, a large living room with fireplace and a rustic kitchen. With parquet floors and panelled ceilings.
210,000 euros   **MOR**
(£131,250) GP

(90)
A raised single-storey building with five rooms. Offers a marble entrance hall, double living room, three bedrooms and one-bedroom basement flat. In a quiet country setting with a tree-filled garden.
206,500 euros   **MOR**
(£129,065) GP

(90)
A renovated farmhouse featuring exposed beamed ceilings and a wooden staircase. Comprises four bedrooms, a large rustic-style kitchen and adjoining barn. Set in 2,650m² of fenced rural land.
201,500 euros   **MOR**
(£125,940) GP

(25)
An 18th-century farmhouse with views of a medieval château. In a rural setting and standing in 1,400m² of garden laid to lawn. Offers three bedrooms, a living room, study and fitted kitchen.
150,000 euros   **BPS**
(£93,750) S

(39)
Situated in Arbois, a characterful house standing in 10,300m² of woodland garden. Benefiting from a heated swimming pool and tennis court, the property features a fitted kitchen and four bedrooms.
455,000 euros   **MAO**
(£284,375) GP

(39)
Set on the outskirts of a pretty village, this stone-built home dates from the 18th century. Near Dole, the property comes with a second attached house and stands in 1,500m² of woodland.
187,512 euros   **MAO**
(£117,195) GP

(90)
On the outskirts of a residential area, this spacious six-bedroom house stands in a small private garden. Features mosaic parquet floors, tiled walls and a balcony, boasting south-facing, rural views.
185,000 euros   **MOR**
(£115,625) GP

(25)
In a town near Besançon, a massive private mansion. With 1,243m² of habitable space, the property has 39 rooms and enjoys a peaceful location, looking out over countryside surroundings.
907,073 euros   **MER**
(£566,920) GP

(90)
This renovated farmhouse stands in a picturesque village and boasts several outbuildings. Comprises a living room, drawing room, five bedrooms and a large veranda. Set in land of 7,384m² with views.
194,500 euros   **MOR**
(£121,565) GP

Price Guide

(90)
This rustic villa stands in a large, enclosed garden. Located in a quiet country area, it features five bedrooms, a fully equipped kitchen and a terrace with south-facing views. In a village setting.
177,000 euros   **MOR**
(£110,625) GP

(39)
An old semi-detached farmhouse dating from the 1830s. Close to Orgelet, the building is in need of total renovation and currently offers four rooms. Outside there is a flagstoned barn and stable block.
35,100 euros   **MDF**
(£21,940) GP

(90)
Built in 1982, this five-bedroom house with a south-facing terrace. Located in 1,050m² of quiet country gardens in a secluded spot. Features two bedrooms and an L-shaped living room.
169,500 euros   **MOR**
(£105,940) GP

(39)
In a village setting close to Lake Vouglans, a large detached house in need of a little work. Set in a pretty garden with a stable and barn, the property has been split into three separate apartments.
106,000 euros   **MDF**
(£66,250) GP

(90)
Close to Giromagny, a restored stone-built house with exposed beams, garage and 3,360m² of land. Comprises four bedrooms, a drawing room, kitchen and dining room. With brick-tiled floors.
145,500 euros   **MOR**
(£90,940) GP

(39)
South facing, a detached wooden chalet. Enjoys stunning views over Lake Vouglans and 765m² of woodland garden. In a tranquil and secluded setting, with three bedrooms and fitted kitchen.
116,000 euros   **MDF**
(£72,500) GP

(90)
This two-bedroom house is located close to Belfort. Offers parquet floors, an oak kitchen, living room, open terrace, two garages and a tiled bathroom. Set in a very peaceful neighbourhood.
130,000 euros   **MOR**
(£81,250) GP

(90)
Facing west, this semi-detached home features a paved terrace, six rooms and a fenced garden. Set on the edge of a village, it comprises four bedrooms, a living room and a fitted kitchen.
136,000 euros   **MOR**
(£85,000) GP

(90)
In need of some renovation, a stone-built house. Situated in the centre of a village, it offers four bedrooms, a kitchen, living room and scullery. Features a wooden staircase, open beams and a cellar.
65,000 euros   **MOR**
(£40,625) GP

Alsace, Lorraine & Franche-Comté

(39)
Near a small town, a renovated semi-detached farmhouse. In a private situation within grounds of 6,500m², the property offers a kitchen, two bedrooms, bathroom, living room and outbuildings.
120,000 euros   **MDF**
(£75,000) GP

(39)
A former square tower, this small property has been converted into a five-room home. Set in a garden of 2,800m² with stunning rural views. Close to the town of Saint-Laurent-la-Roche and shops.
121,195 euros   **MDF**
(£75,750) GP

(39)
This detached house boasts all modern conveniences and comes with four spacious bedrooms. Set in a secluded spot, with land of 8,250m² filled with trees and shrubs. Close to a market town.
190,561 euros   **MDF**
(£119,100) GP

(39)
Just south of Arbois, a renovated farmhouse featuring 5,170m² of agricultural land. Boasting 200m² of living space and set in a quiet location, with an adjoining studio apartment and several garages.
211,904 euros   **MAO**
(£132,440) GP

(39)
In the heart of a village lies this 18th-century home with many original features. Set around a courtyard and surrounded by trees, the property benefits from a quiet situation. Several outbuildings.
349,108 euros   **MAO**
(£218,195) GP

(39)
Surrounded by hilly countryside, a large semi-detached property with five rooms. The property also has two self-contained holiday apartments. It is centrally heated and stands in a courtyard garden.
221,000 euros   **MDF**
(£138,125) GP

(25)
In the centre of Arc-et-Senans in a quiet residential area, this bungalow has a colourful garden planted with trees and flowers. Comprises three bedrooms, kitchen, dining room and garage.
105,189 euros   **MAO**
(£65,745) GP

(90)
On the outskirts of Belfort, this renovated mansion has 260m² of living space and is set in land of 9,200m² with a car park and garage. Features a large paved veranda and moulded ceilings.
267,500 euros   **MOR**
(£167,190) GP

(39)
This contemporary villa with a large heated swimming pool. Situated in a landscaped garden of 2,500m² with trees and shrubs, the property includes three vast bedrooms, wine cellar and garage.
327,765 euros   **MAO**
(£204,855) GP

Price Guide

(39)
Surrounded by land of almost 7,960m², this grand house is in need of some work. Comprises 12 principal rooms and a separate apartment. Entered via a private driveway lined with mature trees.
**365,900 euros   MAO
(£228,690) GP**

(25)
In the area of Arc-et-Senans, a detached house in a quiet and secluded situation. At the rear of the home is a terrace looking out on to a small garden. Comprises three bedrooms, cellar and garage.
**211,196 euros   MAO
(£132,000) GP**

(68)
A 1930s house that has been modernised throughout. This property has ample parking on a large forecourt, pretty, well-maintained gardens of 700m² and an airy interior with exposed beams.
**221,051 euros   SIG
(£138,160) GP**

(39)
Dating from the 18th century, an old farmhouse in need of some work. Comprises a main house with a cellar, several outbuildings suitable for conversion and a large studio apartment for renovation.
**150,900 euros   MAO
(£94,315) GP**

(25)
This large detached house stands in a garden of 1,920m² with mature trees, secure parking and a patio area. Features 155m² of living space, three bedrooms, attic for conversion and an outbuilding.
**134,156 euros   MAO
(£83,850) GP**

(68)
Standing in 15,000m² of well-maintained gardens, a renovated country house and barn. The property is set in a peaceful secluded location near a small village and enjoys spacious rooms.
**205,806 euros   SIG
(£128,630) GP**

(39)
Just outside Salins-les-Bains, a stone-built house with 300m² of habitable space. Set in grassland of 19,350m² planted with trees and totally enclosed. Offers five bedrooms and a vast living room.
**326,240 euros   MAO
(£203,900) GP**

(39)
Totally renovated, this large house offers 200m² of living space and modern amenities. Situated in a residential area close to a small town. Nordic interior design, several bedrooms and a garage.
**320,142 euros   SIG
(£200,090) GP**

(39)
On the outskirts of an old town, this house has 150m² of living space. Looks out across a road to fields and countryside. Standing in 1,800m² of land, which is to the side and rear of the property.
**178,365 euros   MAO
(£111,480) GP**

Alsace, Lorraine & Franche-Comté

(39)
Situated on the edge of a village, a house built from stone and dating from the 18th century. Restored and privately located, it offers a living room, dining room, office, mezzanine and four bedrooms.
336,000 euros   **MAO**
(£210,000) GP

(39)
A large house dating from the 1930s set in a bustling village. This centrally heated and well-maintained property is impressively presented with a host of original details throughout.
205,806 euros   **SIG**
(£128,630) GP

(39)
Close to Bletterans, a bungalow comprising a vast basement, cellar and living room overlooking a small garden. Centrally heated and with a garage, the property is set in a peaceful neighbourhood.
154,965 euros   **MAO**
(£96,855) GP

(39)
Enjoying a large enclosed garden, featuring a pond with ornamental fountain, a house split over two floors, boasting a terrace with superb views, barbecue area, large woodstore and a double garage.
152,150 euros   **MAO**
(£95,095) GP

(68)
A typical Alsatian house. Isolated and secluded, the property offers six rooms, including a fully-fitted kitchen. Centrally heated, with a courtyard and outbuildings. Set in 10,000m² of sunny countryside.
368,926 euros   **SIG**
(£230,580) GP

(39)
In a picturesque village setting a short distance from Arbois, this two-storey home overlooks a lake and stands in 30,000m² of land. Comprises a dining room with fireplace, two bedrooms and cellar.
330,750 euros   **MAO**
(£206,720) GP

(39)
Set in a charming village, a house built from stone offering 210m² of habitable space. Secluded and rustic, the property is in need of a little work and looks out on to a country road. In a rural setting.
114,000 euros   **MAO**
(£71,250) GP

(39)
Surrounded by greenery and hilly countryside, this wooden house stands in an enclosed garden of 1,800m². Features a fully-fitted kitchen, living room opening on to a terrace and swimming pool.
190,000 euros   **MAO**
(£118,750) GP

(39)
Ancient and historic, an ensemble of houses and outbuildings. Set in 4,670m² of land, planted with trees and bordered by a river. The property enjoys an idyllic setting and consists of two small houses.
407,801 euros   **SIG**
(£254,875) GP

Price Guide

(67)
Set in the town of Bischwiller, a large apartment with three rooms. In a secluded spot, surrounded by woodland and greenery. The property has 65m² of living space on one level and a fitted kitchen.
64,790 euros   **KLS**
(£40,495) GP

(68)
A renovated stone house with a large, totally enclosed garden of 2,350m² planted with mature trees. Comprises two bedrooms, two bathrooms, mezzanine, garage and large attic suitable for conversion.
259,163 euros   **MAO**
(£161,980) GP

(67)
A small country villa with five rooms including a cellar. Arranged over two floors with 100m² of living space. Fronted by a small lawned garden, featuring a pond with an ornamental fountain.
152,450 euros   **KLS**
(£95,290) GP

(39)
In the centre of the pretty town of Arbois, this bungalow provides plenty of space and comes with a self-contained studio, separate apartment, garage and several outbuildings. Ready to move in to.
258,600 euros   **MAO**
(£161,625) GP

(67)
In the heart of a busy town, a half-timbered detached house with five main rooms. Close to all amenities and arranged over three floors, it offers a cellar, laundry room and several outbuildings.
190,561 euros   **KLS**
(£119,100) GP

(67)
Situated in the peaceful town of Haguenau, a villa with four rooms. Set in a colourful garden of 1,000m² and offering secure parking and a cellar. Split over two levels and ready to move in to.
140,500 euros   **KLS**
(£87,815) GP

(67)
Just outside Schirrhoffen, a villa with five bedrooms. Enjoying a terrace with panoramic views and 5,000m² of garden with a lawn and mature trees, it features a large cellar and secure car parking.
221,052 euros   **KLS**
(£138,160) GP

(67)
In the heart of Marienthal town, an L-shaped villa boasting 26 principal rooms. Split over two storeys and situated in 4,000m² of gardens featuring a courtyard and planted with flowering shrubs.
853,716 euros   **KLS**
(£533,575) GP

(67)
Set just back from a country road, this four-room villa is in need of a little work. Privately situated in a residential area and close to a village. It is surrounded by 840m² of enclosed garden laid to lawn.
192,850 euros   **KLS**
(£120,530) GP

Alsace, Lorraine & Franche-Comté

(70)
Near the town of Lure, a detached house on one level. Standing in 12,000m² of enclosed land, the house enjoys a secluded spot in a residential area close to shops and all amenities. Ready to move in to.
118,910 euros   **PYI**
(£74,320) S

(70)
A small house surrounded by 11,000m² of rural land, planted with trees and set deep in the country. Detached and isolated, close to Vauvillers, it enjoys rural views and a secluded situation.
47,259 euros   **PYI**
(£29,535) GP

(70)
Just outside Lure, a renovated farmhouse standing in 32,000m² of land. The first floor comprises a kitchen, dining room, lounge and bathroom, while upstairs are two bedrooms and a large attic.
75,462 euros   **PYI**
(£47,165) GP

(70)
Close to Ronchamp, a tiny house surrounded by greenery and set in 6,000m² of wooded land, looking out over an idyllic lake. Furnished, the home comprises one bedroom, corner-kitchen and shower room.
33,539 euros   **PYI**
(£20,960) GP

(70)
In Saulnot, a renovated farmhouse and several outbuildings suitable for conversion. Entered via the kitchen, the property comprises a dining room with fireplace, two bedrooms, bathroom and an attic.
128,049 euros   **PYI**
(£80,030) GP

(70)
A bungalow and garage a short distance from a market town. Includes a large entrance hall, two bedrooms, dining room, lounge and bathroom. Set in an enclosed garden with a small outbuilding.
115,099 euros   **PYI**
(£71,935) GP

(88)
In the heart of Vosges, this large mill is undergoing renovation. Situated in 14,000m² of land with woodland and outbuildings. Features a large kitchen and three rooms arranged over two floors.
106,098 euros   **PYI**
(£66,310) GP

(70)
Standing alone, an old farmhouse built from stone. Renovated and secluded, the building offers four bedrooms, a mezzanine, bathroom and three outbuildings. Features a garage and ancient bread oven.
231,723 euros   **PYI**
(£144,830) GP

(88)
Surrounded by forest and hilly landscape, a restored farmhouse. Comprises a kitchen, dining room, lounge with fireplace, two bedrooms and mezzanine. Set in 10,000m² of land with stables.
180,671 euros   **PYI**
(£112,920) GP

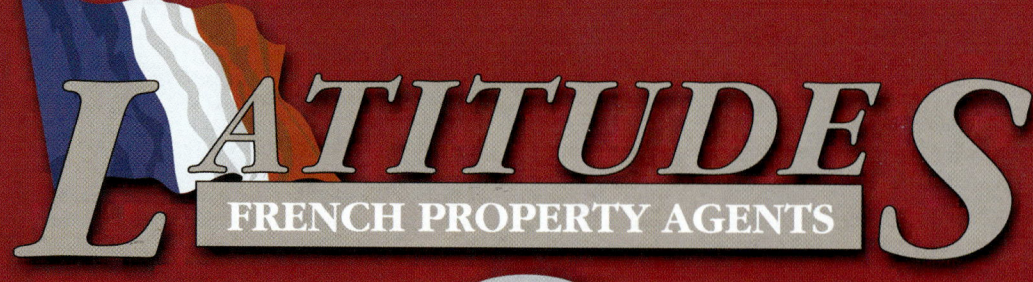

Latitudes
FRENCH PROPERTY AGENTS
2003

Latitudes offers a large selection of all types of property in the following areas:

Pas de Calais (including Le Touquet & Hardelot)	Charente	Lot	Aude
Normandy	Charente Maritime	Lot et Garonne	Herault
Brittany	Correze	Tarn	Gard
Burgundy	Dordogne	Tarn et Garonne	Provence
Deux Sevres	Gironde	Gers	Var
Haute Vienne	Landes	Languedoc Roussillon	Vaucluse
	Pyrenees Atlantiques	Pyrenees Orientales	Cote d'Azur

Website: http://www.latitudes.co.uk

Telephone: 020 8951 5155   Fax: 020 8951 5156   E-mail: sales@latitudes.co.uk
Grosvenor House, 1 High Street, Edgware, Middlesex HA8 7TA

 FOPDAC

THE LOIRE

Price Guide

(37)
Two restored farmhouses situated on the outskirts of the medieval market town of Loches. The first cottage features a lounge, kitchen and three bedrooms. The second has two bedrooms and a kitchen.
335,400 euros   LVL
(£209,625) GP

(85)
On the edge of a rural village and looking out across a large lake, this detached one-bedroom home is ready to move in to. Set among woodland and fields, the property enjoys peaceful surroundings.
89,316 euros   VEF
(£55,825) GP

(85)
With two bedrooms and a large garden, this character house is set on the outskirts of a pretty village. Standing on its own, the home benefits from a secluded spot, but is only a short walk from a village.
180,804 euros   VEF
(£113,005) GP

(37)
Near the village of Loches, a 19th-century house with tower. Set in 5,700m² of garden with a cellar and garage. The property boasts four bedrooms, a library, two lounges and a summer room.
166,440 euros   LVL
(£104,025) GP

(37)
An ancient farm with numerous stone outbuildings. The main house features an open fireplace, two small rooms suitable for bedrooms, rear kitchen/larder, shower room and a comfortable lounge.
176,840 euros   LVL
(£110,525) GP

(85)
This four-bedroom home boasts lots of character and is situated on the edge of a rural village. With a garden featuring a courtyard, the house is approached by a gravel driveway. Set in a quiet spot.
787,360 euros   VEF
(£482,100) GP

(36)
Just a 10-minute drive from Argenton-sur-Creuse, this small *fermette* with 800m² of land needs restoration. Features an attached barn and single garage, plus an attic room ready for conversion.
32,015 euros   LRP
(£20,010) GP

(36)
An old mill house in the beautiful Creuse Valley. Fully restored and set in grounds of 1,000m², the property features four bedrooms, a separate self-contained apartment, cellar and various outbuildings.
272,884 euros   LRP
(£170,555) GP

(36)
Charming restored farmhouse with well-appointed kitchen, large living room with open fireplace and exposed beams, terrace, four bedrooms and barn attached. Extensive gardens of 2,500m².
113,623 euros   LRP
(£71,015) GP

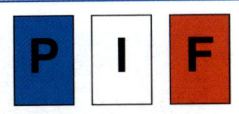

Loire Valley

We are a British owned, French registered Estate Agency. We have been established in this accessible, mild region for 16 years helping clients buy properties directly and in conjunction with Notaires and other French Estate Agents. We are on hand here in France to translate, assist, offer advice, legal or otherwise, mortgages and free restoration estimates with Notaires, Banks and a Maître d'Oeuvre respectively. After purchase we offer surveillance, maintenance and letting services.

Ask for our general brochure today.

SARL PIF

Properties in France

La Croix de Noël, 49390 Mouliherne, France

Our UK Tel No. is 0121 744 0820

Fax: 00 33 2 41 52 02 47

Email: pif@compuserve.com

Website: propertiesinfrance.com

Carte professionelle: 49-349

AGENCE TRANSIMMO

Tel: **00 33 2 41 89 16 94**

Email: **transimmo@aol.com**

Looking for a house in our area, between Angers and Saumur, in the Loire Valley?

Do not hesitate to contact us.

www.edenimmo.com/transimmo

Allez Français

For quality property in the Poitou Charente
Specialising in Mills, Logis & Fermettes

• **French property at French prices** •

Specialist services throughout France
Foreign Currency Exchange, Mortgages
Title insurance and other insurances

Allez Français are a refreshing new style business marketing French property, offering property in the Poitou Charente, specialising in the Deux Sevres department, with a complete range of financial and insurance services to provide a one stop shop.

Allez Français pride themselves in being very selective about the property that they view with clients. We do not offer a range of property that is out of date or unsuitable just because it is within a selected price range. Two out of three viewers with Allez Français make offers for the property that they view in France. Don't waste your time – call us today.

e-mail: allez-francais@wanadoo.fr

Tel: **05 49 27 01 22 from France**

Tel: **0871 717 4176 from the UK**

www.allez-francais.com

LRP Associates

Property finding agent in Central France, dept. 36

Contact details: **Carol Carpenter**

Tel: **00 33 2 54 25 35 60**

Fax: **00 33 2 54 25 35 59**

Ref: 18 **Price: 111,218€**

Large character property in excellent external condition needing a little 'help' & decoration to its interior. Central Heating. Kitchen, dining room, lounge, 6 beds, bathroom, WC, loft, large attached barn, seperate barn, oldblacksmiths shop (in poor condition) & a well. Almost 8,000m^2 land, bordered by river.

www.findingfrance.co.uk

Price Guide

(53)
A stone-built house with a small garden. Offering stunning views and a rural position, the property has an open-plan kitchen with parquet flooring and two spacious bedrooms with exposed beams.
65,000 euros   **LAT**
(£40,625) GP

(37)
Located in Chinon, this country dwelling is beamed throughout with rustic *tomette* tiles. Offers two bedrooms on the first floor and a further two above. Comes with a small house for renovation.
193,000 euros   **LVL**
(£120,625) GP

(37)
Built in 1850, this ancient cottage is in need of some renovation. Set in a quiet hamlet, the property offers three bedrooms with open fireplaces, the cottage also features a woodburning stove and garden.
91,200 euros   **LVL**
(£57,000) GP

(53)
A restored south-facing house, with garages and a garden. Offers three bedrooms, kitchen, dining room with tiled floor and exposed beams. Outbuildings include a converted barn and woodstore.
95,000 euros   **LAT**
(£59,375) GP

(37)
Quiet and tucked away, a restored farmhouse in an enclosed garden of 3,500m². With two staircases, the property comprises three bedrooms, a playroom and an oak kitchen. Close to a pretty stream.
229,000 euros   **LVL**
(£143,125) GP

(37)
Four large farm buildings suitable for conversion. Built around a courtyard, the property is set in 25,000m² of land. One building has been completed and is ready for occupation. Close to Loches.
228,673 euros   **LVL**
(£142,920) GP

(37)
A detached cottage set in a quiet hamlet close to Loches. On the ground floor there are two rooms, along with a cellar, shower room and lounge/diner. On the first floor are three further bedrooms.
124,855 euros   **LVL**
(£78,035) GP

(53)
A south-facing stone building set in a courtyard. Partially habitable, the property currently comprises a kitchen, bathroom living room and bedroom. Features a stable block and outbuildings.
53,500 euros   **LAT**
(£33,440) GP

(53)
A detached south-facing home for conversion. Set in 3,000m² of land with a well. The building is currently divided into a barn and stable area with a large attic. Services have yet to be connected.
53,357 euros   **LAT**
(£33,350) GP

The Loire

(53)
A rustic south-facing home with outbuildings and 7,280m² of land. Comprises a kitchen and two bedrooms with balconies. Features include exposed walls, stables, a pigsty and stone outbuildings.
144,000 euros   **LAT**
(£90,000) GP

(85)
This secluded country residence is located near a market town. Set in immaculate gardens of 8,000m² with views, the property features a billiards room, three bathrooms and secure parking for four cars.
646,236 euros   **MER**
(£403,900) GP

(53)
This detached stone-built house is set in over 1,430m² of gardens. Features tiled floors, traditional window shutters and exposed beams. With two bedrooms and a living room. In a village setting.
136,000 euros   **LAT**
(£85,000) GP

(18)
An old stone-built house with a barn, garage and outbuildings. Set in the heart of a market town. On the ground floor there are two small store rooms and a kitchen. Upstairs features one bedroom.
43,600 euros   **LIN**
(£27,250) GP

(18)
A massive barn for conversion, and a house in need of complete renovation. Situated in a pretty rural spot in a secluded garden with mature trees and vines that grow up the side of the house.
50,308 euros   **LIN**
(£31,445) GP

(53)
Newly built, this character house is set in over 1,000m² of garden, with a garage. Comprising a basement, entrance hall, kitchen, living room and two bedrooms. Features a small wooden veranda.
131,000 euros   **LAT**
(£81,875) GP

(85)
A traditional house dating from 1827 in a conservation area. This four-bedroom property has many original features including a bread oven. 1,600m² of tranquil grounds filled with plants and trees.
140,250 euros   **MAQ**
(£87,655) GP

(49)
Dating from the 19th century, a large house set in a landscaped garden with a swimming pool. Accommodation is spacious and includes four bedrooms. With beamed ceilings throughout.
182.939 euros   **FWY**
(£114,335) GP

(85)
In Vendée, a stone-built property in a quiet area though close to a town. Surrounded by a stone wall, there are two bedrooms, a studio apartment and kitchen. Features a 13th-century stone staircase.
253,000 euros   **LIN**
(£158,125) GP

Price Guide

(53)
A modern detached house with 1,060m² of garden. Set in beautiful countryside, the house has two double bedrooms and room for more. Boasts a sun room, outbuildings and garage.
212,700 euros   LAT
(£132,940) GP

(37)
Boasting a private garden, strewn with fruit trees and entered by electric gates, this house features a cellar under an office, a fitted oak kitchen and two bedrooms. Set on the edge of a busy town.
203,000 euros   LVL
(£126,875) GP

(37)
On the outskirts of Bléré and set in a peaceful hamlet, this house offers five bedrooms, four of which need completion. Exposed beams throughout. Features a dining room with open fireplace.
139,000 euros   LVL
(£86,875) GP

(37)
A large château dating from the 18th century. Sitting on the banks of the River Creuse in parkland with meadows and woodland. The château has 15 bedrooms, four bathrooms, farmhouse and cottage.
1,650,000 euros   SIF
(£1,031,250) GP

(53)
A three-bedroom barn in need of restoration. With spacious rooms, the property boasts a large lake, veranda, cathedral-style ceilings and 20,000m² of orchards. Near to the waterside town of Mayenne.
232,500 euros   BIS
(£145,315) GP

(49)
A small village house that has been recently restored and offers two bedrooms. Around the back of the house is an enclosed garden and garage. There is also a studio apartment in need of renovation.
90,708 euros   FWY
(£56,695) GP

(37)
Dating from the 19th century, a restored house set on the edge of a stream in 20,000m² of land with a lake. Featuring three bedrooms, the house boasts exposed beams, tiled floors and and wood fires.
225,234 euros   WAT
(£140,770) GP

(18)
This old stone cottage comes with a large attached barn and needs a new roof. Set in 2,000m² of garden. The ground floor offers a dining room, lounge and kitchen that leads into a spacious loft.
25,384 euros   LIN
(£15,865) GP

(49)
Close to Angers, a partially restored 16th-century manor house. Set in 16,250m² of land, with a dovecote, well and pigsty. The renovated ground floor has three bedrooms and a kitchen.
652,482 euros   FWY
(£407,800) GP

The Loire

(37)
Looking out over a stream and surrounded by woodland, these old mill buildings are currently being converted into gîtes. Close to an old town and set in grounds, with outbuildings and meadows.
339,290 euros   FWY
(£212,055) GP

(53)
North of Ernée and situated at the end of a small lane, a house with several stone outbuildings set in 1,500m² of land. In need of renovation, the house is partially habitable with services connected.
72,400 euros   FWY
(£45,250) GP

(37)
An older house that has been recently renovated. Set in enclosed woodland of 1,900m², in an area of outstanding natural beauty. Features three bedrooms, veranda and barn decorated with old tiles.
180,000 euros   FPL
(£112,500) GP

(49)
This partially restored farmhouse sits in the centre of 8,000m² of woodland, with a pond, stables, and barn. Features exposed beams, terracotta tiles, open fires and slaked lime mortar throughout.
195,000 euros   FPL
(£121,875) GP

(37)
A water mill and outbuildings, dating from the 17th century. Set beside a lake in 30,000m² of land. Currently features a bake oven room, billiard room, living room, a kitchen and three bedrooms.
411,612 euros   WAT
(£257,260) GP

(53)
A former village forge with a bread oven, recently converted into a two-bedroom house. The property is fronted by a forecourt and equipped to sleep up to six people. Comes with furniture.
55,254 euros   FPL
(£34,535) GP

(53)
In a small village, a semi-detached cottage situated in a cul-de-sac. With a large lounge, a fully-fitted kitchen, three bedrooms and a bathroom. Features a secluded walled garden. Close to Caen.
95,585 euros   FPL
(£59,740) GP

(41)
With exceptional views across the Loire Valley, this character house boasts numerous bedrooms and a large garden. Set a short distance from the village of Chambord. Benefits from quiet surroundings.
385,000 euros   FPL
(£240,625) GP

(37)
This restored water mill is set in 10,000m² of land. The property benefits from a swimming pool and comprises a fitted kitchen, drawing room, three large en-suite bedrooms, a garage and barn.
381,123 euros   WAT
(£238,200) GP

Price Guide

(23)
This listed 16th-century château comes with a large terraced house divided into three properties. The main château comprises a living room, veranda, scullery and three bedrooms with exposed beams.
1,850,000 euros   **SIF**
(£1,156,250) GP

(85)
Close to Luçon, a centrally heated house with five bedrooms. Set in 45,000m² of garden, boasting a garage, courtyard and horse boxes. The main building offers a living room, fitted kitchen and cellar.
236,295 euros   **HIF**
(£147,685) GP

(49)
Dating from the 15th century, an impressive château with a tower. Bordering a river, on the edge of a village. Comprises a caretaker's cottage, stables and outbuildings. Located in a winemaking region.
1,272,500 euros   **CUR**
(£795,315) GP

(72)
A renovated house set in 850m² of wooded land. Features exposed beams, open fireplaces and a bread oven. Comprises three bedrooms, one family bathroom, cellar and a large barn in need of renovation.
140,000 euros   **FPL**
(£87,500) GP

(45)
Dating from the 18th century, a restored farmhouse built from limestone and brick. Boasting oak beams and sloping ceilings. Set in a tiny hamlet of just five houses. Offers two mezzanine bedrooms.
144,100 euros   **CUR**
(£90,065) GP

(85)
With three bedrooms, a 1970s house enclosed by 1,760m² of tree filled garden with plenty of space for parking and a garage. Comprises three bedrooms, living room, shower room and kitchen.
131,106 euros   **HIF**
(£81,940) GP

(44)
A spacious modern house with a good-sized garden. Situated in the medieval town of Guérande. On the ground floor is a kitchen and three bedrooms. Upstairs are three more bedrooms and a bathroom.
176,000 euros   **CUR**
(£110,000) GP

(85)
Totally renovated, this detached house stands in 1,020m² of land. On the ground floor is a kitchen, utility room, living room and a workshop. Upstairs is a bathroom and three spacious bedrooms.
105,190 euros   **HIF**
(£65,745) GP

(85)
Situated in Saint-Jean-de-Monts, a bungalow close to the sea. In an enclosed and shaded garden of 1,400m². Comprises three large bedrooms, a living room, kitchen, bathroom and a double garage.
97,262 euros   **HIF**
(£60,790) GP

The Loire

(72)
A country house situated on the edge of a typical French village. Surrounded by mature parkland of 1,500m², the property comprises a main house, two guest houses and features a stone-built cellar.
476,910 euros   **PPC**
(£298,070) GP

(53)
A renovated house boasting open beams, a spiral staircase, log fires and a jacuzzi. Set in 2,300m² of land with a second property that requires some finishing-off. The house offers two bedrooms.
83,847 euros   **HAM**
(£52,405) GP

(85)
Close to l'Hermenault, an Alpine-style house overlooking a private lake and vineyard. Set in 30,000m² of land, surrounded by countryside and woodland. With three bedrooms and large veranda.
240,869 euros   **HIF**
(£150,545) GP

(85)
A fully-renovated house a short distance from the beach. At the rear of the property is an enclosed garden. Situated in Saint-Jean-de-Monts, with a corner-kitchen, four bedrooms and shower room.
89,335 euros   **HIF**
(£55,835) GP

(28)
Comprising three main houses, split over three floors, this large property is surrounded by mature parkland, boasting orchards, a guest house and spacious barn. Set in a quiet country location.
640,000 euros   **PPC**
(£400,000) GP

(49)
Dating from the 16th century, a priory and small manor house. Set in flower gardens and paddocks of 30,000m². Boasts a spiral staircase, old beams and a pool. Offers four bedrooms and three studio flats.
1,204,347 euros   **VAL**
(£752,720) GP

(37)
Just south of the historic town of Chinon, a restored farmhouse with outbuildings and gardens featuring woodland and paddocks. This unusual character property has an ancient ruined tower.
228,675 euros   **VAL**
(£142,920) GP

(49)
Dating from the 19th century, a château with a wealth of original character. Situated on the side of a valley, with paddocks and wooded land. Boasts a swimming pool, 11 bedrooms and a house to restore.
530,523 euros   **LPS**
(£331,575) GP

(49)
A charming water mill dating from the 18th century. The grounds of the property feature a stream running through woodland as well as a small lake with an island. Features two bedrooms.
202,550 euros   **VAL**
(£126,595) GP

203

Price Guide

(18)
Totally restored, an old farmhouse and garden. Set in a small hamlet in a valley. Tiled throughout, with old beams and stone walls. Offers four bedrooms, a fitted kitchen, terrace and a private driveway.
**220,550 euros   CUR
(£137,845) GP**

(53)
Boasting rural views and close to a river, this detached house is surrounded by private, fenced land. Comprises a living room, dining room, three bedrooms, fitted kitchen, garage and outbuildings.
**213,306 euros   SIN
(£133,315) GP**

(18)
A restored 19th-century château in a tranquil, rural environment, close to a forest. Set in mature parkland of 50,000m². Boasts a fishing lake with a central island, numerous bedrooms and a pool.
**848,400 euros   CUR
(£530,250) GP**

(37)
A small *maison de maître* located in a quiet hamlet. Fully restored, the property boasts a fitted kitchen, two bedrooms, loft and several outbuildings for conversion. Set in rural countryside.
**152,000 euros   SOU
(£95,000) GP**

(85)
Ready to move in to, this detached house has a sunny, enclosed garden of 2,000m² filled with trees and flowering shrubs. Close to the area of Fontenay-le-Comte, with two bedrooms and outbuildings.
**112,812 euros   HIF
(£70,510) GP**

(49)
Partly renovated, a stone *longère* boasting 160m² of living space. Close to Combrée, the property features five bedrooms, a living room, kitchen, two bathrooms and cellar. Set in 2,000m² of grounds.
**150,920 euros   SIN
(£94,325) GP**

(36)
A small partly restored farmhouse, set in a small hamlet. Featuring several barns and outbuildings. The property is set in an idyllic rural spot overlooking a river and is a short distance from a village.
**560,000 euros   SOU
(£350,000) GP**

(49)
Close to the town of Angers and surrounded by scenic countryside, a 15th-century manor house and farmhouse. Situated in mature parkland of 2,000m² with a moat and a heated swimming pool.
**420,000 euros   EDE
(£262,500) GP**

(36)
This small restored farmhouse is set in a quiet hamlet. Situated in 2,500m² of land with large barns and outbuildings. Partly restored, the property sits in open farmland and boasts unrestricted views.
**57,000 euros   SOU
(£35,625) GP**

The Loire

(49)
A short drive from the historic town of Angers, a family home dating from the 1970s. Set in a garden of 1,500m² with a terrace, heated pool and garage. Offers four bedrooms and a mezzanine.
242,394 euros **VAL**
(£151,495) GP

(49)
A restored property in a quiet, sunny country location. On the edge of a small village north of Saumur. Features an independent guest house and its grounds boast two wells and a stone pigsty.
218,002 euros **VAL**
(£136,250) GP

(49)
In a village setting, a large detached residence dating from the late 19th century. Set in landscaped gardens with a heated swimming pool. Comprises four bedrooms and a mezzanine.
182,939 euros **VAL**
(£114,340) GP

(49)
A modern house on the edge of a village close to the market town of Saumur. The village is surrounded by orchards and forests. South-facing, this well-presented house offers five bedrooms and a cellar.
210,734 euros **VAL**
(£131,710) GP

(37)
With a garden running down to a small stream, a one-bedroom house with terracotta tiled floors, exposed beams, a *tuffeau* fireplace and fitted kitchen. Situated in a rustic village, with all amenities.
54,020 euros **VAL**
(£33,765) GP

(37)
Dating from the 19th century, a *maison de maitre* with extensive stone outbuildings. Set a short distance from a village, the house stands in 2,500m² of garden and comes with a detached cottage.
105,952 euros **LPS**
(£66,220) GP

(49)
In a small market town, a restored and spacious house. Situated in an enclosed garden with converted outbuilding and a vaulted cellar. Features six bedrooms, a kitchen, dining room and games room.
242,394 euros **VAL**
(£151,495) GP

(49)
This renovated two-storey house is situated on the edge of a small village and comes with a cottage. In need of some finishing-off work. Benefits from having three bedrooms, pool and outbuildings.
97,567 euros **LPS**
(£60,980) GP

(49)
A 19th-century farmhouse in a tranquil location. Renovated and close to a riverside market town, the property comprises three bedrooms, two receptions, stables and barn. Set in 2,000m² of land.
195,135 euros **LPS**
(£121,960) GP

Price Guide

(49)
An 18th-century house with a lake. The grounds include a well, covered playground, cellar and trees. Recently restored, the house boasts four bedrooms, terracotta floors and exposed beams.
355,400 euros   **VAL**
(£222,125) GP

(37)
Currently under restoration, an ensemble of old mill buildings. Looking out over a stream and surrounded by woodland. Features three units, with a kitchen and three to four bedrooms each.
339,290 euros   **VAL**
(£212,055) GP

(53)
A characterful cottage with a veranda. Set in 10,000m² of land, the cottage boasts a well-equipped kitchen, dining room with open fire and two bedrooms. Centrally heated, with a double garage.
103,366 euros   **MSE**
(£64,605) GP

(37)
A small single-storey house with two bedrooms and an enclosed garden. Outside is an outbuilding, garage and covered terrace. Set in a rural village, close to all major routes. Boasts a quiet location.
90,607 euros   **VAL**
(£56,630) GP

(49)
On the outskirts of a small village, a restored farmhouse with an attached *gîte*. With 100m² of land and a garage. The main house boasts five bedrooms, an external staircase and wine cellar.
151,135 euros   **VAL**
(£94,460) GP

(53)
A *longère* set in 9,000m² of rural land, boasting a lake and several outbuildings. Comprises three bedrooms, a dining room and a loft for conversion. Set in scenic countryside close to a village.
102,300 euros   **MSE**
(£63,940) GP

(37)
On the north bank of the River Loire, a restored south-facing home in a rural landscape. In the heart of a winemaking region. Features marble floors, exposed *tuffeau* walls, a gallery and cellar.
402,724 euros   **VAL**
(£251,705) GP

(49)
This 16th-century house is set in a quiet riverside hamlet just south of Saumur. Boasts many character features and stands in a garden of 100m², with a vaulted cellar and workshop. Offers three bedrooms.
136,442 euros   **LPS**
(£85,275) GP

(49)
Set at the end of a quiet country lane, a sunny farmhouse. Totally restored, the property features a vaulted cellar, three bedrooms and south-facing kitchen. Comes with a second house for renovation.
155,219 euros   **VAL**
(£97,010) GP

The Loire

(49)
On the side of a rural valley and in a hamlet, a house in need of some decorative work. Set a short distance from a village. Features three bedrooms, split over two floors and several outbuildings.
105,190 euros **LPS**
(£65,745) GP

(44)
In a small rural community with views over the Nantes-Brest canal, this former coaching inn needs some interior work. It has eight bedrooms and two bathrooms. Benefits from 2,300m² of gardens.
161,595 euros **NON**
(£101,000) GP

(49)
A spacious *maison de maitre*. Set in a quiet hamlet a short distance from a historic town. Standing in 3,849m² of land with extensive outbuildings and a pond. Several bedrooms and a single garage.
82,322 euros **LPS**
(£51,450) GP

(18)
An old farmhouse set in a rural area. In need of modernisation, the first floor features one small and one large bedroom. Upstairs there is one large room. Set in a private garden with mature trees.
96,957 euros **LIN**
(£60,600) GP

(49)
Dating from the 12th century, a fortified château with 14 rooms and a vaulted cellar. This spacious home has undergone renovation and features several outbuildings, including a chapel and dovecote.
218,002 euros **LPS**
(£136,250) GP

(49)
In a tranquil region of forest and orchards, an 18th-century house and barn. Situated in a manicured garden of 3,170m² with a pool. Boasts three bedrooms, a dining room and a four-bedroom gîte.
320,143 euros **LPS**
(£200,090) GP

(72)
A small 17th-century farmhouse with character. Features a large gîte and stables. Set on the edge of a picturesque village in land of 35,000m². Enjoys an idyllic and secluded location with open views.
114,337 euros **EDE**
(£71,460) GP

(85)
Dating from the 18th century, a six-bedroom *longère* with a small tower. Standing in 67,000m² of open land boasting two large lakes. Comes with several barns. Approached via a long driveway.
561,750 euros **FRA**
(£350,980) GP

(37)
An ancient estate surrounded by forest. Set in a secluded spot, the property has been fully restored and has several outbuildings. Features four bedrooms and a generous 35,000m² of land.
312,000 euros **SLP**
(£195,000) GP

Price Guide

(37)
A small château on the outskirts of a village. Situated within woodland grounds with several outbuildings and a separate guest house. Features three bedrooms, parquet floors and open fireplaces.
381,122 euros   DEE
(£238,200) GP

(49)
Dating from the 19th century, a four-bedroom farmhouse with a separate three-bedroom gîte. Set in a region of forest, a short walk from a village. The house features four bedrooms, a garage and cellar.
320,143 euros   LPS
(£200,090) GP

(18)
Dating from the 13th century, a feudal castle on the outskirts of a small village. Set on a rocky spur offering panoramic views over the surrounding countryside. Features a watch tower and terraced garden.
1,524,490 euros   DEE
(£952,805) GP

(49)
A farm cottage, recently extended. Set in a pretty hamlet close to a village in an attractive rural area. Features a living room, kitchen, four bedrooms and 4,000m² of land with several small barns.
104,428 euros   LPS
(£65,270) GP

(49)
Dating from 1900, a detached house in a village setting. In need of some renovation and in a quiet street, bordered by a stream. Set in a small garden. Comprises two bedrooms and a garage.
37,350 euros   LPS
(£23,345) GP

(53)
Located in a pretty hamlet, a modest country home featuring a fitted kitchen with tiled floors and exposed beams, a sitting room and three bedrooms. Set in a small plot of land surrounded by fields.
125,600 euros   LAR
(£78,500) GP

(49)
A renovated and detached home, dating from the 18th century. The property has retained much of its original charm and comes with three bedrooms, kitchen and a small garden with a paved terrace.
82,322 euros   LPS
(£51,450) GP

(53)
This traditional country cottage has been substantially improved to offer two bedrooms. Adjacent to the main house there is a gîte ready for letting. Boasts open fires, oak beams and a slate roof.
160,000 euros   BIS
(£100,000) GP

(49)
In the heart of a quiet, historic village, this 16th-century manor house boasts a walled garden of 1,570m² with outbuildings. In need of some modernisation, with four bedrooms, cellar and parking.
320,143 euros   LPS
(£200,090) GP

The Loire

(53)
Situated in a secluded location within the Mayenne forest. With this property comes 2,000m² of land and a carp-stocked lake. Featuring three bedrooms, the home is situated close to a village.
168,000 euros   **BIS**
(£105,000) GP

(49)
Offering 210m² of living space, a spacious property draped in vines. Comprises five bedrooms, living room and kitchen. In a very quiet location in the country. Set in 10,000m² of open rural land.
480,216 euros   **AMP**
(£300,135) GP

(49)
A *fermette* with a courtyard set in 1,933m² of open land, on the edge of a village. Features a vast kitchen, four bedrooms, living room, study and several large outbuildings, cellars and garages.
269,720 euros   **AMP**
(£168,575) GP

(49)
An ancient water mill offering two apartments. Set in tree-filled grounds of almost 20,000m² and surrounded by farmland and rural countryside. Features 10 main rooms, garages and outbuildings.
400,180 euros   **AMP**
(£250,115) GP

(49)
For restoration, a detached and secluded house with a chapel, cellar and 6,600m² of land. The house is a short drive from a small town. Offers various outbuildings and 700m² of accommodation.
369,765 euros   **AMP**
(£231,105) GP

(49)
On the edge of a forest, this large house sits in 25,000m² of land with stables, outbuildings and a pond. Comprises a living room, kitchen and four bedrooms. With views across an idyllic stream.
272,122 euros   **AMP**
(£170,075) GP

(45)
Set between Orléans and Blois and a short distance from the town of Beaugency, a recently renovated stone house with exposed beams, three bedrooms, kitchen, dining room and two bathrooms.
97,636 euros   **FPL**
(£61,025) GP

(49)
A contemporary house built on 1,200m² of land. Comprises a living room, fitted kitchen, four bedrooms and mezzanine. Set in a secluded, private location, a short distance from the town of Angers.
449,801 euros   **AMP**
(£281,125) GP

(53)
The northern side of this château looks out over a village and river. Situated on high in a beautiful landscaped garden. Features an underground chamber, chapel, 25 bedrooms and a guest cottage.
1,067,143 euros   **DEE**
(£666,965) S

Price Guide

(49)
In Savennières, a large detached bungalow with six main rooms. Boasts three bedrooms, a kitchen and terrace, looking out on to an enclosed lawned garden. Comes with a garage and outbuilding.
201,691 euros　　　　　**AMP**
(£126,055) GP

(49)
A three-bedroom detached house in Angers. Features a vast, well-equipped kitchen, office and living room. Outside boasts land of 1,450m² with a double garage and several stone outbuildings.
193,686 euros　　　　　**AMP**
(£121,055) GP

(49)
Built in the 19th century, a vast home with *tuffeau* stone walls. Fully renovated, with a south-facing courtyard and terrace leading to landscaped gardens. A restored tapestry hangs in the lounge.
403,989 euros　　　　　**DEE**
(£252,495) GP

(49)
In a tourist village, this extensive property boasts three bedrooms, a vast reception room, office, two bathrooms and mezzanine. Set in a garden with a swimming pool, patio area and a large garage.
224,100 euros　　　　　**AMP**
(£140,065) GP

(49)
Dating from the 1960s, a large detached residence. Composed of a living room with open fireplace and terrace, three bedrooms and a bathroom. In open countryside surroundings, with a large lawn.
203,200 euros　　　　　**AMP**
(£127,000) GP

(72)
A listed, fully-restored 17th-century home protected by watch-towers surrounded by moats. 15,000m² of grounds with several outbuildings including a listed chapel. Stunning original features.
646,383 euros　　　　　**DEE**
(£403,990) GP

(53)
A manor house built during the 15th century. Comprises five bedrooms, a panelled hall and reception room. Set in 110,000m² of landscaped grounds featuring two lakes. Surrounded by hills.
518,326 euros　　　　　**DEE**
(£323,955) GP

(49)
An old house, recently renovated. With five bedrooms, cellar, large kitchen and living room. Features *tomette* tiles, exposed beams and a massive ornamental fireplace. In a small garden, with superb views.
227,350 euros　　　　　**AMP**
(£142,095) GP

(49)
A *fermette* with a vast entrance hall, living room and kitchen. Fronted by a colourful courtyard and garden, which is also to the side and rear of the buildings. Offers four bedrooms and office.
233,598 euros　　　　　**AMP**
(£146,000) GP

The Loire

(49)
A bright, sunny house with four bedrooms. Composed of eight main rooms, including a living room and kitchen. Benefits from having a large terrace with views. Set in a pretty lawned garden.
177,679 euros   AMP
(£111,050) GP

(49)
Boasting superb views over the countryside surroundings and set in 4,500m^2 of tree-filled garden, a renovated house. Boasts three bedrooms, a modern, well-equipped kitchen and large garage.
185,683 euros   AMP
(£116,050) GP

(49)
A historic abbey on the banks of the River Loire. Dating as far back as the 12th century, the abbey is composed of *tuffeau* stone walls, it features a library, kitchen, 38 bedrooms and 12 monks' cells.
1,051,898 euros   DEE
(£657,435) GP

(49)
A modern bungalow with a large basement. Features an entrance hall, living room, kitchen and three bedrooms. Set in a large garden with a terrace giving spectacular south-facing views.
124,856 euros   AMP
(£78,035) GP

(49)
A listed château on top of a small hill overlooking the countryside. A fantastic medieval setting featuring nine bedrooms, a dressing room, 13th-century tower, spiral stone staircase and vaulted corridors.
548,816 euros   DEE
(£343,010) GP

(49)
This semi-detached house has three bedrooms, study, veranda, kitchen and living room. Centrally heated, the property is split over two floors and is situated in a small garden in a residential area.
145,665 euros   AMP
(£91,040) GP

(44)
Dating from the 15th century, a listed windmill and contemporary house. Set in a park of 35,000m^2 featuring woodland and meadows. Divided into 10 main rooms, the house boasts five large bedrooms.
594,001 euros   MER
(£371,250) GP

(49)
An old renovated house featuring an open-plan main living room and kitchen, four bedrooms, an office and garage. Boasts exposed beams and stone walls. Comes with an independent apartment.
137,661 euros   AMP
(£86,040) GP

(49)
Close to Angers, a house with three bedrooms, kitchen, living room and garage. Enjoys a large lawned garden boasting a terrace with views. In a residential area close to a picturesque village.
112,851 euros   AMP
(£70,530) GP

Price Guide

(49)
Ready to move in to, an old house with a living room, back-kitchen, kitchen and two bedrooms. Set in a pretty garden, with a garage and shed. Features a wooden roof. Benefits from a secluded location.
70,432 euros   **AMP**
(£44,020) GP

(49)
Situated on the edge of a village on a main road, a house with four rooms. Comprises a lounge, one bedroom, bathroom and kitchen. Standing in a garden of 900m², with plenty of space for parking.
59,151 euros   **AMP**
(£36,970) GP

(44)
Built back in the 18th century, this manor house sits a short drive from Nantes and offers 10 main rooms, split over two levels. Features four bedrooms with high ceilings and 2,140m² of parkland.
428,001 euros   **MER**
(£267,500) GP

(49)
In a quiet village setting, a large residence offering four bedrooms with beams, and a lounge with a fireplace. Standing in wooded parkland and fields of 2,500m², and dating from the 17th century.
256,000 euros   **MER**
(£160,000) GP

(85)
A country house benefiting from a peaceful environment. Standing in an extensive garden boasting a swimming pool, paddocks and woodland. Split over two floors and on the edge of a quiet village.
273,600 euros   **LAR**
(£171,000) GP

(85)
A large house close to the sea yet in the heart of a country town. Features a reception room with parquet floors and a monumental fireplace. Set in wooded parkland, enjoying a pool and mature trees.
445,152 euros   **MER**
(£278,220) GP

(53)
A large château dating from the 16th century and split over three floors. Totally renovated but retaining many original details. Set in land of 60,000m², with a swimming pool, pool house and pavilion.
823,226 euros   **MER**
(£514,515) GP

(49)
Dating from the 1970s, a large three-bedroom house with a kitchen, cellar, garage and terrace. Set in 550m² of land planted with shrubs and trees. In a quiet neighbourhood, close to a village.
113,650 euros   **AMP**
(£71,030) GP

(49)
An extensive half-timbered *maison de maître*. Enjoys a pool, tennis court and sauna. Provides spacious accommodation and offers seven bedrooms, an office, cellar and three sitting rooms.
990,920 euros   **MER**
(£619,325) GP

The Loire

(37)
A lovely cottage situated in a hamlet close to a village with all amenities. The property is fully restored and ready for occupation. Recent central heating system and planning permission for a pool.
118,500 euros   SLP
(£74,065) GP

(37)
Extensively renovated house with several outbuildings, close to a small village. The main house has four bedrooms and a huge attic, while the outbuildings have the potential to form a gîte complex.
295,000 euros   SLP
(£184,375) GP

(36)
A substantial property constructed in the 1970s. Set in a tranquil, rural location, the property is finished to the highest standards and benefits from a high-efficiency heating system and land of 20,000m^2.
450,000 euros   SLP
(£281,250) GP

(37)
An unusual property consisting of two houses joined by an arched passage. Habitable but in need of some improvements, there is huge scope here. A number of outbuildings and 1,800m^2 of land.
90,500 euros   SLP
(£56,565) GP

(37)
This semi-detached three-bedroom house is located at the centre of a lovely village. The house boasts a mooring on the River Aigronne bordering the rear of the property. Courtyard garden.
82,500 euros   SLP
(£51,565) GP

(37)
Just 15 minutes from the city of Tours, a beautifully restored 18th-century *longère*. With grounds of 35,000m^2 including an orchard and large barn, this seven-bedroom home is an idyllic gem.
374,500 euros   SLP
(£234,065) GP

(37)
A property situated in the central square of a market town, this former office needs work to realise its potential as a three-bedroom house. Many original features, attic, central heating and courtyard.
70,000 euros   SLP
(£43,750) GP

(37)
This unusual house consists of two properties that have been joined together. Partly habitable but in need of total renovation. There is a small triangular garden and a further plot of land nearby.
41,000 euros   SLP
(£25,625) GP

(37)
In the centre of a small market town, this cottage has been fully restored, requiring only kitchen fittings and decoration. With two bedrooms, kitchen, lounge and bathroom. Small courtyard to side.
39,500 euros   SLP
(£24,690) GP

Price Guide

(36)
A large restored stone-built house near Argenton-sur-Creuse. Set in 3,000m² of parkland, the centrally heated property benefits from five/six bedrooms, a huge living room and a self-contained annexe.
205,806 euros   LRP
(£128,630) GP

(36)
In the medieval town of Saint-Benoît-du-Sault, this beautiful house in need of restoration. With five rooms on two floors plus attic, cellar, terrace and charming courtyard. Services connected.
45,238 euros   LRP
(£28,275) GP

(36)
An 18th-century post house in 1,800m² of grounds. With 22 rooms, garage and assorted outbuildings, this property oozes potential. The town of Argenton-sur-Creuse is a short drive away.
131,107 euros   LRP
(£81,940) GP

(36)
Pretty house in hamlet 2km from amenities. Sitting and dining rooms with exposed beams. Two bedrooms with potential to add one/two more. Barn attached and outbuildings on nearby land.
44,000 euros   LRP
(£27,500) GP

(36)
A restored *fermette* with glorious views offering three bedrooms and a separate gîte with four/five rooms. The property also benefits from a generous 6,000m² of land, a large barn and a small lake.
106,715 euros   LRP
(£66,700) GP

(36)
A small semi-detached cottage with a well-equipped kitchen, one bedroom, bathroom and separate WC. The property also has a garage attached and there is a small garden close to the property.
24,239 euros   LRP
(£15,150) GP

(53)
A detached bungalow fronted by a garden of 550m² that faces the road. Comprises a kitchen, two bedrooms, cellar and a dining room with a tiled floor. Set in rugged countryside, close to town.
74,000 euros   LAT
(£46,250) GP

(37)
Situated close to the medieval village of Loches. A farmhouse, currently undergoing renovation. The ground floor offers three bedrooms, a lounge and kitchen. Upstairs are two further bedrooms.
141,777 euros   LVL
(£88,610) GP

(53)
A detached south-facing house. Features a small courtyard and garden on the other side of the road. Comprises a kitchen with fireplace, two bedrooms and study. Set close to a market town.
56,500 euros   LAT
(£35,315) GP

BURGUNDY

Price Guide

(89)
An ancient watermill complex with large grounds and a restored house. Features nine rooms and a separate farmhouse in need of renovation. The property borders a river and is set close to a village.
282,030 euros   **BUR**
(£176,270) GP

(71)
This spacious house comprises five bedrooms and a self-contained one-bedroom apartment. Set in a quiet village, it offers land of 10,000m² with mature pine trees and several outbuildings.
763,000 euros   **BUR**
(£476,875) GP

(89)
A property comprising a house, garages and separate gîte. The main house enjoys a veranda with open views, three bedrooms and a summer room. The gîte features two bedrooms and a shower room.
243,918 euros   **LAT**
(£152,450) GP

(58)
A renovated mill complex set in 60,000m² of meadows with a river, gardens and tennis court. Close to a village, the property comprises a *maison de maître*, guesthouse, cottage and a pond.
243,918 euros   **SIF**
(£152,450) GP

(58)
Located in a small village, this barn has been converted into a home and sits in grounds of 1,100m². The interior is in need of refurbishment, but is ready to move in to and boasts nice views.
59,000 euros   **BUR**
(£36,875) GP

(58)
A picturesque cottage with an adjoining workshop, situated in a quiet, rural village. The property has been mostly renovated and offers two bedrooms. Features original oak beams and open fires.
50,309 euros   **FPL**
(£31,445) GP

(58)
Close to the River Loire and Canal du Nivernais, this two-bedroom home features a veranda, garage and cellar. Set in 4,000m² of land, the property enjoys access to local amenities and is habitable.
75,462 euros   **BUR**
(£47,165) GP

(21)
Dating from 1878, this isolated house in 2,000m² of landscaped grounds boasts a swimming pool and a second self-contained house. Offers 468m² of living space and open views of the countryside.
800,000 euros   **FPP**
(£500,000) GP

(71)
Located to the north of Mâcon on the edge of a pretty hamlet. This small farmhouse is in need of renovation. Situated in 700m² of land, the property offers 45m² of living space and two bedrooms.
50,300 euros   **BUR**
(£31,440) GP

Burgundy 4 U

We can help you find a house and settle in South Burgundy;

The area between Beaune and Macon.
We are English speakers & work "sur place".

www.burgundy4u.com

tel: 00 33 3 85 98 96 24

email: info@burgundy4u.com

Price Guide

(58)
A renovated house just south of Morvan Regional Park. Enjoying 800m² of grounds in calm and picturesque surroundings, this property features two bedrooms and boasts a small pretty garden.
75,462 euros   **BUR**
(£47,165) GP

(71)
With outstanding views, this character house is situated a short drive from Autun. Features two bedrooms, a living room with open fireplace and kitchen. Set in a large garden with meadows.
88,500 euros   **BUR**
(£55,315) GP

(71)
A house with a self-contained studio apartment and garden of 5,000m². The main property offers two bedrooms, while the studio features two main rooms. Benefits from stunning panoramic views.
96,500 euros   **BUR**
(£60,315) GP

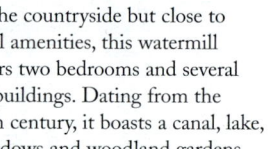

(21)
Arranged over three floors, this house comprises a bathroom and five bedrooms, each with a balcony. The ground floor features a large, well-equipped kitchen and living room. Pleasant gardens.
83,000 euros   **BUR**
(£51,875) GP

(58)
This detached house and studio apartment sit within 1,000m² of garden. Situated close to local shops, the house comprises two large bedrooms, an outbuilding, vaulted cellars and a triple garage.
74,500 euros   **BUR**
(£46,565) GP

(71)
In the countryside but close to local amenities, this watermill offers two bedrooms and several outbuildings. Dating from the 19th century, it boasts a canal, lake, meadows and woodland gardens.
427,000 euros   **BUR**
(£266,875) GP

(21)
A two-storey house with parquet floors and many original features. Offering 70m² of living space, the building comprises two bedrooms on the first floor. A garden of 2,000m² surrounds the property.
68,600 euros   **BUR**
(£42,875) GP

(21)
In the Côte-d'Or vineyards, this traditional town house has five main rooms arranged over two floors. Features three bedrooms, a kitchen and living room. With two cellars and a 970m² garden.
67,000 euros   **BUR**
(£41,875) GP

(71)
In a village 15km from Beaune, this old house has recently been renovated and comprises two bedrooms, a cellar and workshop. Set in a garden, with a second building in need of renovation.
145,000 euros   **BUR**
(£90,625) GP

Burgundy

(71)
On the edge of an old village, this two-bedroom house has a large living room and garden of nearly 3,000m². South-facing, the house is fully furnished, enjoys open views and is ready to move in to.
145,000 euros   BUR
(£90,625) GP

(71)
West of Mâcon, this stone-built house has numerous bedrooms and a covered gallery. The interior of the house is in need of some work. Situated in 900m² of garden with mature fruit trees.
190,000 euros   BUR
(£118,750) GP

(58)
Enjoying views over beautiful countryside, this house has four bedrooms and grounds of nearly 4,000m². Close to Autun, the house has gas-fired heating. With two rooms still to be renovated.
145,000 euros   BUR
(£90,625) GP

(71)
Set in 2,000m² of land, this former farmhouse benefits from views over a country landscape. Sold fully furnished, the property has one bedroom, a summer living room, stables and a cellar.
105,000 euros   BUR
(£65,625) GP

(71)
This large house, situated in front of a church and next to shops, has been converted from a restaurant into a family home. Set in a small village, the property has a lawned garden and several bedrooms.
106,700 euros   BUR
(£66,690) GP

(58)
A farmhouse with 100m² habitable space located near a forest. The property comprises two large bedrooms and a convertible loft. Outbuildings include a large cellar, garage, workshop and horse boxes.
137,204 euros   BUR
(£85,755) GP

(71)
A gothic stone-built property set in a winemaking area. Benefiting from an enclosed courtyard, the residence is arranged over two floors. Comprises three bedrooms with another room for conversion.
120,000 euros   LAT
(£75,000) GP

(58)
Located in a rural hamlet, this restored watermill sits in 1,000m² of land. With three bedrooms and a large veranda looking out across a quiet stream. This house also benefits from a garage and cellars.
108,240 euros   BUR
(£67,650) GP

(71)
Set in a winemaking village, this traditional house has a covered terrace and landscaped garden that overlook the vineyards. The house comprises of three bedrooms and needs renovating.
134,400 euros   BUR
(£84,000) GP

Price Guide

(21)
With views over orchards and vineyards, this property comprises a main house with a fitted kitchen, dining room and three bedrooms. There are several barns and outbuildings for renovation.
137,000 euros   **BUR**
(£85,625) GP

(71)
A stone-built farmhouse with a courtyard. Completely renovated, the property is set in 7,000m² of land, close to the town of Cluny. Comprises three bedrooms, an adjacent barn and extensive cellars.
290,000 euros   **LAT**
(£181,250) GP

(71)
A modern house located close to a village. Enjoys nearly 7,500m² of grounds and open views over the rural surroundings from a wooden veranda. Boasts two bedrooms, two bathrooms and a conservatory.
185,000 euros   **BUR**
(£115,625) GP

(71)
This single-storey house is set around a courtyard with several outbuildings. Composed of a tiled sitting room, kitchen and two bedrooms. The house features exposed beams and open fires.
89,000 euros   **LAT**
(£55,625) GP

(71)
A farm with assorted outbuildings in the Auxois. The main house offers four bedrooms and is ready to move in to. Enjoying land of 6,000m², the property also features two Dutch barns and three stables.
120,000 euros   **BUR**
(£75,000) GP

(71)
A large residence standing in 700m² of garden with a garage. Boasting southwesterly views, the house comprises three large bedrooms and is set in a quiet village with a school and shops.
273,000 euros   **LAT**
(£170,625) GP

(71)
In a village surrounded by vineyards, this 19th-century house has been renovated and offers seven spacious bedrooms. The house features a mature garden with an orchard and a dovecote.
380,000 euros   **BUR**
(£237,500) GP

(71)
A four-bedroom house close to the market town of Chagny. Set in grounds of 320m², the property features spacious rooms and a large garage. It is ready to move in to and is set in a peaceful area.
140,000 euros   **BUR**
(£87,500) GP

(58)
These two watermills look out across a trout-filled river and waterfall. Set in 33,000m² of land, the first watermill comes with two bedrooms, while the second has three bedrooms and a bread oven.
180,000 euros   **BUR**
(£112,500) GP

Burgundy

(71)
Located in Châlonnais, a well-presented modern four-bedroom property. An airy, spacious house, it is situated close to local amenities and has a 900m² garden with a patio and space for parking.
194,000 euros   BUR
(£121,250) GP

(71)
Just north of Mâcon. Located in a village with shops and a school, this two-bedroom period house features large, light-filled rooms. The property benefits from a secluded, well-maintained garden.
182,000 euros   BUR
(£113,750) GP

(71)
Dating from the 19th century, a manor house with 4,000m² of garden looking out over a river. Features three bedrooms, a fitted kitchen, wine cellar and garage. Set close to a medieval village.
534,000 euros   LAT
(£333,750) GP

(71)
Dating from the 17th century, a fortified stone-built house set around a courtyard. The property enjoys extensive views and 5,000m² of colourful gardens with a well. Features an original vaulted cellar.
500,000 euros   LAT
(£312,500) GP

(71)
This renovated farmhouse has been transformed into a family home. The property comes with four bedrooms and a large main living room. Outside there is an old stable, barn and single garage.
183,000 euros   BUR
(£114,375) GP

(21)
North of Beaune, this renovated three-bedroom house benefits from spectacular views over the Ouche Valley. Features an original bread oven, and outbuildings including barns and stabling.
175,000 euros   BUR
(£109,375) GP

(71)
Set in a town, a bungalow with wine cellars underneath the entire building. Offers six main rooms, including a living room and two bedrooms. Boasts an enclosed garden with views over vineyards.
195,000 euros   BUR
(£121,875) GP

(71)
A former holiday camp in need of renovation. This small château sits in peaceful countryside with open views. Split over two storeys, it is full of authentic detail and comes with 30,000m² of wooded garden.
290,000 euros   BUR
(£181,250) GP

(21)
Set in a rural landscape, these two houses have been renovated to form one property. Comprises two bedrooms, large barns, garages and two cellars. Situated in a quiet location, in grounds of 5,700m².
165,000 euros   BUR
(£103,125) GP

Price Guide

(71)
On the edge of a large village, this restored house comprises four bedrooms. Benefiting from a heated swimming pool, the property sits in a small, well-maintained flower garden.
256,000 euros   **BUR**
(£160,000) GP

(71)
Dating from the beginning of the 20th century, this character house offers three bedrooms and plenty of space for further renovation. Sits in grounds of 1,400m^2 in a quiet village with all amenities.
227,150 euros   **BUR**
(£141,970) GP

(71)
Set among vineyards, this large house with a studio apartment boasts panoramic views over the surrounding area. The main house offers three bedrooms, while the apartment comes with an office.
256,114 euros   **BUR**
(£160,070) GP

(71)
Dating from 1695, this ancient dwelling has been renovated and offers 125m^2 of living space, four bedrooms and a cellar. There is also a garage at the back of the property. Ready to move in to.
213,000 euros   **BUR**
(£133,125) GP

(71)
An 18th-century property situated in grounds of 8,000m^2, featuring a chapel, caretaker's cottage and outbuildings. Boasts 16 bedrooms, numerous bathrooms, a stone staircase and original oak beams.
445,000 euros   **LAT**
(£278,125) GP

(71)
This renovated house and farm sits in a forested area. The house boasts many original features and has three bedrooms. There is stabling on the extensive farmland offered with the property.
256,114 euros   **BUR**
(£160,070) GP

(21)
This ancient rectory is set in its own plot of land. With plenty of character, the property has been fully restored and offers three bedrooms. Features living space of 140m^2 and comes with a garage.
229,000 euros   **BUR**
(£143,125) GP

(21)
In between Semur-en-Auxois and Montbard. This character house is currently being renovated and boasts many original features including ancient Burgundy flagstones. Offers four bedrooms.
240,000 euros   **BUR**
(£150,000) GP

(21)
This restored watermill offers 275m^2 of living space and is set in 16,000m^2 of land. Comprises a living room, kitchen, bathroom, WC and one bedroom. There are three further rooms for renovation.
260,000 euros   **BUR**
(£162,500) GP

Burgundy

(71)
This fortified farmhouse has lots of character and spectacular views over the local countryside. Features many authentic details, including a tower, archways and rustic tiles. Offers seven bedrooms.
267,500 euros   BUR
(£167,190) GP

(21)
Surrounded by a moat, this house with stone walls boasts 4,500m² of land with mature gardens. On the ground floor there are three rooms to be renovated. Also offers three bedrooms and a convertible attic.
242,000 euros   BUR
(£151,250) GP

(21)
A renovated farmhouse offering four bedrooms and set in grounds of 31,500m². With a swimming pool, pond and woods, the house is situated in a peaceful area and benefits from panoramic views.
333,000 euros   BUR
(£208,125) GP

(21)
This three-bedroom stone-built house enjoys superb views over a medieval village. Features original beamed ceilings and stone floors. Terrace and garden with ornamental pool. Some renovation required.
169,676 euros   BPS
(£106,050) S

(71)
A recently built four-bedroom apartment with private parking and benefiting from the use of a swimming pool. Standing in 150m² of enclosed garden within the grounds of a large château.
335,388 euros   LAT
(£209,620) GP

(71)
Dating from the 19th century, this large house has two wings, each offering six main rooms. Set in grounds of 40,000m², the property features a stone fireplace, period floors and a long covered terrace.
435,000 euros   BUR
(£271,875) GP

(71)
This house and barn is in need of some renovation. Dating from the early 17th century, the property offers three good-sized bedrooms. The large adjacent barn offers a convertible area of 130m².
366,000 euros   BUR
(£228,750) GP

(71)
This character property comes with a garage and outbuildings. Set in an elevated position, the house is surrounded by 2,500m² of enclosed woodland. Offers nine bedrooms and a studio apartment.
305,000 euros   LAT
(£190,625) GP

(21)
This modern house is set in a tranquil location and boasts a heated swimming pool and tennis court. Additionally, the property offers five main rooms, a fitted kitchen and an attractive garden.
320,143 euros   BUR
(£200,090) GP

Price Guide

(21)
Set in a medieval village this stone mansion offers 370m² of accommodation including reception, dining, library, breakfast rooms and six bedrooms. In landscaped gardens making a magical setting.
450,000 euros   **BPS**
(£281,250) GP

(21)
A business opportunity comprising two period houses. House one features a dining room, mezzanine and two bedrooms. House two is ideally suited for use as a six-bedroom gîte. Set in 3,000m² of land.
183,000 euros   **BPS**
(£114,375) GP

(71)
A château classified as a historic monument. Boasting eight large bedrooms, all with bathrooms, this property is bordered by a moat and reached by a drive lined with mature oak and lime trees.
1,222,000 euros   **BUR**
(£763,750) GP

(21)
This mansion overlooks a valley and has seven bedrooms, five bathrooms and two separate one-bedroom studios. Fully renovated, the property features a chapel, cellar, courtyard, fountain and tower.
1,220,000 euros   **BUR**
(£762,500) GP

(21)
In good order, this property comprises three apartments, two studios and a loft for conversion into a fourth apartment. Standing in well-maintained gardens, this is a sound investment opportunity.
157,000 euros   **BPS**
(£98,125) S

(58)
Located in a regional park with 70,000m² of land, this château dates from the 18th century and boasts 17 en-suite bedrooms and several outbuildings. It is in need of some decoration but habitable.
915,000 euros   **BUR**
(£571,875) GP

(89)
This stone-built village house is located in a hamlet. Set in a small garden, the property is arranged over two levels and features three vaulted rooms on the first floor, a stone fireplace and sink.
66,315 euros   **MOD**
(£41,450) GP

(21)
At the heart of a delightful village, this four-bedroom stone-built house has been partly restored and retains many original features. Enjoys a large walled garden to the rear of the property.
69,000 euros   **BPS**
(£43,125) GP

(21)
This elegant château, dated 1642, is set in 48,000m² of parkland. Features a clock tower, 12 en-suite bedrooms, panelled reception/dining rooms, manor house and stables. Ideal family/professional use.
1,219,500 euros   **BPS**
(£762,190) GP

Burgundy Property Specialists

PLANNING YOUR RETIREMENT?
BUYING A SECOND HOME?

YOU WANT TRANQUILITY, MORE SECURITY AND A BETTER PROPERTY FOR YOUR MONEY?

THEN BURGUNDY'S FOR YOU! THIS WORLD FAMOUS WINE REGION OFFERS RICHLY VARIED LANDSCAPES, 550 PROTECTED NATURE PARKS AND HISTORIC CITIES SUCH AS DIJON AND BEAUNE WITH A WEALTH OF MAGNIFICENT ARCHITECTURE.

BUYING?
Whether you are buying a second home, or a principal residence, BPS offers a wide selection of properties. Need help with your visit. Call us.

BPS2 - Home Investment   221,000€

BPS38 - Period farmhouse   112,500€

INVESTMENT?
Are you looking for an investment opportunity, chambre d'hote/gite, appartments to let permanently, or management of & income from your second home? Call us.

FINANCE?
We recently negotiated a client's loan at 3.8% for year 1 (ex.ass.) with a variable rate fixed for each subsequent year based on Euribor 12 months + 0.9%. We do not charge for this service. Call us.

BPS14 - Farm with 20 acres   236,296€

BPS11 - Elegant mansion   450,000€

RENOVATIONS?
We can assist you with your restoration conversion project from quotations to completion. We only work with skilled artisans incl. Compagnon roofers & carpenters. Call us.

PLEASE CONTACT PETER COLLINS IN BURGUNDY.

TELEPHONE: 00 33 3 80 84 35 21   MOBILE: 00 33 6 09 43 23 19
FAX: 00 33 3 80 24 03 87   EMAIL: burgundyproperty@aol.com

Price Guide

(58)
Fronted by a large lawned area, an extensive château boasting many original details including two towers and a moat. Dating from the 16th century and standing in mature parkland of 34,000m².
701,265 euros   **SIF**
(£438,290) GP

(58)
Set in gently rolling countryside, an 18th-century château in need of some interior renovation. Built over three storeys, the château has a vast living room, open kitchen, billiard room and six bedrooms.
490,000 euros   **DEE**
(£306,250) GP

(89)
On the edge of a small village, a 17th-century château flanked by two round towers. Surrounded by 22,000m² of landscaped grounds with several outbuildings. Boasts two pavilions and 10 bedrooms.
800,357 euros   **DEE**
(£500,225) GP

(21)
An old stone house located in the heart of a quiet country village. Full of character and privately situated, it offers three bedrooms, dining room and living room with fireplace. Set in a small garden.
89,200 euros   **BPS**
(£55,750) GP

(21)
South of the town of Montbard, a charming restored 19th-century mill. In a magical setting overlooking a river, the property features seven bedrooms and a cast-iron staircase designed by Eiffel.
487,850 euros   **BPS**
(£304,905) GP

(21)
A former presbytery dating from the 16th century. Restored and retaining many original details, such as exposed beams, stone floors and curving staircases. The property offers a pool and garden.
295,000 euros   **BPS**
(£184,375) GP

(89)
Restored in 1986, this farmhouse sits on land of 4,230m² laid to lawn. Benefits from a terrace with south-facing views. Situated in a very peaceful area, just south of a small village with all amenities.
153,600 euros   **FPL**
(£96,000) GP

(89)
A renovated farmhouse on the outskirts of Chablis offering stunning rural views. Composed of several spacious rooms, it sits in a large, well-maintained garden planted with trees and shrubs.
160,000 euros   **FPL**
(£100,000) GP

(71)
This detached house is situated in a small village on the edge of the Morvan Regional Park. It boasts three bedrooms with oak floors, a fully-fitted kitchen with tiled floor, lounge and courtyard.
120,000 euros   **FRA**
(£75,000) GP

Burgundy

(58)
A renovated farmhouse with lots of character. Boasting three large bedrooms, a sunny terrace with uninterrupted country views, and several outbuildings. Stands in 2,335m² of cultivated farmland.
140,250 euros   FRA
(£87,655) GP

(58)
This listed 17th-century château is approached via an avenue framed by outbuildings and lime trees. Arranged over three levels and set around four square pavilions. Boasts a chapel and vaulted cellars.
3,811,225 euros   DEE
(£2,382,015) GP

(89)
A property with a pool, dating from the 16th century. Features a fitted kitchen and living room with terracotta tiles, open beams and bread oven. Offering two bedrooms and a small garden.
160,071 euros   ACM
(£100,045) GP

(71)
Situated in a pleasant village, this *maison de maître* was built at the beginning of the 18th century around an enclosed courtyard. It consists of a main house on two floors, barns, stables and dovecote.
200,000 euros   FRA
(£125,000) GP

(89)
This watermill with 20,000m² of gardens and woodland lies at the entrance of a small village. Facing south, the mill boasts limestone walls and oak wood floors. With seven bedrooms and a basement.
609,796 euros   DEE
(£381,125) GP

(79)
In a small village, a country house with a fitted kitchen, living room with fireplace, and shower room. The property offers two bedrooms. Set in 800m² of garden, with a cellar and outbuildings.
81,561 euros   ACM
(£50,975) GP

(71)
This seven-bedroom manor house is set in a landscaped park that includes a trout river. The property comprises a gatehouse and several outbuildings, including a stone mill house and dovecote.
768,000 euros   FRA
(£480,000) GP

(71)
Located in Autun, this dwelling offers one bedroom with a shower room, a summer living room, stables and a vaulted cellar. The property is fully-furnished and set in 2,000m² of grassy fields.
105,000 euros   BUR
(£65,625) GP

(89)
A contemporary house a short drive from Avallon. Features an entrance hall, kitchen, living room with fireplace, and two bedrooms. Set in 600m² of well-maintained garden with a covered terrace.
70,889 euros   ACM
(£44,305) GP

Price Guide

(21)
Charming and authentic, a stone farmhouse with a family room, two spacious bedrooms, kitchen, bathroom, large terrace and vaulted cellar. Set in a 10,000m² garden, featuring a stable and barn.
198,184 euros   ACM
(£123,865) GP

(21)
A two-bedroom stone-built house arranged over two floors. Set around a courtyard and with a garden of 2,500m². Offers an attached barn, cellar and sitting room. In a secluded location.
105,952 euros   ACM
(£66,220) GP

(89)
In Avallon, a contemporary home with five bedrooms. Comprises a sitting room with fireplace and exposed beams, bathroom, shower room and dressing room. Boasts a terrace looking out across a river.
1,800,000 euros   ACM
(£1,125,000) GP

(21)
A short walk from the centre of a medieval town, this 18th-century residence stands in 5,000m² of land enjoying magnificent views over the country. Offers seven bedrooms and a vast dining room.
525,949 euros   ACM
(£328,720) GP

(21)
A detached period house set in grounds of over 2,700m². Located in a village, the house has 160m² of habitable space, including several bedrooms and bathrooms. With spectacular country views.
179,890 euros   ACM
(£112,430) GP

(21)
Dating from the 18th century and bordered by a large lake, an old manor house currently run as a bar and hotel. Boasts several large bedrooms and bathrooms. In a quiet, secluded country setting.
434,479 euros   ACM
(£271,550) GP

(89)
A small villa standing in 2,200m² of garden planted with trees. On one level and featuring two large bedrooms, living room with open fireplace, and kitchen. Outside is a garage and small outbuilding.
89,945 euros   ACM
(£56,215) GP

(89)
An old stone house comprising a kitchen, dining room with open fireplace, sitting room, study, three bedrooms and a bathroom. Boasts an inner courtyard and garden of 1,100m² with a barn and garage.
213,428 euros   ACM
(£133,390) GP

(89)
In a typical Burgundy village, a home with unimpeded panoramic views over a rural valley. Features a large kitchen, sitting room, three bedrooms, bathroom and a cellar. Comes with an outbuilding.
800,000 euros   ACM
(£500,000) GP

Burgundy

(21)
Next to the River Seine, this old mill features a dining room with porthole windows overlooking the river and a water wheel. With three bedrooms, a cellar, three further rooms and attached barn.
381,123 euros BPS
(£238,200) GP

(21)
Charming village house with period features in walled gardens with open views of the countryside and neighbouring château. Three bedrooms, salon and dining room. Barn/stable conversion possible.
81,000 euros BPS
(£50,625) GP

(71)
Close to Mâcon, this large private residence is draped in vines and stands in 300m² of garden. Offering 14 main rooms including several bedrooms, a fitted kitchen, bathrooms and vast outbuildings.
384,172 euros MER
(£240,110) GP

(58)
An ancient watermill overlooking a pretty stream. Accessed via a small bridge, the property occupies a countryside setting surrounded by hills and wooded land. In need of some renovation.
427,681 euros MER
(£267,300) GP

(21)
Ideal as a small hotel, a farmhouse built from stone. In need of some restoration. The property features a kitchen with oak beams, study, three bedrooms and a cellar. Set around a large stone courtyard.
170,000 euros BPS
(£106,250) GP

(89)
In the town of Saint-Agnan, this extensive château stands in grounds of nearly 7,000m² with mature trees, meadows and rural land. Features 13 main rooms, a tower and numerous outbuildings.
815,603 euros MER
(£509,750) GP

(21)
An elegant early 20th-century villa set in an enclosed 6,000m² woodland park. The property offers 200m² of accommodation, including six bedrooms, a dining room, library and two bathrooms.
175,500 euros BPS
(£109,690) S

(58)
In the heart of a small peaceful town. This ancient dwelling stands in 9,445m² of land with panoramic views. Features include a tower and dining room with wooden panelling and chandeliers.
329,290 euros MER
(£205,805) GP

(89)
In open farmland close to a town, this L-shaped *fermette* with six main rooms features three large bedrooms and a farmhouse-style kitchen. Set in agricultural land of 100,000m² with outbuildings.
329,300 euros MER
(£205,810) GP

Price Guide

(21)
Set in Morvan Regional Park, a carefully-restored mill house dating from the 19th century. Features a dining room with views across a private lake, master bedroom suite and a guest apartment.
495,000 euros **BPS**
(£309,375) GP

(21)
For restoration, a detached character house with four bedrooms, salon, dining room and study. Set in delightful walled gardens beside a river in a pretty village. Ideal permanent or second home.
122,000 euros **BPS**
(£76,250) GP

(71)
In a busy town, this detached farmhouse stands in 2,600m² of garden laid to lawn and with far-reaching views. Boasts 222m² of living space featuring eight main rooms, including four bedrooms.
350,701 euros **MER**
(£291,190) GP

(58)
A large castle with four towers set in the heart of ancient woodland. Fronted by an extensive lawn with a gatehouse. Offers 15 rooms with many original details, including pitched ceilings and oak beams.
1,417,778 euros **MER**
(£886,110) GP

(71)
In the town of Mâcon, a *maison de maitre*. The façade of the building has retained many architectural features with all of the windows boasting traditional shutters. Offers spacious accommodation.
587,234 euros **MER**
(£367,020) GP

(71)
A country cottage standing in 24,000m² of land featuring trees and flowers. Close to a quiet rural village and the town of Diou, this traditional residence comprises eight spacious rooms and a barn.
411,613 euros **MER**
(£257,260) GP

(21)
Charming 18th century farmhouse. Large salon/dining room, fitted kitchen, two/three bedrooms and separate guest house. Set in 4,000m² of gardens with a double garage. Excellent order throughout.
251,540 euros **BPS**
(£157,210) GP

(21)
A substantial farm property in a superb location. Comprising salon/dining rooms, two en-suite bedrooms, fitted kitchen and vaulted cellar. Complete with barn, stable and two apartments.
221,000 euros **BPS**
(£138,125) GP

(21)
A restored country cottage in a hillside setting. On the ground floor is a dining room, kitchen, cellar and shower room. Upstairs are two beamed bedrooms and a bathroom. Ideal second home.
121,197 euros **BPS**
(£75,750) GP

POITOU-CHARENTES

Price Guide

(17)
This recently-renovated farmhouse backs on to vineyards and enjoys views across the River Gironde. Set in 2,000m² of gardens, the property offers three bedrooms and a family bathroom.
131,150 euros **LAF**
(£81,970) GP

(16)
A restored cottage with many original features. The property has three bedrooms and is ready to move in to. Set within 1,300m² of mature gardens with a large detached barn and open views.
131,150 euros **LAF**
(£81,970) GP

(86)
An old house located in a small village near a town. The property is in need of renovation and offers eight main rooms. To the rear of the house is a courtyard and a garden with several outbuildings.
61,932 euros **LIN**
(£38,710) GP

(16)
Offering grounds of more than 10,000m², this detached house is set in a pretty hamlet. There are numerous bedrooms and open views over the countryside. The property is ready to move in to.
532,755 euros **VEF**
(£332,970) GP

(16)
Close to Rouillac, this former school has been renovated to create a four-bedroom home. Set in a quiet rural area, the property enjoys open views and a heated pool. It is ready for occupation.
196,659 euros **LAF**
(£122,910) GP

(79)
A country house with the option of purchasing 1,700m² of land. Comprises a kitchen, scullery, shower room, lounge with fireplace and five bedrooms. The grounds offer a barn and stables.
175,317 euros **LIN**
(£109,575) GP

(17)
A stunning 18th-century house located to the west of Cognac. With many original features, this large property offers 450m² of living space and 20,000m² of grounds with several outbuildings.
947,091 euros **FPY**
(£591,930) GP

(16)
Located near a small town, this beautifully-renovated farmhouse offers four bedrooms, a large living room, three bathrooms and well-appointed gardens of 12,000m² planted with trees.
314,600 euros **FPY**
(£196,625) GP

(16)
This stone-built period house is set near the town of Jarnac. It has been restored to a high standard and features three bedrooms, a living room, dining room, sun terrace and immaculate gardens.
261,803 euros **FPY**
(£163,625) GP

La Fonciere Charentaise

An established agency with 15 years experience

A wide range of property throughout the Poitou-Charente

Contact: **David or Vanessa Leake**

Tel: **00 33 5 45 21 78 38**

Fax: **00 33 5 45 21 78 39**

Email: **lfc-aigre@wanadoo.fr**

14 bis Grand Rue, Aigre 16140 FRANCE

Charente Property Services

For access to properties in the Poitou Charente Region of France, go to www.charenteproperty.co.uk
Or telephone/write to us direct and Guy Sparrow, who is English, will happily speak with you about your aims.

30 Rue Fareze 16700 Nanteuil en Vallee
00 33 5 45 85 49 93
Email: info@charenteproperty.co.uk

Fine Property - France
www.finepropertyfrance.com

Selected cottages, houses, chateaux from
£50,000 to £2 million
South Western France
Tel/Fax: 0033545 67 28 16
E-mail to info@finepropertyfrance.com
www.finepropertyfrance.com

L'Affaire Francaise
www.French-Property-net.com
UK Tel: 0208 570 9844
e-mail: FrenchProp@aol.com

CHARENTE
8 bedroom country house with 2 hectares of land, swimming pool and lovely views
Ref: 21657
Price: 396,675€

CHARENTE MARITIME
Restored 4 bed farmhouse, guest cottage, outbuildings, heated pool & 5000m² land
Ref: 21652
Price: 476,225€

English Estate Agents registered in France
Professional Card No 57 (Charente)
25 Grand Rue 16200 JARNAC France
Tel: 00 33 5 45 81 76 79 Fax: 00 33 5 45 35 09 52
Properties in the Charente, Charente Maritime, Dordogne and Limousin

Price Guide

(79)
A detached farmhouse located in a small town. Enjoying scenic views and a quiet location, the property has one large bedroom and stands in land of 2,800m². All main services are connected.
74,980 euros   **PAP**
(£46,865) GP

(16)
Set in a rural hamlet, this property dates from 1763 and has been converted from a coachhouse. Features 14 bedrooms, a small lake stocked with carp, stables, a dovecote and a swimming pool.
727,000 euros   **SIF**
(£454,375) GP

(86)
A classic three-bedroom French farmhouse that has been recently renovated. Features include oak floorboards and exposed beams. The property is set in a small hamlet, close to a market town.
131,200 euros   **PAP**
(£82,000) GP

(16)
A traditional two-bedroom stone-built farmhouse set in the country. Offers a garden of 1,700m² with a pond, terrace, courtyard and outbuildings. With open views, the property is habitable immediately.
121,631 euros   **LAT**
(£76,020) GP

(17)
This four-bedroom farmhouse has been completely renovated. Set in 18,000m² of land with a swimming pool and an attached gîte. Within a short drive of La Rochelle and local amenities.
348,244 euros   **LAF**
(£217,655) GP

(16)
Set in 500,000m² of meadows and woodland, this property features a kitchen, lounge and two bedroom suites. There is a gîte within the grounds, together with a barn and a huge wine cellar.
540,813 euros   **FWY**
(£338,010) GP

(16)
This small stone-built cottage is the perfect renovation project. Full of character, the property features a large attached barn, more than 4,000m² of land and impressive, panoramic views.
50,000 euros   **FDC**
(£31,350) GP

(16)
A three-bedroom house with a second house to finish renovating. This property features a swimming pool and 10,000m² of land, and is a short walk to the village and a stone's throw from a river.
280,000 euros   **FDC**
(£175,000) GP

(16)
In a mature garden of 1,600m², this detached house offers three double bedrooms, a fitted kitchen, living/dining room and a family bathroom. Features an attached barn for further conversion.
150,000 euros   **FDC**
(£93,750) GP

French Discoveries

Charente Office

Telephone our office in Charente for less than 10p/minute
on 0871 717 4164 or e-mail: Charente@french-discoveries.com

The *French Discoveries* offices are run by English couples who have been helping people to purchase property in France for more than 10 years.

Supported by our dedicated French and English teams, we offer a friendly, professional service, including translation and legal advice.

We invite you to visit our website on:

www.french-discoveries.com

which is up-dated weekly, or to chat in English with the people who have actually visited the properties.

Associate offices in Brittany and Normandy.

Offices opening soon in Burgundy, Languedoc and Loire.

Leggett Immobilier
S.A.R.L • Transactions Immobilières

Ref: CL322 Price: 42,686€ - Large house to renovate situated in a small hamlet in a very pretty area of the Charente. The house has electricity and water connected and is structurally sound. 900m² of adjoining land.

Ref: CP374 Price: 100,650€ - Renovated country cottage in need of finishing, with barn (200m²), outbuildings and roughly 5,000m² of land. Situated in a beautiful isolated and wooded spot of the south east Charente with fine views. The house (170m² habitable) comprises: large living room with tiled floor wood burner and exposed beams, kitchen with wood-fired range, bathroom, WC, three bedrooms, workshop and wood-fired central heating.

Ref: CB336 Price: 134,384€ - Renovated country house in excellent condition situated in a peaceful area, with barn and 3,700m² of land. The house has 3 bedrooms, a kitchen, bathroom, an open-plan lounge and dining room. There is oil-fired central heating in the house.

Ref: CP357 Price: 196,658€ - Pretty collection of farm buildings, including a main house, gite and barn, situated in a very calm area in 5,000m² of land. The main house comprises of kitchen, lounge, dining room, bathroom, WC and 3 bedrooms. The gite has a lounge, kitchen, bathroom/toilet and 2 bedrooms. The main house is heated by wood fired central heating. The whole property has been re-roofed recently and is all in excellent condition.

Tel: **00 33 5 53 56 62 54**
Fax: **00 33 5 53 56 62 57**
email: **sales@frenchestateagents.com**
www.frenchestateagents.com

Muret Immobilier
Rue du Puits de L'Appent 16560 Coulgens

Whether you are seeking a holiday home, a peaceful haven for your retirement or even buildings to convert into gîtes, then look no further than our beautiful department, situated between the vineyards of Cognac and the gateway to the Dordogne area.

QUALITY SERVICE and **EFFICIENCY** have been our motto for many years.

WE AWAIT YOUR CALL!!!!

Tel: **00 33 5 45 70 32 74**
Fax: **00 33 5 45 91 42 66**
email: **muretmichel@wanado.fr**

Podium Habitat

Agence de Saint Maixent
15 Place du Marché
Tel: 00 33 5 49 17 00 22 Fax: 00 33 5 49 17 09 11

Agence de Melle
5 Grand' Rue
Tel: 00 33 5 49 27 24 10

www.podiumhabitat.com

As featured in Channel 4's 'A Place in the Sun!'

Price Guide

(79)
A characterful watermill for renovation. Within 16,000m² of land, the property comprises a millhouse, gatehouse, separate single-storey building and miller's house, all set around a stone courtyard.
116,500 euros   **MAM**
(£72,815) GP

(16)
Situated in rolling grassland of 40,000m² close to picturesque lakes, this barn and small house are in need of renovation. The house offers three main rooms, and services have been connected.
117,386 euros   **FWY**
(£73,365) GP

(17)
Located in a village, this period home is set in 200m² of gardens with a terrace and mature trees. An unusual property, this house features two towers that accommodate eight large bedrooms.
263,431 euros   **LIN**
(£164,645) GP

(79)
A family home on the banks of the River Sèvre and close to a picturesque village. Benefiting from a tranquil rural setting, this property offers a mature garden with trees and four bedrooms.
182,000 euros   **MAM**
(£113,750) GP

(17)
Set in a village with swimming and horse riding facilities, this detached stone-built house offers living space of 130m². The house features a terrace, garage and three bedrooms with wooden floors.
75,462 euros   **LIN**
(£47,165) GP

(17)
Located in a hamlet, this old farm building is set in a quiet area. Partially restored, with new windows and shutters, this home has a rustic garden planted with trees and offers four main rooms.
50,308 euros   **LIN**
(£31,445) GP

(79)
With the potential for six bedrooms, this property is currently a bar and restaurant. In need of renovation, the building offers wooden floors, large garages, storage rooms and a wine cellar.
121,000 euros   **MAM**
(£75,625) GP

(16)
In a hamlet surrounded by vineyards, this renovated farmhouse stands in grounds of 4,670m². Benefits from a swimming pool and library, and offers four bedrooms and a separate small house.
278,000 euros   **LIN**
(£173,750) GP

(79)
A detached house and a second house with a barn and garage. Set in 3,860m² of lawned gardens, the main house offers three bedrooms. The property is located close to the village of Celles-sur-Belle.
211,700 euros   **PAP**
(£132,315) GP

Poitou-Charentes

(79)
A renovated cottage with a guest-house to finish. Set in 9,000m² of land with horse-riding, golf and cycling facilities close by. Offers a terrace that overlooks a lake, and three large en-suite bedrooms.
193,350 euros   MAM
(£120,845) GP

(16)
An old stone-built house with an enclosed garden. On the ground floor is a kitchen, dining room and WC, while the first floor offers two bedrooms. Complete with a large barn for conversion.
80,000 euros   LIN
(£50,000) GP

(17)
An old stone Charentais house with a 5,000m² garden. Parts of the property are in need of some work but are perfectly habitable. Offers four large bedrooms, two bathrooms and one shower room.
117,386 euros   MAM
(£73,365) GP

(79)
A fully-renovated house standing in large established grounds of 7,300m² with a well-stocked lake. On the outskirts of a small town, the property offers a dining room, three bedrooms and a small study.
214,000 euros   MAM
(£133,750) GP

(79)
A cottage located in peaceful, rural surroundings. With three bedrooms, the property sits on a 2,290m² plot and enjoys open views. A short drive from the village of Clussais-la-Pommeraie.
100,500 euros   PAP
(£62,815) GP

(79)
A detached house in Exoudun with a 1,800m² plot. The house features six bedrooms with rural views and five bathrooms. Outside there are outbuildings, a courtyard and a heated swimming pool.
316,700 euros   PAP
(£197,940) GP

(16)
Located in a pretty rural hamlet 10km from a market town and set in a large meadow. This ensemble of buildings includes five stone outbuildings in need of renovation and a small cottage with a well.
58,693 euros   LIN
(£36,685) GP

(79)
Offering 100,000m² of land with a river running through it, this farm features two houses with central heating and several stone outbuildings that could be converted into gites or stabling.
222,250 euros   MAM
(£138,905) GP

(86)
A town house set in Civray within easy reach of local amenities. To the rear of the property there is a small courtyard, while the house features three good-sized bedrooms and is ready for occupation.
80,272 euros   PAP
(£50,170) GP

Price Guide

(16)
A four-bedroom detached stone house with a triple garage and outbuildings set in nearly 1,500m² of well-maintained gardens. The property features a large living room, kitchen and bathroom.
159,525 euros   **LAT**
(£99,705) GP

(16)
A character house with a large garden located in a rural hamlet. This property enjoys open views and comprises four bedrooms. The house is ready to move in to and has all services connected.
190,366 euros   **VEF**
(£118,980) GP

(79)
A picturesque character château offering 16 bedrooms. Set in grounds of 20,033m² close to Gournay-Loizé, the château features several spacious rooms and is approached via a long drive.
595,500 euros   **PAP**
(£372,190) GP

(16)
This detached house is located close to a village. Set in grounds of nearly 30,000m² with four mobile homes for letting, the house offers three bedrooms and open views. Close to Exideuil.
169,300 euros   **PAP**
(£105,815) GP

(16)
A stone house with a garage and a garden of nearly 900m². The ground floor comprises a living room, dining room and kitchen. On the first floor are a bathroom, separate WC and three bedrooms.
137,350 euros   **LAT**
(£85,845) GP

(16)
A three-bedroom farmhouse that is ready to move in to. This property features a small well-maintained garden with a barn and is located on the outskirts of a typical Charentais hamlet.
90,202 euros   **VEF**
(£56,375) GP

(16)
In the town of Confolens, this terraced house offers five spacious light-filled bedrooms. The property is within easy access of local amenities and is ready to move in to. All services are connected.
203,246 euros   **PAP**
(£127,030) GP

(16)
Enjoying 3,000m² of gardens with country views, this house has been recently renovated. Set in a village, this property has two good-sized bedrooms and a third room that could be converted.
96,691 euros   **LAF**
(£60,430) GP

(16)
This character house is located in a hamlet on the Charente-Limousin border. With three bedrooms and many original features, the property is set in a large garden and is ready for occupation.
196,409 euros   **VEF**
(£122,755) GP

Poitou-Charentes

(16)
Set near the Charente-Limousin border, this character property is currently being run as a restaurant. Offering several bedrooms, it is located on the edge of a town and features a barn in its grounds.
332,285 euros   **VEF**
(£207,680) GP

(86)
This detached bungalow is located close to Availles-Limouzine and has a parking space for one car. Standing in 10,000m^2 of land with trees and a patio area, this property offers three bedrooms.
117,700 euros   **PAP**
(£73,565) GP

(85)
Set in a quiet village, this terraced house offers three bedrooms and a single garage. The property benefits from being close to local amenities and has a small garden of 820m^2 to the rear of the house.
49,500 euros   **PAP**
(£30,940) GP

(86)
Approached via a gravel drive, this detached three-storey house offers several bedroom suites. The property is located in a small town and enjoys open views. Set in a garden planted with mature trees.
135,366 euros   **VEF**
(£84,605) GP

(79)
A characterful country cottage in tranquil surroundings. Located close to the village of Clussais-la-Pommeraie, this property offers three bedrooms and stands in a well-maintained garden of 820m^2.
100,500 euros   **PAP**
(£62,815) GP

(79)
This country cottage offers two bedrooms, an outbuilding and a garden planted with trees and shrubs. The property enjoys open rural views and is just a short distance from the village of Ensigné.
71,000 euros   **PAP**
(£44,375) GP

(86)
Close to a stunning forest, this traditional country cottage enjoys rural views and a garden of 1,072m^2 with lawns and mature trees. The property has four large bedrooms and a family bathroom.
152,400 euros   **PAP**
(£95,250) GP

(86)
Set in the village of Persac, these two small properties could be converted into one main house. The first building offers a large room with a fireplace, the second has a bedroom and a bathroom.
22,562 euros   **LIN**
(£14,100) GP

(16)
Set in a hamlet close to Alloue, this detached stone-built house offers a second house in need of complete renovation. The main house comprises three bedrooms and stands in 3,000m^2 of gardens.
47,600 euros   **PAP**
(£29,750) GP

Price Guide

(86)
Set near the village of Pressac, this detached former mill house with an outbuilding stands on land of approximately 30,000m². The house offers four bedrooms and enjoys a swimming pool.
284,800 euros   **PAP**
(£178,000) GP

(17)
This single-storey house offers an open-plan kitchen, living room, two bedrooms and a shower room with separate WC. Benefits from a terrace leading onto an enclosed garden with a double garage.
65,706 euros   **FWY**
(£41,065) GP

(86)
A grand stone-built house standing in a well-maintained garden of 2,500m². The property features 12 bedrooms and a stable block. Set in a tourist area, just a short drive from the Atlantic coast.
480,000 euros   **FPL**
(£300,000) GP

(16)
A semi-detached house with traditional wooden shutters. The ground floor offers a large living room, fully-fitted kitchen and cellar. On the first floor there are three bedrooms and a bathroom.
100,600 euros   **LAT**
(£62,875) GP

(79)
Located near the village of Aubigné, this property comprises several large barns in need of complete renovation. Set in a rural location, the property benefits from open views and a garden.
41,921 euros   **PAP**
(£26,200) GP

(86)
This period house near Poitiers comprises a kitchen, dining room, bathroom and three bedrooms. Set in land of 2,500m² with an orchard, several outbuildings and potential for development.
122,000 euros   **FPL**
(£76,250) GP

(17)
Close to the town of Saint-Jean-d'Angély, a large watermill in need of restoration. The property offers a large living area and several outbuildings set in extensive open grounds of 45,000m².
379,751 euros   **APN**
(£237,345) GP

(17)
A large renovated farmhouse with a separate studio apartment set in the tranquil surroundings of the Gartempe Valley. Features five bedrooms, a swimming pool, stone staircase and attached barn.
285,841 euros   **FPL**
(£178,650) GP

(16)
One hour from Bordeaux, this farmhouse features a swimming pool, four bedrooms and a barn for renovation. Located near a village in 12,000m² of gardens with mature trees and open views.
208,500 euros   **FPL**
(£130,315) GP

Poitou-Charentes

(16)
A renovated *fermette* located a short distance from a busy market town. With a well-maintained garden, this property comprises a dining room, three bedrooms, a bathroom and double garage.
120,000 euros   **FPL**
(£75,000) GP

(16)
Located in a riverside village, a restored house comprising four spacious bedrooms and several outbuildings. The property boasts rural views and is set in a walled garden of 2,800m² with trees.
409,707 euros   **LAF**
(£256,065) GP

(17)
This restored farmhouse with a large enclosed courtyard is set in the idyllic hamlet of Bresdon. Comprising three bedrooms, the property has a covered entrance, driveway and attached barn.
409,707 euros   **LAF**
(£256,065) GP

(16)
A traditional farmhouse with a detached barn and 7,000m² of enclosed land. Comprises four bedrooms and set on the edge of a picturesque village with a school, shops and all facilities.
294,989 euros   **LAF**
(£184,370) GP

(17)
In an isolated rural spot close to the small village of Migron, this farmhouse offers 5,000m² of land and a separate partially-restored cottage. The farmhouse features three spacious bedroom suites.
172,000 euros   **LAF**
(£107,500) GP

(17)
A four-bedroom house with large outbuildings and a heated pool. Set in 30,000m² of gardens with mature trees and plenty of room for parking. The property is situated in open, rural surroundings.
409,707 euros   **LAF**
(£256,065) GP

(79)
Located in the village of Pioussay close to local amenities, this property comprises a farmhouse and a separate cottage. The main house offers three bedrooms and stands in a garden of 1,238m².
213,800 euros   **PAP**
(£133,625) GP

(16)
A restored two-bedroom cottage located in a pretty hamlet close to the town of Villebois-Lavalette. Enjoying open country views and a small garden, this property is ready for occupation.
57,931 euros   **LAF**
(£36,205) GP

(16)
Dating from the 18th century, this recently-restored watermill offers two bedrooms and a separate barn for conversion. Close to the town of Rouillac and set in garden of 11,000m² with mature trees.
311,377 euros   **FPL**
(£194,610) GP

Price Guide

(17)
This traditional farmhouse is set near a quiet rural village in 10,000m² of mixed land. Enjoying views to the Gironde Estuary, the property benefits from several outbuildings for conversion.
263,375 euros   **LAF**
(£164,610) GP

(16)
A Charentais house with a Dutch barn. Set in 3,500m² of mature grounds that include a swimming pool, dovecote and outbuilding for conversion. The house offers two large bedrooms.
270,900 euros   **LAF**
(£169,315) GP

(17)
This restored house with three bedrooms and three bathrooms features spacious rooms with lots of light. Set in rural surroundings of 4,000m², the property enjoys open views and a quiet setting.
262,964 euros   **LAF**
(£164,355) GP

(17)
Dating from the 17th century, this five-bedroom dwelling offers land of 12,000m² with a barn and a self-contained apartment. Located near a small village, the property is ready for occupation.
467,088 euros   **LAF**
(£291,930) GP

(17)
A restored watermill with six bedrooms. Located in a quiet hamlet and currently run as a hotel, it offers a one-bedroom gîte, outbuildings for conversion and is set in 10,500m² of land.
426,775 euros   **LAF**
(£266,735) GP

(17)
Located in Genac, this character house with three bedrooms. Set in a small fenced-in garden, the property has one bathroom and is ready to move in to. All mains services have been connected.
246,574 euros   **LAF**
(£154,110) GP

(17)
Set beside a river in gardens of 22,000m², this imposing château boasts 14 bedrooms and three independent apartments. Features include a chapel, old well and several large outbuildings.
1,541,250 euros   **LAF**
(£963,280) GP

(17)
This large detached house comes with five good-sized bedrooms and a heated swimming pool. Set in the village of Villars-en-Pons with 10,000m² of gardens and plenty of space for car parking.
397,750 euros   **LAF**
(£248,595) GP

(16)
A renovated house in a village location. With four bedrooms, a family bathroom and a courtyard, the property is ready to move in to and features a small garden with views over the countryside.
180,271 euros   **LAF**
(£112,670) GP

Poitou-Charentes

(79)
An ensemble of two houses close to a town. House one has been recently renovated and comprises three bedrooms. House two is in need of some finishing-off work, and could offer three bedrooms.
284,375 euros   <u>ALZ</u>
(£177,735) GP

(86)
This former presbytery offers six bedrooms and a spacious attic for conversion. Enclosed in a walled garden of 3,600m² featuring a patio area and mature trees. In a quiet spot, close to a village.
292,000 euros   <u>ALZ</u>
(£182,500) GP

(17)
Close to Saintes, a large *longère* offering 200m² of living space. Comprises four bedrooms, a study, two living rooms and two outbuildings. Stands in a garden of 4,248m² with mature trees.
371,671 euros   <u>APN</u>
(£232,295) GP

(16)
A restored farmhouse offering four bedrooms, two bathrooms and a dovecote for conversion. The property enjoys a heated swimming pool and is set in a large well-maintained garden.
415,000 euros   <u>AZL</u>
(£259,375) GP

(79)
An impressive château featuring 17 en-suite bedrooms. Ideal as a hotel, the property is set in land of 20,000m² featuring mature trees and a large lawned area. In need of a some interior work.
553,400 euros   <u>ALZ</u>
(£345,875) GP

(16)
This *maison de maitre* boasts 10 bedrooms, five bathrooms and three outbuildings. Set in land of 10,000m² with a swimming pool and two detached gîtes with views and a quiet location.
724,132 euros   <u>AND</u>
(£452,585) S

(16)
An old village house with a garage and courtyard. The property features a living room, fully-fitted kitchen, three bedrooms and a bathroom. Set in a small garden to the front and side of the house.
97,567 euros   <u>LAT</u>
(£60,980) GP

(86)
Overlooking a beautiful valley, this farmhouse offers five bedrooms and a studio apartment. Set in 5,000m² of land with a large barn. Enjoys a heated swimming pool and sun terrace.
326,350 euros   <u>ALZ</u>
(£203,970) GP

(16)
A stone-built terraced house with a courtyard and garden. Offers a dining room, two bedrooms and a kitchen. In need of some work, the property comes with a well, dovecote and large bread oven.
46,811 euros   <u>LAT</u>
(£29,255) GP

Price Guide

(79)
This three-bedroom dwelling has been recently restored. Features a large living room of 95m², outbuildings and tree-filled gardens of 2,800m². Enjoys a quiet country location with splendid views.
274,000 euros   ALZ
(£171,250) GP

(16)
On the banks of the River Charente, a *maison de maitre* arranged over three floors. Comprises nine bedrooms with en-suite facilities, a studio apartment, cellars and a tennis court.
729,800 euros   LAT
(£456,125) GP

(16)
A restored manor house set in 15,000m² of land. Currently divided into two dwellings, the property comprises five bedrooms, two bathrooms, two fitted kitchens and several outbuildings.
409,575 euros   WAT
(£255,985) GP

(16)
A south-facing house situated in a quiet village. Set in 1,300m² of land with several outbuildings, it features an open-plan kitchen and living room, master bedroom and two further double bedrooms.
403,989 euros   LAT
(£252,495) GP

(79)
A classic *maison de maitre* with six bedrooms. Set in large wooded and lawned grounds with several outbuildings and a second house. Features large reception rooms, a kitchen and extensive library.
480,215 euros   ALZ
(£300,135) GP

(16)
Approached via a long drive, a Charentais-style house with a one-bedroom annexe. Set in over 4,200m² of grounds, the property features exposed beams, four large bedrooms and a huge living room.
389,220 euros   LAT
(£243,265) GP

(16)
Set in a hamlet, an old farmhouse with a courtyard and adjoining outbuilding. Requiring complete renovation, the property currently comprises two large ground-floor rooms and a convertible attic.
19,200 euros   CUR
(£12,000) GP

(79)
A stone-built house with three large bedrooms. Set in a tourist area and overlooking a lake, the property enjoys attractive lawned gardens. Located in a quiet country area, close to a lively village.
245,639 euros   ALZ
(£153,525) GP

(16)
Dating from the 19th century, a *maison de maitre* with an outbuilding that could be converted into a gîte. Set in an enclosed garden laid to lawn with mature trees, a pond, fountain and a well.
208,000 euros   CUR
(£130,000) GP

Poitou-Charentes

(17)
A modern villa with a swimming pool set in 3,300m² of land. A short distance from a quiet village, the villa comprises an open-plan kitchen and living room, three double bedrooms and a garage.
229,513 euros   WAT
(£143,445) GP

(16)
A renovated town house standing in 2,500m² of grounds featuring a double garage and a small house for total renovation. The main house features three bedrooms, a kitchen, dressing room and cellar.
241,173 euros   HIF
(£150,735) GP

(79)
A small gîte complex comprising three cottages. Located in a hamlet within easy reach of a lake and swimming facilities, the property features pitched ceilings, exposed beams and an orchard.
309,725 euros   CUR
(£193,725) GP

(16)
A four-bedroom detached house with a veranda, fitted kitchen, corner-kitchen and garage. Set in a shaded garden of 3,000m² with stunning country views. On the ground floor is a studio apartment.
131,715 euros   HIF
(£82,320) GP

(86)
A fully-restored farmhouse dating from 1778. Features stone walls, wooden doors and exposed beams. Surrounded by woodland, the property boasts a garden with a flood-lit pool and fruit trees.
317,000 euros   CUR
(£198,125) GP

(16)
This restored farmhouse is set in a lawned garden of 3,000m² with open views. Offers a fitted kitchen, sitting room and three bedrooms and features a courtyard and outbuildings for conversion.
165,240 euros   HIF
(£103,275) GP

(19)
A restored farmhouse set in the countryside near a village. With a swimming pool, pond, orchard, terraces and two fields, the property comprises four bedrooms, an artist's studio and a gallery.
288,100 euros   CUR
(£180,065) GP

(86)
A large house and four gîtes set around a courtyard with an adjacent meadow. In easy reach of a historic town and the coastal resorts, the property offers private gardens and a swimming pool.
592,300 euros   CUR
(£370,190) GP

(17)
Formerly a mill complex, this large house is situated in a hamlet with open views over the countryside and a river. Sits in parkland of 15,000m² featuring two islands, terraces and a stone-built bridge.
426,100 euros   CUR
(£266,315) GP

Price Guide

(17)
A three-bedroom stone-built house set in 2,000m² of gardens. In easy reach of the beach and a town, the property retains many original features including plaster mouldings and ceiling roses.
608,187 euros   **CUR**
(£380,115) GP

(17)
This six-bedroom manor house is set on the banks of the River Charente. Situated in open land, the estate offers two islands and private moorings Features a swimming pool covered by a dome.
640,000 euros   **CUR**
(£400,000) GP

(79)
A 17th-century manor house and four-bedroom gîte. The main house offers five bedrooms and a large reception area, and the entire property enjoys splendid views across a river and 3,000m² of land.
465,000 euros   **ALZ**
(£290,625) GP

(16)
A converted barn standing in 2,500m² of lawned gardens with mature trees, shrubs and a sun terrace. Comprises a large living room, kitchen and mezzanine, and offers lots of additional space.
151,229 euros   **HIF**
(£94,520) GP

(16)
Dating from the 18th century, a large château surrounded by open parkland of 49,000m². Offering nine bedrooms, a caretaker's residence, two separate lodges, two small lakes and a swimming pool.
576,258 euros   **POD**
(£360,160) GP

(16)
In the centre of a town, a totally-renovated house with a heated pool. Comprises an enclosed courtyard garden, three bedrooms, a fitted kitchen and living room. Adjoining the property is a barn.
194,700 euros   **CHA**
(£121,690) GP

(17)
A traditional Charentais house comprising three bedrooms. Set in an enclosed tree-filled garden of 6,800m², it features a terrace, living room, fitted kitchen, laundry room and a convertible attic.
158,699 euros   **HIF**
(£99,190) GP

(17)
Located in a small a village, this house offers two bedrooms, a dressing room, fitted kitchen, living room and wine store and stands in a shaded, enclosed garden of 1,546m² with a garage.
98,100 euros   **HIF**
(£61,315) GP

(16)
Enjoying unrestricted views overlooking a lake and beautiful countryside, this period house features three attached cottages. Each cottage has its own entrance and offers two to three bedrooms.
575,000 euros   **CHA**
(£359,375) GP

Poitou-Charentes

(16)
This large property, a former farmhouse, offers many unique design features. Complete with a barn for conversion into a separate guest cottage, a heated swimming pool and 9,000m² of grounds.
526,750 euros   LAF
(£329,220) GP

(16)
An imposing farmhouse dating from the 18th century. Totally restored, the property comprises five bedrooms, a swimming pool and several outbuildings. Surrounded by 8,000m² of land.
411,725 euros   LAF
(£257,330) GP

(16)
A typical Charentais-style house with an open-plan lounge and dining room, kitchen, bathroom, four bedrooms and several large outbuildings. Stands in enclosed woodland of nearly 2,000m².
114,337 euros   NON
(£71,460) GP

(17)
Set on the outskirts of a typical Charentais village and a short walk from a river, this modern bungalow enjoys an enclosed garden of 1,425m² and is surrounded by farmland and countryside.
796,555 euros   HIF
(£497,845) GP

(16)
Dating from 1900, a stone-built house close to shops and the town of Saint-Aulaye. Comprising four bedrooms, an entrance hall, dining room, study and pantry, the property is set in a garden of 2,000m².
132,871 euros   SIN
(£83,045) GP

(16)
Built in the 17th century, this property comprises a main three-bedroom house and two smaller houses in need of some work. Set in land of 2,000m² with orchards, a garden and a swimming pool.
290,000 euros   SIN
(£181,250) GP

(16)
A restored watermill located in the heart of the country. Offers four bedrooms, two reception rooms, a kitchen and a very large garden enjoying stunning views. Benefits from a quiet situation.
292,245 euros   FRA
(£182,655) GP

(16)
This country residence has been totally renovated and comes with an attached barn. Surrounded by a landscaped parkland garden with a swimming pool. The property boasts six en-suite bedrooms.
274,500 euros   CHA
(£171,565) GP

(16)
Located on the edge of a village near the town of Chalais, this property stands in a well-maintained garden and enjoys excellent countryside views. The house offers three bedrooms and cellar.
110,000 euros   HIF
(£68,750) GP

Price Guide

(79)
This renovated farmhouse offers three bedrooms and comes with a four-bedroom gîte. With lots of room for extension, the property enjoys a secluded, private location, a swimming pool and patio area.
170,500 euros   ALZ
(£106,565) GP

(17)
A short drive from the coast, this large character house offers two spacious bedrooms overlooking the garden. Features a study and living area of 149m^2. Set in a garden with outbuildings.
210,075 euros   APN
(£131,300) GP

(79)
Dating from the 15th century, this old fortified building has been partly restored and is set in large grounds. The main house features many original stone carvings and three bedrooms.
230,000 euros   ALZ
(£143,750) GP

(17)
An 18th-century château set in the heart of the countryside. With 20 main rooms and numerous bedrooms, the property features many original details and stands in 30,000m^2 of mature parkland.
564,586 euros   APN
(£352,865) GP

(79)
A very large mill house located close to Niort. With various barns and outbuildings, the property has been well restored and enjoys a heated swimming pool. Stands in a tree-filled garden laid to lawn.
559,500 euros   ALZ
(£349,690) GP

(79)
Near a small village, this mill house dates from the 18th century. Completely restored, with three bedrooms, two bathrooms and a kitchen, it is set in 2,000m^2 of gardens with a large pond.
400,000 euros   ALZ
(£250,000) GP

(79)
Recently renovated, this riverside dwelling comprises five bedrooms and three bathrooms. Featuring an indoor swimming pool, the house is set close to a village and has extensive gardens of 2,000m^2.
320,000 euros   ALZ
(£143,750) GP

(79)
An old priory dating from the 14th century with five bedrooms and a large vaulted cellar. Set in 10,000m^2 of grounds with a barn, the property is complete with a second house for renovation.
360,000 euros   ALZ
(£225,000) GP

(17)
Near the town of Saintes, this 19th-century estate comprises a main house, gîte, swimming pool and outbuildings. Stands in 4,370m^2 of landscaped gardens set within a forest and meadows.
403,990 euros   APN
(£252,495) GP

LIMOUSIN & AUVERGNE

Price Guide

(87)
A restored farmhouse comprising three bedrooms and a gîte to be let out. Set in 9,000m² of land with mature gardens and open views. The house is split over two levels and boasts spacious rooms.
295,625 euros **LAF**
(£184,765) GP

(87)
Close to Châlus and set on the outskirts of a village, this large traditional house with an attached barn offers three bedrooms. Set in 2,500m² of landscaped garden, the house is bordered by woodland.
197,800 euros **LAF**
(£123,625) GP

(87)
A traditional farmhouse built in stone. Dating from 1641 and set in gardens of 8,000m² with trees and shrubs. The property enjoys unrestricted views and boasts many original architectural details.
197,800 euros **LAF**
(£123,625) GP

(87)
This presbytery-style farmhouse, built in stone, is close to the town of Bessines-sur-Gartempe. Newly renovated, the property has three bedrooms and enjoys 200m² of living space. Set in a small garden.
195,134 euros **FWY**
(£121,960) GP

(87)
Dating from the 15th century, this large, semi-restored convent is set in 2,000m² of land with a private lake and swimming pool. Features a stone staircase, six bedrooms and three large reception rooms.
368,927 euros **FWY**
(£230,580) GP

(87)
A farmhouse set in 12,300m² of land on the outskirts of a typical Limousin hamlet. The buildings form a U-shape with a courtyard in the middle. There are five main rooms and numerous outbuildings.
167,700 euros **FWY**
(£104,815) GP

(87)
Located on the Limousin-Dordogne border, a barn for conversion. Situated on the edge of a small hamlet in a national park, the property is surrounded by fields of 4,500m² with open views.
27,440 euros **FWY**
(£17,150) GP

(87)
Dating from the 15th century, a *maison de maitre* for renovation. Boasting large spacious rooms, the property comprises two bedrooms and features a stone staircase, large fireplaces and exposed beams.
83,850 euros **FWY**
(£52,405) GP

(23)
Surrounded by greenery and set beside a river, a house comprising two kitchens, sitting room, two bedrooms, bathroom and terrace. Close to a medieval village. With a separate two-room apartment.
109,763 euros **VAN**
(£68,600) GP

Limousin & Auvergne

(23)
Ready to move in to, a detached house with four bedrooms. Set close to a village, the property benefits from a small private garden that is bordered by a pretty meadow and wooded area.
96,799 euros **VEF**
(£60,500) GP

(87)
A historic 17th-century manor house with nine bedrooms. Many original details are still in place, including a stone spiral staircase and open fireplaces. Set in land of 28,000m² with outbuildings.
575,125 euros **LAF**
(£359,455) GP

(87)
A terraced bungalow with a large garden. Set in a pretty hamlet in a quiet location. The property enjoys open views and comprises three spacious bedrooms. Comes with an attached outbuilding.
87,019 euros **VEF**
(£54,385) GP

(23)
This detached house in Creuse has a large, pretty garden with lawns, trees and a swimming pool. Set in a secluded area, the property offers four bedrooms, several bathrooms and open rural views.
338,979 euros **FPP**
(£211,860) GP

(87)
A period town house with two striking towers. This property enjoys spacious rooms and boasts five bedrooms. Surrounding the house are gardens of 1,800m² with mature trees and open views.
349,375 euros **LAF**
(£218,360) GP

(87)
This detached house with two bedrooms is set in a small hamlet. Featuring a private garden and an underground garage, the property is ready to move in to and offers two bedrooms and a small terrace.
127,143 euros **VEF**
(£79,465) GP

(23)
This large detached house is situated on the outskirts of a pretty hamlet. In a tranquil rural location, the property offers several bedrooms and is set in a well-maintained garden with a garage.
524,000 euros **VEF**
(£327,500) GP

(87)
Offering numerous bedrooms, this large château is set in a secluded location. Approached by a long drive, the property enjoys extensive grounds of 200,000m² and is surrounded by woodland.
545,082 euros **VEF**
(£340,675) GP

(23)
A small cottage with a secluded garden. On one level, the property offers a kitchen, dining room, bedroom, and lounge. Original features include an open fireplace, outside cellar and stone archways.
30,490 euros **LIN**
(£19,055)

Price Guide

(23)
A restored mill with a lake, gîte and chalet. The mill features three bedroom suites and a mezzanine. The chalet offers two bedrooms, a terrace overlooking the lake and a dining room with granite fireplace.
712,000 euros   **LIN**
(£445,000) GP

(87)
Situated in a small hamlet, a stone-built house comprising a kitchen, cellar, two bedrooms and one bathroom. To the rear of the property is a private garden of 1,700m² with two outbuildings.
44,473 euros   **LIN**
(£27,795) GP

(87)
An 18th-century château close to a historical village. Set in land of 25,000m² with outbuildings and a swimming pool. Features a tower, marble fireplace, orangery, 11 bedrooms and five bathrooms.
727,000 euros   **SIF**
(£454,375) GP

(19)
Close to a river, this 17th-century property enjoys 89,000m² of woodlands with a stream and small lake. Offering five bedrooms, the home has a spiral staircase, library, casement windows and a terrace.
1,131,172 euros   **MOD**
(£706,985) GP

(87)
A traditional stone-built barn for conversion. Electricity and water are nearby and ready to connect. Close to a town, the property has 100m² of living space, a garden and separate grounds of 3,000m².
21,500 euros   **LIN**
(£13,440) GP

(19)
Near Vignols, a house dating from 1800. Set in a quiet, rural location, the property features a double garage, barn, bread oven and workshop. With 1,900m² of land. Offers three large bedrooms.
149,000 euros   **LIN**
(£93,125) GP

(87)
Situated in a pretty village, this house comprises a hall, kitchen, sitting room and two bedrooms. Attached to the house is a garage and workshop. Set in a garden with a well and small outbuilding.
63,500 euros   **FPL**
(£39,690) GP

(87)
A large house on the edge of a quiet village. The ground floor comprises a fitted kitchen, sitting room and dining room. At the top of a marble staircase there are four bedrooms and a bathroom.
145,000 euros   **FPL**
(£90,625) GP

(87)
A modern house in the country. Benefiting from three bedrooms, the property features a large living room with fireplace, bathroom, fitted kitchen, summer-kitchen and garage. Set in a large garden.
118,147 euros   **FPL**
(£73,840) GP

Limousin & Auvergne

(87)
Close to a river, a village house with three bedrooms. Features include exposed beams, fireplaces and a fitted kitchen. Upstairs are three bedrooms. Set in 1,200m² of gardens with open country views.
84,600 euros **FPL**
(£52,875) GP

(87)
Set in an isolated location, a listed 12th-century chapel. Comprising two houses, stables, five barns and numerous outbuildings. In need of complete renovation, the property sits in land of almost 8,000m².
165,000 euros **FPL**
(£103,125) GP

(87)
A large farmhouse, 19th-century château, gardener's house, various barns, outbuildings and a chapel, approached by a private driveway. In 39,000m² of pasture, including a separate farm and picturesque lake.
963,500 euros **FPL**
(£602,190) GP

(19)
This character house with two bedrooms and a double garage sits in a garden of 650m². Offers a living room with fireplace, two shower rooms and a sitting room. Set in a peaceful environment.
105,572 euros **LIN**
(£65,980) GP

(87)
A farmhouse with 34,000m² of agricultural land. Approached by a long open drive, the property is habitable but in need of extensive renovation. Close to a village and surrounded by rural countryside.
57,930 euros **FPL**
(£36,205) GP

(87)
This character house is set in a hamlet, close to the small town of Bellac. Comprising two houses that could be converted into one four-bedroom house. Comes with a tree-filled garden and a barn.
33,500 euros **FPL**
(£20,940) GP

(19)
On the Haute-Vienne/Creuse border. Currently a popular bar and restaurant, this property comprises three bedrooms, a living room, shower room, attic and a small garden. In need of renovation.
164,000 euros **FPL**
(£102,500) GP

(87)
Close to a small town, this house is set in a garden of 500m² and comes with the possibility of buying further land. There are four bedrooms arranged over two floors and a large living room.
70,000 euros **FPL**
(£43,750) GP

(87)
By the side of a railway, this small cottage is situated on the outskirts of a quiet hamlet. The property comprises two rooms on the ground floor and two rooms upstairs. Set in a small garden.
21,300 euros **FPL**
(£13,315) GP

Price Guide

(87)
A large renovated house with vast landscaped gardens of 15,000m². Boasting numerous bedrooms and bathrooms, the property benefits from a private swimming pool and enjoys open woodland views.
338,500 euros　　　　**FPL**
(£211,565) GP

(19)
Dating from the 17th century, a property standing in gardens of nearly 800m². Comprising two south-facing reception rooms, a separate kitchen, four bedrooms and a cellar. In need of some work.
211,000 euros　　　　**LAT**
(£131,875) GP

(87)
In a small village close to lakes and rivers. This house comprises a joint living room and kitchen, dining room, bathroom and two bedrooms. Set in a garden with a small house for renovation.
94,350 euros　　　　**FPL**
(£58,970) GP

(03)
An ancient farmhouse with a barn on one side and stables on the other. In need of restoration, it stands in 2,800m² of land in a quiet village setting. Comprises four rooms. Comes with a cottage.
60,980 euros　　　　**AUV**
(£38,110) GP

(87)
A small character farmhouse and barn for renovation. Situated in a small garden on the edge of a pretty hamlet. Set on high, the farmhouse enjoys open views of a nearby river and meadows.
23,000 euros　　　　**FPL**
(£14,375) GP

(23)
Built in 1966 and set in almost 1,560m² of garden with a swimming pool. Enjoying magnificent country views, this property comprises three large bedrooms, a fitted kitchen and single garage.
187,000 euros　　　　**LAT**
(£116,875) GP

(03)
Situated in a small hamlet near Gannat, this small, two-bedroom farmhouse with a bread oven is ripe for restoration. With one barn at the rear and a smaller house at the side. Great potential.
70,127 euros　　　　**AUV**
(£43,830) GP

(87)
Three cottages and a barn in need of renovation. Set in spacious grounds, the property features an old bread oven and water pump. The property is habitable and is close to a small, pretty hamlet.
54,000 euros　　　　**FPL**
(£33,750) GP

(03)
A period house situated in a village between Montmarault and Saint-Pourçain-sur-Sioule. Comprises a kitchen, three bedrooms, living room, bathroom and garage. Wonderful open views.
80,798 euros　　　　**AUV**
(£50,500) GP

Limousin & Auvergne

(19)
Dating from the 19th century, an ancient stone-built barn for total renovation. Situated close to the village of Turenne, the barn offers 210m² of potential living space. Located in 1,643m² of rural land.
45,734 euros   **LAT**
(£28,585) GP

(87)
In a rural setting, close to a busy town. Comprises a main house and a large attached barn. Set in a walled garden with mature fruit trees. The main house boasts oak floors, three bedrooms and a cellar.
128,100 euros   **CUR**
(£80,060) GP

(19)
A large property surrounded by almost 40,000m² of rural and wooded land. Accommodation is on three levels and comprises five spacious bedrooms. Boasts a pool and a secluded location.
406,000 euros   **LIN**
(£253,750) GP

(23)
This large restored house is set in a hamlet alongside five traditional houses. Close to the market town of Bellac, the residence offers two bedrooms and a lawned garden of 8,000m² with a vegetable plot.
199,500 euros   **CUR**
(£124,690) GP

(23)
For conversion, a 14th-century dwelling in a countryside setting. Formerly an abbey, the property offers an attached barn and large garden. Features a spiral staircase and several good-sized bedrooms.
137,204 euros   **VAN**
(£85,750) GP

(63)
Situated in scenic countryside in a tourist region, this house with guest wing boasts an indoor pool, sauna, jacuzzi, gym and games room. Comprises 11 bedrooms and 1,000m² of mature gardens.
457,000 euros   **PRV**
(£285,625) GP

(87)
A restored water mill with several outbuildings, set in 20,000m² of land with a stream. Features four bedrooms, three bathrooms, living room and kitchen. In the heart of a bustling market town.
272,121 euros   **WAT**
(£170,075) GP

(03)
An old cottage, built from stone. In a picturesque village setting, with sweeping country views. On the ground floor is a living room and kitchen. Upstairs are a shower and two bedrooms with fireplaces.
98,602 euros   **AUV**
(£61,625) GP

(03)
Close to a village, a two-bedroom bungalow set in 2,000m² of enclosed garden. Comprises a fully-fitted kitchen, terrace, dining room and lounge. Newly built, the property has a single garage.
101,379 euros   **AUV**
(£63,360) GP

Price Guide

(03)
Under a slate roof, two buildings comprising a reception room, three dining rooms, four further rooms, kitchen, ten bedrooms and several small bathrooms. Set in forested parkland of 3,200m².
518,327 euros   **AUV**
(£323,955) GP

(63)
Just south of Clermont-Ferrand, a collection of buildings and a barn. The first house comprises five en-suite bathrooms. Boasts a converted stable block. Set in woodland with mountain views.
402,465 euros   **AUV**
(£251,540) GP

(03)
A château in 11,000m² of enclosed grounds with mature trees and a bridleway, featuring a guest house and numerous outbuildings. Surrounded by quiet countryside, with stunning panoramic views.
663,153 euros   **MAQ**
(£414,470) GP

(63)
In the hills near Combrailles, two houses with several outbuildings. Situated in 12,000m² of farmland and boasting four fishing lakes. The first house offers five bedrooms while the second has six.
350,632 euros   **AUV**
(£219,145) GP

(63)
A pretty manor house, standing in 20,000m² of land bordered by the River Loire. A private lake graces the front of the property, which comprises a guest cottage, two bedrooms and outbuildings.
396,367 euros   **AUV**
(£247,730) GP

(23)
Dating from the 18th century, a historic castle with medieval foundations. Set in 12,000m² of parkland, boasting a dovecote, woods and orangery. Featuring a spiral staircase and many rooms.
937,561 euros   **MAQ**
(£585,975) GP

(63)
A 15th-century rectory set on high ground next to a pretty church. In the centre of a small village surrounded by unspoilt country. Boasts hand-painted wood panels and vaulted cellars.
304,898 euros   **AUV**
(£190,560) GP

(63)
A grand château with a dungeon and round corner tower. With seven bedrooms, stables, a guest cottage and garage. Situated in landscaped gardens of 50,000m², surrounded by idyllic countryside.
1,167,759 euros   **MAQ**
(£729,850) GP

(63)
This fortified château dates from the 14th century and has more than 400m² of living space. Featuring two towers, it sits in a rural valley in 21,000m² of grounds with a swimming pool.
998,475 euros   **MAQ**
(£624,045) GP

Limousin & Auvergne

(19)
A stone-built manor house with a small lake and heated swimming pool. Accessed via a long drive flanked by trees, and set in land of 30,000m². Features eight large bedrooms and a terrace with views.
442,102 euros   **VAN**
(£276,315) GP

(03)
Standing in 1,000,000m² of parkland, a magnificent 13th-century château with a watchtower. With stunning views across beautiful landscape, it boasts a spiral staircase and wood-panelled walls.
1,051,898 euros   **MAQ**
(£657,435) GP

(63)
Just outside a small town, a secluded château. Set in 70,000m² of land with an orangery, cottage and stables. Boasts nine en-suite bedrooms, monumental fireplaces and an elaborate dining room.
1,349,173 euros   **MAQ**
(£843,235) GP

(03)
A spacious half-timbered manor house. Close to the River Loire and in the heart of a large village. Comes with a separate small guest house and caretaker's cottage. Offers a well-stocked lake.
419,235 euros   **HOM**
(£262,020) GP

(03)
Dating from the 18th century, a large residence boasting ancient towers, wood panelling, stone fireplaces and a room decorated in Burgundy stone. Features six bedrooms and 10,000m² of land.
686,020 euros   **MAQ**
(£428,760) GP

(23)
Set around a courtyard, this large château offers 14 spacious rooms with wood panelling and stone fireplaces. Standing in private grounds of 30,000m², enjoying gorgeous countryside scenery.
487,836 euros   **MAQ**
(£304,900) GP

(63)
In the heart of a small medieval village and in need of some interior work. Arranged over three floors, the house features two en-suite bedrooms, three further bedrooms, wine cellars and a fitted kitchen.
251,540 euros   **MAQ**
(£157,210) GP

(19)
An enormous house in a church square boasting a beautiful flower garden. Set in the heart of a small, historic town with all amenities. Features a kitchen, several large bedrooms and a vast dining room.
150,400 euros   **VEF**
(£94,000) GP

(23)
This 16th-century château offers a tower and ancient fortress. Set in a wooded park featuring an old moat. With two spiral staircases, flagstone floors, open fires, an old chapel and a large boating lake.
839,994 euros   **MAQ**
(£524,995) GP

Price Guide

(19)
A restored farmhouse in a quiet country setting. Comprises a living room with mezzanine and inglenook fireplace, kitchen, four bedrooms, cellar and terrace. In a landscaped garden of 6,300m².
285,842 euros   **VAN**
(£178,650) GP

(23)
In Saint-Germain-Beaupré, a stone house with three bedrooms. In a peaceful setting, with a garden to the rear and opposite. Comprises a kitchen, dining room and lounge. Set on a country road.
290,000 euros   **HOM**
(£181,250) GP

(03)
A manor house dating from the 13th century and situated a short distance from a village. Split over three floors and in need of some renovation. Set in 500,000m² of land, with stunning country views.
239,163 euros   **MAQ**
(£149,475) GP

(19)
A short drive from the market town of Aubusson, this stone house has a garden of 210m². Comprising an entrance hall, fitted kitchen, dining room, lounge and two spacious bedrooms.
90,000 euros   **HOM**
(£56,250) GP

(19)
Formerly a school, this large five-bedroom house is in need of interior renovation. Features a small tower and several large rooms with pitched ceilings. Set on the edge of a pretty village.
76,200 euros   **VAN**
(£47,625) GP

(87)
A stone-built terraced house with an attached barn. Comprises four bedrooms, kitchen, lounge and garage. Outside the property is a small enclosed back garden with a large workshop and cellar.
53,357 euros   **HOM**
(£33,350) GP

(87)
A large restored house in a rural location just south of Bellac. Set in a garden planted with mature lime trees and laid to lawn. Boasts exposed stone walls and pitched ceilings. Features two bedrooms.
199,500 euros   **CUR**
(£124,690) GP

(23)
A stone-built terraced cottage standing in a pretty hamlet. Offers a living room, kitchen, cellar and three bedrooms. Features an original fireplace and small courtyard, with a garden and woodstore.
301,087 euros   **HOM**
(£188,180) GP

(23)
For renovation, a large stone farmhouse with two separate barns. Standing in a garden of 20,000m², the house offers two bedrooms, a kitchen, lounge with open fireplace and dining room.
90,000 euros   **HOM**
(£56,250) GP

Limousin & Auvergne

(23)
Dating from the 17th century, a large château on the outskirts of a town. Set in 29,000m² of beautiful landscaped gardens and woodland. Boasts two towers, cellars, an original kitchen and well.
487,836 euros DEE
(£304,900) S

(23)
A main house and gîte standing in 9,000m² of mature garden with lawn, trees and shrubs. A stream runs through the grounds, which also feature a barn that has been converted into an artist's studio.
266,786 euros HOM
(£166,740) GP

(23)
Three stone-built houses and a two-storey outbuilding, offering three main rooms with fireplaces and four bedrooms. Recent roofs, but some work still required. Small gardens to front and rear.
53,357 euros HOM
(£33,350) GP

(23)
A stone *fermette* in a small hamlet. Features a kitchen with open fire and exposed beams, open-plan lounge and study, three bedrooms and an attached barn. Outside is a small garden to the side and rear.
90,707 euros HOM
(£56,690) GP

(87)
South of Bellac, an ancient house with 2,350m² of land. The main house offers two bedrooms and boasts exposed stone walls. There is also a second smaller stone house standing to the rear of the property.
205,245 euros HOM
(£128,280) GP

(87)
Boasting five en-suite bedrooms, a separate guest wing and a pool, this renovated stone house stands in 8,950m² of land. Comprises a corner-kitchen, large lounge, dining room and a mezzanine.
327,765 euros HOM
(£204,855) GP

(23)
This château features four round towers and is entered via a double staircase. Located in a forested area with many lakes, the château offers several bedrooms, a double garage and a vast tiled terrace.
327,765 euros DEE
(£204,855) S

(23)
A five-bedroom house and old water mill for renovation. Set in 2,500m² of land with extensive views, bordered by a small stream. Comprises five bedrooms, an entrance hall, lounge and attic.
146,351 euros HOM
(£91,470) GP

(19)
Located in the south of Corrèze and surrounded by countryside and woodland. A house with a large living room, four bedrooms and a kitchen. Enjoys a swimming pool, pool house and open views.
290,000 euros VAN
(£181,250) GP

Price Guide

(23)
Two houses set in 4,900m² of land with a garage. The first house has a fitted kitchen, living room and two bedrooms. The second offers a dining room, kitchen, three bedrooms and a workshop.
167,694 euros   **HOM**
(£104,810) GP

(19)
A manor house set in landscaped grounds with many rare species of plants. Located in a small town, the property has been split into three separate accommodations, each offering four large bedrooms.
747,000 euros   **DEE**
(£466,875) GP

(23)
Isolated and peaceful, this stone house and attached barn are set deep in the countryside. Boasts an oak kitchen with a woodburning stove, three bedrooms, and a large garden with a summer-kitchen.
213,428 euros   **HOM**
(£133,390) GP

(19)
This ancient farmhouse is located close to a village with all shops and services. Situated in a landscaped garden offering views over mountains. Comprises three bedrooms, living room and cellar.
381,122 euros   **DEE**
(£238,200) S

(23)
An entirely renovated stone-built house with an extension. The property comprises a fully-fitted kitchen, bread oven, large lounge with open fireplace and four bedrooms. Set in a secluded garden.
228,673 euros   **HOM**
(£142,920) GP

(19)
A four-bedroom house arranged over two levels with 1,875m² of land. Comprises a lounge, dining room with open fireplace and two bedrooms. Boasts an external set of stairs and vaulted cellars.
132,631 euros   **HOM**
(£82,895) GP

(63)
Dating from the 19th century, a large town house in the centre of a health resort. Arranged over four floors, the property features eight main rooms including five large bedrooms. With a pretty garden.
326,250 euros   **MER**
(£203,905) GP

(23)
Situated in Naillat, this renovated stone house offers a fully-fitted kitchen, lounge, two bedrooms, veranda and a mezzanine. The garden to the rear features an attractive stream and an old barn.
129,582 euros   **HOM**
(£80,990) GP

(87)
A renovated *fermette* close to Saint-Pardoux lake. Set in 10,000m² of land with a paddock. Comprises a kitchen, lounge with fireplace and exposed beams, one bedroom and adjoining barn.
104,424 euros   **HOM**
(£65,265) GP

Limousin & Auvergne

(23)
Dating from the 17th century, a partially renovated château. Set in 14,000m² of parkland and woods, with a separate guest cottage. It offers several bedrooms, reception rooms and two vaulted cellars.
600,000 euros HOM
(£375,000) GP

(23)
This fully renovated house with a detached two-bedroom cottage sits on the edge of a picturesque village. Features a figure-of-eight pool, terrace, studio apartment, oak beams and marble fireplace.
259,163 euros HOM
(£161,975) GP

(63)
On the edge of small village. A restored manor house dating from the 15th century, with a separate caretaker's cottage. Boasts a garden with a fountain, springs, several ponds and mature trees.
680,001 euros MER
(£425,000) GP

(63)
Built in 1992, a villa with eight main rooms. Featuring five large bedrooms, a spacious kitchen and living room. Situated in 5,000m² of tree-filled gardens. Benefits from a peaceful and secluded spot.
375,000 euros MER
(£234,375) GP

(23)
In Naillat, a renovated *fermette* with two attached barns and a small stone house standing in its own garden. The main residence boasts three en-suite bedrooms, a barn, kitchen and lounge area.
267,000 euros HOM
(£166,875) GP

(23)
In northwest Creuse, a farm with 186,000m² of land. Comprises a large main house, two smaller houses and several outbuildings needing renovation. Offering a cellar, garage and livestock.
640,286 euros HOM
(£400,180) GP

(23)
A renovated stone *fermette* set in 16,000m² of wooded ground and meadows. Boasts a large entrance hall, fitted kitchen with access to an attached modern barn and three bedrooms with rural views.
335,387 euros HOM
(£209,620) GP

(43)
Dating from the 19th century, a large house standing in 4,910m² of grounds. With 22 main rooms and 1,296m² of living space. Located in open countryside on the outskirts of a small village.
257,600 euros MER
(£161,000) GP

(23)
In a village setting, a stone-built house sitting in a private walled garden. Comprises a large family kitchen, living room, music room, cellar, bathroom and three vast bedrooms. Boasts open fireplaces.
102,689 euros HOM
(£64,180) GP

Price Guide

(63)
Offering many unusual and original features, a castle with a large tower, 21 main rooms and a swimming pool. Standing in 10,000m² of secluded land with mature trees. Approached via a private drive.
1,468,086 euros   **MER**
(£917,555) GP

(63)
Dating from the 19th century, a traditional period house with nine main rooms. Features two garages, six bedrooms, a terrace and a woodstore. Set in a very quiet location in 2,500m² of land.
407,801 euros   **MER**
(£254,875) GP

(63)
A former monastery with 14 main rooms and 650m² of living space. Boasts an L-shaped terrace, a cloister, 3,000m² of enclosed garden with a spring and many original architectural details.
503,083 euros   **MER**
(£314,430) GP

(63)
A large *maison de maitre* boasting 11 main rooms and almost 900m² of habitable space. Set in 2,500m² of enclosed landscaped parkland, with a separate guest house, barn and several large outbuildings.
1,305,002 euros   **MER**
(£815,630) GP

(23)
This semi-detached house sits on the outskirts of a quiet village. On the ground floor is a kitchen with lounge, bathroom and French doors to a small garden. Upstairs are two good-sized bedrooms.
39,600 euros   **HOM**
(£24,750) GP

(43)
On the edge of a busy village, a 19th-century home. Standing in 2,500m² of gardens with a tennis court and outbuildings, the house features nine main rooms with views. Split over three storeys.
182,939 euros   **MER**
(£114,340) GP

(63)
This *maison de maitre* sits within 80,000m² of gardens featuring several outbuildings. Boasting 15 main rooms and dating from the early 20th century, the property overlooks open fields and forest.
457,348 euros   **MER**
(£285,845) GP

(63)
This listed 13th-century castle stands on an ancient site. Offering 18 main rooms, including several bedrooms and a kitchen. Set in more than 40,000m² of parkland, with outbuildings and a cottage.
1,143,369 euros   **MER**
(£714,605) GP

(19)
Set on high, a contemporary stone house standing in 12,000m² of landscaped and enclosed grounds with three ponds. Features a guest cottage, five bedrooms, fitted kitchen, living room and garage.
1,220,002 euros   **MER**
(£762,500) GP

Limousin & Auvergne

(63)
In a village setting close to a town, this three-bedroom house stands in a small garden. Centrally heated, the property offers a large kitchen, living room and attached barn. Benefits from a quiet spot.
152,500 euros   **VIC**
(£95,310) GP

(23)
A village house comprising a summer-kitchen, cellar, living room, two bedrooms and a shower room. Centrally heated and set in a small garden, which is to the front and side of the property.
65,553 euros   **HOM**
(£40,970) GP

(23)
In Fleurat, a stone house with a large basement and a paddock of 7,000m². On the ground floor is a garage, dining room, kitchen and three bedrooms. Upstairs, a games room and two further bedrooms.
105,189 euros   **HOM**
(£65,745) GP

(23)
This renovated end-terrace house comes with a small stone house for renovation. Set in an enclosed rear garden with a paved terrace. The main property comprises two bedrooms, lounge and kitchen.
41,161 euros   **HOM**
(£25,725) GP

(23)
A three-bedroom bungalow comprising a fitted kitchen, lounge with an open fire, three bedrooms, bathroom, cellar and conservatory. In an enclosed garden with apple trees and vines.
84,000 euros   **HOM**
(£52,500) GP

(23)
A detached house with two bedrooms and a large basement. Set in a large garden of 1,000m², with plenty of space for parking. Offers a kitchen, lounge, balcony and bathroom. In a residential area.
81,561 euros   **HOM**
(£50,975) GP

(23)
A group of stone buildings close to Dun-le-Palestel. Features a stone house with one large room and boasting an open fireplace and two bedrooms. Set in a private garden with a second smaller house.
32,014 euros   **HOM**
(£20,010) GP

(63)
Close to Clermont-Ferrand, a villa with three bedrooms. Within easy reach of all amenities, the villa boasts spacious and light-filled rooms. Set on high in a garden, overlooking fields and woodland.
208,900 euros   **VIC**
(£130,560) GP

(63)
A stone-built villa located close to a train station and shops. Features three bedrooms, fitted kitchen and living room. Split over three floors and facing a quiet road. Standing in a garden planted with trees.
82,300 euros   **VIC**
(£51,440) GP

Price Guide

(23)
In the town of Guéret, a castle with 12 main rooms. Surrounded by woodland and benefiting from a secluded location, the property offers 2,220m² of habitable space. Situated in parkland of 24,000m².
815,601 euros   **MER**
(£509,750) GP

(23)
Split over two levels, a *maison de maître* with nine rooms, including two bathrooms, four bedrooms and two cellars. Centrally heated, it boasts extensive grounds of 5,270m². Set close to a busy town.
246,970 euros   **MER**
(£154,355) GP

(63)
A four-bedroom villa near a busy market town. Situated in a tree-filled garden with a large swimming pool, terrace and two garages. Boasts a veranda with fantastic views of the countryside.
285,000 euros   **VIC**
(£178,125) GP

(19)
Situated on the edge of a small hamlet, this pretty manor house is set in parkland of 6,000m² with spectacular views. Comprises six bedrooms, drawing room, tiled living room and fitted kitchen.
335,245 euros   **VAN**
(£209,530) GP

(23)
An extensive estate standing in 125,000m² of agricultural land and woodland. Approached via a lane flanked with mature oak trees. Features two lakes, springs, stables and a forge. In a secluded location.
2,989,525 euros   **VAN**
(£1,868,455) GP

(19)
Built in the 1970s, a large house with a cellar, garage for three cars, living room with fireplace, five double bedrooms and a kitchen. Set in 30,000m² of land, offering views across a lake and fields.
228,680 euros   **VAN**
(£142,925) GP

(23)
A manor house built with a slate roof in the 1930s, set in nearly 50,000m² of parkland. Features a living room with parquet floor, drawing room, kitchen, cellar and eight bedrooms. In a quiet spot.
182,940 euros   **VAN**
(£114,340) GP

(19)
On the top of a hill, a small château with views over a river valley. Comprises three cellars, a tower room with a vaulted ceiling and six further rooms. With a pool and a secluded, walled garden.
564,000 euros   **VAN**
(£352,500) GP

(19)
An 18th-century château situated in enclosed, wooded parkland with a lake and several springs. Numerous bedrooms, a professional kitchen and a swimming pool. Offers a private location.
884,205 euros   **VAN**
(£552,630) GP

Limousin & Auvergne

(23)
Close to the town of Montluçon, an ancient priory dating from the 12th century. Standing in 2,500m² of land, the property boasts five bedrooms and is centrally heated. Set at the end of a country lane.
263,432 euros   **MER**
(£164,645) GP

(87)
An impressive castle boasting 17 main rooms, including nine large bedrooms and several bathrooms. Surrounded by 70,000m² of land, featuring fields and woods. On the edge of a busy market town.
734,043 euros   **MER**
(£458,775) GP

(87)
A house close to the town of Bellac. Located in a peaceful area, the property boasts two spacious bedrooms and stands in a small, enclosed garden a short distance from local shops and amenities.
49,600 euros   **LAR**
(£31,000) GP

(87)
Located between two busy towns, this 19th-century castle sits on a hilltop in a pretty hamlet. Set in nearly 30,000m² of landscaped gardens, with views stretching as far as the Auvergne volcanoes.
564,061 euros   **DEE**
(£352,540) GP

(87)
Situated between Angoulême and Limoges. In a quiet and secluded area, this vast wooded estate stretches along an 18-hole golf course. Includes a restored 17th-century house and several barns.
1,829,391 euros   **MER**
(£1,143,370) GP

(23)
Renovated and cosy, this country home sits on the edge of a hamlet. In a quiet location, but near a town, the property features a living room with exposed beams and open fireplace, three bedrooms and a terrace.
114,337 euros   **VAN**
(£71,460) GP

(23)
A 16th-century château with 19 main rooms and a large swimming pool. Features a separate apartment, drawing room, vaulted cellar, round tower and stabling. Set in 23,000m² of mature parkland.
747,000 euros   **VAN**
(£466,875) GP

(03)
Listed as a historic monument, this feudal fortress is located at the entrance of a small village. Set in vast, hilly landscaped grounds, with a separate guest cottage and a tower at the gate of the estate.
929,939 euros   **DEE**
(£581,210) S

(19)
Built during the 15th century, a château in a small village. Set in parkland with a field and orchard. Features a spiral staircase, vaulted cellar, living room, summer dining room and five spacious bedrooms.
1,250,000 euros   **VAN**
(£781,250) GP

Vive la France
c'est Fantastique!

The only FRENCH LIFESTYLE, TRAVEL and PROPERTY Exhibition in the UK

Come and visit the exhibition in January at London Olympia

Discover French Regions • Champagne Tasting • Play Boules • French Markets
Great Value Holidays • Wine Seminars • Hidden Secrets of France • Chic Fashions
Jean-Christophe Novelli's Cookery Theatre • Café de la Musique • **A Great Day Out**

Call the ticket hotline now on
0870 902 0444
or book online www.vivelafrance.co.uk

www.vivelafrance.co.uk

In association with Maison de la FRANCE
www.franceguide.com

RECOMMENDED BY CLASSIC fm

THE RHONE-ALPS

Price Guide

(42)
An extensive property standing in a garden planted with trees and shrubs. This house offers three bedrooms, a fitted kitchen, bathroom, sitting room with open fireplace and a self-contained studio.
45,735 euros   **MDF**
(£28,543) GP

(74)
A former café with an adjoining chalet, this stone house features three cellars, a kitchen, bar, study, dining room and lounge. The property offers nine bedrooms, each with a south-facing balcony.
409,300 euros   **FPL**
(£255,815) GP

(07)
This four-bedroom villa stands in 2,600m² of enclosed tree-filled gardens. Privately located in woodland, the property features a patio, cellar, garage and living room with a large open fireplace.
257,639 euros   **MDF**
(£161,024) GP

(74)
A renovated farmhouse at the foot of a mountain. This 100-year-old property has metre-thick walls, five bedrooms, two bathrooms and a wine cellar. Located just 15 minutes from Lake Geneva.
280,000 euros   **FPL**
(£175,000) GP

(74)
This two-bedroom apartment is set in the heart of a small village surrounded by mountains. A short drive from a major ski centre, the apartment offers two bedrooms with balconies and Alpine views.
186,200 euros   **VEF**
(£116,375) GP

(74)
Located in Châtel, this duplex apartment with eight bedrooms boasts panoramic views over the Abondance Valley and has 280m² of living space. The property features a sauna and four bathrooms.
503,000 euros   **FPL**
(£314,375) GP

(01)
An unusual L-shaped house in the town of Divonne-les-Bains. Set in tranquil gardens of 1,870m², the property offers five bedrooms, a garage and cellar, plus a self-contained apartment.
640,000 euros   **ASB**
(£400,000) GP

(01)
A wooden chalet for nature lovers set in the countryside near the town of Gex. This four-bedroom property offers a living room with open fire and a mezzanine. Set in 5,300m² of gardens with a pool.
687,000 euros   **ASB**
(£429,375) GP

(74)
A chalet apartment set in the beautiful alpine village of Praz-sur-Arly. The apartment features two bedrooms, a fully-fitted kitchen, bathroom, balcony with views and tiled floors throughout.
76,072 euros   **MNI**
(£47,545) GP

ERA ACPI IMMOBILIER

39 rue Maurice Meyer, Montelimar, 26200 FRANCE

Email: **jean-charles-rey@wanadoo.fr**

Specialist in Stone Houses & Mas, either side of the Rhone, in Ardèche & Drôme.

We have a large selection of properties available, but if we don't have the property you are looking for, we would be delighted to find it for you.

Tel: **00 33 4 75 00 65 65**
Fax: **00 33 4 75 00 65 69**

PANGON IMMOBILIER

77 rue de President-Wilson, 26240 SAINT-VALLIER
21 avenue Gambetta 38270 BEAUREPAIRE

VALLEE DU RHONE

Between Lyon & Valence. A magnificent mansion of 400m² habitable space set in about 6,000m² of grounds overlooking the Rhone. Entrance hall, dining room, sitting room, 6 bedrooms, Cocktail room, corridors, storage space & cupboards, cellars, garage & swimming pool. **Price: 800,360€**

Tel: **00 33 4 75 23 02 09**
Fax: **00 33 4 75 23 54 39**

www.pangon-immobilier.com

FRENCH ALPS: LAKE GENEVA

"Buyers Guide" & particulars of new and older property with photos from £40,000 to £500,000+

BEACHES INTERNATIONAL PROPERTY

3/4 Hagley Mews, Hagley Hall, West Midlands DY9 9LQ

Tel: **01562 885181**   Fax: **01562 886724**

Email: **info@beachesint.co.uk**
www.beachesint.co.uk

(74)
A recently-constructed three-bedroom chalet close to the ski centre of Morzine. This Alpine property enjoys sweeping mountain views and is set in a small village with all amenities.
355,000 euros **APP**
(£221,875) GP

(74)
This detached chalet lies at the foot of a mountain and enjoys magnificent views across the Alps. Situated in a slightly isolated area, the chalet offers three bedrooms, two shower rooms and two WCs.
244,000 euros **APP**
(£152,500) GP

(74)
Two newly-built chalets offering excellent sweeping vistas over wooded mountainsides. Built to a high standard and benefiting from three airy bedrooms, balconies and open-plan living space.
350,000 euros **APP**
(£218,750) GP

(74)
A traditional Alpine apartment within easy access of ski slopes and a small town. The chalet offers five bedrooms, including one with en-suite facilities. Also features a garage and veranda.
496,000 euros **APP**
(£310,000) GP

(07)
In a tranquil rural environment, this villa with five main rooms and a terrace is surrounded by woodland. Close to a busy market town, it stands in 500m^2 of garden set beside a quiet country lane.
129,600 euros **OPM**
(£81,000) GP

(74)
This large two-bedroom farmhouse offers 6,500m^2 of land and assorted outbuildings. The property is in need of some renovation, but is ready to move in to as all services are connected.
210,000 euros **APP**
(£131,250) GP

(74)
This newly-built chalet is set within a landscaped garden. Offering four large bedrooms, one bathroom, two shower rooms and a garage, it affords idyllic views of the surrounding forests and hills.
282,030 euros **APP**
(£176,270) GP

(74)
In need of renovation and with land of 3,000m^2, this small house is set in a quiet location close to a traditional Alpine village. No services are connected so a fair amount of work is required.
69,000 euros **APP**
(£43,125) GP

(01)
This spacious, fully-renovated villa is set in the town of Thoiry. Offering five principal rooms, four bedrooms and a kitchen with open fire, the house stands in a colourful garden planted with shrubs.
350,000 euros **OPM**
(£218,750) GP

EQUIN●XE Immobilier

6 rue Gambetta, 24000 Perigueux

Contact: **Dominic Faccini**

Tel/Fax: **00 33 5 53 60 55 17**   Mobile: **00 33 6 73 18 46 04**

Working throughout Dordogne, Charente, Haute Vienne, Corrèze and Lot, Equinoxe Immobilier is a dynamic French agency with bilingual staff who specialize in rural properties: Second Homes, Gites, Chambres d'hote, Lakes, Farms or Renovation projects.... We always try and get you the best deal!

DORDOGNE (24)

Ref: 1467

Cosy restored farmhouse with large living room with fireplace and pointed stones. Ten hotel rooms with bathrooms en suite. 12 x 6 swimming pool. Small lake.

Price: 520,000€ inlcuding fees.

HAUTE VIENNE (87)

Ref: 1457

Delightful mill house in granite stone. 3 bedrooms. Tastefully restored in traditional manner. 2 large barns. Great gardens with waterfalls.

Price: 215,000€ inlcuding fees.

LOT (46)

Ref: 1486

2 superbly restored traditional stone houses with immense character. Currently a very upmarket guesthouse. Large swimming pool. Set in 2 hectares overlooking dreamy landscapes. Sold fully furnished.

Price: 700,000€ including fees.

www.perigord-property.com

Prices include agency fee. Carte professionnelle transaction sur immeubles et fonds de commerce N 346. Caisse de garantie FNAIM.

Price Guide

(73)
On the piste with views of tree-lined ski slopes, a one-bedroom apartment in a development located away from the more traditional resorts. Offers a fully-equipped kitchen, garage and large cellar.
86,437 euros　　　　　　**MNI**
(£54,025) GP

(73)
A recently-built traditional-style chalet in an up-and-coming resort with its own system of lifts and great off-piste skiing. Close to a pretty Alpine village, and less than half an hour from Val d'Isère.
149,600 euros　　　　　　**SAS**
(£93,500) GP

(74)
A deluxe five-bedroom chalet-style apartment set in the centre of a popular Alpine resort. Featuring open fireplaces, a balcony and en-suite facilities, car parking facilities are also available.
795,000 euros　　　　　　**AAA**
(£496,875) GP

(07)
Near a historic village in the Rhône Valley, this large stone-built farmhouse is in need of interior work. The property stands in a remote location and is set in rural land of 50,000m².
327,760 euros　　　　　　**ERA**
(£204,850) GP

(07)
On the Ardèche Plateau, a large farmhouse with many original architectural details. With 290m² of living space and outbuildings, it is situated in 10,000m² of woodland in a quiet farming district.
236,296 euros　　　　　　**ERA**
(£147,685) GP

(73)
Built in 1992 for the Winter Olympics, a chalet set in a small village with links to the Three Valleys area. Features a cellar, four en-suite bedrooms and a large kitchen. Boasts mountain views.
602,180 euros　　　　　　**MNI**
(£376,363) GP

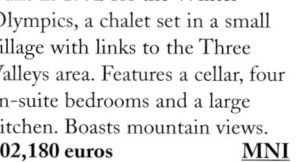

(69)
Set on a hilltop overlooking a large lake and river, this 16th-century Renaissance fortress features two towers with spiral staircases. The property offers 16 main rooms arranged over two floors.
304,898 euros　　　　　　**DEE**
(£190,560) S

(73)
This south-facing chalet with magnificent mountain views has been fully renovated. In a small village close to the ski resort of Méribel, it offers two large bedrooms and a studio apartment.
427,000 euros　　　　　　**CUR**
(£266,895) GP

(26)
This château to the south of Valence is set in 17,000m² of enclosed, landscaped grounds. With 10 bedrooms, stabling, a courtyard and ornamental lake, it features Venetian chandeliers.
838,469 euros　　　　　　**DEE**
(£524,045) S

The Rhône-Alps

(07)
Standing in 14,000m² of cultivated land with countryside views, this large farmhouse with a swimming pool is ideal for conversion to a small hotel. The property is set in a quiet village location.
327,765 euros   ERA
(£204,855) GP

(69)
A country house with five main rooms plus an open-plan living room and kitchen, laundry room and garage. With lovely views and a quiet location, the house is set in 317m² of tree-filled gardens.
335,400 euros   MER
(£209,625) GP

(07)
Currently run as a small hotel, this ensemble of two buildings is set in 57,000m² of wooded land and meadows. Features an indoor pool, numerous bedrooms and a peaceful and secluded location.
673,500 euros   ERA
(£420,940) GP

(69)
This large two-storey villa is in a secure location close to the city of Lyon. With 12 main rooms, the house also offers a laundry room, store room, pool house and cellar. Features several bedroom suites.
2,200,003 euros   MER
(£1,375,000) GP

(38)
A historic castle with a tower located near the town of La Tour-du-Pin. Standing in 25,000m² of land with numerous outbuildings, the property features 15 main rooms and a swimming pool.
587,001 euros   MER
(£366,875) GP

(38)
Enjoying a rural setting in the heart of Isère surrounded by forest and hills, this villa offers ten main rooms arranged over two floors. Features 400m² of living space, car parking and 40,000m² of land.
534,001 euros   MER
(£333,750) GP

(69)
Near Dardilly, this farmhouse is set in gardens of 2,200m² featuring a heated swimming pool. The property is privately situated and offers seven main rooms, including three spacious bedrooms.
560,251 euros   MER
(£350,155) GP

(38)
Standing in 9,438m² of land set on the edge of a pretty village, this *maison de maître* offers a pool and pool house. The house enjoys outstanding views and is surrounded by forest and farmland.
496,001 euros   MER
(£310,000) GP

(38)
A *longére* with nine rooms set deep in the countryside. Close to a town with all amenities, it offers a cellar, secure parking and nine main rooms. Benefits from a quiet location and picturesque views.
274,410 euros   MER
(£171,506) GP

Putting down new roots?
So are we...

With the winning combination of Eurostar™ and efficient French rail – our network in France is growing every year. Offering both direct Eurostar™ and TGV services, often involving just one simple change of trains in Paris or Lille – Eurostar™ Plus puts over 60 French destinations within your reach.

Enjoy the flexibility of frequent services and a wide choice of connections from London or Ashford, with a scenic, relaxing journey that takes you smoothly from city-centre to city-centre – right into the real heart of France. And for more space and comfort try our First Class option.

For information and to book...
Call **08705 186 186***
Visit **eurostar.com**

*Calls charged at national rate.

AQUITAINE

Price Guide

(24)
A restored farmhouse with a guest cottage and mature gardens of 2,900m². Comprises a large living room, attached barn and three good-sized bedrooms. Located in the charming town of Ribérac.
199,230 euros   **LAF**
(£124,520) GP

(24)
Recently restored, this traditional farmhouse with lots of character features three bedrooms and is set in the village of Verteillac. The property has plenty of room for parking and a 39,000m² garden.
152,424 euros   **LAF**
(£95,265) GP

(24)
On high ground, this farmhouse comprises three bedrooms and sits in 8,000m² of gardens. Located in the centre of a pretty village, with a large attached barn, several outbuildings and a garage.
147,654 euros   **LAF**
(£92,285) GP

(24)
With views of beautiful countryside, a majestic, well-restored château dating from the 13th century. Offering extensive accommodation and 105,000m² of land in the heart of Dordogne.
1,293,200 euros   **CHS**
(£808,250) GP

(47)
A country residence comprising a stone-built house, guest cottage, barn and swimming pool, all set in a well-maintained garden. Features exposed beams, terracotta floors and three double bedrooms.
539,081 euros   **VIA**
(£336,925) GP

(47)
Set in the country and dating from 1687, this property features a kitchen with fireplace, three bedrooms, a barn and gardens of 1,000m². The house is built of stone and in need of restoration.
150,200 euros   **VIA**
(£93,875) GP

(24)
This beautifully restored traditional farmhouse is close to the town of Périgueux. The property benefits from spacious accommodation, a selection of outbuildings and a large swimming pool.
500,951 euros   **CHS**
(£313,095) GP

(47)
A stone-built country house with a swimming pool. Boasts large rooms with tiled floors, open wood beams and a terrace with BBQ area. Comprises four double bedrooms, orchards and stables.
384,200 euros   **VIA**
(£240,125) GP

(47)
Near Laroque-Timbaut, this country home offers three bedrooms and 1,100m² of woodland. In a private, secluded location, the property also features two gîtes, a pool, two springs and paddocks.
457,000 euros   **VIA**
(£285,625) GP

Andrew Bishop FRENCH PROPERTIES

Tel: 00 33 5 57 46 27 06
Fax: 00 33 5 57 46 38 10

36, Rue de la Republique, 33220 Sainte Foy La Grande, France

Email: andrewbishop@wanadoo.fr   Web: www.andrew-bishop.com   Web: www.aquitaineassociates.com

AB 22022 - Situated on the top of a valley, 1Km from the charming market town of Vergt (24) with a good variety of shops and restaurants, near the regional capital, Perigueux. Bergerac and airport 20 mins away, with Bordeaux and the International airport, less than 1 hr. A beautiful 17thC. stone built Perigordine ensemble comprising a large family house, spacious gite, pool, large barn, delightful pigeonnier & terrace with fabulous views down the valley. The property has been sympathetically restored to a very high standard, and retains all its original features, in a marvellous tranquil, private setting with land of 3 hectares (over 7 acres). The accommodation includes large living room with fireplace, fully equipped kitchen and dining room, 3 bedrooms, 2 bathrooms, laundry, wine-cave with original bread oven. The gite has 2 bedrooms, living room, and bathroom and kitchen. There is a large barn, used as a games room, opening onto the pool (12m x 6m) and terrace. Services: Mains water, electricity, oil central-heating, telephone, satellite TV.
Price: 640,286€ F.A.I.

AB 22024 - Situated a few kms from the charming Bastide town of Beaumont (24) with a good variety of shops and restaurants, the property is in an idyllic waterside setting. Bergerac and International airport 30 minutes away. A most attractive 17thC. stone built Perigordine house forming an enclosed private courtyard with its outbuildings, entered by a stone archway. The property is situated in 7 hectares (17 acres) of land bordered by a stream, with its own small lake. The ensemble comprises a large family house, annexe, large barn, garage and prune oven. There are 2 further large open stone barns to the rear of the property. The accommodation includes living room with fireplace, kitchen, dining room, 3 bedrooms, bureau/4th bedroom, bathroom, and dressing room. The annexe has 2 bedrooms and a bathroom, which could easily be enlarged. The main barn has been partially converted into accommodation, and would provide two 3 bedroom gites. Services: Mains water, electricity, oil central-heating, telephone.
Price: 609,796€ F.A.I.

AB 22027 - Situated 3 kilometres from the large village of Sigoules (24) with a good variety of shops and restaurants, the property is in an elevated setting with panoramic views over vineyards. Bergerac and International airport 25 minutes away. Description: An attractive 19thC. 6 bedroom stone house, ideal for Chambres d'Hote, which has just been completely renovated, with new swimming pool. The property is situated very privately in gardens of 3500 m² (nearly an acre) approached by a long drive. The accommodation includes living room with fireplace, fully equipped kitchen, laundry, dining room, 6 bedrooms, and 4 bathrooms. There is a very large covered terrace and two open terraces, and one which surrounds the 10.5 m x 7.5m salt filtration pool. Services: Mains water, electricity, oil central-heating, telephone.
Price: 422,193€ F.A.I.

WATERSIDE PROPERTIES INTERNATIONAL LTD

Haute-Vienne - Near Dordogne border - restored water mill with substantial outbuildings in 2.5 hectares with mill stream 4 bedrooms, 3 bathrooms, living/dining room (90m²), kitchen. Versatile property with potential and immense charm. Near delightful town. Ref: WPI/87/001   Price: 272,121€

Pyrenees-Atlantiques - 18th century Chateau, farm house and numerous outbuildings set in 4.86 hectares (garden, kiwi plantation, meadows). Superb original features, 3 reception rooms, kitchen, 6 bedrooms, 3 bathrooms. Lovely hilly countryside, 6 kms from lively town. Ref: PAU/403   Price: 945,000€

Remarkable selection of beautiful properties throughout Poitou-Charentes, Aquitaine, Midi-Pyrénées & the Touraine. In other regions only exceptional waterside properties.

   Tel: 01892 750011   Fax: 01892 750033

Email: sales@watersideproperties-int.co.uk   Web: www.watersideproperties-int.co.uk

Price Guide

(24)
This traditional three-bedroom home with modern facilities is in a quiet and secluded location near the town of Mareuil. The property offers a garden of 7,200m² with stunning panoramic views.
180,271 euros   **LAF**
(£112,670) GP

(24)
A five-bedroom family house with many original features and a swimming pool. Set in 20,000m² of beautiful gardens, the accommodation offers wonderful views over the surrounding countryside.
262,212 euros   **LAF**
(£163,885) GP

(24)
A stone-built village house with an attached barn. Features front and rear courtyard gardens. Offers three bedrooms and boasts many original details, including tiled floors. In need of modernisation.
107,000 euros   **LAT**
(£66,875) GP

(47)
This semi-detached house in the centre of a quiet village offers four bedrooms and a small garden at the rear of the building. The property is ready to move in to and all services are connected.
135,870 euros   **VEF**
(£84,920) GP

(24)
This manor house with land of 27,000m² is located in the country near a small village and offers four spacious bedrooms. Approached by a drive, the house comes with several barns and outbuildings.
245,824 euros   **LAF**
(£153,640) GP

(19)
This 18th-century manor house is set on a hilltop and boasts stunning views. The property features a traditional dovecote, barn and guest cottage and benefits from 17,000m² of tree-filled parkland.
655,750 euros   **LAF**
(£409,845) GP

(47)
This six-bedroom character house is set on the outskirts of a pretty village. Offering a large garden and a single garage, the property is ready to move in to. Just a short walk from local amenities.
252,270 euros   **VEF**
(£157,670) GP

(24)
A traditional, fully-restored country house near a small village. The property comprises four bedrooms and a family bathroom, and is set in land of 2,500m² with a pool and panoramic views.
327,553 euros   **LAF**
(£204,720) GP

(47)
Set in a garden of 10,000m², this château lies on the outskirts of a quiet village and currently offers six bedrooms, with the possibility of converting more. Complete with a barn and outbuildings.
548,570 euros   **VEF**
(£342,855) GP

Leggett Immobilier
S.A.R.L • Transactions Immobilières

Ref: DC280 Price: 70,432EUR - Small house and 2 hectares of land situated in a quiet village in the Dordogne. The house, which comprises of 3 rooms, one which is currently used as a kitchen; and a bathroom/WC. There is a barn across the lane, and another outbuilding. The main house has a small garden attached to it. The remaining land consists of woodland and grassland and is situated on the edge of the village.

Ref: SL366   Price: 111,385€ - Bungalow with 1 hectare of well kept land, and an outbuilding of 160m². The house has 3 bedrooms, a kitchen, lounge/dining room with a wood-burning stove, bathroom, and separate WC. The bungalow has electric central heating throughout. There is also a good sized garage and utility room.

Ref: DB354   Price: 237,575€ - Old water mill with renovated house, two barns and roughly 5,000m² of land and pretty garden. All in very good order, oil-fired central heating, shops and services nearby. The house comprises three bedrooms, bathroom, WC, kitchen, lounge and dining room, cellar and loft which could be converted.

Ref: DH376 Price: 343,000€ - Renovated stone house, with a one bed-roomed gite, barn and pool, situated in a pretty village in the North Dordogne. The main house has a lounge with the original stone fireplace, fitted kitchen, dining room, entrance hall, utility and WC on the ground floor. On the first floor there are 3 good sized bedrooms and 2 bathrooms. Above this is a large loft. This wonderful property is situated in 1.75 hectares of extremely well kept land.

Tel: **00 33 5 53 56 62 54**
Fax: **00 33 5 53 56 62 57**
email: **sales@frenchestateagents.com**
www.frenchestateagents.com

L'Affaire Francaise
www.French-Property-net.com
UK Tel: 0208 570 9844
e-mail: FrenchProp@aol.com

DORDOGNE
Maison de Maitre 4 bedrooms with en-suite bathrooms, pool, 1 ha land & pretty views
Ref: 51137
Price: 295,625€

HAUTE VIENNE
Beautiful 5 bedroom, 4 bathroom country house with 3 furnished gites, pool & 8 acres land
Ref: 40060
Price: 578,452€

English Estate Agents registered in France
Professional Card No 57 (Charente)
25 Grand Rue 16200 JARNAC France
Tel: 00 33 5 45 81 76 79 Fax: 00 33 5 45 35 09 52
Properties in the Charente, Charente Maritime, Dordogne and Limousin

---

Jon Coshall A.N.A.E.A.

7, rue de Temple, 24500 EYMET
Tel: 00 33 5 53 74 50 40
Fax: 00 33 5 53 74 50 41
Email: info@eymet-immobilier.com

Le Bourg, 24240 SIGOULES
Tel: 00 33 5 53 73 53 15
Fax: 00 33 5 53 73 53 16
Email: info@eymet-immobilier.com

EYMET IMMOBILIER

www.eymet-immobilier.com

The agency is a small locally owned British concern. All properties are personally visited by us, thus ensuring that you only receive the best selection. We can arrange everything on your behalf - your appointment to view properties, guide you through the buying process, reserve accommodation. We will also organise for finance, restoration, planning, etc, all with a personal touch.

We are situated in the charming old Bastide town of Eymet in the heart of the Bergerac vineyards, approx half an hour south of Bergerac, in an area surrounded by other Bastides, and the superb countryside of the southern Dordogne, northern Lot et Garonne.

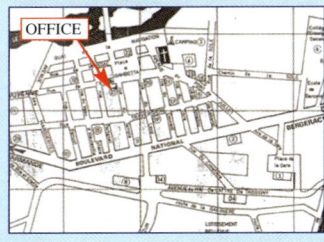

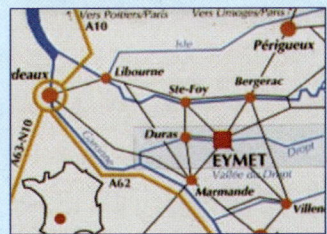

Price Guide

(47)
A 19th-century château with five bedroom suites. Features include an office with oak parquet floors and moulded ceilings, a billiards room and a gym. Set in parkland of 3,000m² with swimming pool.
762,245 euros VIA
(£476,405) GP

(24)
Featuring a fully-fitted kitchen and a period fireplace, this five-bedroom country cottage also offers three bathrooms. The garden comprises a terrace, lawn and mature shrubs and trees.
112,000 euros FFF
(£70,000) GP

(47)
This 18th-century stone-built house has been completely renovated. Featuring six bedrooms and a large swimming pool, it is set in 9,700m² of gardens and is within easy access of an airport.
427,000 euros FPL
(£266,875) GP

(24)
In a picturesque hamlet setting, this detached home offers a large garden and barn for conversion. The house is ready to move in to and benefits from stunning views over the surrounding countryside.
97,256 euros VEF
(£60,785) GP

(47)
This 18th-century château with a classical Napoleonic façade has been renovated to provide six double bedrooms. The property offers a guest house and features a chapel carved out of bedrock.
655,531 euros VIA
(£409,705) GP

(24)
Located in a quiet hamlet and approached by a private drive, this château sits in over 24,000m² of woodland gardens. Features several en-suite bedrooms with open views over the countryside.
793,902 euros VEF
(£496,190) GP

(47)
Built in 1771, this stone-built farmhouse offers three gîtes which sleep up to 20 people. Set in a landscaped garden with fruit trees, vegetable plot, swimming pool and a pond. Features a wine store.
555,000 euros FPL
(£346,875) GP

(47)
This four-bedroom stone-built farmhouse enjoys sunny gardens and a figure-of-eight shaped swimming pool. The property features wood-beamed ceilings, open fires and a shady terrace.
182,000 euros VIA
(£113,750) GP

(24)
Offering two bedrooms, this characterful house is set in a quiet hamlet. A large well-maintained garden to the front, side and rear of the house features a selection of mature trees and shrubs.
189,329 euros VEF
(£118,330) GP

GRANDCHAMP IMMOBILIER

ZC LE MAINE 24160 EXCIDEUIL

Large selection of properties in Perigord

Tel: 00 33 5 53 62 04 80
Fax: 00 33 5 53 62 89 61

email: grandchamp.immo@wanadoo.fr
www.perigord-immobilier.com

CHARLES LOFTIE IMMOBILIER
Place Hugues Salel, 46250 Cazals France
Tel: 00 33 5 65 22 83 50   Fax: 00 33 5 65 22 88 71

We offer a wide selection of top quality properties in Lot & Dordogne

L/4194 - LOT
Attractive stone built house, restored to a high standard with outbuildings and swimming pool set in 2.3 ha of land.

Price: 383,100€

L/4204 - LOT
Rare opportunity to acquire a prestigious property currently run as a high quality chambre d'hote set in 3 ha of parkland.

Price: 954,000€

 Full property details and photographs of all our properties can be found on our website:

www.charles-loftie-immo.com

The French Property Shop

Clergy House • Churchyard • Ashford • Kent TN23 1QG

• Tel: 01233 666 902   • Fax: 01233 666 903

• Email: sales@frenchpropertyshop.com

We specialise in South West France, with emphasis on the Departments of: Vienne (86), Charente (16), Charente Maritime (17), Dordogne (24), Gironde (33), Haute Vienne (87), Lot (46), Lot-et-Garonne (47), Tarn-et-Garonne (82), and Deux-Sèvres (79).

www.frenchpropertyshop.com

CONTACT: **PIPPA ROBSON** AT

AGENCE IMMOBILIERE
HERMAN DE GRAAF

LE BOURG - 24800 SAINT JEAN DE COLE

WE WILL HELP YOU FIND YOUR PERFECT HOME, FROM A COTTAGE TO A CASTLE.

Ref: 1134 - Small, simply restored farmhouse, quietly situated in garden with a lovely view. Living room (25m^2) with fireplace, kitchen (20m^2), WC with basin, bathroom (WC, bath & basin) & 2 bedrooms. Basement with cellars, storage space & boiler room with oil-fired central heating. Adjoining barn (18m^2) & small outbuilding.

Price: 120,000€ F.A.I.

TEL: 00 33 5 53 62 38 03
FAX: 00 33 5 53 55 08 03
EMAIL: agence@immobilier-dordogne.com
www.immobilier-dordogne.com

Price Guide

(24)
A *maison de maitre* in need of some work. Set in a picturesque location, the property boasts four bedrooms, a fitted kitchen and a heated swimming pool. A garden of 10,000m² surrounds the house.
295,625 euros   LAF
(£184,765) GP

(47)
This ensemble of stone-built house and several outbuildings is set in a large garden with open views. Approached by a private drive, the property offers three bedrooms and a swimming pool.
305,580 euros   VIA
(£190,990) GP

(24)
This well-situated farmhouse has been fully restored. Retaining many of its original features, the house has five spacious bedrooms, a swimming pool and a garden of 4,200m² with stunning views.
295,625 euros   LAF
(£184,765) GP

(47)
This four-bedroom town house features a stone staircase and lounge with a chandelier but is in need of some renovation. Offers a fully-furnished dining room, bathroom and a small rear garden.
198,000 euros   VIA
(£123,750) GP

(24)
This detached house with a double garage enjoys superb views over the surrounding countryside and vineyards. Featuring a garden of 5,000m² laid to lawn, three bedrooms, a balcony and cellar.
99,000 euros   LAT
(£61,875) GP

(47)
A stone barn located in a pretty hamlet close to Beauville. Newly roofed, the property is in need of conversion work to become a two-bedroom home. Features traditional tiling and open views.
35,100 euros   VIA
(£21,940) GP

(47)
A renovated stone-built house with stunning views over a rural valley. Well situated in a pretty *bastide* village, the property offers three spacious bedrooms, a small rear courtyard and a large cellar.
134,400 euros   VIA
(£84,000) GP

(24)
Overlooking a small lake, this detached four-bedroom house is set in a quiet hamlet in Dordogne. This character property offers many original features, a large garden and stunning views.
186,433 euros   VEF
(£116,520) GP

(47)
A country house with gardens. Recently renovated, the house offers spacious accommodation and has four double bedrooms. Features include a rear patio area, high ceilings and a beamed lounge.
241,000 euros   VIA
(£150,625)

Aquitaine

(47)
This period country house with 1,000m² of garden offers light and spacious accommodation. The property is located in a rural area and boasts three double bedrooms and cellars beneath the house.
151,000 euros   VIA
(£94,375) GP

(47)
Close to the town of Tournon-d'Agenais, this modern three-bedroom house enjoys an upstairs patio that overlooks the garden and swimming pool. Features a lounge with woodburning fire.
762,245 euros   VIA
(£476,405) GP

(47)
Located in a quiet rural village, a two-storey semi-detached dwelling offering four bedrooms and a small garden to the rear. The house is ready to move in to, with all services connected.
135,870 euros   VEF
(£84,920) GP

(33)
Surrounded by vineyards and set in a peaceful location, a waterside property with two cottages and a swimming pool. Featuring five bedrooms, a paved terrace, wine cellars and woodland gardens.
609,255 euros   WAT
(£380,785) GP

(47)
A fully-renovated stone house with gîtes and a swimming pool, set in large gardens with views over a valley. The main house features two en-suite bedrooms, an open-plan kitchen and lounge.
402,000 euros   VIA
(£251,250) GP

(47)
A characterful, stone-built six-bedroom house located on the edge of a rural village. The property enjoys a small garden and single garage and is just a short drive from local amenities.
252,270 euros   VEF
(£157,670) GP

(24)
A classic stone-built converted barn retaining many of its original features. With a swimming pool and garden of 700m², the property offers views over beautiful countryside and the River Dordogne.
99,646 euros   LAT
(£62,280) GP

(33)
This detached brick-built house is set in 2,500m² of land. The ground floor comprises a living room, kitchen, bathroom and two large bedrooms. The second floor offers a study and three bedrooms.
252,565 euros   LAT
(£157,855) GP

(24)
A gîte complex with three houses and two barns. Partially furnished, the main house sleeps up to six people. Featuring a tennis court, the property is set in hilly countryside among fields and woods.
512,000 euros   FFF
(£320,000) GP

Price Guide

(33)
A detached house with a garage, set in grounds of nearly 1,700m². The ground floor comprises a living room with fireplace, two bedrooms, bathroom and kitchen. Upstairs are two further rooms.
253,300 euros   **LAT**
(£158,315) GP

(47)
A farmhouse in need of some modernisation. Currently offering two bedrooms, shower room and kitchen, the property has plenty of scope for conversion. Set in a small garden with attached barn.
126,000 euros   **VIA**
(£78,750) GP

(47)
This magnificent 18th-century *chartreuse* is set in 12,000m² of gardens with a swimming pool. Fully renovated, the property boasts terracotta-tiled floors and has five en-suite double bedrooms.
449,300 euros   **VIA**
(£280,815) GP

(33)
A picturesque, recently-restored stone-built farmhouse with views across the countryside, a heated swimming pool and converted barn. Offers a main house, several apartments and garage.
517,280 euros   **MOD**
(£323,300) GP

(47)
Set in parkland and boasting six garages, a lake, spring, well and a small vineyard. This property comprises three stone houses and features original tiling, four bedrooms and a summer-kitchen.
1,143,368 euros   **LAT**
(£714,605) GP

(47)
An ensemble of farmhouse, barn and cottage for renovation. Situated in an orchard and meadow, the farmhouse offers four double bedrooms, two bathrooms and a heated swimming pool.
442,000 euros   **VIA**
(£276,250) GP

(64)
This 19th-century farmhouse is set in 6,100m² of gardens offering open views stretching as far as the Pyrenees. Surrounded by vineyards, this extensive property is approached by a private driveway.
548,000 euros   **LEB**
(£342,500) GP

(64)
An attractive stone-built house located in the hills of the Madiran winemaking region. The property offers spacious accommodation and is situated in the heart of a small village with all amenities.
69,000 euros   **LEB**
(£43,125) GP

(47)
A country residence dating from 1580 and set in 28,000m² of mature parkland with orchards, stone barns and a well. Features include open fires and terracotta floors. Offers five large bedrooms.
539,670 euros   **VIA**
(£337,295) GP

Aquitaine

(47)
A renovated country residence set in 2,000m² of mature gardens with a fenced-in pool and patio. Offering five double bedrooms, the property features oak parquet floors and a walnut fitted kitchen.
231,291 euros   **VIA**
(£144,560) GP

(64)
A character farmhouse with many original features and open views over the countryside. Approached by a long gravel drive, the property has several outbuildings and a large courtyard.
260,000 euros   **LEB**
(£162,500) GP

(47)
A large 19th-century manor house located close to the town of Agen. Offers 12 bedrooms, five bathrooms, three reception rooms and many original architectural details. Set in extensive parkland.
381,123 euros   **LAT**
(£238,200) GP

(24)
A renovated barn with gîte and gardens of nearly 4,400m². With stunning views over fields and woodland, the house comprises a kitchen, shower room, bathroom, two bedrooms and a large lounge.
139,300 euros   **FWY**
(£87,065) GP

(64)
A small house currently arranged over the ground floor but with potential to create further accommodation in the attic. Offers living space of 100m². A character home set in an attractive garden.
160,070 euros   **LEB**
(£100,045) GP

(24)
A five-bedroom house and gîte in Ribérac. Set in a 1,800m² garden with a well, garages, workshop and sheds. Offers four bedrooms and a family bathroom. Located in a very quiet neighbourhood.
139,300 euros   **FWY**
(£87,065) GP

(33)
This large 18th-century *demeure* offers 350m² of habitable living space with 14 main rooms and four partially renovated bathrooms. The property also features several outbuildings and stabling.
211,904 euros   **FPP**
(£132,440) GP

(64)
On high ground with views of the Pyrenees, this house dates from the 18th century and is constructed from riverstones. With a new slate roof, it offers 660m² of living space arranged over three floors.
428,750 euros   **LEB**
(£267,970) GP

(40)
A restored farmhouse in the middle of an oak forest. A short drive from the Landaise coast, this extensive property features a swimming pool and a stream that runs through the grounds.
650,000 euros   **LEB**
(£406,250) GP

Price Guide

(33)
A contemporary villa located in a peaceful area close to the coast. Boasting 10 main rooms, the property features a swimming pool, a garden of 1,170m² and a spacious well-equipped kitchen.
564,061 euros   **FWY**
(£352,540) GP

(64)
This character property features a large swimming pool and is surrounded by woodland. Fronted by an immaculate lawn, it offers a second house that could be let out. Set in a quiet rural area.
850,000 euros   **LEB**
(£531,250) GP

(33)
An old house in need of some work. Offering 10 main rooms and two bathrooms, it is set in a hamlet near Blaye. The property benefits from easy access to local amenities and a quiet location.
138,738 euros   **FWY**
(£86,710) GP

(33)
In the heart of a village close to Saint-Savin, this house has five main rooms and is in need of total renovation. Comprising a living room, lounge, kitchen and the possibility of three bedrooms.
29,727 euros   **FWY**
(£18,580) GP

(64)
Located high in the Madiran hills, this restored house enjoys views over a valley and is surrounded by woodland. The property is approached by a drive and fronted by a pretty lawned garden.
419,000 euros   **LEB**
(£261,875) GP

(33)
In a peaceful location in the town of Cavignac, this house offers seven main rooms and two large bathrooms. Recently rewired and ready to move in to, the property benefits from a pleasant garden.
242,394 euros   **FWY**
(£151,495) GP

(33)
Set in the country, a house with outbuildings and mature gardens of 3,900m². Offering a terrace, courtyard and swimming pool, this property features stone walls, open fires and beamed ceilings.
304,898 euros   **FWY**
(£190,560) GP

(64)
A stone-built *maison de maitre* with a swimming pool. Set in an enclosed park with easy access to Pau and Biarritz. This property boasts unrestricted views and several good-sized bedrooms.
321,000 euros   **LEB**
(£200,625) S

(24)
Located in Black Périgord, this property comprises five stone barns set around a main farmhouse. Situated in 250,000m² of land with a natural spring running into lakes stocked with trout.
382,000 euros   **EQU**
(£238,750) GP

Aquitaine

(24)
Between Limoges and Périgueux, this property comprises a house and three gîtes. The house offers four bedrooms, while each gîte sleeps between four and 10. Set in a garden with swimming pool.
390,000 euros   **EQU**
(£243,750) GP

(24)
A converted farmhouse located in a quiet hamlet five minutes from a town. The main house offers three bedrooms, and the property comes with a second house for restoration and a lovely garden.
240,000 euros   **EQU**
(£150,000) GP

(47)
A stone-built cottage situated in wooded countryside. In need of some renovation, the existing accommodation comprises a large dining room, sitting room and a traditional farmhouse kitchen.
20,581 euros   **CAB**
(£12,865) GP

(24)
A completely renovated house in a small hamlet. The property offers three bedrooms, one bathroom and a sitting room with exposed beams. Set in 6,500m² of land with a rock garden and well.
180,000 euros   **EQU**
(£112,500) GP

(24)
Nestling against a wooded hill this traditional 16th-century château boasts several bedrooms, a spiral staircase leading to an oak library and a painted antechamber depicting colourful classical scenes.
720,000 euros   **EQU**
(£450,000) GP

(24)
A large gîte complex located close to a picturesque village and surrounded by woodland and meadows. There are four gîtes and several outbuildings all built in the traditional style of the region.
450,000 euros   **EQU**
(£281,250) GP

(47)
An old water mill situated on the edge of a village. Comprising four bedrooms, two shower rooms and one bathroom, the property is set in 3,300m² of land bordered by a stream and mature woodland.
250,474 euros   **SEL**
(£156,545) GP

(47)
Located on a plateau with open views, this property comprises a main house, a one-bedroom studio apartment at garden level and a barn that has been converted into a gîte with two bedrooms.
517,280 euros   **FPP**
(£323,300) GP

(64)
Dating from the 14th century, a partially restored residence within a short distance of a village and mountains. Boasting panoramic views, the property features seven bedrooms and terracotta tiling.
153,000 euros   **LAT**
(£95,625) GP

Price Guide

(24)
A two-bedroom bungalow set on 500,000m² of land with mature woods and meadows. Comprises a converted granary, lounge and kitchen. The property also offers a large cellar beneath the house.
540,813 euros   **FWY**
(£338,010) GP

(64)
Located in an elevated position this manor house boasts open views and is surrounded by a garden. Offering several bedrooms, the property is ready to move in to and is close to a small village.
530,000 euros   **LEB**
(£331,250) S

(24)
In a peaceful spot, this property is set in 30,000m² of land with a swimming pool and terrace. It features a monumental fireplace, *colombage* walls, tiled floors and a 17th-century wooden staircase.
339,352 euros   **FWY**
(£212,095) GP

(24)
A south-facing farmhouse in need of renovation. Situated on the outskirts of a busy market town and in a tourist area well known for its water sports. The property has a 10,000m² garden and a barn.
48,780 euros   **FWY**
(£30,490) GP

(40)
On the outskirts of a market town this traditional village house benefits from a swimming pool. Suitable for use as a hotel or gîte complex, the property has a small garden surrounding the house.
290,000 euros   **LEB**
(£181,250) GP

(24)
An extensive gîte complex set in fenced grounds of over 20,000m² with a pond, two tennis courts and a swimming pool. Comprises two houses and five apartments to be let out. Close to a small village.
485,000 euros   **EQU**
(£303,125) GP

(24)
This vast villa is set in wooded grounds of 40,000m² with a lake and swimming pool. Approached via a private driveway, this property features a cellar, 12 bedrooms and two en-suite bathrooms.
720,000 euros   **EQU**
(£450,000) GP

(24)
A renovated ensemble of stone buildings that overlooks the Périgord nature reserve. Offering a main house and two fully-furnished independent gîtes that can each sleep four to six people.
300,000 euros   **EQU**
(£187,500) GP

(64)
This restored house is set on the outskirts of Pau and boasts stunning views stretching as far as the Pyrenees. Offering an extensive garden with trees and shrubs, the house benefits from large rooms.
397,000 euros   **LEB**
(£248,125) GP

Aquitaine

(64)
A 1920s house with a garage and office building set in 3,200m² of land in a Bearnaise village. The property features a living room opening onto a terrace, a sitting room and eight large bedrooms.
245,000 euros   **LAT**
(£153,125) GP

(64)
Dating from the 16th century, a character house in over 7,000m² of land. The property is partially restored and offers four bedrooms, a living room with stone fireplace and a fully-equipped kitchen.
272,000 euros   **LAT**
(£170,000) GP

(24)
This ivy-clad house with two barns is set in a large garden close to a quiet village. Comprising a beamed living room, kitchen, two bedrooms and a terrace. Enjoys parquet floors and stunning views.
161,647 euros   **LAT**
(£101,030) GP

(24)
A large gîte complex comprising a main house with four double bedrooms, four gîte buildings, a barn and a swimming pool. Set in 30,000m² of garden with a patio area, shrubs and mature trees.
575,000 euros   **ALZ**
(£359,375) GP

(24)
A five-bedroom *maison de maitre* standing in a small garden laid to lawn and planted with mature trees. This spacious residence enjoys two bathrooms, a sunny terrace and many original features.
192,085 euros   **AND**
(£120,055) S

(33)
This historic château offers 11 good-sized bedrooms and eight bathrooms. Benefiting from a heated swimming pool, the house is set in 25,000m² of tree-filled land and is near a busy town.
754,622 euros   **AND**
(£471,640) S

(24)
In a historic village with all amenities, this large cottage offers six bedrooms and three bathrooms. Standing in a small garden with panoramic views and featuring a heated swimming pool.
242,400 euros   **AND**
(£151,500) GP

(33)
This restored manor house dates from the 19th century and comes with several large outbuildings. Situated in 15,000m² of land, the property features five bedrooms, a study, living room and lounge.
729,240 euros   **LAT**
(£445,775) GP

(24)
A former farmhouse with two bedrooms, a fitted kitchen and a living room arranged over the ground floor. Upstairs is an attic for conversion. Set in 5,000m² of grounds with a shed and barn.
195,897 euros   **HIF**
(£122,435) GP

Price Guide

(33)
A classic *maison de maitre* with five good-sized bedroom suites, two bathrooms and many original architectural details. The house is set in a large well-maintained garden with panoramic rural views.
254,590 euros   **AND**
(£159,120) S

(24)
Close to the town of La Roche-Chalais, a spacious farmhouse with four bedrooms. Comprises a kitchen, living room, garage and a small outbuilding. The property is set in a mature garden of 2,300m^2.
99,701 euros   **HIF**
(£62,315) GP

(24)
A Périgordine-style house with a swimming pool and detached garage. The house is set in shaded grounds of 2,350m^2 and features three bedrooms, a sunny terrace, living room and a corner-kitchen.
194,372 euros   **HIF**
(£121,485) GP

(24)
A fully-renovated village house featuring three bedrooms, shower room, kitchen and sitting room. Adjoining the house is a garage and a small terrace. Within a short distance of local amenities.
60,522 euros   **HIF**
(£37,825) GP

(24)
This large villa enjoys panoramic views and boasts a swimming pool. Comprises three en-suite bedrooms, a study, kitchen, living room, cellar, wine store and tidy lawned gardens of 6,000m^2.
609,186 euros   **HIF**
(£380,740) GP

(33)
Dating from the 19th century, a country residence with two guest cottages, outbuildings and a swimming pool. Set in an enclosed garden of 9,600m^2, the property features five bedrooms.
884,204 euros   **LAT**
(£552,625) GP

(24)
Standing in 1,000m^2 of garden planted with trees and shrubs, this restored farmhouse offers nine bedrooms, five bathrooms and one outbuilding. Wonderful country views and a quiet surrounding.
140,253 euros   **AND**
(£87,660) GP

(33)
Close to the small town of Arveyres, a typical 18th-century house standing in gardens of 6,000m^2. The residence features a renovated living room, six bedrooms, study, attic and open fires.
890,860 euros   **LAT**
(£556,790) GP

(24)
A restored stone-built house set in 8,000m^2 of partially wooded land with a swimming pool. The house features a fitted kitchen with exposed beams and tiled floor, two en-suite bedrooms and a cellar.
195,897 euros   **LAT**
(£122,435) GP

Aquitaine

(24)
A 15th-century stone-built house with a moat and towers. This extensive property features an original drawbridge and interior courtyard. Situated in an elevated position in 4,500m² of grounds.
672,300 euros   **LAT**
(£420,185) GP

(33)
A large farmhouse currently comprising three bedrooms, two bathrooms and several outbuildings. In a tranquil woodland setting of 20,000m² with a small stream and impressive panoramic rural vistas.
297,275 euros   **AND**
(£185,795) S

(47)
Located in 12,000m² of woodland with a swimming pool, lake and tennis court, this nine-bedroom 17th-century château features a stone staircase and wooden floors. The property also offers a lodge.
1,375,000 euros   **SIF**
(£859,375) GP

(33)
This large château offers several bedroom suites, a self-contained caretaker's cottage and a number of large outbuildings. Standing in 120,000m² of tree-filled rural land with a small lake and open views.
600,000 euros   **LAT**
(£375,000) GP

(47)
Set in the countryside close to a village, a six-bedroom country home with a swimming pool built inside a converted barn. The house also offers a drawing room, study and south-facing garden.
600,000 euros   **SIF**
(£375,000) GP

(24)
A château set on a hilltop standing in 10,000m² of parkland. This impressive building features original architectural details including stained-glass windows and towers. Complete with a pool and terrace.
599,920 euros   **LAT**
(£374,950) GP

(33)
A seven-bedroom farmhouse with two bathrooms. Set in 2,000m² of garden laid to lawn with a patio area, swimming pool and three outbuildings. The property enjoys stunning panoramic rural views.
259,163 euros   **AND**
(£161,975) S

(33)
A restored four-bedroom farmhouse and gîte set in 3,000m² of land. The property has two reception rooms and a dining room. Comes with a garage, barn and a swimming pool. Close to a river.
510,399 euros   **LAT**
(£319,000) GP

(47)
This renovated farmhouse is set in a small garden with a swimming pool. Boasting views across the surrounding countryside, the property features three bedrooms and several brick outbuildings.
149,400 euros   **AND**
(£93,375) S

Price Guide

(47)
Dating from the 18th century, a family house draped with vines. Located in the country, the property has a garden of 5,800m² with a tennis court and ample parking. Features six bedrooms and a cellar.
808,000 euros   **SIF**
(£505,000) GP

(24)
Set on the banks of a river, this large mill house offers four spacious bedrooms. With 60,000m² of land, outbuildings and a large swimming pool, the property enjoys outstanding rural views.
426,857 euros   **AND**
(£266,785) GP

(24)
An extensive farmhouse surrounded by woodland and meadows. This property features a large living room with exposed beams and stone walls and a sitting room in the unusual tower structure.
509,179 euros   **LAT**
(£318,235) GP

(24)
A village house comprising seven spacious bedrooms and five bathrooms set in enclosed land of 1,000m². The property benefits from a heated swimming pool and comes with a separate gîte.
403,990 euros   **AND**
(£252,495) S

(33)
This renovated stone-built home dates from the 18th century and offers an outdoor swimming pool. Situated in undulating grounds of 2,000m² with several outbuildings. Features three spacious bedrooms.
486,500 euros   **LAT**
(£304,065) GP

(24)
A farmhouse with four bedrooms and two bathrooms. Enjoying two swimming pools, the property is located down a secluded lane and sits in 3,500m² of gardens with an outbuilding and two letting gîtes.
403,990 euros   **AND**
(£252,495) S

(47)
Fronted by an open courtyard, this large manor house comprises five spacious bedrooms and three bathrooms. Set in grounds of 1,600m² with several outbuildings including a separate dovecote.
396,367 euros   **AND**
(£247,730) S

(24)
In a hilltop setting, a stone-built house standing in 5,900m² of land with a swimming pool. Comprises three bedrooms, a fully-fitted kitchen and three cellars. Features the original wooden staircase.
436,003 euros   **LAT**
(£272,500) GP

(24)
A traditional three-bedroom *maison de maître* set in a small garden planted with mature trees and laid to lawn. With many original features, this idyllic home also offers an outbuilding and a pool.
373,500 euros   **AND**
(£233,435) S

Aquitaine

(33)
A partially restored three-bedroom character house set in 20,000m² of land in a quiet neighbourhood. The property retains period features including tiled floors and dressed stonework.
244,000 euros   **WAT**
(£152,500) GP

(33)
This six-bedroom *maison de maître* has four bathrooms and many original features. The house is set in a small garden planted with trees and shrubs and enjoys a swimming pool and outbuildings.
442,102 euros   **AND**
(£276,315) GP

(47)
Approached via a long drive, this traditional house offers seven bedrooms and three bathrooms. Set in 6,000m² of garden with a large heated pool and a gîte, the house is located close to a busy town.
541,500 euros   **AND**
(£338,435) GP

(24)
A charming *maison de maître* in need of some work. Featuring a swimming pool and 10,000m² of wooded grounds. The property offers four en-suite bedrooms, a covered terrace and a large salon.
295,625 euros   **WAT**
(£184,765) GP

(24)
A traditional farmhouse with six bedrooms. Set in a garden of 10,000m² featuring a swimming pool, patio area, outbuildings and a gîte. The main house offers a fitted kitchen and four bathrooms.
450,000 euros   **AND**
(£281,250) GP

(47)
Approached via a private drive, a farmhouse with five large bedrooms. Surrounded by open farmland and rolling countryside, the property benefits from panoramic views and a large swimming pool.
404,000 euros   **AND**
(£252,500) GP

(33)
Dating from the 18th century, a restored house set in 4,500m² of natural woodland. Located in a peaceful hamlet close to a village. Offers a sauna, summer dining room, pool and a guest wing.
322,195 euros   **WAT**
(£201,370) GP

(47)
An eight-bedroom château with five spacious bathrooms and several outbuildings. Just a short distance from a pretty village, the property is set in grounds of 13,000m² with a swimming pool.
880,394 euros   **AND**
(£550,245) GP

(47)
This detached farmhouse has seven bedrooms, six bathrooms and two outbuildings. Benefiting from a secluded spot, it stands in 1,000m² of land with a gîte and a heated pool. Near a small village.
352,157 euros   **AND**
(£220,100) GP

Price Guide

(47)
This farmhouse comprises four bedrooms, two bathrooms and one outbuilding. The property enjoys a swimming pool and a mature garden of 3,000m². Just a short distance from a village.
358,225 euros   **AND**
(£223,890) S

(24)
A traditional manor house with five bedrooms, three bathrooms and two outbuildings. Set in a tree-filled garden to the front and side of the house, the property also features a swimming pool.
289,653 euros   **AND**
(£181,035) GP

(64)
This large house with several outbuildings was built in the early 1900s. A short drive from the cathedral city of Pau, the house features two bathrooms, a two-storey barn and swimming pool.
410,000 euros   **WAT**
(£256,250) GP

(47)
In an elevated position and benefiting from southwesterly views, a house with a swimming pool set in 7,000m² of land. This home features tiled floors, beams and three large en-suite bedrooms.
323,142 euros   **LAT**
(£201,965) GP

(47)
A stone-built farmhouse boasting a figure-of-eight swimming pool. Set in the heart of a small town, the property features four spacious bedrooms, three bathrooms and a 1,000m² garden with outbuildings.
282,030 euros   **AND**
(£176,270) GP

(24)
With a tower, a pool with a terrace surround and two modern barns, this restored four-bedroom farmhouse is set in land of 20,000m². Close to a quiet village and with lovely country views.
320,142 euros   **LAT**
(£200,090) GP

(64)
This 1960s-style villa comprises a living room, terrace, kitchen and five large bedrooms. Carpeted throughout and south-facing, the property enjoys mountain views and is set in woodland.
914,659 euros   **LAT**
(£571,660) GP

(24)
On the banks of a river, this large *maison de maitre* comprises six bedrooms, two bathrooms and several outbuildings. Set in a mature lawned garden with a swimming pool and patio area.
396,367 euros   **AND**
(£247,730) S

(40)
Surrounded by wooded grounds of 5,000m² and bordered by a stream, a château offering high ceilings, parquet floors, a marble fireplace and an extensive cellar. Features 13 en-suite bedrooms.
646,600 euros   **LAT**
(£404,125) GP

Aquitaine

(24)
A restored farmhouse comprising five bedrooms, three bathrooms and one large outbuilding. Set in over 3,000m² of rural land with a swimming pool and a letting gîte. Enjoys a private, secluded spot.
496,221 euros   **AND**
(£310,140) GP

(24)
This 1960s town house is located in the centre of Nontron. The house comprises five bedrooms, a large drawing room, study and living room. Standing in well-maintained gardens of 12,000m².
274,661 euros   **FPP**
(£171,665) GP

(24)
This detached *longère* comprises three bedrooms and two bathrooms. It is set in a lawned garden with an outdoor swimming pool. In a tranquil location just a short distance from a small village.
131,500 euros   **AND**
(£82,185) GP

(47)
A sympathetically renovated 18th-century manor house featuring terracotta tiles, oak flooring and a dovecote. Enjoys a pool heated by solar energy and a self-contained guest cottage.
595,000 euros   **LAT**
(£371,875) GP

(64)
Dating from the 19th century, an L-shaped house with several outbuildings, swimming pool and a large tree-filled garden. With four bedrooms, the property is located close to a picturesque village.
327,765 euros   **FRA**
(£204,855) GP

(64)
A traditional house with a large adjoining garage. Standing in a south-facing winter garden of 7,700m², the property features a living room with an open fireplace and original floor tiles.
426,857 euros   **LAT**
(£266,785) GP

(24)
Dating from the 18th century, a country residence comprising six bedrooms, three receptions and two bathrooms. Features a guest cottage and several outbuildings. Boasts spectacular rural views.
650,000 euros   **SIF**
(£406,250) GP

(64)
A restored terraced house with a veranda. Includes a fitted kitchen, living room, bathroom and three bedrooms. Located a short drive from Biarritz in a private garden at the end of a quiet cul-de-sac.
373,500 euros   **LAT**
(£233,440) GP

(64)
This unusual house stands in over 13,000m² of woodland gardens with mountain views. The property features tiled halls, marble fireplaces, parquet floors and seven bedrooms. Set in a quiet village.
530,000 euros   **LAT**
(£331,250) GP

Price Guide

(24)
A south-facing villa set in an enclosed garden of 2,500m² with a swimming pool and garage. Newly-built, the property features tiled floors, three bedrooms and an open-plan kitchen and lounge.
275,000 euros   LAT
(£171,875) GP

(64)
An ancient farm set on a hill in a forested area. Comprising three bedrooms, the building features tiled floors, an open fireplace and woodburning stove. Set in land of 6,500m² with panoramic views.
211,904 euros   FWY
(£132,440) GP

(24)
Located in a small town, this recently-built stone house is set in a 3,650m² garden. Offering tiled floors and a double garage, the property features two large bedrooms with walk-in wardrobes.
227,912 euros   LAT
(£142,445) GP

(24)
A detached stone house set in a garden of 4,000m². Features an entrance hall, fitted kitchen with a fireplace, rear terrace, dining room and three bedrooms. Situated close to a bustling market town.
148,000 euros   LAT
(£92,500) GP

(33)
This 18th-century mansion is approached by a long gravel drive and is set in 7,000m² of secure parkland with a swimming pool and a gîte. Benefits from a secluded location and countryside views.
566,400 euros   FPP
(£354,000) GP

(24)
Dating from the 12th century, this house retains many original features including period fireplaces and exposed stone walls and beams. Bordered by a stream and complete with a small garden.
195,961 euros   LAT
(£122,475) GP

(24)
A well-executed barn conversion with several good-sized bedrooms. Set on a hilltop overlooking the Dordogne countryside. Situated in 1,000m² of land with a large pool and a separate gîte for rental.
240,000 euros   FPP
(£150,000) GP

(24)
A traditional village house enjoying a large garden with a pool, two terraces, a greenhouse and open views. The house features a tiled living room with a bar, exterior staircase and four bedrooms.
195,897 euros   LAT
(£122,435) GP

(24)
An old stone house with an attached garage located in over 85,000m² of land. The exterior of the property is in need of some renovation. Inside is a woodburning fire and original beams.
162,000 euros   LAT
(£101,250) GP

THE MIDI-PYRENEES

Price Guide

(82)
Situated in Tarn-et-Garonne, a two-bedroom stone-built house with a tower and swimming pool. Comprises two double bedrooms, one shower room and a traditional dovecote. Set in a 1,000m² garden.
295,000 euros   VIA
(£184,375) GP

(09)
This stone-built house is in need of renovation and comes with nearly 1,000m² of garden. Set in a quiet location with views over fields and meadows. Services have yet to be connected but are nearby.
33,500 euros   CAT
(£20,940) GP

(32)
Close to the town of Auch, this single-storey, stone-built house comprises three bedrooms and is set in 250m² of lawned garden with a patio area. Enjoys open views across the local countryside.
223,300 euros   DAV
(£139,565) GP

(31)
Just south of Saint-Gaudens, in a small market town, this village house, built of stone with nearly 700m² of enclosed land, offers three bedrooms. Outside there are numerous outbuildings and barns.
83,000 euros   LIN
(£51,875) GP

(82)
Boasting views over a rural valley, this stone house comprises three double bedrooms, one bathroom and a small fruit garden with a patio and spring. Features exposed beams and a wood burning stove.
142,775 euros   VIA
(£89,235) GP

(09)
Close to Saverdun, this house is arranged over two levels and situated near a town. Currently the ground floor is let out. The first floor is in need of renovation and benefits from spacious rooms.
42,000 euros   CAT
(£26,250) GP

(82)
This stone house has been fully renovated and boasts terracotta tiled floors, beamed ceilings and exposed stone walls. Offering five en-suite bedrooms, it is set in a garden with a pool and woodland.
803,000 euros   VIA
(£501,875) GP

(81)
A vast estate close to a medieval village. Comprises a house with four bedrooms, a separate two-bedroom guest cottage and several outbuildings. Set in 34,000m² of woodland and fields.
403,989 euros   DEE
(£252,495) S

(82)
A main house with vaulted cellars plus a second old house for renovation. The main house offers four double bedrooms, with views across a valley. Features a bread oven and a tobacco-drying barn.
305,580 euros   VIA
(£190,990) GP

The FRENCH, English speaking Estate Agent

ACTION Habitat

Najac

Properties in South West France:
- The right property for **you** at the right price
- **Free** legal advice

Aveyron, Tarn, Tarn et Garonne, Lot & more.

Contact: **Madeleine Vallet or Pierre Bateson**
Tel: **00 33 5 65 29 74 74**
Fax: **00 33 5 65 29 75 92**
Email: **actionhabitat@yahoo.com**
Le Faubourg 12270 Najac FRANCE

www.myswfrancehome.com

AUDE & ARIEGE

ARE YOU LOOKING FOR PROPERTY WITHIN EASY REACH OF TOULOUSE, CARCASSONNE AND PERPIGNAN AIRPORTS, SKIING AND MEDITERRANEAN BEACHES?

WE HAVE A WIDE SELECTION OF PROPERTIES FOR SALE IN THIS VARIED AND BEAUTIFUL REGION OF FRANCE

CONTACT: JEREMY CAMPBELL
Email: frenchproperty@wanadoo.fr

TEL: 00 33 4 68 69 35 61
FAX: 00 33 4 68 69 35 61

www.catharcastles.com

CHARLES LOFTIE IMMOBILIER
Place Hugues Salel, 46250 Cazals France
Tel: 00 33 5 65 22 83 50   Fax: 00 33 5 65 22 88 71

We offer a wide selection of top quality properties in Lot & Dordogne

L/4180 DORDOGNE
Majestic, well restored 13th C. Chateau set in 10.5 ha of land with spectacular views.

Price: 1,293,200€

L/4189 DORDOGNE
Beautifully restored traditional Perigordine farmhouse with outbuildings and swimming pool.

Full property details and photographs of all our properties can be found on our website:

www.charles-loftie-immo.com

SOUTH WEST FRANCE

Lot et Garonne, Aquitaine
Spacious, 5 bedroom country house set in 16 acres gardens, paddocks and oak woodland. Very peaceful spot. Centrally heated accom with 45m² lounge, huge living/kitchen. 13x5m swimming pool. Lovely family home **Price: 384 200€**

Tarn et Garonne,
Midi Pyrennees
Attractive Quercy stone farmhouse with Pigeonnier, set in an acre gardens with swimming pool and views. Spacious 4 bedroom accomm with beamed lounge, living room, kitchen/dining room, 2 shower rooms. BBQ patio. Outbuilding. Possible income
Price: 395 000€

Ask for brochure and colour details. Over 300 properties for sale.
CHECK OUT OUR WEB SITE: **WWW.VIALEX.COM**

VIALEX INTERNATIONAL
47470 Beauville France
Tel: 00 33 553 95 46 24
Fax: 00 33 553 95 46 25
Email: French@vialex.com

Price Guide

(09)
A village house in the Lèze Valley. The property comprises a living room, kitchen, bathroom and two large bedrooms. Set in a small private garden with trees and a garage and panoramic views.
56,500 euros   **CAT**
(£35,315) GP

(82)
A farmhouse set in 7,500m² of rural landscape. Featuring an oak-beamed lounge, exposed stone walls and a fireplace. The property has three double bedrooms, a kitchen, swimming pool and pretty garden.
253,000 euros   **VIA**
(£158,125) GP

(12)
A restored stone house in a pretty hamlet setting. Standing in land of 2,500m² with a pool. Features two staircases, a cellar, kitchen, four bedrooms and a vast veranda. Boasts tiled floors and a cellar.
274,402 euros   **ACT**
(£171,500) GP

(81)
In rolling countryside, an ancient stone-built property with a tower dating from the 16th century. Isolated and peaceful, with several spacious rooms in need of a total renovation. Enjoys open views.
448,000 euros   **ACT**
(£280,000) GP

(82)
A country residence set in over 8,000m² of garden with a salt water pool and carport. Features four double bedrooms, terracotta tiled floors, beamed ceilings and a pool house. Set in a quiet location.
262,000 euros   **VIA**
(£163,750) GP

(09)
A modern house with a garden of 1,300m². Offers four bedrooms, one bathroom and a dining room, which leads out on to a small terrace with views over the local area. There is also a single garage.
106,800 euros   **CAT**
(£66,750) GP

(12)
A four-bedroom farmhouse with a swimming pool. Situated in the heart of a medieval village. It has been fully restored and features four double bedrooms. Boasts a sunny terrace and large orchard.
300,000 euros   **PRV**
(£187,500) GP

(46)
This village house with a guest wing is situated close to shops and local amenities. Features three double bedrooms. The guest wing is reached via a raised terrace and offers a spacious double bedroom.
126,000 euros   **VIA**
(£78,750) GP

(32)
Fronted by a vast lawn, this light, spacious residence boasts a quiet situation, close to a village. Offers a kitchen, several bedrooms and a huge living room. Enjoys sweeping views across the open countryside.
250,000 euros   **GAS**
(£156,250) GP

Midi-Pyrénées

(12)
A characterful farmhouse with many original features, including stone fireplace, open beams and high ceilings. Situated in rural farmland, close to a village. With several bedrooms and a garden.
192,000 euros   <u>ACT</u>
(£120,000) GP

(82)
This spacious stone farmhouse with an old water mill alongside is set in over 9,000m² of land and bordered by a stream. The main house has been restored and offers five bedrooms with wooden floors.
215,000 euros   <u>VIA</u>
(£134,375) GP

(09)
In Ariège, a small barn suitable for conversion. Situated close to a quiet village, this property comes with a small garden offering open views over the surrounding area. Services have yet to be connected.
10,671 euros   <u>CAT</u>
(£6,670) GP

(82)
In the historic town of Caylus, this renovated house comprises seven bedrooms, a library, dining room with fireplace and winter garden. Built in 1870, the house boasts fruit trees and a patio area.
219,530 euros   <u>FPP</u>
(£137,205) GP

(09)
This gîte complex comprises five large gîtes and a main house. Featuring a large swimming pool and plenty of space for parking. The property is set in a small garden close to a busy village.
609,796 euros   <u>CAT</u>
(£381,125) GP

(65)
Dating from the 17th century, this stone-built house is set at the end of a long, secluded lane. Featuring four bedrooms, the property offers several barns and outbuildings. Benefits from a large garden.
160,000 euros   <u>LEB</u>
(£100,000) S

(09)
North of Mirepoix, a farmhouse in the process of renovation. This property comprises a living room, kitchen, dining room, bathroom and four bedrooms. Set in land of 95,000m² with a barn and a shed.
157,000 euros   <u>CAT</u>
(£98,125) GP

(65)
Set on high, a character stone house with a swimming pool. Boasting many original features and stunning views over the Pyrenees. Situated a short drive from the busy town of Marciac.
245,000 euros   <u>LEB</u>
(£153,125) GP

(46)
Dating from the 18th century, a manor house with a walled garden. In a small village between Gramat and Figeac. Boasts spacious rooms and high ceilings. Features five bedrooms and a separate chapel.
375,200 euros   <u>SIF</u>
(£234,500) GP

Price Guide

(82)
This renovated stone cottage is set in 2,000m² of peaceful meadows in a nice location with open views. The cottage offers three double bedrooms and space for a fourth. Features terracotta floors.
182,000 euros   VIA
(£113,750) GP

(32)
This fully-restored 19th-century château sits in its own private park with mature trees and a large swimming pool. Featuring 10 bedrooms, numerous bathrooms, a stable block and a long drive.
1,800,000 euros   LEB
(£1,125,000) GP

(65)
A traditional Gascon residence with three bedrooms and a large irrigation lake. Set in 2,500m² of land, with sweeping views towards the Pyrenees. Outside are several brick barns and outbuildings.
4,000,000 euros   LEB
(£2,500,000) S

(81)
This fully-restored house is set in a quiet village and features a large swimming pool. Comes with a separate guest cottage and a sunny mature garden with mature trees. Situated in an elevated position.
240,000 euros   UNI
(£150,000) GP

(82)
This country estate boasts a lake, numerous bedrooms and a heated swimming pool. Set in 20,000m² of land, with a courtyard, lawn and woodland area. Features a fully-fitted kitchen and a dovecote.
649,000 euros   UNI
(£405,625) GP

(46)
A restored house, boasting a pretty garden of 2,500m². Featuring a covered veranda, the property is split over three floors and enjoys spacious, light-filled rooms. With open views and close to a village.
401,000 euros   UNI
(£250,625) GP

(46)
Situated in countryside close to a large village and bordered by a stream, a water mill surrounded by its own land. Features four bedrooms, dressing room, study and cellar. Boasts exposed beams.
490,000 euros   SIF
(£306,250) GP

(82)
This stone-built farmhouse is set on a hill at the edge of a pretty village. Offering 10,000m² of land with a detached barn. The house is in need of general renovation and a short drive from the airport.
99,090 euros   CAB
(£61,930) GP

(32)
A restored hill-top farm with great views. Features four bedrooms, a barn, several outbuildings and 15,000m² of parkland. Enjoys rural surroundings and is situated in a peaceful spot, close to shops.
488,000 euros   GAS
(£305,000) GP

AGENCE GIRMA MOULY
90 rue du Portal Alban 46 000 Cahors
Tel: **00 33 5 65 35 21 42** Fax: **00 33 05 65 35 93 83**
www.mouly-immobilier.com

Authentic Quercy House located between Lot & Dordogne, 2 hectares of land with a fantastic view. First floor: Fully equiped kitchen and living room with a stone fire place and wooden beams, 3 bedrooms and 2 bathrooms with parquet flooring. Attic: 2 more bedrooms. A very nice and equiped gite with its barns. A Huge Swimming pool with a large terrace. **PRICE: 485,000€**

Agence Girma Mouly was established 35 years ago in Quercy **(South West of France)**
We offer you a wide range of properties. Feel free to contact us

le bonheur

MY FRENCH PROPERTY is designed to facilitate the process of buying a home in France. We provide up to date, selected listings of French property for sale, quality rental properties and a wide range of practical background information relative to purchasing property and living in France.

MY FRENCH PROPERTY

Contact: Edward Landau, My French Property,
Quartier Cutorte, Larreule, 65700 Maubourguet.
T: 00 33 5 62 96 94 27   F: 00 33 5 62 96 94 33
M: 00 33 6 07 80 06 21   E: le-bonheur@wanadoo.fr

le bonheur

www.myfrenchproperty.com

The Perfect Setting in South-West France
Tarn, Tarn et Garonne, Lot and Aveyron

For a superb selection of Cottages, Farmhouses, Country homes & Chateaux, in all price ranges - simply contact Charles & Jane Smallwood at Agence L'Union

• Tel: 00 33 5 63 30 60 24   • Fax: 00 33 5 63 68 24 67

• Email: info@agencelunion.com   • Web: www.agencelunion.com

Price Guide

(65)
Set in wooded parkland of nearly 4,200m², this character stone house enjoys sweeping views over the Pyrenees and also boasts a private swimming pool. The house offers numerous bedrooms.
380,000 euros   **LEB**
(£237,500) GP

(09)
Near to Foix, a large farmhouse with four bedrooms. Set in land of 95,000m² with two barns. Offers four bedrooms, a study, laundry room, bathroom and kitchen. Is in need of some finishing-off work.
176,500 euros   **CAT**
(£110,315) GP

(82)
In the medieval market town of Moissac, this large house over three storeys sits on a pretty riverbank. Situated 60km from Toulouse airport. The property comprises four large bedrooms.
105,190 euros   **CAB**
(£65,745) GP

(65)
A large house currently run as a hotel. Boasting a large garden and numerous en-suite bedrooms, the property is situated close to the Madiran winemaking region and benefits from unrestricted views.
360,000 euros   **LEB**
(£225,000) S

(82)
A house and garden situated in a hill-top village, close to the market town of Castelsarrasin. At present two rooms on the ground floor are used as bedrooms. There are two rooms upstairs for renovation.
106,715 euros   **CAB**
(£66,700) GP

(65)
Set in the foothills of the Pyrenees, a village house for renovation. With a small garden planted with trees and shrubs, the property offers several bedrooms and benefits from a quiet location.
344,000 euros   **LEB**
(£215,000) GP

(82)
On the outskirts of a hilltop village beside the River Garonne, this four-bedroom house boasts open views and is surrounded by a garden of 2,600m². Benefits from a tranquil, rural setting.
118,910 euros   **CAB**
(£74,319) GP

(32)
A historic château surrounded by a fort. Set in the foothills of the Pyrenees, with stunning views and close to a small village. Boasts numerous rooms, outbuildings for conversion and a large garden.
457,300 euros   **LEB**
(£285,815) GP

(82)
A period house with character set in a small village between Lavit and Saint-Nicolas-de-la-Grave. The house has been restored and retains its original terracotta floor tiles and massive oak beams.
120,435 euros   **CAB**
(£75,270) GP

Midi-Pyrénées

(82)
A completely restored riverside residence situated close to the busy city of Toulouse. The property features numerous rooms and is set in a small garden with trees. Ready for occupation.
132,630 euros   **CAB**
(£82,895) GP

(82)
A large farmhouse set in 3,000m^2 of land. Close to a picturesque hill-top village, this large property comprises a tiled sitting room with oak beams, a large open-plan kitchen and four bedrooms.
144,820 euros   **CAB**
(£90,515) GP

(82)
A traditional Gascon farmhouse, with four bedrooms and two bathrooms. Located close to a medieval river port, the property is set in a large, mature garden with two garages and a well.
147,875 euros   **CAB**
(£92,420) GP

(65)
Close to a busy market town, this cottage is set in a small hamlet. The cottage boasts a garden of 2,500m^2 with trees and shrubs. Enjoys unrestricted views that stretch as far as the Pyrenees.
90,000 euros   **LEB**
(£56,250) GP

(47)
An old country cottage set high up on the walls of a medieval *bastide*. A sitting room, dining room and kitchen make up the ground floor. On the first floor there is one en-suite bedroom.
25,154 euros   **CAB**
(£15,720) GP

(82)
Dating from 1965, a house on the outskirts of a bustling market town. Situated close to the River Garonne, this residence offers two bedrooms, a shower room and a small flower garden.
121,960 euros   **CAB**
(£76,225) GP

(65)
Situated on the outskirts of a busy market town, this village house features numerous bedrooms and is well placed for open views. Set in lawned garden, the property is approached by a long gravel drive.
289,000 euros   **LEB**
(£180,625) GP

(82)
A country residence to the south of Valence. Boasts a sitting room with woodburning stove and casement windows that open on to a veranda. Set on high ground with stunning panoramic views.
71,650 euros   **CAB**
(£44,780) GP

(65)
Set on the outskirts of a pretty village, this traditional country farmhouse stands on its own. Featuring a stable block, the house is a short drive from airports, stations and local shops.
289,000 euros   **LEB**
(£180,625) GP

Price Guide

(46)
A hillside residence close to Lauzerte. Comprising a stone-built home and barn, the property is in need of some work, but is habitable. Set in nearly 500m² of land, in a secluded rural area.
144,286 euros   **CAB**
(£90,180) GP

(82)
Situated among vineyards in the hills above the market town of Moissac, this L-shaped home enjoys extensive, panoramic views. Set in a well-established garden with lawns and mature trees.
157,022 euros   **CAB**
(£98,140) GP

(32)
A large renovated house in Haute-Garonne featuring four bedrooms and a well-stocked garden. Located among vineyards in the popular winemaking region of Saint-Sardos. Ready to inhabit.
205,800 euros   **FPP**
(£128,625) GP

(32)
A period town house arranged over three storeys. Situated within the walls of a medieval *bastide*. A cottage adjoins the house and is in need of some modernisation. In easy reach of the local ski slopes.
193,610 euros   **CAB**
(£121,005) GP

(31)
Dating from the 19th century, this bourgeois manor house offers four bedrooms, a summer-kitchen, pool house and bathroom. Outside are a large swimming pool, single garage and several outbuildings.
548,816 euros   **SEL**
(£343,010) GP

(32)
Set in a garden with a swimming pool, this stone-built house has been totally renovated. Close to the medieval town of Fleurance and within easy distance of local shops and the Pyrenees ski slopes.
320,140 euros   **CAB**
(£200,090) GP

(32)
This *maison de maître*, constructed from stone and brick, sits in wide parkland. Approached by a long private driveway flanked by trees. Boasting 360m² of living space and set on high, with open views.
548,816 euros   **LEB**
(£343,010) S

(82)
Dating from the 17th century, a water mill with open fireplaces and four bedrooms. In an idyllic location among weeping willows and beside a stream. Features a sitting room and dining room.
411,612 euros   **CAB**
(£257,260) GP

(65)
A restored house with a heated swimming pool. Set in over 40,000m² of enclosed parkland with mature trees. The property boasts three large bedrooms and is situated close to a quiet village.
510,000 euros   **LEB**
(£318,750) GP

Midi-Pyrénées

(82)
This three-bedroom house is set in a small village close to a large market town. Features a sitting room with terracotta tiled floors and massive oak beams, a dining room and a large kitchen.
53,357 euros   **CAB**
(£33,350) GP

(46)
A village house set in 3,200m² of land with a separate barn. Offers two spacious bedrooms, a large bathroom and kitchen. A short drive from the local market town. Benefits from a quiet situation.
106,940 euros   **SEL**
(£66,840) GP

(82)
A stone-built farmhouse with 2,700m² of land. Close to the area of Beaumont-de-Lomagne. The building is set on high ground and boasts views of the Pyrenees. Features three large bedrooms.
202,757 euros   **CAB**
(£126,725) GP

(82)
A restored stone house dating from the 18th century. Set in 6,100m² of garden with trees and lawn. Bordered by a stream, the house features three underground cellars and a detached workshop.
236,448 euros   **SEL**
(£147,780) GP

(82)
Originally a school, this period house is set in a quiet village and has been recently renovated. Features an open-plan kitchen, with dressed stone walls, three bedrooms and a swimming pool.
190,561 euros   **CAB**
(£119,100) GP

(32)
Dating from the 17th century, a manor house with two towers. Set around a small courtyard garden, close to Auch. Boasts several light and spacious bedrooms. On the edge of a picturesque village.
424,000 euros   **GAS**
(£265,000) GP

(82)
A typical stone-built farmhouse of this region situated on the edge of a picturesque village. Offers two large bedrooms and a shower room. Original details include terracotta tiles and exposed beams.
193,610 euros   **CAB**
(£121,005) GP

(12)
A country cottage with superb views across the rural landscape of Aveyron. In need of some internal modernisation, the cottage is set close to a lively village. Features a shepherd's hut, barn and pigsty.
118,224 euros   **SEL**
(£73,890) GP

(65)
Standing on its own, this family house with a swimming pool is set in an idyllic country setting. With numerous bedrooms and a large garden, the property is close to a village with all amenities.
215,000 euros   **LEB**
(£134,375) S

Price Guide

(46)
A detached house with a large barn. Special features include an ancient bread oven and a stone sink. Set in a lawned garden with trees and an outbuilding. Comes with an attached chicken house.
371,636 euros   **SEL**
(£232,275) GP

(46)
This stone-built property is set on the outskirts of a small hamlet. Offers four spacious bedrooms and a swimming pool with a retractable roof. Set in 2,500m² of land with woods and a patio area.
220,686 euros   **SEL**
(£137,930) GP

(12)
A two-bedroom property with three gîtes, each containing a shower or bathroom. Set in nearly 4,100m² of land with open views. Located in a hamlet close to a small village with all amenities.
427,000 euros   **SEL**
(£266,875) GP

(82)
A semi-detached house set on a hill-top village overlooking the Garonne Valley. Featuring three bedrooms, a sitting room with a woodburning stove and a dining room with an open fireplace.
89,182 euros   **CAB**
(£55,740) GP

(46)
Dating from the 18th century, a character property with period features. Set in an idyllic location, close to the River Lot, the château boasts a landscaped garden with fruit trees and a swimming pool.
320,890 euros   **SEL**
(£200,555) GP

(46)
An ancient family home that has been recently restored. Set in 3,500m² of land, close to a quiet village and shopping facilities. Comprises two bedrooms, a children's playroom and a cellar.
146,280 euros   **SEL**
(£91,425) GP

(46)
A château currently being run as a hotel. Set in mature parkland of 80,000m² with woodland, a golf course and swimming pool. Boasts several outbuildings, an indoor pool and 33 spacious bedrooms.
1,470,000 euros   **AZF**
(£918,750) GP

(82)
An extensive property comprising a small house and a stone-built barn. Nestling in woodland hills, with 1,700m² of land and open views. Accommodation has yet to be created or services connected.
193,610 euros   **CAB**
(£121,005) GP

(46)
A traditional country dwelling, dating from the 18th century. In a quiet location, the house looks out across a pretty valley. Comprises three bedrooms, one bathroom, one shower room and two WCs.
163,760 euros   **SEL**
(£102,350) GP

Midi-Pyrénées

(82)
A stone-built cottage situated close to the town of Beaumont-de-Lomagne. Set upon a hill with views that stretch as far as the Pyrenees. Features a terraced garden with a pond and a well.
179,890 euros　　　　**CAB**
(£112,430) GP

(12)
A country residence that has been restored externally but is in need of internal completion. Set in 1,300m² of land with open views and a nearby village. Offers five rooms and a large wine cellar.
83,545 euros　　　　**SEL**
(£52,215) GP

(82)
A traditional Gascon farmhouse, situated a short distance from a medieval *bastide*. The building has been entirely renovated and offers three bedrooms with a fourth on a mezzanine floor.
228,673 euros　　　　**CAB**
(£142,920) GP

(12)
Bordered by 7,500m² of oakland and meadows, this property comprises a restored barn requiring internal completion and two gîtes. Offers three bedrooms, two bathrooms and a heated pool.
533,572 euros　　　　**SEL**
(£333,485) GP

(12)
An old water mill in 20,000m² of peaceful landscape. Surrounded by meadows and woodland, the mill retains many of its original details, including a stone sink, bridge and stream flowing under the house.
360,000 euros　　　　**SEL**
(£225,000) GP

(82)
A *maison de maitre* dating from the 19th century. Built in the classical style by local artisans and in a small hill-top village. Features a wide corridor leading to a sitting room and two bedrooms.
228,670 euros　　　　**CAB**
(£142,919) GP

(12)
A four-bedroom character house set in land of 3,000m². Bordered by woodland and fields, the house benefits from a secluded location. and boasts exposed beams and original stonework.
219,222 euros　　　　**SEL**
(£137,015) GP

(82)
A detached town house set above a medieval river port beside the River Garonne. Carefully restored to retain its original architecture, the property boasts massive oak beams. Comprises two bedrooms.
79,273 euros　　　　**CAB**
(£49,545) GP

(82)
A recently renovated house, with five bedrooms and a single garage. Situated in a small market town, the property boasts a large flower and vegetable garden. Within a short drive of Toulouse airport.
228,670 euros　　　　**CAB**
(£142,919) GP

Price Guide

(81)
This recently restored house is split over two storeys and features eight bedrooms. Set in land of 20,000m², with a swimming pool and patio area. The property is fronted by a long private drive.
762,246 euros　　　　　**AZF**
(£476,405) GP

(81)
Dating from the 19th century, this large château boasts stunning architectural details, including two towers and large exposed beams throughout. With 15 principal rooms and a tiled swimming pool.
804,981 euros　　　　　**AZF**
(£503,115) GP

(31)
A restored farmhouse, reached by a long private drive and set close to a small village. Surrounded by woodland and meadows. With five bedrooms, the house features a pool, workshop and garage.
510,000 euros　　　　　**AZF**
(£318,750) GP

(82)
A large *maison de maitre* with three bedrooms. Set in 15,000m² of land with a small cottage for total renovation and a large stone-built barn. Comprises a fitted kitchen, living room and utility room.
350,633 euros　　　　　**HIF**
(£219,145) GP

(32)
A traditional Gascon farmhouse in need of complete renovation. Set in 2,500m² of land with open views over the surrounding rural area. Features numerous bedrooms and an outbuilding for conversion.
360,000 euros　　　　　**LEB**
(£225,000) S

(82)
A renovated Gascon farmhouse set in a south-facing garden with a terrace. Features four bedrooms, two drawing rooms and a dining room. Boasts a veranda with views over the countryside and river.
242,393 euros　　　　　**HIF**
(£151,495) GP

(32)
This farmhouse and vineyard are situated a short distance from a village and set in 265,000m² of open land. Approached by a long drive, the property features six bedrooms and five bathrooms.
808,000 euros　　　　　**SIF**
(£505,000) GP

(82)
A traditional Gascon farmhouse with three bedrooms. Completely renovated, the residence features a mezzanine, living room, kitchen and bathroom. Surrounded by a pretty, mature garden of 5,000m².
198,183 euros　　　　　**HIF**
(£123,865) GP

(32)
This small stone-built hamlet comprises several residences set in 16,000m² of land. Benefiting from a large swimming pool and garden, the main house features a kitchen and five big bedrooms.
360,000 euros　　　　　**LEB**
(£225,000) S

Midi-Pyrénées

(31)
A recently restored mill featuring six bedrooms, a guest house and caretaker's cottage. Set in nearly 25,000m² of landscaped gardens with a dovecote, swimming pool and 600m² of outbuildings.
990,000 euros   AZF
(£618,750) GP

(12)
With five bedrooms, this restored property boasts a lake, swimming pool and a quiet stream which runs under the house. Set in over 15,000m² of calm surroundings, with numerous outbuildings.
564,000 euros   AZF
(£352,500) GP

(31)
A château lying in the foothills of the Pyrenees and set in 30,000m² of meadow and parkland. On the banks of a quiet fishing river, the château boasts two towers, a pool, stables, an aviary and two gîtes.
690,000 euros   SIF
(£431,250) GP

(46)
Enclosed in 1,860m² of garden, a stone house in Luzech. Boasts a tower, three bedrooms, a study and a covered terrace. Features a living room with terracotta tiled floors and a large summer-kitchen.
277,000 euros   WAT
(£173,125) GP

(82)
A detached farmhouse surrounded by 2,000m² of garden with two garages and a workshop. Boasts four good-sized bedrooms, a large living room, kitchen and dining area. Set in a medieval river port.
147,875 euros   HIF
(£92,420) GP

(81)
A historic 18th-century manor house with outbuildings and large garden leading down to a river. The house has been restored and features vaulted cellars, eight bedrooms and a music room.
1,000,000 euros   LAT
(£625,000) GP

(32)
A character house dating from the 18th century. Boasting spacious accommodation, the property has three bedrooms, a study, cellar and kitchen. The pretty garden has a spring-fed lake. Set in a village.
335,000 euros   WAT
(£209,375) GP

(46)
Dating from 1855, a stone-built house with a pool and numerous outbuildings. Boasting an original fireplace, the house benefits from a terrace and has four bedrooms. Set in a garden in a quiet location.
297,276 euros   LAT
(£185,790) GP

(82)
Bordered by a stream, a large farmhouse and mill set in land of 35,000m². Totally renovated, the main house offers five bedrooms, while the water mill has a new roof and is split over three floors.
215,000 euros   HIF
(£134,375) GP

Price Guide

(46)
An old restored farmhouse and barns set on the banks of a river. On the ground floor are five large bedrooms, a study and bathroom. Upstairs is a terrace, living room, fitted kitchen and a mezzanine.
326,240 euros   WAT
(£203,900) GP

(32)
A single-storey house enjoying panoramic views. Close to a busy town, the property has been renovated and features three bedrooms, a fully-fitted kitchen and a living room. Set in a garden of 4,000m².
280,800 euros   LAT
(£175,500) GP

(32)
Dating from the 16th century, a renovated house set in 20,000m² of parkland with a tennis court, stone barn and shed. Features four bedrooms, a fitted kitchen and a two-bedroom apartment.
538,462 euros   HIF
(£336,540) GP

(82)
A stone-built house and garage set in 2,000m² of land. Enjoying sweeping vistas over surrounding countryside, the property features four bedrooms, a dining room and breakfast area. Close to a town.
223,200 euros   LAT
(£139,500) GP

(81)
Three stone-built dwellings with an interior courtyard and two swimming pools. Set in 11,600m² of land ideal for gîtes. Features three bedrooms, an old house for renovation and a barn conversion.
275,000 euros   LAT
(£171,875) GP

(82)
Situated in a small village a short distance from Toulouse airport. In need of some interior work, the house features a dining room with terracotta tiles, a sitting room of similar decor and three bedrooms.
53,357 euros   HIF
(£33,350) GP

(32)
An old stone-built house full of character. Standing in grounds of 47,000m². The property is in need of restoration work and comprises six rooms. Features a barn and several other outbuildings.
180,200 euros   LAT
(£112,625) GP

(46)
In the hills above a village, a large house built in 1972. Comprises five bedrooms, a dovecote and sunny terrace. Stands in a garden of 1,000m², boasting panoramic views over the surrounding area.
258,097 euros   LAT
(£161,310) GP

(32)
In a village setting, this restored farmhouse has many original architectural features and a garden of 1,100m² with space for a pool. The accommodation offers three bedrooms and a dressing room.
182,939 euros   LAT
(£114,335) GP

Midi-Pyrénées

(81)
A traditional house for renovation comprising two bedrooms, a kitchen and living room. Set in 200,000m² of quiet countryside with great views. Situated a short distance from the town of Albi.
235,000 euros **LAT**
(£146,875) GP

(32)
An ensemble of stone houses set in 10,000m² of rural land. In need of restoration, the property offers five rooms with new woodwork. Boasts 600m² of living space and benefits from a beautiful location.
245,600 euros **LAT**
(£153,500) GP

(32)
Close to Dunes, a bungalow with three bedrooms. Features a covered veranda and large sun terrace. Set in a garden of over 4,000m², boasting sweeping views over the surrounding countryside.
195,897 euros **HIF**
(£122,435) GP

(32)
Set in a medieval hilltop village close to the town of Montréal, this stone house has a garden and a terrace with superb views over the surrounding area. Comprises three bedrooms and a kitchen.
83,880 euros **HIF**
(£52,425) GP

(32)
A country residence with several outbuildings and a garage set in wooded grounds of 3,500m². The house has been totally restored and includes a living room, three bedrooms and space for two more.
228,674 euros **LAT**
(£142,920) GP

(82)
Close to a busy market town and near a large lake, this four-bedroom house is in need of some interior decoration and sits in a garden of 2,000m² with a barn. Features a log-burning fire.
82,322 euros **HIF**
(£51,450) GP

(46)
A mill house and outbuildings set in 6,000m² of grounds, bordered by a stream, with a stone barn and a cow shed. Comprises a vast kitchen, three bedrooms and living areas. Village location.
180,200 euros **LAT**
(£112,625) GP

(32)
A carefully restored house with some work to do. Set in 3,000m² of wooded land with a small pond, garage and a shed. The property has four bedrooms and is set in tranquil surroundings.
257,000 euros **LAT**
(£160,625) GP

(46)
In a village close to Luzech and within easy reach of a town, this renovated house is bordered by a stream and boasts a small, pretty garden. Comprises an open-plan living area and three bedrooms.
151,700 euros **HIF**
(£94,815) GP

Price Guide

(46)
A stone-built house with a tower and dovecote, set in mature grounds of 2,200m². Comprises a kitchen, two small cellars and three bedrooms. Features include stone walls and panelled ceilings.
162,054 euros   **LAT**
(£101,285) GP

(46)
Dating from 1800, a fully-restored farmhouse with a separate gîte in a small hamlet setting. Features a wooden staircase and old beams throughout. To the side of the house is a pool set in a terrace.
219,700 euros   **CUR**
(£137,315) GP

(82)
Close to a river, a brick house with an attached barn. With a garden of 2,000m², the property is on the edge of a village. Offers two reception rooms, a beamed kitchen and four large bedrooms.
150,925 euros   **LAT**
(£94,330) GP

(32)
Dating from the 17th century, a former water mill standing in 8,000m² of pasture and parkland, the main house is complemented by two further buildings, stabling, a swimming pool and orchard.
640,000 euros   **GAS**
(£400,000) GP

(32)
A restored house with a swimming pool, gîte and assorted outbuildings for conversion. Standing in over 20,000m² of land, the property enjoys a sun terrace and offers four bedrooms.
487,600 euros   **LAT**
(£304,750) GP

(32)
A skilfully restored stone-built house with many original features. The property benefits from a splendid terrace incorporating a pool and barbecue area. Has three bedrooms and 20,000m² of land.
365,000 euros   **GAS**
(£228,125) GP

(32)
A *maison de maitre* with beautiful gardens and a pool. Featuring four bedrooms and two bathrooms, this house is full of character. Two barns provide a development opportunity, 60km from Auch.
640,000 euros   **GAS**
(£400,000) GP

(32)
A professionally restored manor house set in a hamlet. With six bedrooms and four bathrooms, plus two-bedroom annexe. Has 47,400m² of impressive wooded grounds, garaging and pavilion.
1,212,000 euros   **GAS**
(£757,500) GP

(32)
Dating from the 19th century, a classic *maison de maitre* set in a 17,000m² arboretum. This four-bedroom house has far reaching views and retains the original poplar planking on the upper floor.
570,000 euros   **GAS**
(£356,250) GP

Midi-Pyrénées

(82)
Dating from the 17th century, a half-timbered brick house with a guest suite. Set in a small garden with a lawn, the property offers three bedrooms and a mezzanine library. Boasts original tiled floors.
149,705 euros   LAT
(£93,565) GP

(32)
A terraced house with a garden and courtyard. In a village setting, the property comprises three bedrooms, a sitting room and reception room. Adjoining the building is a second house for renovation.
148,668 euros   LAT
(£92,920) GP

(46)
A stone house set in 10,000m^2 of grounds with delightful views. A short distance from town, the property offers five bedrooms, a kitchen, study and a living room. The house is centrally heated.
403,380 euros   LAT
(£252,115) GP

(32)
A large restored house with a swimming pool and separate guest apartment. Set in wooded land of 14,000m^2. The residence features a library, several bedrooms and a living room with marble fireplace.
646,384 euros   LAT
(£403,990) GP

(46)
This restored house with barns stands in a garden of 1,000m^2. A traditional property featuring oak beams and a cathedral-style ceiling, it offers two bedrooms, a small terrace and dining room.
130,344 euros   LAT
(£81,465) GP

(81)
A *maison de maître* surrounded by 2,750m^2 of enclosed woodland. The ground floor has recently been rewired and boasts parquet floors. Fronted by an ornamental fountain. Offers five bedrooms.
411,610 euros   LAT
(£257,255) GP

(32)
A villa set in 7,500m^2 of grounds. Boasting marble floors, eight large bedrooms, two kitchens and three bathrooms. With a living area of 300m^2, the property is located a short distance from a small village.
407,200 euros   LAT
(£254,500) GP

(32)
This restored 18th-century house benefits from a swimming pool and an enclosed garden. Boasting a stone staircase, living room with wood panels and four bedrooms, plus a four-bedroom guest wing.
678,703 euros   LAT
(£424,190) GP

(81)
A classic château set in a partly-wooded estate of 5,000m^2 with a small stream. In good condition, the property offers 13 en-suite bedrooms and many original features including marble fireplaces.
646,600 euros   LAT
(£404,125) GP

Price Guide

(82)
Dating from the 15th century, a water mill complex with several outbuildings set in over 2,000m² of land bordered by a river. Offers five bedrooms, a study, stables, a large annexe and fitted kitchen.
594,551 euros   LAT
(£371,595) GP

(46)
Attractive stone-built house restored to a high standard. This property benefits from a swimming pool and a number of outbuildings. A generous 23,000m² of land and glorious views.
383,100 euros   CHS
(£239,440) GP

(46)
Rare opportunity to acquire this prestigious property currently run as a hotel. Set in 30,000m² of beautiful parkland with magnificent views, this large house has serious business potential.
954,000 euros   CHS
(£596,250) GP

(82)
This spacious house is set around a courtyard and bordered by a river. Approached via a driveway flanked with trees, the residence is set in land of 50,000m² with a veranda, stables and several barns.
457,347 euros   LAT
(£285,840) GP

(12)
A four-bedroom farmhouse with a swimming pool. Situated in the heart of a medieval village, it has been fully restored and features four double bedrooms. Boasts a sunny terrace and large orchard.
300,000 euros   PRV
(£187,500) GP

(46)
Built in 1723, this restored house benefits from a large heated pool, terrace, garage and visitor parking. Set in mature parkland of 10,000m². Original details include exposed walls and stone fireplaces.
514,211 euros   LAT
(£321,380) GP

(64)
An old house set in 30,000m² of ground, with a swimming pool and pool house. Features a living room with a parquet floor, three bedrooms, a long terrace and a study. Near Villeneuve-sur-Lot.
34,000 euros   LAT
(£21,250) GP

(46)
A stone-built house with a pool and garage. Standing in 2,495m² of land and completely restored. Comprises a kitchen, dining room with exposed beams, study and four spacious bedrooms.
322,125 euros   LAT
(£201,330) GP

(32)
Dating from the 18th century a stone house with a dovecote. Set in 18,000m² of woodland and meadows, with a pond and several outbuildings. In an elevated spot, offering sweeping rural views.
304,899 euros   LAT
(£190,560) GP

Midi-Pyrénées

(12)
This former farmhouse stands in 10,000m² of grounds with a barn, ancient well and vaulted cellar. In need of a total restoration, the house boasts exposed oak beams, wood floors and three bedrooms.
135,680 euros ACT
(£84,800) GP

(12)
This U-shaped farmhouse is set in 10,000m² of land. Comprises a main house, guest house and vast two-storey barn. Boasts a stone staircase, covered patio, pool and four en-suite bedrooms with views.
579,306 euros ACT
(£362,070) GP

(31)
An old farmhouse with numerous outbuildings for renovation. The ground floor offers a living room and kitchen. Upstairs are two bedrooms and in the garden an enclosed orchard and two barns.
83,000 euros LIN
(£51,875) GP

(65)
A *maison de maitre* with two reception rooms, four bedrooms and two bathrooms. Set in a large garden planted with trees and with a well. Features a covered terrace with stunning views.
327,765 euros SIF
(£204,855) GP

(12)
Offering views over valleys and hills, this stone-built house is in need of total restoration. Standing in 4,000m² of land, the building comprises an attached barn, kitchen and one large bedroom.
33,539 euros ACT
(£20,960) GP

(46)
A restored stone-built house and barn. Comprising three bedrooms, a reception room, two bathrooms and a large kitchen. In attractive countryside close to a town. With a well and extensive grounds.
375,180 euros SIF
(£234,490) GP

(12)
A former farmhouse, dating from the 18th century. Features include stone archways and original terracotta floors. Set in 4,000m² of land with a barn. Comprises four bedrooms, terrace and kitchen.
184,615 euros ACT
(£115,385) GP

(12)
A listed 15th-century residence in countryside on the edge of a regional park. Set on the side of a hill with many mature trees. Features 14 rooms and retains much of its original character.
480,000 euros SIF
(£300,000) GP

(12)
In the village of Savignac, a stone house standing in land of almost 3,000m². Boasts stunning rural views, four bedrooms, veranda and dovecote. Features stone floors and arches, and exposed beams.
198,190 euros ACT
(£123,870) GP

LANGUEDOC-ROUSSILLON

Price Guide

(11)
Dating from the 14th century, an old water mill set in 10,000m² of meadows with a waterwheel and a stream suitable for bathing. The main house offers three bedroom suites and a games room.
600,000 euros FPL
(£375,000) GP

(11)
A traditional farmhouse with several outbuildings set in 12,000m² of enclosed gardens planted with shrubs and trees. The house enjoys a swimming pool and a secluded location.
427,000 euros FPL
(£260,875) GP

(11)
This semi-detached house comprises a kitchen, dining room, bathroom and lounge. Set in a village with all amenities, the property has two bedrooms and a large attic. It is ready to move in to.
54,000 euros FPL
(£33,750) GP

(11)
Surrounded by fields, this newly-built chalet comprises a one-bedroom apartment with a dining room and kitchen. The property also offers also two gîtes, 10 stables and a mature garden.
138,000 euros FPP
(£86,250) GP

(11)
Set in a landscaped garden in open countryside, this property comprises one large building that has been converted into letting cottages, a further cottage, tennis court and a large swimming pool.
815,600 euros FPL
(£509,750) GP

(11)
Overlooking a river, this *maison de maître* features high ceilings and spacious rooms. Offering four bedrooms, a living room, dining room, two kitchens, a study, large terrace and dressing room.
66,300 euros CAT
(£41,440) GP

(11)
West of Limoux, an unusual two-bedroom village house featuring a large rooftop terrace with stunning panoramic views. The property also offers a living room, bathroom and a small workshop.
99,092 euros CAT
(£61,935) GP

(66)
This south-facing village house has been completely renovated and offers 140m² of living space. With stunning views, the house features an oak staircase, sitting room, garden and three bedrooms.
120,000 euros FPL
(£75,000) GP

(11)
Located west of Quillan, this terraced house comprises a spacious dining room, kitchen, cellar, three large bedrooms and a shower room. Fronted by a garden and set in a village with amenities.
79,273 euros CAT
(£49,545) GP

AUDE IMMO FUTUR

4 rue de Verdun, 11000 CARCASSONNE
(opposite the museum & library)

Tel: 00 33 4 68 71 23 70
Fax: 00 33 4 68 71 18 70
email: aude-immo-futur@wanadoo.fr

TEAM OF PROFESSIONALS AT YOUR SERVICE

CONTACT US FOR EXPERT ADVICE

YOUR FUTURE PROPERTY FOUND WITH CONFIDENCE

Please contact us via email or by fax

www.aude-immo-futur.com

HARRISON STONE
Properties, Services, Financial
FRANCE

Specialising in the Languedoc Roussillon, Midi Pyrenées & Brittany.

Harrison Stone can select houses, barns, farms, gites, vineyards etc, from various French Immobilieres, notaires and private sellers.

We can offer a personal service to serious buyers through our experience in the business and excellent local knowledge.

We can also arrange mortgages, currency, accommodation and car hire. English speaking notaire available.

Selection for Sale & Rent on:
www.harrisonstone.co.uk
t + f: **01798 342776**
e: **info@harrisonstone.co.uk**

Le Moulin de la mer

Villas with gardens on the Mediterranean sea in a resort with a swimming-pool

Contact your adviser
Mobile : 00 33 608 163 669

1, Place des Alliés
34500 BEZIERS
Tél. 00 33 467 492 244
Fax 00 33 467 498 575
Website : lemoulindelamer.com
e.mail : moulinmer@magic.fr

Price Guide

(11)
Near the border with Ariège, close to a river. Currently offering four rooms that are habitable, this house with outbuildings is in need of renovation. The property enjoys open views of the Pyrenees.
411,612 euros   **FPL**
(£257,260) GP

(11)
With land of 11,000m², this farmhouse enjoys views stretching as far as the Pyrenees and Black Mountains. The house features two bedrooms, a dining room and a fully-fitted oak kitchen.
290,320 euros   **FPL**
(£181,450) GP

(11)
This four-bedroom village house with an enclosed courtyard is set close to a busy market town. In need of some work, the property offers an entrance hall, dining room, kitchen and a small garden.
80,000 euros   **CAT**
(£50,000) GP

(34)
This building is in need of renovation as accommodation has yet to be laid out. Benefits from spacious rooms and set in a busy village with all amenities, a short drive from the town of Lodève.
99,100 euros   **MED**
(£61,940) GP

(11)
At the foot of a mountain, this rustic village house offers five bedrooms. Set in a small garden with a terrace, the house enjoys a secluded location and features a large living room and basement.
106,000 euros   **CAT**
(£66,250) GP

(11)
Dating from 1810 and set in the Black Mountains, this spacious home features six en-suite bedrooms, a living room and kitchen. Stands in a garden with a courtyard, a covered terrace and garage.
229,146 euros   **FPL**
(£143,215) GP

(11)
Located in a small village a short drive from Revel, this large family residence features a swimming pool and patio area. The property benefits from uninterrupted views of the surrounding countryside.
381,123 euros   **FPL**
(£238,200) GP

(11)
Standing in a garden of 14,500m², this impressive residence features several bedroom suites and a terrace with splendid open views. Located in a village, the house benefits from a private setting.
565,616 euros   **MED**
(£353,510) GP

(11)
An up-and-running gîte complex set in 120,000m² of land a short drive from a village and the town of Razès. This extensive property enjoys a secluded location and offers spacious accommodation.
655,531 euros   **FPL**
(£409,705) GP

LA MERIDIENNE INTERNATIONALE

Estate Agent

Our dedicated staff at La Meridienne International will help and guide you through the property market, to find the personal, individual, dream property, for which you have been searching. La Meridienne has bilingual staff, so you can be assured of a thoroughly professional experience and complete peace of mind

Mandat 223 - Price: 640,300€
Three buildings, 35 minutes from Montpellier, this extraordinary property offers 800m² of living accommodation on more than 4 hectares of land a part of which is constructible.

Mandat 287 - 795,000€ - Languedoc 'mas' built in local stone and beautifully restored. The property is located 55 kms North of Montpellier and 6 kms from the A75 motorway. This totally isolated property has 280m² of living space plus outhouses and stands in 13 hectares of land bordered, for the most part, by a stream.

Mandat 307 - 534,240€ - 0.5 hr from Montpellier, this is a rare opportunity to purchase a stone property, retaining many original features. These include fine tiled floors or terrazzo in all rooms. Decorative state is excellent throughout, there is 260m² of habitable space plus a large stone vaulted 16th century cellar & many outbuildings.

Mandat 305 - 968,840€ - This impeccable 1977 chalet style villa is set in 10,000m² beautiful gardens with a large variety of mature trees and bordering the river Mare stocked with Trout, outbuildings including a small stone gatehouse, covered car port, workshop, the property benefits from a sophisticated intruder alarm system, video cctv access and electrically operated main gates and 14 hectares.

www.lameridienne-immo.com
email: rene@lameridienne-immo.com

We are here

7, place de la Halle
DARDE 34700
Lodeve France

Tel: **00 33 4 67 44 33 81**
To speak in English

Tel: **00 33 4 99 91 02 10**
Pour parler en Francais

www.france1st.com

Price Guide

(34)
Approached via a private drive and standing in 130,000m² of gardens, this large house offers several bedroom suites. The property enjoys stunning rural views and is set in a quiet rural location.
795,000 euros　　　　　MED
(£496,875) GP

(11)
A *maison de maître* and five gîtes surrounded by 14,200m² of woodland. Features a large swimming pool and offers up to eight bedrooms. Within a short drive of a town and Carcassonne airport.
884,204 euros　　　　　FPL
(£552,630) GP

(11)
Built in the 1970s, this village house offers five bedrooms, two bathrooms, a sitting room and a double garage. Approached by a private drive, the house stands in a garden of 3,742m² with trees.
178,365 euros　　　　　FPL
(£111,480) GP

(34)
A former farmhouse that has been partially renovated in local stone. The main building is surrounded by meadows and comprises five bedrooms. The property is bordered by a river and woodland.
444,000 euros　　　　　LIN
(£277,500) GP

(11)
This large country house is set in the Black Mountains, a short drive from Carcassonne airport. The property features three lakes in its large woodland grounds and offers a separate gîte and barn.
724,132 euros　　　　　FPL
(£452,585) GP

(34)
Located near a village, this large house is bordered by a river. Offering a kitchen, dining room, lounge and four bedrooms, the property enjoys stunning views of the surrounding countryside.
102,170 euros　　　　　LIN
(£63,855) GP

(34)
A traditional village house currently arranged as three apartments and offering two kitchens, two living rooms and four bedrooms. The house is set in a small garden planted with shrubs.
243,918 euros　　　　　LIN
(£152,450) GP

(34)
Comprising two houses, this residence enjoys panoramic views over a rural valley and features four bedrooms, two terraces and a dining room with fireplace. Stands in a garden with a large patio area.
216,038 euros　　　　　LIN
(£135,025) GP

(11)
In a pretty village, not far from Carcassonne, this 13th-century property has been well renovated and is set around a courtyard. It has two bedrooms, two separate apartments and a vaulted cellar.
533,572 euros　　　　　HAM
(£333,480) GP

Languedoc-Roussillon

(34)
Just five minutes from the beach, this modern three-bedroom home features a fitted kitchen, jacuzzi and a terrace. Entered by electric gates, the property is set in a garden planted with palm trees.
503,000 euros   **LIN**
(£314,375) GP

(34)
Set at the bottom of a hill near the town of Bédarieux, this detached villa features three bedrooms and a library. The villa offers a wine cellar, wooden floors and an extensive lawned garden.
231,720 euros   **LIN**
(£144,825) GP

(11)
Close to Carcassonne and located in a tourist village, this building is currently a popular restaurant. The property is being sold as a going concern, complete with a car and all kitchen equipment.
381,123 euros   **FPL**
(£238,200) GP

(34)
This property is located in the town of Vias, just a few minutes from the coast. Offering two three-bedroom apartments, each with kitchens, the house is set in 1,700m² of gardens with stabling.
594,550 euros   **LIN**
(£371,595) GP

(11)
A spacious house set on a hill near the town of Castelnaudary. This residence comprises a large kitchen, sitting room, cellar, four bedrooms and a bathroom. Offers a small garden with a garage.
195,745   **FPL**
(£122,340) GP

(11)
Near a village in Aude, this historic castle enjoys stunning views of the Pyrenees. With sections of the building dating from the 13th century, the property offers extensive accommodation.
489,366 euros   **FPL**
(£305,855) GP

(30)
This three-bedroom villa is set in mature secluded gardens of 4,000m² with open views over the surrounding area. Near a small village, close to the town of Uzès, the villa is ready to move in to.
595,000 euros   **DAV**
(£371,875) GP

(34)
In a quiet location on the edge of a pretty village and within easy reach of the coast. This large house offers five bedrooms, a study, lounge and kitchen. Set in a small garden with a single garage.
92,000 euros   **MII**
(£57,500) GP

(30)
Dating from the 13th century, this 12-bedroom château features an internal courtyard, moat and towers. The estate offers a farm and lodge, and the grounds contain a lake and freshwater spring.
3,201,429 euros   **SIF**
(£2,000,895) GP

Price Guide

(11)
In a rural village in hilly countryside, this three-bedroom property offers an adjoining barn that has been converted to provide four further bedrooms. Stands in a mature garden with a terrace.
609,000 euros   MII
(£380,625) GP

(34)
This residence is set in a quiet village close to the coast and offers six bedrooms, a large garden backing onto vineyards and a paved courtyard. Features a conservatory and fully-fitted kitchen.
199,000 euros   MII
(£124,375) GP

(34)
This *maison de maitre* stands in mature parkland of 1,200m². Approached via a private drive, this extensive property features a self-contained studio apartment with one large bedroom.
396,400 euros   MED
(£247,750) GP

(34)
An old house close to the city of Béziers. The property comprises two bedrooms, dressing room, a shower room, large lounge, kitchen, cellar and a hallway leading out to a small lawned garden.
69,364 euros   MED
(£43,350) GP

(34)
Set at the edge of a small village within easy reach of Saint-Chinian, this four-bedroom villa features an open-plan living area and a mature tree-filled garden with a large swimming pool.
327,765 euros   MII
(£204,855) GP

(34)
This traditional farmhouse features a kitchen with an open fireplace, an office and extensive grazing land currently used for rearing sheep. The property also offers a chalet set in a garden.
280,201 euros   MED
(£175,125) GP

(34)
A three-bedroom apartment in a *maison de maitre*. Featuring a spacious lounge with a marble fireplace and a dining room with high ceilings and wood floors, the property is ready for occupation.
66,470 euros   MED
(£41,545) GP

(34)
In the heart of a picturesque village, a small house arranged over three floors. Currently offering a kitchen, living room and one bedroom, the property features a large attic for conversion.
29,000 euros   MII
(£18,125) GP

(11)
Dating from the 16th century, this listed château with open views offers nine spacious bedrooms. Set in rural land of 120,000m² with a swimming pool, barn, three stone buildings and a small dovecote.
1,850,000 euros   AZF
(£1,156,250) GP

SUBSCRIBE TO french magazine

FOR ONLY £19.50 FOR SIX ISSUES*

Over 200 pages in every issue packed with inspirational editorial and properties to buy and let

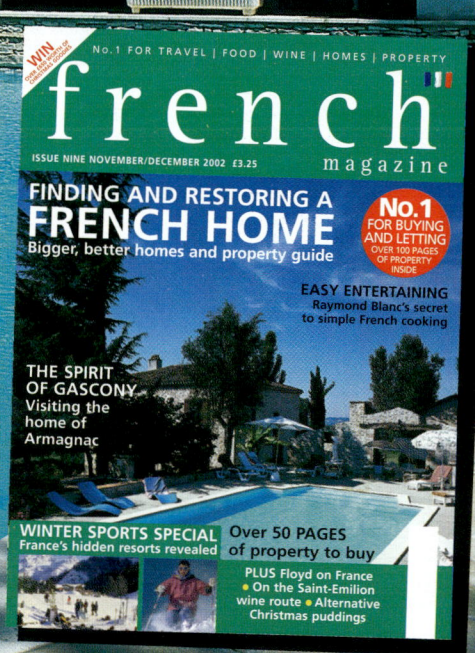

Call the order hotline on:
01225 786844

* (UK price)

Price Guide

(11)
A fully-renovated semi-detached bungalow in Carcassonne. With a kitchen, two bedrooms, a study and garage, the property also features a terrace with pleasant views over a lawned garden of 6,000m².
120,000 euros   **HIF**
(£75,000) GP

(11)
A new development of terraced villas enjoying views of the sea and the Pyrenees. Within a short drive of Narbonne, the villas offer an open-plan living room and kitchen area and two bedrooms.
132,478 euros   **PRP**
(£82,780) GP

(66)
Located in a traditional southern wine village close to Perpignan, a luxury apartment in a complex boasting panoramic views over lagoons and the sea. There are two swimming pools on site.
119,000 euros   **FEE**
(£74,375) GP

(11)
A third-floor apartment with sea views located in a small residential complex with a swimming pool and tennis courts. Set close to the beach, the apartment offers one bedroom and is fully furnished.
54,880 euros   **PRP**
(£34,300) GP

(11)
A modern detached house in a landscaped garden of 2,000m². On the ground floor is a games room, en-suite bedroom and a garage. Upstairs are two bedrooms, study, a fitted kitchen and living room.
230,000 euros   **HIF**
(£143,750) GP

(66)
A spacious apartment with a sea view just a short walk from the town centre. Offering a secluded private garden, it is located in a tourist area with all amenities close to the beach and harbour.
191,000 euros   **FEE**
(£119,375) GP

(30)
Close to the city of Nimes and near the coast, this *bastide*-style house is surrounded by mature pine and oak trees. Features four double bedrooms and a terrace leading to a swimming pool.
640,285 euros   **ACT**
(£400,180) GP

(11)
This fully-restored 18th-century farmhouse features six bedrooms. Enjoying a small lake, swimming pool and separate guest cottage, the farmhouse is set in a large garden in idyllic surroundings.
775,000 euros   **AZF**
(£484,375) GP

(11)
Located a short walk from the beach and local shops, this three-storey villa with a garden enjoys open sea views. Features five bedrooms, a fitted kitchen and large sun terrace with a barbecue area.
465,000 euros   **PRP**
(£290,625) GP

Languedoc-Roussillon

(11)
A modern villa converted into a two- and a three-bedroom studio apartment. Set in a 1,000m² garden and benefiting from the use of an indoor swimming pool, each apartment has a modern kitchen.
213,428 euros   **HIF**
(£133,395) GP

(11)
A large house for restoration set in a picturesque village bordered by the Canal du Midi. Arranged over four floors, the house offers three bedrooms with tiled floors, a dining room and sitting room.
118,000 euros   **PRP**
(£73,750) GP

(34)
Dating from the 12th century, a partly-renovated home classified as a historic monument. Boasts exposed walls, a gallery, drawing room, stained-glass windows, a study and three large bedrooms.
528,236 euros   **HAM**
(£330,145) GP

(11)
This small villa is set around a courtyard in a complex with a swimming pool. Close to the beach, the villa offers a mezzanine-style bedroom with recessed sleeping area and a fitted kitchen.
50,500 euros   **PRP**
(£31,565) GP

(34)
An ensemble of buildings in the heart of the countryside. Standing in extensive grounds of 35,000m² with horse boxes, a tennis court and heated pool. Comprises three houses, all ready to move in to.
807,980 euros   **HIF**
(£504,990) GP

(11)
A splendid apartment in a large château surrounded by the idyllic countryside of the Black Mountains. Offers two bedrooms, fitted kitchen and use of shared gardens and a swimming pool.
121,000 euros   **HAR**
(£75,625) GP

(11)
A four-bedroom apartment set in the heart of Narbonne. Comprises a kitchen, living room and a large sitting room. Steps lead up to a spacious mezzanine. Features parquet floors and exposed beams.
160,000 euros   **PRP**
(£100,000) GP

(34)
Centrally heated, this L-shaped villa enjoys a swimming pool and private garden of 2,000m². Near Pézenas, the villa features five bedrooms arranged over two floors and a sun terrace with open views.
381,123 euros   **HIF**
(£238,200) GP

(66)
Dating from the 19th century, a spacious villa with a swimming pool, several outbuildings and a large wooded garden. Boasts four light-filled bedrooms. In a quiet residential area close to a village.
327,765 euros   **FRA**
(£204,855) GP

Price Guide

(11)
Dating from the 19th century, a stone-built village house with a terrace. Set around a courtyard, the property features terracotta tiled walls and floors, a sun terrace and three spacious bedrooms.
101,200 euros   **PRP**
(£63,250) GP

(34)
An old house in a fortified village. Enjoying superb views over a river, the house comprises three bedrooms and features two reception rooms, a small corner-kitchen, cellar and store rooms.
134,146 euros   **HIF**
(£83,840) GP

(11)
A ground floor apartment facing the port at Gruissan. A short walk from the beach, the apartment is fully furnished and offers one double bedroom. Features a large open-plan living area and terrace.
50,308 euros   **PRP**
(£31,445) GP

(34)
Dating from the 18th century, this large *maison de maitre* offers seven bedrooms over two floors. The property stands in an enclosed garden of 1,200m² featuring a gymnasium and a swimming pool.
411,583 euros   **HIF**
(£257,240) GP

(11)
Set in a quiet village, this small single-storey house is in need of some work. Accommodation has yet to be created, but could comprise three bedrooms. Standing in a small field, facing the Pyrenees.
66,470 euros   **HAR**
(£41,545) GP

(34)
An old château dating from the 17th century. Set beside a river, the property features two original towers, 34 rooms and a sunny terrace. Also offers a large basement in need of some renovation.
1,051,829 euros   **HIF**
(£657,395) GP

(11)
Dating from the 19th century, a totally restored country house standing in 9,000m² of land. Features a swimming pool and five en-suite bedrooms with open views over rural countryside.
420,200 euros   **PRP**
(£262,625) GP

(11)
A character house in need of partial restoration located in a village. Benefiting from three bedrooms and two attic rooms, the residence has retained many original details including a 19th-century staircase.
41,923 euros   **PRP**
(£26,200) GP

(11)
A country house set on a hillside. Stone-built and recently renovated, the house is surrounded by fields and woodland with a spring. The property enjoys panoramic views of the Black Mountains.
101,000 euros   **HAR**
(£63,125) GP

Languedoc-Roussillon

(11)
A two-storey villa a short walk from the beach and all amenities. Newly built, the property has two bedrooms and stands in a small garden laid to lawn. Centrally heated and ready to move in to.
61,490 euros   **PRP**
(£38,430) GP

(66)
A luxurious Mediterranean-style five-bedroom villa built in 1966. Set in 1,600m² of established garden planted with palm and fig trees. Features mountain views, a jacuzzi, pool and a small tower.
738,000 euros   **FEE**
(£461,250) GP

(66)
On a plot of 5,000m² and close to the beach and village centre, a renovated house arranged over two levels. Features a veranda, study, winter-kitchen and lounge. Offers three spacious bedrooms.
303,000 euros   **FEE**
(£189,375) GP

(30)
Set on a hillside in the Cevennes Mountains, an ancient monastery built in 1029. Standing in a large enclosed garden of 4,000m² with natural springs and a reservoir. Comprises three large bedrooms.
480,214 euros   **HAR**
(£300,135) GP

(11)
On the third floor of an apartment complex, this duplex-style flat benefits from the use of a heated swimming pool and comes with two good-sized bedrooms. Just a short walk from the beach.
67,073 euros   **PRP**
(£41,920) GP

(66)
Set on a mountainside, this stone-built residence has been totally renovated. Isolated and quiet, the house features three bedrooms, a sunny veranda and swimming pool. Enjoys stunning rural views.
628,000 euros   **FEE**
(£392,500) GP

(66)
In the Perpignan suburbs close to the beach, this three-bedroom villa was built in 1976. Located in a residential area, the property features a private garden with pine trees, a sun terrace and a garage.
360,000 euros   **FEE**
(£225,000) GP

(66)
Dating from the 19th century, a Tuscan-style villa built by an Italian architect. Set in a valley with orchards and vineyards, close to the town of Prades. The property features nine large bedrooms.
1,008,000 euros   **AHF**
(£630,000) GP

(66)
A short distance from the coast and a small village, this stone-built house is surrounded by vineyards and open countryside. Over 300 years old, the property offers four bedrooms and open fires.
410,000 euros   **FEE**
(£256,250) GP

Price Guide

(11)
Dating from the 19th century and set in a picturesque village, this terraced house is within easy reach of Narbonne and the coast. Featuring a courtyard garden, the property offers three bedrooms.
114,337 euros   **PRP**
(£71,460) GP

(66)
In the heart of a village, a group of traditional stone houses dating from the 18th century. Boasting many original features and stone walls, each house offers two to six bedrooms. In need of renovation.
353,000 euros   **FEE**
(£220,625) GP

(66)
Nestling at the foot of a mountain, an ensemble of four buildings in a remote setting. The properties date from 1600 and are in need of some renovation. Bordered by a river and forest.
263,373 euros   **FEE**
(£164,610) GP

(34)
Located in a village, this terraced four-storey villa offers two bedrooms, plenty of convertible space and a large living room and kitchen. The villa is in need of a little work, but is totally habitable.
54,881 euros   **HIF**
(£34,300) GP

(66)
A Catalan-style villa in the heart of a traditional village. Enjoying mountain views, a pool and three bedrooms, it is set in a mature south-facing garden planted with fruit trees. Features a sun terrace.
540,800 euros   **FEE**
(£338,000) GP

(34)
Set in a village close to the town of Lamalou-les-Bains, this renovated house is arranged over three floors and comprises a kitchen, dining room, balcony, terrace and two bedrooms with open fires.
55,000 euros   **HIF**
(£34,375) GP

(34)
On the outskirts of a town, this one-bedroom stone-built house is ready for occupation. In need of a little work and modernisation, the property features a covered terrace, kitchen and living room.
57,000 euros   **HIF**
(£35,625) GP

(66)
A character house set in a cul-de-sac in a market town. Offering four bathrooms and a bungalow currently used as a storehouse, the house features a swimming pool, tower and mountain views.
328,000 euros   **FEE**
(£205,000) GP

(34)
A large château with a swimming pool, currently comprising a dining room, kitchen, terrace, five bedrooms, a separate guest house, conservatory and old forge. This property enjoys stunning views.
914,694 euros   **FPP**
(£571,685) GP

Languedoc-Roussillon

(66)
A short drive from Perpignan, this detached house comprises four bedrooms and a bathroom. In need of some work, the property features an open-plan kitchen and veranda. Set in 6,000m² of land.
196,000 euros   **FEE**
(£122,500) GP

(30)
An old stone house in need of restoration. Features 490m² of habitable space, comprising 10 rooms and a converted flat. Set in 1,000m² of wooded grounds, with views over the surrounding area.
251,540 euros   **DAV**
(£157,215) GP

(66)
In need of some renovation, a large house in Port-Vendres. Currently comprising a self-contained three-bedroom flat on the top floor, an office, veranda and six bedrooms on the ground floor.
267,000 euros   **FEE**
(£166,875) GP

(11)
This house is set in a village near the Black Mountains. While habitable, it is in need of renovation. Surrounded by 3,000m² of land with pleasant open views, it offers a kitchen and convertible attic.
76,224 euros   **HIF**
(£47,640) GP

(11)
With views of the Pyrenees, this newly-built villa is located in a small village. The property offers three double bedrooms, a living room and open-plan kitchen area. Features farmhouse-style interiors.
180,273 euros   **FEE**
(£112,670) GP

(30)
This stone-built house is in need of some renovation. Situated high up on a wooded hillside, it enjoys stunning views of the valley below. Comprises four bedrooms, salon, dining room and kitchen.
484,800 euros   **DAV**
(£303,000) GP

(30)
A small hamlet of three houses and outbuildings in need of total renovation. Featuring a quiet rural location and a private swimming pool, the property is set in about 1,000m² of land with open views.
487,850 euros   **DAV**
(£304,905) GP

(66)
In the heart of a village close to Collioure, this large penthouse apartment is a short walk from the beach. Comprises a dining room, living room, bar, kitchen, study and four spacious bedrooms.
328,000 euros   **FEE**
(£205,000) GP

(11)
A house with a garden set in the heart of Carcassonne. Features a kitchen, living room, three bedrooms and a cellar. Comes with a garage and several large outbuildings, including a workshop.
129,600 euros   **HIF**
(£81,000) GP

Price Guide

(30)
This fully-restored property is set close to a golf course in 3,000m² of landscaped gardens enjoying open views over the surrounding area and a heated pool. Features five bedrooms and two receptions.
560,000 euros   **DAV**
(£350,000) GP

(66)
Close to the beach, this large villa is set in 12,000m² of private parkland with an abundance of Mediterranean trees and flowers. Enjoys a swimming pool, sun terrace and five large bedrooms.
2,250,000 euros   **FEE**
(£1,406,250) GP

(11)
A *maison de maitre* offering two large reception rooms and five bedrooms. With many original features including stone fireplaces and exposed beamed ceilings. Set on the edge of a pretty village.
395,150 euros   **SEH**
(£246,970) GP

(30)
This character stone-built property dates from the 11th century and comprises a main house and two self-contained guest houses. Situated in 11,000m² of idyllic forested countryside near a river.
594,550 euros   **DAV**
(£371,595) GP

(66)
This fisherman's house is located on a private beach and is close to an old village and port. Enjoying sea views and in a quiet neighbourhood, the property also offers a separate three-bedroom studio.
250,000 euros   **FEE**
(£156,250) GP

(66)
On the outskirts of a quiet village, this Provençal-style house is set on a large plot of land with fruit trees and a swimming pool. The property features three bedroom suites and a fully-fitted kitchen.
410,000 euros   **FEE**
(£256,250) GP

(11)
Dating from the 1980s, this small house is surrounded by quiet countryside and enjoys open views. The property is south-facing and features two spacious bedrooms and a small garden.
130,000 euros   **HIF**
(£81,250) GP

(30)
Built in the 18th century, this traditional house is located close to a busy market town and is surrounded by woodland. The house features two reception rooms, six bedrooms and a small garden.
594,552 euros   **DAV**
(£371,595) GP

(11)
On the outskirts of an old town, this single-storey villa features four bedrooms, living room and kitchen. Benefits from a large veranda with stunning views and a garage. Set in a residential area.
130,000 euros   **HIF**
(£81,250) GP

Languedoc-Roussillon

(30)
Set in a secluded spot on the edge of a medieval village, a newly-built villa with a fitted kitchen and three bedrooms. Features a landscaped garden with a heated swimming pool and olive trees.
595,000 euros   **DAV**
(£371,875) GP

(11)
A traditional house in the heart of Limoux. Semi-detached, the property stands in an extensive, tree-filled garden and features three bedrooms, a summer-kitchen, kitchen and living room.
147,880 euros   **HIF**
(£92,425) GP

(30)
Dating from the 19th century, an Italian-style villa located a short distance from a market town. Set in 22,000m² of mature gardens and farmland, it features seven bedrooms and four bathrooms.
1,963,500 euros   **DAV**
(£1,227,190) GP

(66)
Built in the 18th century, this farmhouse with outbuildings stands in 4,000m² of meadows. Offers many original details, three reception rooms and six bedrooms. Set in hilly countryside.
945,000 euros   **WAT**
(£590,625) GP

(11)
On the outskirts of a busy town, this semi-detached house stands in a quiet shaded garden with several outbuildings. The property comprises three bedrooms, fitted kitchen, veranda and living room.
160,500 euros   **HIF**
(£100,315) GP

(11)
In a small village to the north of Narbonne, a residence with 70m² of habitable space. In need of some modernisation, it offers two bedrooms, a living room and kitchen. Boasts original floor tiles.
45,500 euros   **HAN**
(£28,440) GP

(11)
Set in a quiet village close to the town of Limoux, a renovated stone-built house. Semi-detached, there are gardens to the side, front and rear of the house which features four spacious bedrooms.
152,448 euros   **HIF**
(£95,280) GP

(11)
A *maison de maitre* in a peaceful village. In need of a little work, it features original floor tiles, open fireplaces and light-filled rooms. Comprises six bedrooms, a living room, sitting room and kitchen.
135,000 euros   **HAN**
(£84,375) GP

(11)
Located in the eastern suburbs of Carcassonne, this single-storey house is semi-detached and dates from the 1980s. Centrally heated, the property enjoys a swimming pool and attractive lawned garden.
173,500 euros   **HIF**
(£108,440) GP

Price Guide

(11)
Close to Carcassonne in the heart of a pretty village, a 19th-century house with a garden of 2,500m². Includes a wine store, living room, three bedrooms and games room plus plenty of convertible space.
**175,000 euros   HIF
(£109,375) GP**

(11)
A 19th-century house with 177m² of living space located in a wine-making area. Set in a small garden with a terrace and two adjoining garages, the property features open fireplaces and wood floors.
**195,140 euros   HIF
(£121,960) GP**

(11)
A spacious village house with a garage, set in the foothills of the Black Mountains. This home features five bedrooms, a living room and shower room, and is fronted by a paved courtyard.
**117,500 euros   HAN
(£73,440) GP**

(11)
In the small village of Corbières, this stone-built house is in need of complete renovation. Features two bedrooms, a barn and small enclosed courtyard. Located in a quiet street, close to all amenities.
**50,000 euros   HAN
(£31,250) GP**

(11)
Situated in a winemaking area, a single-storey villa comprising a living room, three bedrooms and terrace with south-facing views. Set in a garden of 7,440m² with a garage and extensive wine store.
**206,000 euros   HIF
(£128,750) GP**

(34)
On the edge of a village close to the Canal du Midi, a detached three-bedroom house with tiled floors throughout. Set in a south-facing lawned garden with mature trees, a vast terrace and a garage.
**182,786 euros   HAN
(£114,240) GP**

(11)
Featuring wood-panelled walls, tiled floors and four bedrooms, this partially renovated village house offers a garage, courtyard, terrace and 1,500m² of gardens. On the outskirts of a small village.
**109,001 euros   HAN
(£68,125) GP**

(11)
In a village with shops close to the town of Carcassonne, this single-storey detached house has two bedrooms, a large terrace and a garage. Set in a south-facing garden planted with fruit trees.
**175,000 euros   HAN
(£109,375) GP**

(66)
Formerly a farmhouse, this small detached rural property stands in a garden of 1,200m² featuring a covered terrace with a summer living room and a garage. Offers three bedrooms and a kitchen.
**70,000 euros   HAN
(£43,750) GP**

Languedoc-Roussillon

(11)
Close to a village, an ensemble of stone-built farm buildings for renovation. Featuring three houses, two workshops, stables and several small outbuildings. Situated in grounds of 15,000m² with a forge.
298,000 euros   **HAN**
(£186,250) GP

(11)
In southern Aude, this old stone-built house enjoys open views and is set in a quiet country village perfect for fishing and hunting. Features a corner-kitchen, two bedrooms and a wine cellar.
228,673 euros   **FWY**
(£142,920) GP

(34)
Set in a village, this old house needs some finishing-off work. The property features a marble fireplace, stone staircase, beamed ceilings, four bedrooms, an artist's studio and a heated plunge pool.
325,000 euros   **HAN**
(£203,125) GP

(30)
Located in a village close to the town of Uzès, this restored stone-built convent comprises three wings set around a U-shaped courtyard. With eight bedrooms and a large garden with a pool.
1,448,266 euros   **SIF**
(£905,165) GP

(11)
South of Carcassonne, this detached house with 240m² of living space overlooks a quiet village. It features four bedrooms, each with a terrace, an L-shaped living room and tiled kitchen.
301,850 euros   **HAN**
(£188,655) GP

(11)
A large, modern house in a small village. In a peaceful location, the property features three bedrooms, two of which are en-suite. Stands in 3,050m² of completely enclosed Mediterranean-style gardens.
335,000 euros   **HAN**
(£209,375) GP

(11)
In a quiet spot, this totally renovated detached farmhouse features a beautiful hand-painted ceiling. The property offers five bedrooms and a beautiful, secluded garden with a well and swimming pool.
419,235 euros   **HAN**
(£262,020) GP

(11)
A historic property dating from the 18th century. Near the coast and a small town, it stands in a private estate of 40,000m² and features a main building with two wings and several bedroom suites.
1,143,367 euros   **DEE**
(£714,605) GP

(11)
Set in beautiful countryside, a large property comprising two bedrooms, an L-shaped kitchen, dining room and double living room. Comes with an adjacent small house and a dovecote.
350,000 euros   **HAN**
(£218,750) GP

PROVENCE, COTE D'AZUR & CORSICA

Price Guide

(06)
Situated close to Cannes, this property benefits from a covered terrace, private garden and a large swimming pool. Offers one en-suite bedroom, four further bedrooms and a family bathroom.
473,000 euros   **HAP**
(£295,625) GP

(06)
This detached house is located in a quiet residential area with sea views. The property boasts marble floors, wine cellars and a heated swimming pool. Set in 7,000m² of land with a spacious terrace.
2,439,024 euros   **LIN**
(£1,524,390) GP

(06)
This Provençal-style property is located in a residential area and enjoys panoramic views. Benefits from a private *pétanque* playing ground, four en-suite bedrooms and a heated swimming pool.
2,515,409 euros   **HAP**
(£1,572,130) GP

(06)
Located in the village of Biot, this south-facing property enjoys stunning countryside views. Offers five en-suite bedrooms, separate guest and caretaker's apartments, and a swimming pool.
1,675,000 euros   **HAP**
(£1,046,875) GP

(13)
This large Provençal-style house, west of Marseille, offers four bedrooms each with en-suite shower or bath facilities and a fully-fitted kitchen. In the generous grounds there are several outbuildings.
487,805 euros   **LIN**
(£304,880) GP

(06)
This two-bedroom portered apartment enjoys sea views and is on the third floor of an Art Deco building. Fronted by a mature garden, the property offers a fitted kitchen and en-suite bathroom.
358,600 euros   **HAP**
(£224,125) GP

(13)
Close to the coast, this detached villa faces south and enjoys views overlooking Marseille. Comprises four bedrooms, terrace and gardens of 650m² with mature trees, shrubs and flower borders.
345,000 euros   **LIN**
(£215,625) GP

(83)
This large 17th-century château is set in a quiet residential area. Benefits from plenty of living space and features 10 bedrooms. All services are connected and the property is ready to move in to.
3,810,000 euros   **DAV**
(£2,381,250) GP

(06)
On a hillside near Saint-Paul, this large Provençal-style villa stands within parkland of 3,000m². Featuring a cathedral-style reception room, the property has open fireplaces and beamed ceilings.
1,143,500 euros   **HAP**
(£714,690) GP

FRENCH ALPS: LAKE GENEVA

"Buyers Guide" & particulars of new and older property with photos from £40,000 to £500,000+

BEACHES INTERNATIONAL PROPERTY

3/4 Hagley Mews, Hagley Hall, West Midlands DY9 9LQ

Tel: **01562 885181** Fax: **01562 886724**

Email: info@beachesint.co.uk www.beachesint.co.uk

Mediterranean Property Search

Guiding you through the process of purchasing property in the South of France.

As a friendly & personal search service, we help you find your dream home in the South of France. We guide you through the sometimes daunting process of purchasing a property saving you considerable time & effort.

With our extensive network of French estate agents, we locate suitable properties & arrange the viewings. Accompanied viewing trips can be arranged.

For further information, please contact:
Mediterranean Property Search
1 Copplestone Road, Budleigh Salterton, Devon, EX9 6DS
Tel: **01395 442689**
Fax: **01395 446866**
email: enquiries@mediterranean-homes.co.uk

L'Agence Bleue
The best way to find your ideal property !

Interested in buying this property? Visit our website Ref: 492

If you are looking for a village house, a villa,
Contact us: **leval-immo@wanadoo.fr**
English estate agents resident in France

Tel: **00 33 4 94 86 49 39**
Superb choice of properties for sale

www.agencebleue.com

www.french-real-estate.com

We are a french real estate company based in Nice and Paris, we market a very wide range of properties in central Paris and on the Riviera most exclusive locations.

You are looking for a home or to invest in properties...

Visit our website !

Conseil Patrimoine
52, boulevard Victor Hugo - 06000 Nice
Tel +33 (0) 497.030.333 - Fax +33 (0) 497.030.334
http://www.french-real-estate.com

Price Guide

(06)
South facing and set in a peaceful wooded location, this property enjoys open views and a heated swimming pool. Offers five bedrooms, an oak-panelled library and a fitted kitchen.
808,000 euros   **HAP**
(£505,000) GP

(83)
Situated close to the town of Lorgues, this Provençal-style villa offers three bedroom suites and a large garden of 7,000m². The property also features a patio area and picturesque views.
3,810,000 euros   **DAV**
(£2,381,250) GP

(06)
Located on a hillside in Saint-Paul, this property enjoys open views, air conditioning and a sauna. Offers six en-suite bedrooms that open onto the garden and covered terraces.
3,155,700 euros   **HAP**
(£1,972,315) GP

(06)
A massive country house offering 900m² of living space and 24 main rooms. Set in 20,000m² of hilly land, the house enjoys a swimming pool and tennis court. In a quiet location, close to a village.
525,949 euros   **HAM**
(£328,720) GP

(13)
This *maison de maître* is located close to Arles and benefits from 450m² of living space. Featuring five bedrooms, five bathrooms and a separate cottage, the property is in need of some restoration.
647,866 euros   **LIN**
(£404,915) GP

(83)
This three-bedroom house is situated in an isolated rural area a short drive from Nice. The property is detached and benefits from a large garden and a single garage. The house is ready to move in to.
537,348 euros   **VEF**
(£335,845) GP

(06)
This three-storey property is set in a quiet residential area know as *La Petite Afrique*. Featuring sea views and a separate caretaker's cottage, there are four bedrooms, three bathrooms and a garden.
3,750,000 euros   **HAP**
(£2,343,750) GP

(13)
This contemporary house is set in a quiet hamlet. The ground floor comprises a kitchen, dining room and sitting room, while the first floor offers four bedrooms. Offers a garden of 2,500m² with a pool.
335,366 euros   **LIN**
(£209,605) GP

(06)
This new stone-built property is located on a private estate. With five en-suite bedrooms, a gym, wine cellar and garage, it offers a self-contained studio apartment with a shower room and kitchen.
2,286,735 euros   **HAP**
(£1,429,210) GP

Ramatuelle - VV429

Bar-Sur-Loup - VV371

Agence Centre Croisette
55, La Croisette - 5th floor. 06400 CANNES

IMMOBILIER DE LUXE
Ventes et Locations
Côte d'Azur

LUXURY REAL ESTATE
Sales and Rentals
French Riviera

Tél. 00 33 (0)4 93 99 13 63   www.amontagu.com   Fax 00 33 (0)4 93 38 52 45

Mougins - VV395

Mons - VV378

Price Guide

(06)
Set in the hills of Saint-Paul, this property enjoys views over the surrounding countryside and features a swimming pool and garden. Comprises two en-suite bedrooms and a fitted kitchen.
1,037,000 euros **HAP**
(£648,125) GP

(06)
Nestling in the hills near a historic village, this south-facing villa enjoys coastal views and a swimming pool. Comprises four bedrooms, a shower room and a self-contained guest apartment.
915,000 euros **HAP**
(£571,875) GP

(06)
This Provençal-style property features large windows opening onto an extensive covered terrace, swimming pool and a lawned garden. The house comprises five bedrooms and three bathrooms.
3,353,878 euros **HAP**
(£2,096,175) GP

(13)
A three-bedroom apartment with spacious accommodation in a portered building. Located in a small town, the property is ready for occupation and benefits from a communal garden and a garage.
217,988 euros **VEF**
(£136,245) GP

(83)
This spacious five-bedroom villa enjoys sea views and a garden of 1,300m². With a recently-installed central heating system, the property features a large garden with two terraces and a barbecue area.
646,383 euros **LIN**
(£403,990) GP

(06)
A charming villa located in a peaceful woodland area close to Cannes. This property benefits from 155m² of living space, three en-suite bedrooms and a large garden with a swimming pool.
732,000 euros **HAP**
(£457,500) GP

(83)
A villa in an elevated position in the town of Saint-Cyr-sur-Mer. With sea views, the villa offers a swimming pool, fitted kitchen, five bedrooms, one with a large terrace, and three washrooms.
647,908 euros **LIN**
(£404,940) GP

(06)
This apartment is set in the secure residence of the Royal Mougins golf club. With use of a pool, the property offers two bedrooms and two bathrooms. Benefits include life membership of the golf club.
512,000 euros **HAP**
(£317,440) GP

(13)
This detached house is located on the edge of a picturesque village. Set in 2,000m² of land with open views, the property is habitable and comprises three good-sized bedrooms and a single garage.
571,189 euros **VEF**
(£356,995) GP

Provence, Côte d'Azur & Corsica

(83)
This property has been completely restored and benefits from open views. Offers a large living room, dining room and eight bedrooms. Set in 2,000m² of lawned gardens, with a swimming pool and patio.
888,778 euros   **LIN**
(£555,485) GP

(83)
This traditional Provençal-style house is located in the heart of the medieval village of Flayosc. The property comprises four bedrooms, three shower rooms, a bathroom and a swimming pool.
533,370 euros   **HAP**
(£333,355) GP

(06)
With views over the sea and mountains, this villa is located in Cannes. Offers four bedrooms, a guest studio and fully-equipped kitchen. Set in mature gardens with a tennis court and pool.
2,000,000 euros   **MAG**
(£1,250,000) GP

(83)
In a secluded woodland location, a Provençal-style house. Features two guest apartments, three large bedrooms, a library, fitted kitchen and dining room. Outside is a well-kept garden with a jacuzzi.
1,300,000 euros   **DAV**
(£812,500) GP

(06)
This luxury stone villa is situated in large grounds on a hillside. Overlooking a picturesque village, the property enjoys sea views and offers six en-suite bedrooms and a self-contained guest apartment.
3,201,500 euros   **HAP**
(£2,000,940) GP

(06)
A luxury poolside villa nestling in the hills of Cannes. Located in a residential area, the property enjoys mature gardens, a plunge pool and summer lounge. Offers four bedrooms and a guest studio.
1,143,500 euros   **MAG**
(£714,690) GP

(06)
This impressive villa with sea views benefits from a quiet situation and has recently been refurbished. Comprises three bedrooms, two bathrooms, a pool, poolhouse and barbecue area.
686,021 euros   **MAG**
(£428,765) GP

(06)
A rustic villa set in a small town just a short drive from Cannes. Comprising two bedrooms and two bathrooms, the villa comes with a separate guest apartment. and 6,700m² of mature gardens.
724,133 euros   **AZF**
(£452,585) GP

(06)
This California-style villa offers spacious rooms, terracotta flooring and southwesterly views. Built on one level, it features open fires, three bedrooms, three bathrooms and a heated swimming pool.
655,530 euros   **HAP**
(£409,705) GP

Price Guide

(06)
Located in a quiet hamlet, this charming detached property benefits from three bedrooms and a large convertible attic. A small garden surrounds the house and to the side is a single garage.
382,341 euros   **VEF**
(£238,965) GP

(06)
Situated on a hillside near Théoule-sur-Mer, a Provençal villa in a stunning setting with a patio and palm trees in the garden. Offers six bedrooms, four bathrooms and a swimming pool.
1,295,816 euros   **AZF**
(£809,885) GP

(06)
Set in a wooded parkland of 30,000m^2, this former olive mill is on the banks of a river. Currently under renovation, the property offers six bedrooms, a swimming pool, spa room and tennis court.
3,050,000 euros   **HAP**
(£1,906,250) GP

(06)
With direct access to a private beach, this villa enjoys a mature garden with a swimming pool, jacuzzi and tennis court. Offers three en-suite bedrooms, a boat house and two studio apartments.
3,049,000 euros   **HAP**
(£1,905,625) GP

(13)
Located on the edge of a small town, this terraced house has numerous bedrooms and a small, well-kept garden. Arranged over three floors, the property is ready to occupy and has a single garage.
147,104 euros   **VEF**
(£91,940) GP

(06)
Nestling in the hills of Saint-Paul, this traditional house enjoys peaceful surroundings with the advantage of a swimming pool. Offers four bedrooms with shower facilities and splendid open views.
1,131,171 euros   **HAP**
(£706,980) GP

(06)
Located in a small town close to Cannes, this villa benefits from four spacious bedrooms with sea views. Near the beach, the property offers a swimming pool and self-contained caretaker's cottage.
1,905,613 euros   **AZF**
(£1,191,010) GP

(06)
Set at the edge of a cliff, this uniquely-placed property boasts nine bedrooms and six bathrooms. With stunning panoramic views, the villa features both an indoor and an outdoor swimming pool.
7,622,450 euros   **AZF**
(£4,764,030) GP

(06)
Close to Menton, this period villa comprises three bedrooms and two bathrooms. Located near the coast and enjoying sea views, the property is set in 2,060m^2 of land with a heated swimming pool.
975,000 euros   **AZF**
(£609,375) GP

Provence, Côte d'Azur & Corsica

(06)
A fully-renovated house close to Cap-d'Ail. With five bedrooms, five bathrooms and a separate guesthouse, the property enjoys stunning sea views and is set in mature gardens of nearly 1,600m².
3,360,000 euros   AZF
(£2,100,000) GP

(06)
Set on a hillside enjoying stunning sea views, this modern villa in Valbonne benefits from a private swimming pool and tennis court. The property features a self-contained studio apartment.
1,525,000 euros   AZF
(£953,125) GP

(06)
In the hills above the medieval village of Eze, this stone-built house comprises six bedrooms, three reception rooms and a triple garage. Original features include an old well and a bread oven.
643,300 euros   HAP
(£402,065) GP

(06)
This large Provençal-style house is set in Antibes. With four bedrooms and four bathrooms, the property enjoys spacious accommodation and light-filled rooms. A short distance from the beach.
1,677,000 euros   AZF
(£1,048,125) GP

(06)
Set on the beachfront, *Le Mouret* comprises two houses. The main house features two en-suite bedrooms, while the one-bedroom self-contained guesthouse benefits from a gym and steamroom.
2,286,000 euros   HAP
(£1,428,750) GP

(06)
Situated in Valbonne, this large *bastide* comprises five bedrooms and five bathrooms and is set in nearly 20,000m² of gardens with trees and a large swimming pool. Located in a quiet residential area.
3,811,225 euros   AZF
(£2,382,015) GP

(83)
In Saint-Tropez, this detached residence offers 12 main rooms. Set in over 18,000m² of land with trees and shrubs, the property enjoys a large swimming pool with a tiled patio area and terrace.
3,811,231 euros   AZF
(£2,382,020) GP

(83)
Standing in gardens of 1,600m² with a large pool, this newly-built villa is situated close to la Croix-Valmer. Fronted by a lawn, the property enjoys open views and is a short distance from the beach.
655,531 euros   AZF
(£409,705) GP

(06)
This villa is set in a quiet residential area of Grasse. The property is arranged over three floors and features four double bedrooms, a tiled swimming pool with poolhouse and a mature garden.
1,067,000 euros   HAP
(£666,875) GP

Price Guide

(06)
In a peaceful residential area, this family home has been completely restored and benefits from light, spacious rooms arranged over three floors. The property has five bedrooms and two bathrooms.
840,000 euros   **HAP**
(£520,000) GP

(84)
Set in Cavaillon, a large property comprising a house with eight bedrooms, two separate gîtes and two swimming pools. Fronted by a gravel drive and featuring a terrace, it stands in 3,800m² of land.
691,500 euros   **AZF**
(£432,190) GP

(13)
Set in 3,830m² of gardens with a swimming pool, this large villa faces south and offers three bedroom suites. In a residential area, the villa is located just a short distance from a village with shops.
838,451 euros   **AZF**
(£524,030) GP

(83)
A traditional country dwelling set in large garden. Currently being run as a hotel with a restaurant and bar, it features 10 bedrooms, 10 bathrooms and a large fitted kitchen. Set in a quiet village.
419,207 euros   **AZF**
(£262,005) GP

(06)
This townhouse overlooks the 11th hole at the Royal Mougins golf club and is surrounded by woodland. Offers two bedrooms, two bathrooms, shower room and use of a shared swimming pool.
535,250 euros   **HAP**
(£334,530) GP

(84)
Close to Pernes-les-Fontaines, this 19th-century dwelling offers seven bedrooms and four bathrooms. The house benefits from a heated swimming pool and stands in 2,000m² of secluded gardens.
564,061 euros   **AZF**
(£352,540) GP

(83)
This five-bedroom house is set in 22,000m² of land with a pool. Close to the town of Lorgues and surrounded by woodland and meadows, it features a separate guest cottage. Ready to occupy.
686,020 euros   **AZF**
(£428,765) GP

(83)
A traditional *bastide* near Flayosc. Located in a quiet hamlet, the property benefits from five bedrooms and has numerous outbuildings. Set in over 5,000m² of woodland, it enjoys rural views.
686,306 euros   **AZF**
(£428,940) GP

(13)
This villa comes with state-of-the-art security and is set in 5,220m2 of beautiful landscaped gardens Offering 200m2 of living space, the property features secure parking and an open fireplace.
510,705 euros   **MER**
(£319,190) GP

Provence, Côte d'Azur & Corsica

(13)
A traditional villa benefiting from double glazing and secure car parking. Set in a mature garden of 680m2, the property features stripped floors, exposed wooden beams and many period details.
357,000 euros   MER
(£223,125) GP

(06)
Within a short drive of the coast, Nice Airport and ski runs, this large villa comprises two fitted kitchens, four bedrooms, a lounge, cellar and balcony. A garden of 393m² surrounds the property.
106,000 euros   HAM
(£66,250) GP

(84)
A large farmhouse in the centre of Luberon. On the ground floor are two living rooms, a kitchen, wine store and shower room. Upstairs offers five bedrooms and a dressing room. Set in 5,000m² of land.
870,000 euros   MAR
(£543,750) GP

(83)
A traditional villa with a lounge and dining room. Close to Garéoult, it comprises four bedrooms, a bathroom, garage and cellar. Set in a tree-filled garden of 1,260m², with a barbecue area.
225,572 euros   HAM
(£140,985) GP

(84)
Close to Cavaillon, a farmhouse with a living room, dining room, kitchen, four bedrooms and three bathrooms. Situated in 3,300m² of land enjoying a swimming pool and unrestricted rural views.
500,000 euros   MAR
(£312,500) GP

(83)
A large farmhouse in Saint-Paul with a separate two-bedroom apartment. Set in an extensive tree-filled garden, it benefits from four spacious bedrooms, a kitchen, living room and two bathrooms.
457,348 euros   MAR
(£285,845) GP

(13)
This bastide comes with 29,000m² of mature parkland with a self-contained guest house and outbuildings. Offering 540m² of living space, a classic example of this type of property.
1,500,002 euros   MER
(£937,500) GP

(83)
In the town of Hyères, this villa comprises a lounge, dining room, four bedrooms, a bathroom and terrace with panoramic views. Stands in a lawned garden of 526m² planted with fruit trees.
274,408 euros   HAM
(£171,505) GP

(83)
An ensemble of gîtes and a large farmhouse standing in land of 6,000m². Comprising three gîtes and a house offering seven rooms, the property enjoys rural views and a heated swimming pool.
548,816 euros   MAR
(£343,010) GP

Price Guide

(83)
In Cogolin, a town house with two bedrooms. Fully renovated, the property features a lounge, kitchen, bathroom and ground floor studio flat. Enjoys a sun terrace leading onto a small garden.
149,000 euros   **HAM**
(£93,125) GP

(06)
In a traditional Niçois building, this third-floor apartment offers three bedrooms and is located in the heart of the city, minutes from the *promenade des Anglais* and the central pedestrianised area.
366,000 euros   **HAP**
(£228,750) GP

(06)
Nestling in the hills of Golfe Juan, this recently-renovated villa stands in a Mediterranean garden overlooking the sea. Features two en-suite bedrooms, dining room and a heated swimming pool.
1,222,500 euros   **HAP**
(£764,065) GP

(83)
This house is close to a small town and stands in grounds of 11,000m². The property features four bedrooms, a small self-contained guest apartment, a garage and a heated swimming pool.
312,520 euros   **MAR**
(£195,325) GP`

(83)
A house situated next to a river in the Saint-Paul area. This property offers a garage, six light-filled bedrooms and two bathrooms, and is set in an elevated position in a picture-book rural location.
381,123 euros   **MAR**
(£238,200) GP

(06)
One hour from Nice, a restored house sitting in a hilltop village. With panoramic views over the surrounding countryside and hills, the property features three large bedrooms and light-filled rooms.
381,122 euros   **FRA**
(£238,200) GP

(83)
Currently undergoing renovation, an old priory with stone-built outbuildings. Set in 40,000m² of woodland and located at the foot of a hill, it benefits from a quiet environment with open views.
556,429 euros   **MAI**
(£347,770) GP

(83)
Dating from the 18th century, a Mediterranean-style house set in 35,000m² of land enjoying a river, meadows and an olive plantation. Featuring three bedrooms, it is in need of some interior decoration.
1,450,000 euros   **DAV**
(£906,250) GP

(06)
This old stone mill-house has been completely restored and offers a corner-kitchen and large bedrooms. It is surrounded by an attractive 735m² garden with a small stream running through it.
320,000 euros   **MAI**
(£200,000) GP

Provence, Côte d'Azur & Corsica

(06)
This large villa enjoys panoramic views over the surrounding hills and the coast. Featuring a living area of 50m² and a swimming pool, the property is set in an enclosed, landscaped garden.
587,000 euros   **MAI**
(£366,875) GP

(83)
This stone-built farm building has been totally renovated and restored. Secluded and peaceful, this residence enjoys stunning views across the surrounding countryside and features a pool.
522,900 euros   **MAI**
(£326,815) GP

(83)
A small village house with three bedrooms. Arranged over two floors, the property features a living room with a fireplace, a large bathroom and dining room. Totally renovated throughout.
150,000 euros   **MAR**
(£93,750) GP

(84)
Located in a quiet rural village, a two-storey house comprising an open-plan kitchen and dining room, living room, bathroom and two bedrooms. This small property features a mezzanine floor.
89,945 euros   **MAR**
(£56,215) GP

(06)
Overlooking Monaco and close to the Italian border, this spacious apartment boasts sea views and is a short distance from the town centre. Features a kitchen, three bedrooms and a large living area.
75,500 euros   **FRE**
(£47,190) GP

(83)
An old bastide with 15,000m² of grounds with an electric gate. This large rustic property has been sympathetically renovated. Large kitchen, outbuildings, open fires and several bedroom suites.
1,175,002 euros   **MER**
(£734,375) GP

(83)
A villa with four bedrooms and a swimming pool. Set in 2,500m² of mature gardens in a quiet residential area, this four-bedroom property has a fitted kitchen, living room with fireplace and garage.
290,000 euros   **MAR**
(£181,250) GP

(83)
This restored house is set close to Draguignan. In a private location and offering 15,000m² of manicured gardens with a swimming pool, it comprises six bedrooms, three receptions and outbuildings.
1,500,000 euros   **DAV**
(£937,500) GP

(83)
A three-storey village house with three rooms on the ground floor, an open-plan kitchen and dining room on the first floor and two spacious bedrooms on the second floor. Fronted by a small garden.
335,000 euros   **DAV**
(£209,375) GP

Price Guide

(84)
This old stone-built farmhouse has been renovated thoughout and offers 320m2 of living space. With period features such as shutters and a traditional kitchen, the house sits in 5,600m2 of land.
685,001 euros   MER
(£428,125) GP

(83)
A modern property surrounded by 10,000m² of vineyards. Offers three bedrooms, a large bathroom and an independent studio flat. Set in a lawned garden with a patio area, garage and workshop.
366,000 euros   DAV
(£228,750) GP

(83)
With a fitted kitchen and large reception room, this single-storey villa offers four bedrooms. South facing and enjoying panoramic views of mountains and forests, it is set in 1,780m² of gardens.
381,100 euros   DAV
(£238,190) GP

(13)
An imposing bastide in very good condition. With original features throughout, including tiled floors and iron banisters, this large property enjoys 11,000m² of landscaped grounds with a pool.
1,135,747 euros   MER
(£709,840) GP

(84)
Standing in 110,000m² of land, this former farmhouse has been fully renovated and offers various outbuildings, a guest house and a swimming pool. The main building has living space of 350m².
930,001 euros   MER
(£581,250) GP

(83)
A stone-built village house offering a garden, self-contained flat and open views. The property features a living room, two bedrooms, fitted kitchen, a secluded garden laid to lawn and a cellar.
404,000 euros   DAV
(£252,500) GP

(83)
South facing, a Mediterranean villa with panoramic mountain views. The house features a study, six bedrooms and a large dining room opening onto a terrace. Set in 6,600m² of tree-filled gardens.
518,330 euros   DAV
(£323,955) GP

(84)
This modern villa stands in well-manicured grounds of 8,325m² with a tennis court and sun terrace. Double glazed throughout, the property offers five main rooms and 180m2 of living space.
655,532 euros   MER
(£409,710) GP

(83)
A restored house on the outskirts of a busy village. Split over three floors, the building features two bedrooms, a roof terrace and a one-bedroom guest flat with salon, dining room and fitted kitchen.
411,600 euros   DAV
(£257,250) GP

Provence, Côte d'Azur & Corsica

(83)
Set around a pool, this modern villa includes five independent studio flats. The main house comprises an open-plan dining room and fitted kitchen, four bedrooms and two bathrooms.
629,600 euros   **DAV**
(£393,500) GP

(13)
A large cottage set in a generous 170,000m2 of beautiful countryside. This property boasts many original details, including shutters, tiled floors and open fires, 250m² of habitable space.
762,246 euros   **MER**
(£476,400) GP

(83)
This spacious villa with a guest-house enjoys panoramic sea views and is set close to village. Features four bedrooms, three terraces and a tree-filled garden of 1,900m² with room for a swimming pool.
800,400 euros   **DAV**
(£500,250) GP

(84)
A traditional stone farmhouse in the popular village of Gordes. With extensive views, this renovated property offers a vast living room and four bedrooms. Stands in 7,000m² of land with a pool.
923,000 euros   **DAV**
(£576,875) GP

(83)
A restored villa a short distance from the picturesque village of La Garde-Freinet. Enjoying country views, the villa comprises five bedrooms, an independent studio apartment and swimming pool.
876,600 euros   **DAV**
(£547,875) GP

(83)
A country residence on the edge of the popular village of Lorgues. Set in extensive grounds with a swimming pool, tennis court and fenced truffle patch. Offers five bedrooms and a summer kitchen.
1,220,000 euros   **DAV**
(£762,500) GP

(84)
Dating from the 18th century, a fully-restored *bastide* in the heart of Vaucluse. Featuring a vaulted dining room, five bedrooms, a study and wine cellars, and set in a garden with a swimming pool.
978,500 euros   **DAV**
(£611,565) GP

(83)
A historic bastide with 450m² of inhabitable space. Restored to high standard, this property features tiled floors and a landscaped garden of 8,000m2 with a swimming pool and sun terrace.
975,001 euros   **MER**
(£609,375) GP

(83)
A modern villa offering generous living quarters. Features three bedrooms, including one en-suite master bedroom leading onto a terrace. Set in a secure residential area, close to the coast and shops.
907,000 euros   **DAV**
(£566,875) GP

Price Guide

(13)
In the town of Aix-en-Provence, this stunning villa is truly a sun trap. With a swimming pool and a terrace, the property has a garden of 5,600m^2 with wonderful views over surrounding countryside.
915,001 euros　　　　　MER
(£571,875) GP

(84)
Located in a peaceful pedestrianised street close to shops, a fully-renovated house comprising a living room, kitchen, dining room, two bedrooms and a cellar. Set in a small garden with trees.
55,095 euros　　　　　DEL
(£34,435) GP

(84)
Standing in 7,000m^2 of immaculate landscaped gardens with a swimming pool and secure parking, this large character house of 350m^2 features tiled floors, and wonderful views.
820,001 euros　　　　　MER
(£512,500) GP

(06)
Set at the end of a country lane on a hillside near Peille, a stone *bastide* in need of some work. Arranged over four levels, the property is south facing and features 20 large bedrooms.
1,600,535 euros　　　　　CAC
(£1,000,335) GP

(83)
A traditional Provençal-style villa with a garage. With three bedrooms, kitchen and two living rooms, the property is centrally heated and set in 2,500m^2 of tree-filled land in a secluded position.
200,592 euros　　　　　HAM
(£125,370) GP

(06)
A stunning *bastide* built on a sunny plateau within 22,000m^2 of woodland and mature gardens. The property features eight bedroom suites, an oval swimming pool and lovely mountain views.
2,439,184 euros　　　　　CAC
(£1,524,490) GP

(83)
A Provençal-style villa located in Cogolin. Featuring three large en-suite bedrooms, each with walk-in wardrobes, the villa is south facing with views over rural valleys. Fully furnished with a shared pool.
219,000 euros　　　　　CAC
(£136,875) GP

(06)
This detached villa is set on the edge of an old village in a peaceful and secluded location. Standing in a garden planted with fruit trees and vines, the property enjoys mountain and sea views.
1,705,488 euros　　　　　CAC
(£1,065,930) GP

(83)
This semi-detached villa is set in a small complex of houses in a village with superb views over the Bay of Cavalaire. Close to the beach and backing onto vineyards, the villa offers two bedrooms.
200,000 euros　　　　　CAC
(£125,000) GP

Provence, Côte d'Azur & Corsica

(83)
This old stone-built farmhouse is set in 10,000m² of sunny gardens and features five bedrooms, three self-contained apartments and a large swimming pool. Offers an additional 80m² for conversion.
960,000 euros   **MPS**
(£600,000) S

(83)
Near the beach in Fréjus, a two-bedroom apartment offering 76m² of habitable space including a kitchen and lounge. Centrally heated, the property is within easy reach of the bustling town centre.
660,419 euros   **HAM**
(£412,760) GP

(06)
A stone-built *bastide* enjoying panoramic views over the sea and countryside. The estate features seven bedrooms, terraces, a courtyard and tennis court. Set in a small town, close to the beach.
1,067,000 euros   **CAC**
(£666,875) GP

(06)
Near a village and set in the heart of a 27,000m² estate with giant oaks, fruit trees and stunning sea views, this château dates from the 19th century and features 12 bedrooms arranged over four floors.
1,707,095 euros   **CAC**
(£1,066,935) GP

(06)
A country estate set in 5,300m² of land with a pool and wonderful views over Cannes. Surrounded by mountains, the property features five bedrooms and comes with a separate one-bedroom cottage.
1,960,000 euros   **CAC**
(£1,225,000) GP

(83)
A large country estate, originally a 14th-century farmstead, set in 10,500m² of grounds with a pool and large sun terrace. This property offers 10 bedrooms, a music room and fully-fitted kitchen.
1,995,000 euros   **CAC**
(£1,246,875) GP

(06)
A large country estate with amazing coastal views. Standing in 12,700m² of mature gardens, it offers 30 large bedrooms and 18 bathrooms. Split over two floors, with a pool and tennis court.
2,290,000 euros   **CAC**
(£1,431,250) GP

(06)
An old *bastide* estate, dating from the 18th century. Set in land of 28,500m² with two houses, a swimming pool, stables, tennis court and vineyards. Features 15 bedrooms and sweeping views.
2,286,000 euros   **CAC**
(£1,428,750) GP

(06)
A villa enjoying stunning views and a quiet location on a hillside in a village. Recently decorated, the property enjoys a pool and is encompassed by a vast lawn, sun terrace and mature olive trees.
784,000 euros   **PRV**
(£490,000) GP

Price Guide

(84)
Renovated to a high standard, this characterful property stands in 35,000m² of grounds with a guest house, swimming pool and amazing views. The main house features a living room with open fire.
602,175 euros   **MER**
(£376,360) GP

(84)
This Provençal-style *mas* enjoys a swimming pool, six bedrooms and three bathrooms. Surrounded by hilly countryside, the house benefits from stunning views and is a short drive from local amenities.
123,680 euros   **LAT**
(£77,300) GP

(83)
This historic residence in the heart of Hyères enjoys unimpeded panoramic views over the local countryside. The property features gothic windows, a period staircase, four bedrooms and cellars.
731,755 euros   **DEE**
(£457,345) GP

(13)
This 18th-century Provençal-style farmhouse stands in 20,000m² of secluded grounds in the heart of a regional park. This large property features roughcast stone walls and eight bedroom suites.
960,500 euros   **DEE**
(£600,310) GP

(04)
An 18th-century residence with views across the Ubaye Valley and the Alps. Set in a small village near the town of Gap, this property offers two bedrooms and two one-bedroom studio apartments.
823,224 euros   **DEE**
(£514,515) GP

(83)
A spacious six-bedroom country home with stunning rural views, a large swimming pool, sun terrace, patio and well-maintained gardens. Close to a village with all amenities and near the coast.
872,000 euros   **SIF**
(£545,000) GP

(83)
A good-sized villa in the town of Sainte-Maxime. With 180m² of living space, this four-bedroom residence offers two reception rooms a swimming pool and well-maintained gardens of 1,200m².
533,500 euros   **MPS**
(£333,435) S

(13)
A traditional cottage with a rustic feel set in 5,630m² of woodland gardens featuring a swimming pool and pool house. This oozes old world charm, yet benefits from air conditioning.
678,001 euros   **MER**
(£423,750) GP

(83)
Near the village of Le Thoronet, this villa is in good condition and offers four bedrooms, a 40m² living room, fitted kitchen, two bathrooms and a double garage. Stands in a garden with a pool.
296,999 euros   **MPS**
(£185,625) S

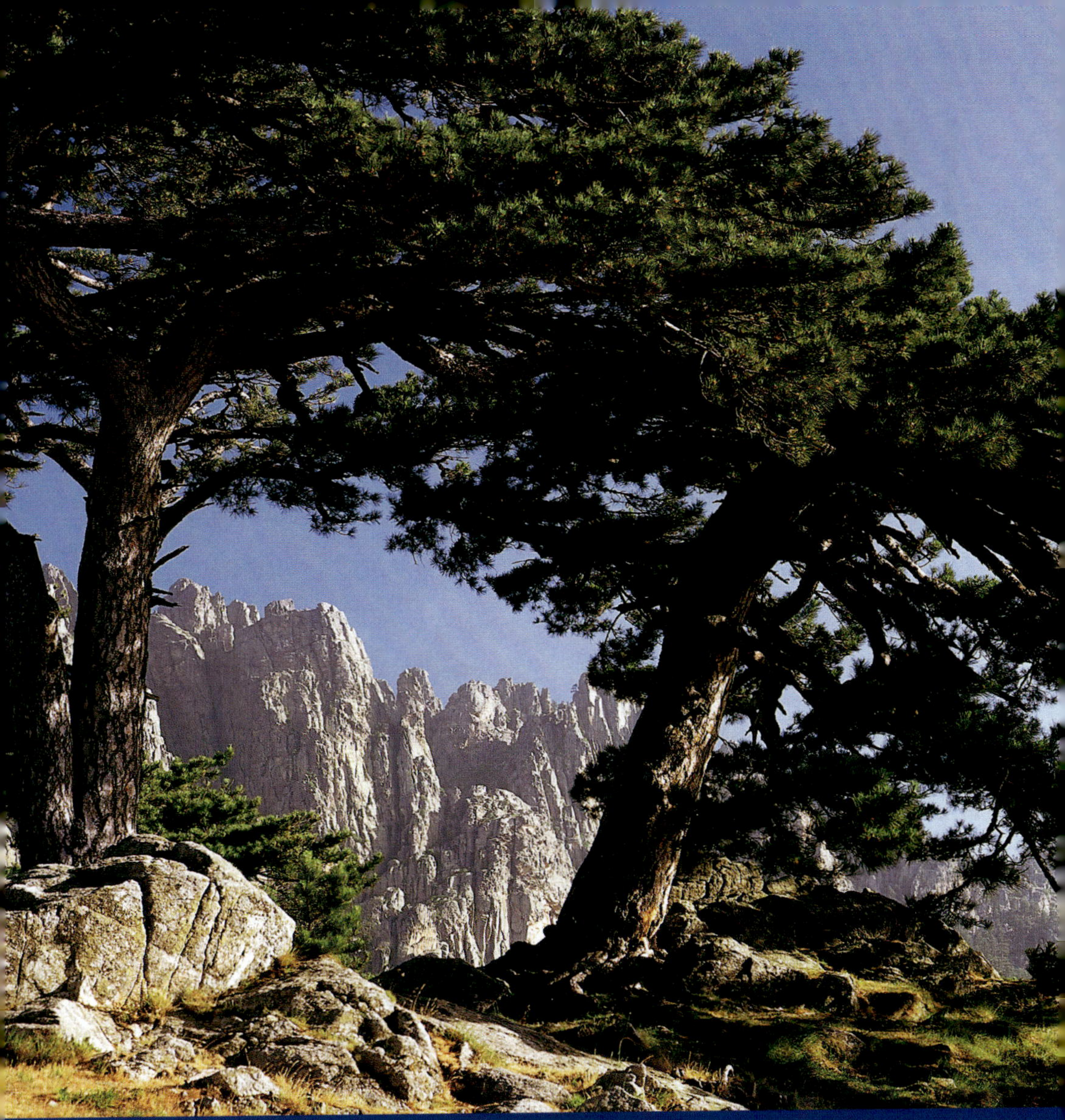

SIMPLY Corsica

The least discovered, most dramatic island in the Mediterranean, Corsica has gorgeous beaches, spectacular mountains and a dash of French sophistication. Our expert knowledge of Corsica has enabled us to put together what we believe to be the best range of accommodation on the island. We offer simple seaside cottages, family-run auberges in the mountains, romantic hideaways in country villages, villas with private pools, world-class hotels, childcare facilities, a watersports centre and a 'Wandering' programme for the more adventurous traveller.

For further information call:
020 8541 2205
or email: corsica@simply-travel.com

BONIFACIO • VALINCO GULF • CARGESE
CALVI & THE BALAGNE • ST FLORENT & CAP CORSE
GULF OF PORTO • PORTO VECCHIO • AJACCIO

HAND-PICKED PROPERTIES...OFF THE BEATEN TRACK

Price Guide

INDEX OF AGENTS

Key to the three-letter codes identifying the agents based both in Britain and France whose properties are featured in the Price Guide

Index of Agents

CODE	NAME & ADDRESS	CONTACT DETAILS
AAA	**Alpine Apartments Agency** Hinton Manor, Eardisland Herefordshire HR6 9BG	Tel: 01544 388234
ACM	**Activimmo** 22 rue de Paris 89200 Avallon, France	Tel: +33 3 86 34 03 44
ACT	**Action Habitat** Le Faubourg 12270 Nagac, France	Tel: +33 5 65 29 74 74
ADL	**Agence des Lacs** 44 rue de l'Ecole Militaire 10500 Brienne le Château France	Tel: +33 3 25 92 63 78
AHF	**A Home in France** The Old Anchor Moat Lane Wingrave Buckinghamshire HP22 4PQ	Tel: 01296 688727
AIB	**Agence IB** 5 rue de Logelbach 75017 Paris, France	Tel: +33 1 42 97 13 06
AIM	**Aims International** Le Bourdonne 53640 Le Horps, France	Tel: +33 2 43 04 26 99
ALI	**Alésia Immobilier** 1 ter rue Léon Bourgeois 51000 Châlons-en-Champagne France	Tel: +33 3 26 68 40 40
ALZ	**Allez Français** La Moinerie 79500 Paizay Le Tort, France	Tel: +33 5 49 27 01 22
AMP	**AMP Loire Immobilier** 43 rue du Vieux Pont 49290 Chalonnes sur Loire France	Tel: +33 2 41 74 13 23
AND	**Andrew Bishop French Properties** 36 rue de la République 33220 Ste Foy la Grande France	Tel: +33 5 57 46 51 29
APN	**Agence Pierre Morin** 2 cours National 17100 Saintes, France	Tel: +33 5 46 98 98 98
APP	**Alpine Property** South Cottage 31 Gloucester Street London WC1N 3AS	Tel: 0161 427 0052

Price Guide

CODE	NAME & ADDRESS	CONTACT DETAILS
APY	**Appy Immobilier** 14 rue Verdun 11000 Carcassonne France	Tel: +33 4 68 25 19 76
ARM	**ARM Immobilier** 1 rue Saulpic 94300 Vincennes, France	Tel: +33 1 43 74 86 86
ASB	**Agence Serge Bastien** Rue des Bains 01220 Divonne les Bains France	Tel: +33 4 50 20 72 61
AUV	**Residences 2 Auvergne**	Tel: +33 4 70 41 33 22 www.residences2.com
AZF	**Azur France** 21 bd Gambetta 06000 Nice, France	Tel: +33 4 93 86 86 58
BIS	**Bishop and Co** Cathedral Quarters 2-3 Queen Street Derby DE1 3DL	Tel: 01332 747474
BPS	**Burgundy Property Specialists** Les Roches 21320 Mont St Jean France	Tel: +33 3 80 84 35 21
BUR	**Burgundy 4 U** 75 rue Reulet 71510 Saint-Leger-Sur-Dheune France	Tel: +33 3 85 98 96 24
CAB	**Cabinet International** Place de la Halle 82120 Lavit, France	Tel: +33 5 63 94 09 44
CAC	**Coast and Country** 71 av de Tournamy 06250 Mougins, France	Tel: +33 4 92 92 47 50
CAT	**Cathers and Castles** Le Caussigne 11230 Rivel, France	Tel: +33 4 68 69 35 61
CHA	**Charente Homes** 4 Grand Rue 16350 Champagne-Mouton France	Tel: +33 5 45 89 12 09
CHS	**Charles Loftie Immobilier** place Hugues Salel 46250 Carzals, France	Tel: +33 5 65 22 83 50
CUR	**Currie French Properties** 2 Fulbrook Road Cambridge CB3 9EE	Tel: 01223 576084

Index of Agents

CODE	NAME & ADDRESS	CONTACT DETAILS
DAV	**David King Associates** 76 Gosberton Road London SW12 8LQ	Tel: 0702 094 0020
DEE	**Demeures de France** 41 rue Baralut 75013 Paris, France	Tel: +33 1 44 17 95 40
DEL	**Delamarche Immobilier** 17 av de Saint-Martin Saint-Martin-de-Brehal 50290 Brehal, France	Tel: +33 2 33 91 40 41
EDE	**Eden Immo** 28 rue Victor Hugo 49150 Bauge, France	Tel: +33 2 41 89 16 94
EJC	**EJC French Property** Les Oliviers 330 Chemin de Repenti 83550 Vidauban, France	Tel: +33 4 94 99 72 00
EQU	**Equinoxe Immobilier** 6 rue Gambetta 24000 Périgueux, France	Tel: +33 5 53 08 40 69
FDC	**French Discoveries Brittany** Moulin de Kerfelix 22390 Pont Melvez, France	Tel: 0871 717 4163
FDC	**French Discoveries Charente** 11 rue de la Gare 16260 Chasseneuil, France	Tel: 0871 717 4164
FDC	**French Discoveries Normandy** Le Vieux Moulin 35420 Le Ferre, France	Tel: 0871 717 4162
FEE	**French Enterprises**	Tel: 020 7531 1214
FFF	**First for French Property** 69 Wealden Way Haywards Heath West Sussex RH16 4DD	Tel: 01444 451250
FPL	**French Property Links** 45 bis rue St Malo 22100 Dinan, France	www.frenchpropertylinks.com
FPP	**French Property Shop** The Clergyhouse Churchyard, Ashford Kent TN23 1QG	Tel: 01233 666902
FPS	**French Property Services** 34 Cambridge Road Hastings TN34 1OT	Tel: 01424 428966

Price Guide

CODE	NAME & ADDRESS	CONTACT DETAILS
FRA	Francophiles Barker Chambers, Barker Road Maidstone, Kent ME16 8SF	Tel: 01622 688165
FRE	FRE Council Patrimoine 52 bd Victor Hugo 06000 Nice, France	Tel: +33 4 97 03 03 33
FWY	French Ways Les Grandes Masures 35420 Monthault, France	Tel: +33 2 99 98 06 89
GAS	Purslow's Gascony Saint-Maur 32300 Mirande, France	Tel: +33 5 62 67 61 50
HAM	Hamilton Estate Agents 2 Burges Close, Thorpe Bay Essex SS1 3JW	Tel: 01702 294691
HAN	Agence Hamilton 30 rue Armagnac 11000 Carcassonne, France	Tel: +33 4 68 72 48 38
HAP	Hamptons International European Department 168 Brompton Road Knightsbridge London SW3 1HW	Tel: 020 7589 8844
HAR	Harrison Stone PO Box 41, Petworth West Sussex GU28 OYZ	Tel: 01798 342776
HEX	Hexagone France Ltd Webster House 24 Jesmond Street Folkestone, Kent CT19 5QW	Tel: 01303 221077
HIF	Homes in Real France 3 Delgany Villas Plymouth, Devon PL6 8AG	Tel: 01752 771777
HOM	Home Finder France 23 place du Marché 23300 La Souterraine France	Tel: +33 5 55 63 59 41
ITT	Initiative Immobilier 34 rue Blomet 75015 Paris, France	Tel: +33 8 10 33 10 33
JBF	JBF French Houses 12 The Friary, Friary Close Selsey, Portsmouth PO5 2LS	Tel: 023 9229 7441
JOS	Josselin Immobilier 19 rue Olivier de Clisson 56120 Josselin, France	Tel: +33 2 97 75 64 78

Index of Agents

CODE	NAME & ADDRESS	CONTACT DETAILS
KLS	Kl'os Immobilier 8a rue Poincare 67240 Bischwiller, France	Tel: +33 3 88 06 26 26
LAC	La Foncière Charentaise 14 bis Grand Rue 16140 Aigre, France	Tel: +33 5 45 21 78 38
LAF	L'Affaire Française 25 Grand Rue 16200 Jarnac, France	Tel: +33 5 45 81 76 79
LAR	La Residence 17 St Martin's Street Wallingford Oxford OX10 OEA	Tel: 01491 838485
LAT	Latitudes 1 High Street, Edgware Middlesex HA8 7TA	Tel: 020 8951 5155
LEB	Le Bonheur My French Property Quartier Cutorte, Lareule 65700 Maubourguet, France	Tel: +33 5 62 96 94 27
LEG	Leggett Immobilier 8 rue Réabrac 24340 La Rochebeaucourt France	Tel: +33 5 53 56 62 54
LIN	Links Property Services Collingwood Business Centre Lower Harding Street Northampton NN1 2JL	Tel: 01604 519412
LPS	Loire Property Services Cabinet Lenfantin 12 place Bilange BP176 49414 Saumur Cedex, France	Tel: +33 2 41 40 50 00
LRP	LRP Associates Ltd Le Champ Vert 36200 Ceaulmont France	Tel: +33 2 54 25 35 60
LUN	Agence L'Union 19 place de la Halle 82140 St-Antonin-Noble-Val France	Tel: +33 5 63 30 60 24
LVL	Loire Vacances Ltd 100 av de Basclos 37600 Loches, France	Tel: +33 2 47 91 91 62
MAG	Magic View Le Beauvallon 107 av du Petit Juas 06400 Cannes, France	Tel: +33 4 92 98 00 99

Price Guide

CODE	NAME & ADDRESS	CONTACT DETAILS
MAI	**Maisons Vacances** 1265 Montee d'Avignon 13090 Aix en Provence France	Tel: +33 4 42 23 82 38
MAM	**M & M International** 14 rue Andre Giannesini 79270 Frontenay France	Tel: +33 5 49 04 37 35
MAO	**Magimmo Groupe Immobilier** 29 place de la Liberté 39600 Arbois France	Tel: +33 3 81 39 99 99
MAQ	**Marquine Immobilier** 36 bd Courtais 03100 Montluçon France	Tel: +33 4 70 09 94 57
MAR	**Marcus House** Hameaux les Alliers 26160 Avignon France	Tel: +33 4 75 46 28 74
MDF	**Maisons de France**	www.maisons-france.com
MED	**La Meridienne Internationale** 7 place de la Halle Darde 34700 Lodève France	Tel: +33 4 67 44 33 81
MER	**Groupe Mercure** 9 place Wilson 31000 Toulouse France	Tel: +33 5 61 21 52 01
MII	**Midi-Maisons** 8 av de la Gare 34310 Capestang France	Tel: +33 4 67 93 43 20
MNI	**Maison Individuelle** 27 Hyde Way Welwyn Garden City Herts AL7 3UQ	Tel: 01707 376255
MOD	**Mondounet Homes** Mondounet Leisure 46800 Fargues France	Tel: +33 5 65 36 96 32
MOR	**Moret Real Estate** 17 rue Thiers 90000 Belfort France	Tel: +33 3 84 28 18 73

Index of Agents

CODE	NAME & ADDRESS	CONTACT DETAILS
MPS	**Mediterranean Property Search** 1 Copplestone Road Budleigh Salterton Devon EX9 6DS	Tel: 01395 442689
MSE	**Maisons Secondaires** 96 Westernlea Crediton Devon EX17 3JE	Tel: 01363 774825
NON	**No Nonsense French Property** 158 Hatch Road Pilgrims Hatch, Brentwood London CM15 9QB	Tel: 01277 374306
OPM	**Open Media** Cloitre immobilier 2046 RN6 73490 Chambéry la Ravoire France	Tel: +33 4 79 71 13 70
PAP	**Papillon Properties** Les Broux 86400 St-Gaudent France	Tel: +33 5 49 87 45 47
POD	**Properties of Distinction** PO Box 10216 Birmingham B38 8XR	Tel: 0121 458 1325
PPC	**Conseil Patrimoine** 105 bd Haussmann 75008 Paris, France	Tel: +33 1 42 66 00 88
PRP	**Propriétés Roussillon** 29 Aversely Road King's Norton Birmingham B38 8PD	Tel: 0121 459 9058
PRV	**Private Properties Abroad** South Hill, Whixley York Y026 8AT	Tel: 01423 323139
PSF	**Property Services France** Saint-Nicolas-des-Bois France	Tel: +33 6 21 39 61 22 www.propertyservicesfrance.com
PYI	**Py Immobilier** 12 av de la République 70200 Lurie France	Tel: +33 3 84 30 06 07
RAV	**Agence Paré** 66-68 rue de Paris 62520 Le Touquet France	Tel: +33 3 21 05 13 13

Price Guide

CODE	NAME & ADDRESS	CONTACT DETAILS
REY	**Reynaud Immobilier** 7 bd Gambetta 34800 Clermont l'Herault France	Tel: +33 4 67 96 08 92
SAS	**Snow & Sea**	Tel: 020 7494 0706 www.snowandsea.com
SEL	**Select Properties** Park Cottage, Lower Hartwell Aylesbury Bucks HP17 8NR	Tel: 01296 747045
SHE	**Select Home**	Tel: 0709 201 5299
SIF	**Sifex** 1 Doneraile Street London SW6 6EL	Tel: 020 7384 1200
SIG	**Sirguey Immobilier** rue du Château 68640 Waldingheffen France	Tel: +33 3 89 07 77 17
SIM	**Simmonds** PO Box 1737, Fordingbridge Hants SP6 3QN	Tel: 01425 653355
SIN	**Sinclair Overseas** The Business Centre PO Box 492 Leighton Buzzard Bedfordshire LU7 2WG	Tel: 01525 375319
SLP	**South Loire Property Search** La Gouarie Bossay Sur Crase 37290 Indre, France	Tel: +33 2 47 94 44 20
SOV	**Sovimmo** 22 rue Emile Roux 16500 Confolens, France	Tel: +33 5 45 85 45 65
SUC	**Success Immobilier** 28 rue d'Hesdin 62130 Saint-Pol-sur-Ternoise France	Tel: +33 3 21 04 58 46
SUC	**Success Immobilier** 32 rue Hamelin 14130 Pont l'Evêque France	Tel: +33 2 31 48 16 31
SUC	**Success Immobilier** Route du Buais 50140 Notre-Dame-du-Touchet France	Tel: +33 2 33 49 83 20

Index of Agents

CODE	NAME & ADDRESS	CONTACT DETAILS
UNI	Agence L'Union 19 place de La Halle 82140 Saint-Antonin France	Tel: +33 5 63 30 60 24
VAL	Agence Vallé Des Rois 23 rue de L'hôtel de Ville 49250 Beaufort-en-Vallée France	Tel: +33 2 41 34 22 22
VAN	Van den Berg Priezac 19130 Saint-Solve France	Tel: +33 5 55 25 28 00
VEF	VEF 4 Raleigh House, Admirals Way London E14 9SN	Tel: 020 7515 8660
VIA	Vialex International rue Messager 47470 Beauville France	Tel: +33 5 53 95 46 24
VIC	Vic Le Comte Immobilier 54 bd du Jeu de Paume 63270 Vic-le-Comte, France	Tel: +33 4 73 69 00 66
VOL	Agence Immobiliere Voillequin 10 rue Jean Roussat 52200 Langes, France	Tel: +33 3 25 87 05 28
WAT	Waterside Properties Int 2 Richmond Terrace Shernford Park, Frant Tunbridge Wells TN3 9DL	Tel: 01892 750011

TO ENSURE THAT YOUR AGENCY APPEARS IN THE 2004 GUIDE, EMAIL:
m.guides@merricksmedia.co.uk

DIRECTORY

Listings of businesses offering services to both the buyers and owners of property in France

Accountants	370
Architects	370
Banks and Financial Advisers	370
Builders and Decorators	372
Building Supplies	373
Car Hire	373
Carpenters	374
Currency Exchange	374
Electricians	374
Exhibitions and Seminars	374
House Inspection, Gardening and Cleaners	374
Insurance	374
Interior Design	375
Kitchen Supplies	376
Language Services	376
Letting Specialists	377
Plumbing and Heating	378
Property Search	378
Removals and Haulage	378
Solicitors and Legal Advisers	380
Surveyors	381
Swimming Pools	381
Television	382
Travel	382
Web Hosting	383

Directory

ACCOUNTANTS

**A E A Antipolis
Experts Associes**
(French equivalent to
Chartered Accountant)
29 avenue Robert Soleau
06600 Antibes
Tel: +33 4 92 90 61 61

Anthony and Company
Vilantipolis 11
473 route des Dolines
06560 Valbonne
Tel: +33 4 93 65 32 23

Arthur D Little France
50 avenue Théophile
75017 Paris
Tel: +33 1 55 74 29 00

**Blevins Franks
Group Limited**
Barbican House
26-34 Old Street
London EC1V 9QQ
Tel: 020 7336 1000

Coopers & Lybrand
32 rue Guersant
75017 Paris
Tel: +33 1 56 57 56 57

Ernst & Young
Tour Ernst & Young
11 allée de l'Arche
92037 Paris la Défense
Cedex
Tel: +33 1 46 93 60 00

Factofrance Heller
Tour Facto
18 rue Hoche
92988 Paris
Tel: +33 1 46 35 70 00

Inter Audit
21 bis rue Lord Byron
75008 Paris
Tel: +33 1 43 59 58 73

PKF (Guernsey) Limited
Sarnia House
Le Truchot
St Peter Port
Guernsey
GY1 4NA
Tel: 01481 727927

Price Waterhouse
Tour AIG
34 place des Corolles
92908 Paris la Défense
Cedex
Tel: +33 1 56 57 58 59

French Tax Services

PKF (Guernsey) Limited has developed a substantial practice advising foreigners on the tax and related implications of connections with France, whether they be non-French residents with property interests in France or people wishing to move there on a permanent basis.

The company's range of tax services includes pre-and-post immigration planning, tax compliance services and estate planning. PKF also publish two highly relevant French tax guides, 'Taxation in France' and 'Letting French Property Successfully'.

For further information about our services or publications, please contact: Kate Brehaut, Virginie Deflassieux or Charles Parkinson.

PKF (Guernsey) Limited
Chartered Accountants
Sarnia House, Le Truchot, St. Peter Port, Guernsey GY1 4NA
Telephone: 01481 727927   Facsimile: 01481 710511
E-mail: french.tax@pkfguernsey.com
Internet: www.pkfguernsey.com

Accountancy and Audit • Trustee Services
Taxation • Company Administration
Management Consultancy • Corporate Finance • Estate Planning

ARCHITECTS

A4 Architects
64 Cours le Rouzic
33100 Bordeaux
Tel: +33 5 56 32 33 66

Adrian Barrett
(Design and Construction
Consultant)
Lower Road, Churchfields
Salisbury SP2 7PN
Tel: 01722 333583

Cedric Mitchell
Bomble Hall
Fesy Lare
Pembroke SA7 14RG
Tel: 01646 681361

David Martyn Architects
rue des Martyrs
24210 La Bachellerie
Tel: +33 5 53 50 57 82

Graham Price
23 bld de l'Ernée
53500 Ernée
Tel: +33 2 43 05 40 06

Iain Stewart
8 rue Pailleron
69004 Lyon
Tel: +33 4 78 30 01 92

James Matthews
71 Hornsey Lane Gardens
London N6 5PA
Tel: 020 8347 5970

Louis Sorridente
808 roue de la Colle
06570 Saint Paul de Vence
Tel: +33 4 93 32 58 26

Pierre M Weingaertner
Le Mas des Couestes
Route de St Canadet
13100 Aix en Provence
Tel: +33 6 60 55 29 74

PSI Sarl
(Chartered Building
Surveyor)
Mas Agora
Place Jules Ferry
84440 Robion
Tel: +33 4 90 76 58 09

Robert Lyell Architects
4 Allée des Maronniers
11300 Limoux
Tel: +33 4 68 31 25 66

BANKS & FINANCIAL ADVISERS

Abbey National
Les Arcades de Flandre
70 rue Saint Sauveur
59046 Lille
Tel: +33 3 20 18 18 18

Anthony & Company
(Overseas Tax Advisers)
7 Villantipolis
473 route des Dolines
06560 Valbonne
Tel: +33 4 93 65 42 45

AXA Mutuelles Unis
William Gérard
5 avenue Tournelli
06600 Antibes
Tel: +33 4 93 34 64 10

Banque Scalbert Dupont
9 rue Royale BP 179
62100 Calais
Tel: +33 3 21 19 11 77

**Barclays France
Champs Elysees**
6 Rond Point des
Champs Elysees
75008 Paris
Tel: +33 1 44 95 13 80

Britline Credit Agricole
15 esplanade Brillaud de
Lujardière
14050 Caen Cedex
Tel: +33 2 31 55 67 89

Charles Hamer
87 Park Street
Thame
Oxfordshire OX9 3HX
Tel: 01844 218 956

Conti Financial Services
(Overseas Mortgage Advisers)
204 Church Road
Hove, Sussex BN3 2DJ
Tel: 01273 772811

**Dun & Bradstreet
International**
345 avenue Georges
Clemenceau
92882 Paris Cedex 9
Tel: +33 141 35 17 00

Eurogroupe
Tour Framatome
92084 Paris la Défence
Cedex
Tel: +33 1 47 96 63 90

www.adrian-barrett.co.uk

**ARCHITECTURE
PROJECT MANAGEMENT**

UK & FRANCE

00 44 (0)17 22 33 35 83

ARCHITECTES
ASSOCIES

Francois CATILLON
Joel   MAESTRO

64 Cours le Rouzic
33100   BORDEAUX

Tel: 00 33 5 56 32 33 66
Fax: 00 33 5 56 40 54 23

Email: a4architectes.fc@wanadoo.fr

Local Professionals

Businesses

Private Individuals

Chateaux

Castles

Renovation

Interior Design

Vast Experience

www.architect.fr
Bilingual services from survey to site direction

Iain Stewart, Architect
8 rue Pailleron, 69004 LYON, France
Tel/Fax: 00 33 4 78 30 01 92
istewart@club-internet.fr

ROBERT
LYELL
ARCHITECTS

- British and French registered, bilingual resident,
- Practising in the Languedoc Roussillon and Midi-Pyrenees,
- Renovation, new build, garden and landscape design,
- Pre-purchase evaluation.

robert.lyell@libertysurf.fr

Tel/Fax : +33 (0)4 68 31 25 66

Directory

Fralex
4 Wimpole Street
London W1G 9SH
Tel: 020 7323 0103

French Mortgage Connection
(French Legal Advisers)
20 Park Road
Fordingbridge
Hampshire SP6 1EQ
Tel: 0800 0745388

HSBC
The Telephone Exchange
5 North Crescent
Chenies St
London WC1E 7PH
Tel: 020 7446 0555

John Siddall International
(Financial/Investment Advice)
Parc Innolin, 3 rue du Golf
33700 Bordeaux-Merignac
Tel: +33 5 56 34 75 51

Kevin Sewell Mortgages
(Investments/Mortgages)
37a Market Place
Devizes
Wiltshire SN10 1JP
Tel: 01380 739198

MFS Partners
(Independent Financial Advisers)
47 Alma Road
Plymouth
Devon PL3 4HE
Tel: 01752 664777

PCS
(Mortgage & Financial Advice)
21b Wellsway
Bath BA2 4RR
Tel: 01225 484846

Porter & Reeves
5 rue Cambon
75001 Paris
Tel: +33 1 42 61 55 77

Simone Paissoni
22 avenue Notre Dame
06000 Nice
Tel: +33 4 93 62 94 95

Templeton Associates
(Mortgage Brokers)
9 Rivers Street Place
Julian Road
Bath
BA1 2RS
Tel: 01225 422282

BUILDERS & DECORATORS

A Neal
Ombrabols
12700 Capdenac Gare
Tel: +33 5 65 64 81 54

Brittany Renovations
(Renovation, Heating, Construction, Decorating)
4 Langedraou
22580 Plouha
Tel: +33 2 96 20 38 11

Central Construction
115 City Road
Norwich
NR1 2HL
Tel: 01603 762804

D Cheeseman
Rouffignac
46600 Montvalent
Tel: +33 5 65 32 56 11

Entreprise Murray
(Renovations)
175 avenue Doménille
75012 Paris
Tel: +33 1 43 44 34 47

Espace Immobilier
15 bld de La Liberté
BP 51 34701 Lodève Cedex
Tel: +33 4 67 96 42 32

Federation of Overseas Property
(Developers' Agents and Consultants)
95 Aldwych
London WC2B 4JF
Tel: 020 8941 558

French Property Select
(Building Repairs: Roofs, Plumbing, Electrical)
Le Pont Caillou
61700 Rouelle-Orne
Tel: +33 2 33 38 11 90

Gedimat
Brunel Freres
ZA La Petrole
127 rue Curie BP116
34400 Lunel
Tel: +33 4 67 71 16 22

Home in South France
11170 Saint Martin La Trile
Le Champ des Oiseaux
09500 Sainte Foi
Tel: +33 4 68 76 01 15

 TEMPLETON ASSOCIATES

• FRENCH PROPERTY FINANCE •

Specialist Mortgage Brokers For France
Offices in France and the UK

MORTGAGES
RE-MORTGAGES

• COMPETITIVE RATES TO SUIT YOU
• LOANS FOR RENOVATION/CONSTRUCTION
• RE-MORTGAGES, EQUITY RELEASE
• INTEREST-ONLY MORTGAGES
• PROFESSIONAL, PERSONAL SERVICE

TEL: **01225 422282**

FAX: **01225 422287**

TEL/FAX: **0033 5 58417433**

Web: **www.templeton-france.com**
Email: **info@templeton-france.com**

PLEASE NOTE: Your home is at risk if you do not keep up repayments on a mortgage or other loan secured on it.
Where a loan is arranged in a foreign currency, the altering equivalent of your liability may be increased by exchange rate movements.

NE BRITTANY

• Renovation
• New build
• Drawings
• Planning permission

The Complete Building Service

 Léhon, Dinan
MIKE WELBY

Tel: **00 33 2 96 87 57 37**
Fax: **00 33 2 96 87 57 36**

Directory

C Hibbert
Quelvehen
6300 Kergrist
Tel: +33 2 97 39 64 34

John Arbuckle
(Solent Services Limited)
2 Sycamore Road
Hordle
Lymington
Hampshire SO41 OYF
Tel: 01425 621036

John Rainforth
Les Puits Neufs
84300 Cavaillon
Tel: +33 4 90 76 28 01

Keith Beaseley & Associates
Les Moellons
Rue des Noyers
La Bonniere
17250 Geay
Tel: +33 5 46 95 37 02

La Foncière Charentaise Sarl
29 avenue Gambetta
16000 Angoulème
Tel: +33 5 45 95 74 10

Le Sabot Bleu
Place de la République
11260 Esperanza
Tel: +33 4 68 74 23 60

Magon Home Improvements
Interior Decoration and Renovation Work
12 rue Corneille
78220 Viroflay
Tel: +33 1 30 24 71 48

Millfield Renovation Company
PO Box 2 Grantham
Lincolnshire NG32 3BF
Tel: 01400 272106

N F Construction
Villeperdue
50170 Sacey
Tel: +33 2 33 68 17 87

Poitou Charentes Building Services
Septic Tanks, General Building, Sandblasting, Electrics
1 rue de Moulin
17470 Contré
Tel: +33 5 46 33 32 04

Radford Consultants
149 Avenue Victor Hugo
75116 Paris
Tel: +33 1 47 55 77 20

Sam Mooney
11220 Riex Enval
Tel: +33 4 68 24 02 94

Societe Cevenole de Travaux Publics
(Ground Works)
Cartels
34700 le Bosc
Tel: +33 4 67 44 13 18

Welby
La Bénardais
22100 Léhon
Tel: +33 2 96 87 57 37

BUILDING SUPPLIES

Brico Lots
Le Jonco
16400 La Couronne
Tel: +33 5 45 67 42 84

CICO Chimney Linings
Freepost Westleton
Saxmundham
Suffolk 1P17 3EF
Tel: 01728 648608

Price Graham
(Roofing)
23 Bld Emée
53560 Emée
Tel: +33 2 43 05 40 06

Solent Services Ltd
2 Sycamore Road, Hordle
Lymington
Hampshire SO41 OYF
Tel: 01425 621036

CAR HIRE

Alamo
Brassmill Lane
Bath
BA1 3JE
Tel: 0870 599 3000

Autos Abroad
11 Archer Street
London
W1D 7B7
Tel: 0870 066 7788

Avis
88 Eversholt
St Euston
London NW1 1BP
Tel: 020 8268 5525

Car Hire Ware House
11 Snowbell Road
Kingsnorth
Ashford
Kent TN23 3NF
Tel: 01233 500464

Easy Autos
PO Box 4795
Earley
Berkshire RG10 9GW
Tel: 0870 054 0200

Eurodrive Car Rental
Drove Road
Weston-Super-Mare
Bristol BS23 3NX
Tel: 0870 160 9060

Europcar UK Ltd
Europcar House
Aldenham Road
Bushey
Watford WD23 2QQ
Tel: 01923 811000

Hertz Car Hire
23 Broadwater Road
Welwyn Garden City
Hertfordshire
AL7 3BQ
Tel: 01707 331433

Holiday Autos House
Pembroke Broadway
Camberley
Surrey GU15 3XD
Tel: 0870 400 0056

Holiday Wheels
Thrifty Car Rental
Head Office
The Old Courthouse
Hughenden Road
High Wycombe
Bucks
HP13 5DT
Tel: 01494 751515

Nova Rent-a-Car
1 Castle Street
Portaferry
BT22 1NZ
Tel: 028 4272 8189

Regent Car Rental
Tel: 01293 511222
Fax: 01293 511333
res@regent-rent.demon.co.uk

Skycars International
41-43 Green Lane
Northwood
Middlesex HA6 3A
Tel: 0870 789 7789

10513

Solent Services Ltd

2 Sycamore Road, Hordle, Lymington, Hampshire, England SO41 0YF

ROOFING CONTRACTORS

New roofing & renovation work, including associated building work, guttering etc., carried out throughout Northern and Mid France.

Tiling and slating craftsmen from the UK South Coast guarantee a reliable & prompt service with top-quality workmanship.

For more information about our range of services or for a quote, contact:

John Arbuckle
Tel: 01425 621036   Mobile: 07866 672048
Fax: 01425 621036
Email: solentservices.com

Directory

The Car Hire Group
Corby Gate Business Park
2 Perth House
Priors Haw Road
Corby
Northamptonshire N17 5JG
Tel: 0870 758 9945

CARPENTERS

Robin Pacey
Leur Vras
2 Heut Pennar Guer
29620 Guimaec
Tel: +33 2 98 67 67 50

Stuart Cook
Valley House
Burne
Bickington
Devon
TQ12 6PA
Tel: 01626 824749

CURRENCY EXCHANGE

Britline
15 esplanade Brillaud
de Laujardière
14050 Caen
Cedex
Tel: +33 2 31 55 67 89

Currencies4Less
Bakery Place
Altenburg Gardens
London
SW11 1JQ
Tel: 020 7228 7667

Currency UK
2 Draycott Court
Westbridge Road
London SW11 3NW
Tel: 020 7738 0777

Exchange Direct Plc
162-168 Regent Street
London W1R 5TB
Tel: 020 7878 1878

Halewood International Foreign Exchange
13 The High Street
Mistress Pages House
Windsor
Berkshire SL4 1LD
Tel: 01753 859159

MoneyCorp
2 Sloane Street
Knightsbridge
London SW1X 9LA
Tel: 020 7235 4200

ELECTRICIANS

Solent Services Ltd
2 Sycamore Road
Hordle, Lymington
Hampshire SO41 OYF
Tel: 01425 621036

Tom Wells
16380 Charras
Tel: +33 5 45 23 05 09

EXHIBITIONS & SEMINARS

Buying Your Dream Home in France
(Workshops/Seminars in the South West)
20 High Street, Honiton
Devon EX14 1PU
Tel: 01404 47830
www.homebuyinginfrance.co.uk

Homes Overseas Exhibitions
(25 exhibitions each year, held in the UK, Scandinavia and Ireland)
Tel: 020 7939 9888

Salon de l'Immobilier de Paris et de l'Ile-de-France
Espace Champerret
1 place Porte Champerret
75017 Paris
Tel: +33 1 43 95 16 92

World of Property
(Three exhibitions each year in the UK)
Tel: 01323 726040

Vive La France
(Annual Show)
Grand Hall, London Olympia
January 17th-19th 2003
Tel: 0870 902 0444

International Property Show
(Shows held throughout the year in London, Bristol and Manchester)
Tel: 01962 736712

HOUSE INSPECTION GARDENING & CLEANERS

Brittany Central
Moulin de Kerlautre
56160 Lignol
Tel: +33 2 97 27 02 96

Brittany Home Care Service
4 Oakfields
Walton-on-Thames
Surrey KT12 1EG
Tel: 01932 247681

Charente Caretakers
Chemin de la Perche
16170 Vaux-Rouillac
Tel: +33 5 45 96 56 41

Chevalier Conservation
(Cleaning and Restoring Carpets and Rugs)
64 bld de la Mission-Marchand
92400 Courbevoie
Tel: +33 1 47 88 41 41

Entreprise Christian Audibert
La Selle d'Andon
06750 Andon
Tel: +33 4 93 60 20 01

Le Jardin Anglais
Tel: 01985 213953

Marine Security
41 Burnley Road
Newton Abbott
Devon TQ12 1YD
Tel: 01626 365282

Valbonne Security
500 route de Nice
06560 Valbonne
Tel: +33 4 93 12 18 79

Vendée Rendez-vous
Le Vicarial
32 rue de la Venise Verte
85420 Oulmes
Tel: +33 2 51 52 49 04

INSURANCE

Agence Eaton
(Continent Assurances)
28 rue du Lieutenant Colonel Maury
BP285
56008 Vannes
Cedex
Tel: +33 2 97 47 31 97

Agençe Tredinnick
(Household, Health, Travel and Mortgage Insurance)
12 Rue Dupy
16100 Cognac
Tel: +33 5 45 82 42 93

INSURANCE

French Property & Motor Policies
English wording
Underwritten @ Lloyds

PROPERTY
Buildings & Contents
(incl. subsidence & tenants liability)

MOTOR
UK plates - Annual Green Card

The Andrew Copeland Group

Call: Maxine Duffin (property)
0208 656 8435
Call: Lisa Cairns (motor)
0208 656 2544

Directory

Andrew Copeland Group
30 Portland Rd
London SE25 4SL
Tel: 020 8656 2544

Anglo-French
Underwriters
5 rue de Liege
75008 Paris
Tel: +33 1 44 70 71 00

Assur' Titre
(London & European Title
Insurance Services Ltd)
Blagrave House
7 Blagrave Street
Reading RG1 1PW
Tel: 0118 957 5000

British Continental
and Overseas Agencies
Assurances
174 bld Saint Germain
75500 Paris
Tel: +33 1 44 39 25 00

Cabinet F X Bordes
11 rue des Desportés
BP 05
24150 Lalinde
Tel: +33 5 53 61 03 50

Chubb Insurance
Company of Europe
6 avenue Matignon
75008 Paris
Tel: +33 1 45 61 73 00

Entrepise Tredennick
2 rue Dupuis
16100 Cognac
Tel: +33 5 45 82 42 93

Eric Blair
3 Bld Princesse Charlotte
BP 265 MC
98005 Monaco Cedex
Tel: +37 7 93 50 99 66
(Monaco)

Europ Assistance
32-38 Leman Street
London E1 8EW
Tel: 020 7204 1444
(or)
1 promenade de la Bonnette
92633 Gennevilliers
Tel: +33 1 41 85 85 85

European Benefits
Administrators
9 rue de Chateaudun
75009 Paris
Tel: +33 1 42 81 97 00

Lark Insurance
(Home Insurance)
Broking Group
Wigham House
Wakering Road
Barking Essex IG11 8PJ
Tel: 020 8557 2300

Lloyds of London
4 rue des Petits Peres
75002 Paris
Tel: +33 1 42 60 43 43

Matthew Gerard TIS Ltd
(Travel Insurance)
MG House
7 Westminster Court
Old Woking
Surrey
GU22 9LQ
Tel: 01483 730900

Norwich Union France
1 rue de l'Union
92843 Rueil Malmaison
Tel: +33 1 41 39 40 23

Saga Services Ltd
(Holiday Home Insurance)
The Saga Building
Enbrook Park
Folkestone
Kent CT20 3SE
Tel: 01303 771111

Title Insurance Services
Minerva House
Valpy Street
Reading RG1 1AQ
Tel: 0118 957 5000

Tyler and Co
12 rue de la Paix
75002 Paris
Tel: +33 1 42 61 63 31

Woodham Group Ltd
Plas Kenrhos
Burry Port
Carmarthenshire
SA16 0DG
Tel: 01554 835252

INTERIOR DESIGN

Art Projet
16 bis rue Segurane
06300 Nice
Tel: +33 4 93 89 50 89

Chaix Decoration
8 rue Paul Deroulède
06000 Nice
Tel: +33 4 93 88 52 02

Darty
(TV and Hi-Fi Equipment,
Household Appliances)
129 avenue Galliéni
93140 Bondy
Tel: +33 1 48 02 32 32

Home Comforts
French Oak Furniture
Chez Deschamps
Route de Medillac
16210 Chalais
Tel: +33 5 45 98 00 97

Hestia-Domus Decoration
11 boulevard Carnot
06000 Nice
Tel: +33 4 93 56 10 43

Ikea
202 rue Henri Barbusse
78370 Plaisir
Tel: +33 8 25 07 88 25

Interior's Design
151 avenue Francis Tonner
06600 Cannes
Tel: +33 4 92 19 47 79

Jadis Carpets
14 rue des Belges
06400 Cannes
Tel: +33 4 92 98 60 16

La Chaise de Provence
1 rue Saint-Pierre
13005 Marseilles
Tel: +33 4 91 47 98 96

La Poterie Sourdive
Le village
26270 Cliousclat
Tel: +33 4 75 63 05 69

Les Toiles de Mayenne
(Interior Decoration, Fabrics)
9 rue Mézière
75001 Paris
Tel: +33 1 45 48 70 77

Loft
(Interior Designers)
25-27 rue de la Buffa
06000 Nice
Tel: +33 4 93 16 09 09

Manuel Canovas
(Interior Decoration,
Fabrics)
223 rue Saint-Honoré
75001 Paris
Tel: +33 1 58 62 33 50

Manufacture des Lauriers
Avenue de la Foux
83670 Varages
Tel: +33 4 94 77 64 79

Directory

Mondo
(The Japanese mattress specialist)
85 bld Beaumarchais
75003 Paris
Tel: +33 1 48 04 04 02

Raineri Decoration
16 rue Biscarra
06000 Nice
Tel: +33 4 93 80 27 89

Sharlyn Interiors
Saddlers House
High St, Bloxham
Oxon OX15 4LU
Tel: 01295 721666

Shogun
71 avenue des Ternes
75017 Paris
Tel: +33 1 40 68 07 61

Societe des Ocres de France
526 avenue Victor Hugo
84400 Vaucluse
Tel: +33 4 90 74 63 82

Souleiado
39 rue Proudhon
13150 Tarascon
Tel: +33 4 90 91 08 80

Taillardat
44 avenue Marceau
75008 Paris
Tel: +33 1 47 20 1712

Urbann Home Design (CINNA)
Angle 123 rue d'Antibes
06400 Cannes
Tel: +33 4 93 68 32 20

Woodstock Fires Ltd
3 Station Road
Heathfield
East Sussex
TN21 8LD
Tel: 01435 868686

KITCHEN SUPPLIES

Ceiling Racks
Dept F
GNU Ltd
The Old Bakery
Pontesbury
Shrewsbury SY5 OPY
Tel: 01743 792900

Cuisine & Cuisinier
35 chemin Puissanton
06220 Vallauris
Tel: +33 4 92 95 37 37

Free Standing Kitchen Units
Woodside Pine
Kings Fram
Maulden, Bedfordshire
Tel: 01525 402266

Godin
(Stoves & Hobs)
Sarl Bauris & Fils
764 route de Grenoble
06200 Nice
Tel: +33 4 93 08 11 08

Mr Pine
Maple Road
Bramhall
Stockport SK7 2DH
Tel: 0161 439 0055

Old Image
41 Gloucester Road
Horfield
Bristol BS7 8TZ
Tel: 0117 975 4434

Woodstock Fires Ltd
(Delivers to FR/UK)
3 Station Road
Heathfield
East Sussex TN21 8LD
Tel: 01435 868686

LANGUAGE SERVICES

Accelerated Learning Systems
50 Aylesbury Road
Aston Clinton, Aylesbury
Bucks HP22 5AH
Tel: 01296 631177

Accent Francais
7 rue de Verdun
34000 Montpellier
Tel: +33 4 67 58 12 68

Accents of America
9 rue Casimir Delavigne
75006 Paris
Tel: +33 1 44 07 05 05

Accord
14 bld Poissonnière
75009 Paris
Tel: +33 1 55 33 52 33

Actilangue
2-4 rue Alexis Mossa
06000 Nice
Tel: +33 4 93 96 33 84

Alliance Francaise
101 bd Raspail
75006 Paris
Tel: +33 1 42 84 90 00

Est. 1982

SADDLERS HOUSE, HIGH STREET, BLOXHAM, BANBURY, OXON. OX15 4LU

For quality soft furnishings supplied & fitted in the South West of France

English or French fabrics, made into curtains, blinds, bedding etc.

Interior design advice if required.

If you would like further information, please contact:

Lynne & Peter French
Tel: *01295 721666*
Fax: *01295 722156*

Email: peter@sharlyn.freeserve.co.uk

Savour Life, Stay & Study in an 18thC French Chateau

Enjoy the convivial, relaxed atmosphere and lovely setting.

Speak French at table,
Relish good French cooking & wine

French Language & Cooking

Residential, immersion courses for adults with small, highly professional classes

Intensive, Private & Very French

Situated 1 hour from Lyon, between Burgundy, Beaujolais & Auvergne

Ecole des Trois Ponts,
Chateau de Matel, 42300 Roanne

Tel(UK): **0871 717 4226**
Tel: **00 33 4 77 71 53 00**
Fax: **00 33 4 77 70 80 01**

www.3ponts.edu email: info@3ponts.edu

Directory

British Institute in Paris
9-11 rue de Constantine
75007 Paris
Tel: +33 1 44 11 73 73

Centre de Pratique de Langues Etrangeres
58 rue de l'Hopital Militaire
59800 Lille
Tel: +33 3 20 63 08 44

Clac
10 Shelford Park Avenue
Great Shelford
Cambridgeshire
Tel: 01223 240340

CFILC
7 rue Duvergier
75019 Paris
Tel: +33 1 40 05 92 42

Département des Etudiants Etrangers
Centre de Francais
Langue Etrangere
Universite Charles de Gaulle/Lille III
BP 149
59653 Villeneuve-d'Ascq
Cedex
Tel: +33 3 20 41 60 00

CPFP
25 rue de Trevise
75009 Paris
Tel: +33 1 45 23 35 68

Ecole des 3 Ponts
Château de Matel
42300 Roanne
Tel: +33 4 77 71 53 00

Ecole Yvelines Langues
2a rue Ducastel
78100 Saint Germain en Laye
Tel: +33 1 30 61 02 08

Eurotalk Limited
315-317 New Kings Road
London SW6 4RF
Tel: 020 7371 7711

French Language Courses
Alexandra and
John Waddington
16110 La Rochefoucauld
Tel: +33 5 45 63 53 07

ICT (Intermediare Consultante Traduction)
Castel Briasse
La Briasse
19310 Ayen
Tel: +33 5 55 25 21 66

ISFP-Clarife
67 bld Vauban
59800 Lille
Tel: +33 3 20 57 92 19

Janet O'Brian
La Croix Lagrise
35120 Cherrueix
Tel: +33 2 99 80 86 55

La Cardere
Petite Gravière
71580 Frontenaud
Tel: +33 3 85 74 83 11

Language in Provence
L'Oustalet
Fontaine de Guby
84490 Saint Saturnin
Tel: +33 4 90 74 23 54
or +33 4 90 75 59 63

Language Studies International
350 rue Saint Honoré
75001 Paris
Tel: +33 1 42 60 53 70

Language Wise
19a Blenheim Gardens
Wallington
Surrey SM6 9PJ
Tel: 020 8773 8794

Lutece langue
31 rue Etienne Marcel
75001 Paris
Tel: +33 1 42 36 31 51

OISE Intensive Language Schools
OISE House
Binsey Lane
Oxford
OX2 OEY
Tel: 0845 601 1157

Paris Langues
30 rue Cabanis
75014 Paris
Tel: +33 1 45 65 05 28

Promolangues
8 rue Blanche
75009 Paris
Tel: +33 1 42 85 19 45

LETTING SPECIALISTS

French Magazine
Charlotte House
Merricks Media Ltd
12 Charlotte Street
Bath
BA1 2NE
Tel: 01225 786800

BOOK DIRECT & SAVE MONEY!

1,000s of holiday properties to choose from at:
www.holidays2france.com

Directory

French Life
Kerry House
Kerry Street
Horsforth
Leeds LS18 4AW
Tel: 0870 444 8877

Meon Villas
Meon House
College Street
Petersfield GU32 3JN
Tel: 01730 230200

Quality Villas
47 Lower Kings Road
Berkhampstead
Hertfordshire HP4 2AB
Tel: 01442 870055

Something Special
Field House
Station Approach
Harlow, Essex CM20 2EW
Tel: 020 8939 5137

Vacances en Campagne
Manor Courtyard
Bignor, Pulborough
West Sussex RH20 1QD
Tel: 01798 869461

PLUMBING & HEATING

Est Paul Gee
(Kitchens, Cookers Central Heating)
Centre Commercial
32410 Castera-Verduzan
Tel: +33 5 62 68 12 48

French Property Select
Le Pont Caillou
61700 Rouelle-Orne
Tel: +33 2 33 38 11 90

Profosse
21 Ker Laurent
RN 164
22570 Gouarec
Tel: +33 2 96 24 80 79

PROPERTY SEARCH

Brittany Properties
Tel : +33 2 96 43 09 94
e-mail: sales@
brittanyproperties.com

**Central France
Property Search**
78 Imperial Avenue
Mayland, Essex CM3 6AH
Tel: 01621 744882

**Charente-Maritime
French-Home-Service**
Tel: +33 5 46 94 48 59
Email: rsayner@
club-internet.fr

Devon International
2 Impasse de La Source
ZA Secterur Gare
13770 Venelles
Tel: +33 4 42 54 68 58

French Discoveries
Tel: +33 2 99 95 19 62

**French Haven
Property Search**
(Northern France)
Tel: +33 3 21 84 54 89

French Property Finder
61 Oxford Street
Cowes
Isle of Wight PO31 8PT
Tel: 01983 240351

**The French
Property Service**
Southgate House
Plough Road Centre
Great Bentley
CO7 8LG
Tel: 01473 439225

Homes in Real France
3 Delgany Villas
Plymouth PL6 8AG
Tel: 01752 771777

J R A
John Roberts
Tel: 01222 665677

**La Foncière
Charentaise Sarl**
14 bis Grande Rue
16140 Aigre
Tel: +33 5 45 21 78 38

Live France Group
BP18
11510 Fitou
Tel: +33 4 68 45 69 62

**London Paris
Dream Home**
Flat 19
St Gabriel's Manor
25 Cormont Road
London SE5 9RH
Tel: 020 7820 1337

LRP Associates
Tel: +33 2 54 25 35 60

**Mediterranean
Property Search**
1 Copplestone Road
Budleigh Salterton
Devon
EX9 6DS
Tel: 01395 442589

**Mediterranean South
East Property**
21 Dartmouth Street
Westminster
London
SW1H 9BP
Tel: 020 7304 4040

Prestige Home Search
(Full mortgage service available)
Tel: +33 5 45 98 41 15

**South Loire
Property Search**
La Gouarie
37290 Bossay sur claise
Tel: +33 2 47 94 44 20

REMOVALS & HAULAGE

**Anglo French
Euro Removals**
146-148 Milton Street
Maidstone
Kent ME16 8LL
Tel: 01622 729911

Armishaws
3 Alfred's Way
Wincanton Business Park
Wincanton
Somerset BA9 9RT
Tel: 01963 34065

**Associated Moving
Services**
1 Pelham Yard
High Street
Seaford
East Sussex
BN25 1PQ
Tel: 01323 892934

Bishop's Move Group
Southern Street
Walkden, Manchester
Lancashire M28 3QN
Tel: 0845 666 3322

Bradsaw International
Units 2-3 Tilson Road
Roundthorn Industrial Estate
Manchester
M23 9PH
Tel: 0161 946 0809

---

prOfOsse

- **Septic Tanks**
- **Soil Tests**
- **Sand Filters**

Andrew Barnes

Brittany Dept: 22, 29, 35, 56

Tel: **00 33 2 96 24 80 79**
Fax: **00 33 2 96 24 84 01**
Mob: **00 33 6 08 62 95 07**
Email: **profosse@wanadoo.fr**

www.profosse.com

Directory

Brookfields
Cesncoch
Nr Welshpool
Powys
SY21 OAQ
Tel: 01938 810 649

Burk Bros
Burk Bros Trading Estate
Foxs Lane
Wolverhampton
West Midlands
WV1 1PA
Tel: 01902 714555

Callington Carriers International
Valentine Road
Callington
Cornwall
PL17 7DF
Tel: 0157 938 3210

Cotswold Carriers
Warehouse No.2
The Walk, Hook Norton Rd
Chipping Norton
Oxon
OX7 5TG
Tel: 01608 730500

David Dale Removals
Dale House
Forest Moor Road
Harrogate HG5 8LT
Tel: 01423 867788

Ede Bros
Nightless Copse, Rusper Road
Dorking, Surrey RH5 5HE
Tel: 01306 711293

Eardley's Removals and Storage
Unit 2 First Avenue
Crewe CW1 6BG
Tel: 01270 588225

Farrer & Fenwick Removals
Park House, 34 Bridge Street
Walton-upon-Thames
Surrey KT12 1AJ
Tel: 01932 253737

F & N International Removals
Unit 14, Autumn Park
Dysart Road
Grantham
Lincolnshire NG31 7DD
Tel: 01476 579210

Franklins Removals Ltd
112 Streetly Lane
Sutton Coldfield
BT4 4TB
Tel: 0121 353 7263

French Connexion
The Old Vicarage
Residential Care Home
Leigh, Sherborne
Dorset DT9 6HL
Tel: 01935 872222

Greens of Suffolk
Tomo Industrial Estate
Creeting Road
Stowmarket
Suffolk IP14 5AY
Tel: 01449 613053

H AppleYard & Sons
Denby Way
Hellaby Industrial Estate
Rotherham Yorkshire
Tel: 01709 549718

Hambleton
Capp House
96d South End
Croydon CR0 1DQ
Tel: 020 8686 1197

Henry's Table
Newnham Court Farm
Bearsted Road
Maidstone
Kent ME14 5LH
Tel: 01386 438159

Homeship ASM
(International Transport/ Removal/Shipping)
Garenor Tour D
BP 360
93616 Aulnais sous Bois
Tel: +33 1 48 65 21 61

Home to Home
UK Head Office
Units W1 & W2
Hazel Road
Southampton
SO19 7GB
Tel: 0800 783 4602

Johnson Henry & Sons
(Customs and Shipping Agent)
5 rue Jacques Kablé
75018 Paris
Tel: +33 1 46 07 94 39

Cotswold Carriers
Removals - Storage
Specialist to the Antique Trade
Moving people with care
Experienced and helpful staff

FULL OR PART LOADS TO AND FROM FRANCE, COLLECTIONS THROUGHOUT UK
FREE ESTIMATES

Warehouse No. 2, The Walk, Hook Norton Rd, Chipping Norton, Oxon OX7 5TG

Tel: **01608 730500**
Fax: **01608 730600**
www.cotswoldcarriers.co.uk

GREENS
OF EAST ANGLIA

- Removals to or from France
- Full or Part Loads
- Free Quotations
- Helpful, Friendly Advice

• Ipswich: 01473 215532 • Diss: 01379 650063
• Stowmarket: 01449 613053 • Felixstowe: 01394 670846
• Bury St. Edmunds: 01284 703811
or • Fax: 01449 770552

Head Office:
Tomo Ind. Est.
Stowmarket
IP14 5AY

email: info@greensremovals.co.uk

Directory

Kidds Services
International House
Kidd Park Cliff Road
Hornsea, Hull
East Yorkshire
HU18 1JB
Tel: 0800 252220

David Powell
The Elephant House
Deykin Avenue
Birmingham B6 7BH
Tel: 0121 326 6008

Langdon Removals Bristol
163 South Liberty Lane
Bristol
BS3 2TL
Tel: 0117 963 7404

Lawlers Removals & Storage
The Dronfield Storage Centre
Wreakes Lane
Dronfield S18 1PN
Tel: 0114 275 1020

Martell's International Removers
Queen's Road
East Grinstead RH19 1BH
Tel: 01342 321303

Metro Removals
Orion Way
Kettering
Northants N15 6NL
Tel: 01536 519450

Monarch UK & Internatonal Movers
Monach House
36 Mestbury Terrace
Upminster
Essex RM14 3LU
Tel: 0800 954 6474

The Personal Moving Service Ltd
110 Ferring Street
Ferring
West Sussex BN12 5JP
Tel: +33 2 33 35 31 80

Reflex Move
Castlegate Busines Park
Old Sarum
Sailsbury SP4 6OX
Tel: 01722 414350

Richman-Ring Ltd
Eurolink Way
Sittingbourne
Kent
ME10 3HH
Tel: 01795 427151

Simpsons of Sussex
Units 1-3 Ditchling Cemmond
Industrial Estate
Burgess Hill
Sussex BN6 8FL
Tel: 0800 027 1958

TBA
2 Strawberry Hill
Bloxham, Banbury
Oxon OX15 4NW
Tel: 01295 720902

Tooth Removals
Unit 1a, Westgate One
Avia Park
Staines Road, Bedfont
Middlesex TW14 8RS
Tel: 01784 251252

Trans Euro Worldwide Movers
2 avenue du Gros Chêne
95610 Eragny
Tel: +33 1 34 48 97 97

United Professional Movers
Chemin des Chaudronniers
94310 Orly
Tel: +33 1 48 92 34 15

White and Company
23 Invincible Road
Farnbrough GU14 7QU
Tel: 01252 541674

SOLICITORS & LEGAL ADVISERS

Bennett & Co Solicitors
Nightingale House
Brighton Road
Crawley
West Sussex RH10 6AE
TEL: 01293 449579

Blake Lapthorn
(Solicitors)
Holbrook House
14 Great Queen Street
London WC2B 5DG
Tel: 020 7430 1709

Dowsons
D52 Rectory Road
West Bridgford
Nottingham
Tel: 0115 910 0600

French Mortgage Connection
20 Park Road, Fordingbridge
Hampshire SP6 1EQ
Tel: 01425 653408

Fox Hayes
(Solicitors)
Bank House
150 Rounday Road
Leeds LS8 5LD
Tel: 0113 209 8922

John Howell & Co
(International Lawyers)
17 Maiden Lane
Covent Garden
London WC2E 7NL
Tel: 020 7420 0400

Kingsfords
(Solicitors)
5/7 Bank Street
Ashford
Kent TN23 1BZ
Tel: 01233 624545

Liliane Levasseur-Hills
69 Pullman Lane
Godalming
Surrey GU7 IYB
Tel: 01483 424303

Mortgages for Business
London Office
53-55 High Street
Sevenoaks TN13 1JF
Tel: 01732 471600

Pannone & Partners
(Solicitors)
123 Deansgate
Manchester M3 2BU
Tel: 0161 909 3000

Pretty Solicitors
Elm House
25 Elm Street
Ipswich
Suffolk IP1 2AD
Tel: 01473 384810

Riddell Croft & Co
(Solicitors)
27 St Helen's Street
Ipswich
Suffolk IP4 1HH
Tel: 01473 384870

Russell-Cooke
2 Putney Hill
London SW15 6AB
Tel: 020 8789 9111

Sean O'Connor & Co
(Bilingual Solicitors)
2 River Walk
Tonbridge
Kent TN9 1DT
Tel: 01732 365 378

LILIANE LEVASSEUR-HILLS

Is a fully qualified French Notaire, resident in the UK, who has been assisting English speaking Clients for over 10 years

Personal service is provided on:
- BUYING & SELLING FRENCH PROPERTY
- FRENCH INHERITANCE LAW
- POSTHUMOUS LEGALITIES REGARDING FRENCH ESTATE
- FRENCH SOCIETE CIVILE IMMOBILIERE
- TAXES RELATING TO FRENCH PROPERTIES

For more details, contact her office:
FRENCH LEGAL CONSULTANCY LTD.
69 PULLMAN LANE,
GODALMING, SURREY GU7 1YB
TEL/FAX: **01483 424303**

Directory

Simone Paissoni
(In France for France)
22 avenue Notre Dame
06000 Nice
Tel: +33 4 93 62 94 95

Stephen Smith Solicitors
(France Limited)
161 Cemetery Road
Ipswich IP4 2HL
Tel: 01473 437186

Taylors
The Red Brick House
28-32 Trippet Lane
Sheffield S1 4EL
Tel: 0114 276 6767

Thring Townsend
(Solicitors)
Midland Bridge
Bath BA1 2HQ
Tel: 01225 340000

Turner & Co
(Solicitors)
Beaufort House
6th Floor
94 Newhall Street
Birmingham
B3 1PB
Tel: 0121 200 1612

Trevor Bennett and Graham Hughes
39 London Road
Alderley Edge
Cheshire
SK9 7JT
Tel: 01625 586937

VEF UK Legal Services
4 Raleigh House
Admirals Way
London
E14 9SW
Tel: 020 7515 8660

SURVEYORS

AlpineSpace Ltd
BP 43
74400 Argentière
Tel: +33 4 50 54 22 81

Burrows-Hutchinson
9 rue du Parc
56160 Ploerdut
Tel: +33 2 97 39 45 53

PSI Sarl
Mas Agora
Place Jules Ferry
84440 Robion
Tel: +33 4 90 76 58 09

Didier Woznicki
Chemin de la Montagne
84110 Faucon
Tel: +33 4 90 46 46 83

Property Center
43 Old Street
Clevedon
Bristol BS21 6DA
Tel: 0870 444 2078

Le Sabot Bleu
Place de la République
11260 Esperanza
Tel: +33 4 68 74 23 60

Curchod Continental
54 Church Street
Weybridge, Surrey
Tel: 01932 823630

James Latter
(Expert Immobilier)
Couvrigny
14700 Saint Pierre du Bû
Tel: +33 2 31 90 17 70

Smith-Woolley & Perry
Chartered Surveyors
130 Sandgate Road
Folkstone CT20 2BW
Tel: 01303 226622

SWIMMING POOLS

Associated Building Properties Ltd
Le Bourg 24340 Mareuil
Tel: +33 5 53 56 68 87

Bob Bakewell
Bakewell Pools
38 Bagley Wood Road
Kennington
Oxford OX1 5LY
Tel: 01865 735205

Claire Pernod-Fantini
119 bd Sadi Carnot
06110 Le Cannet
Tel: +33 4 92 99 01 00

Clearwater Swimming Pools Ltd
The Studio
81 Langley Close
Headington
Oxford OX3 7DB
Tel: 01865 766112

Christal Pools
139 Enville Street
Stourbridge
West Midlands BY8 3TD
Tel: 01384 440990

10540

Burrows Hutchinson
SARL

 CHARTERED SURVEYORS IN FRANCE

- Pre-purchase building surveys
- Architectural and Interior Design
- Planning Consents
- Co-ordinating local builders/artisans

9 Rue du Parc
56160 Ploërdut, France
Tel: **00 33 (0)2 97 39 45 53**
E-mail: **burrowhutch@aol.com**
www.burrows-hutchinson.com

DIY SWIMMING POOL KITS

Video & Manual £30 inc. p&p & VAT
Example: 30ft x 15ft Block & Liner DIY Swimming Pool - All essential items around £3500 incl. VAT & carriage to any UK address.
All basic building materials not incl. These are purchased local to site.
Option available to buy as you build.

For more details:
J W Green Swimming Pools Ltd.
Tel: **01902 42 77 09**
Email: **info@jwgswimming.co.uk**

Directory

Home in South France
11170 Saint Martin le Vieil
Tel: +33 4 68 76 01 15

**JW Green
Swimming Pools Ltd**
Regency House
88a Great Brick Kiln Street
Grainsley
Wolverhampton WV3 OPU
Tel: 01902 427709

**London Swimming Pool
Company**
138 Replingham Road
London SW18 5LL
Tel: 020 8874 0414

**Peter Joyce
Poolstone UK Ltd**
Monks Brook House
Nutburn Road
North Baddesly
Southampton
SO52 9BG
Tel: 0845 128 4373

Piscines du Canal
Michel Roques
Route de Narbonne
34500 Béziers
Tel: +33 4 67 28 33 03

TELEVISION

Big Dish Satellite
Mouriol Milhaguet
87440 Marvel
Tel: +33 5 55 78 72 98

**Finnegar & Hellbach
GmbH**
Le Petit Fouine
16210 Curac
Tel: +33 05 45 98 25 37

French-Help
Lagarde Hachamp
32300 Mirande
Tel: +33 5 62 67 09 21

Susat UK
37 Spencer Mews
London W6 8PB
Tel: 0845 451 3133

TV5 (UK)
PO Box 846
Bristol BS99 5HR
Tel: 0117 954 9189

TV5 (France)
19 rue Cognacq-Jay
75341 Paris Cedex 07
Tel: +33 1 44 18 55 55

UBALDI
272 avenue de la Californie
06000 Nice
Tel: +33 4 93 18 80 88

TRAVEL – AIR

Air France
Terminal 2
London Heathrow Airport
Hounslow
Middlesex
TW6 1ET
Tel: 0845 0845 111

AOM French Airlines
Premiere House
3 Betts Way
Crawley
West Sussex
RH10 2GB
Tel: 01293 596663

Aurigny Air Services
Southampton International
Airport
Southampton
Hampshire
SO18 2NL
Tel: 01481 822886

British Airways
London Luton Airport
Luton
Bedfordshire LU2 9ND
Tel: 01582 424155

British European
Exeter Airport
Clyst
Honiton
Exeter
EX5 2BD
Tel: 0870 567 6676

British Midland
Cargo Building
552 Shoreham Road East
Hounslow
Middlesex TW6 3EU
Tel: 0845 240 0203

Buzz
Endeavour House
Stanstead Airport
Stansted
Essex CM24 1RS
Tel: 0870 240 7070

**EasyJet Airline
Company Ltd**
Easyland Luton Airport
London
Bedfordshire LU2 9LS
Tel: 0870 600 0000

Genie Travel
60 Lansdowne Street
Hove Sussex
Tel: 01273 770453

Lyddair
Lydd International Airport
Lydd
Kent
TN29 9QL
Tel: 01797 320000

Ryanair
Dublin Airport
County Dublin
Tel: 0871 246 0000

TRAVEL – COACH

Eurolines
52 Grosvenor Gardens
Victoria
London SW1W OAU
Tel: 0870 514 3219

TRAVEL – RAIL

Euro Tunnel
P.O. Box 2000
Cheriton Park
Folkestone, Kent CT19 4QS
Tel: 01303 288700

Eurostar
Eurostar House
Waterloo Station
12 Lower Road
London SE1 8SE
Tel: 0870 518 6186

Eurostar
3rd Floor, Kent House
81 Station Road
Ashford, Kent TN23 1AP
Tel: 0870 518 6186

Rail Europe Ltd
34 Tower View
Kings Hill
West Malling
Kent ME19 4ED
Tel: 0870 584 8848

SNCF
23 avenue de la Porte
d'Aubervilliers
75018 Paris
Tel: +33 1 53 90 20 20

TRAVEL – SEA

Brittany Ferries
Milbay Docks
Plymouth
Devon PL1 3EW
Tel: 0870 536 0360

Digiboxes & Satellite Dishes
Installation & Sales
FINNINGER & HELBACH GmbH
Fully installed in France & Germany
Le Petit Fouine, 16210 Curac
Tel/Fax: 00 33 5 45 98 25 37
Email: FinnHans@aol.com
Own Workshop
TV • VIDEO • HIFI
SAT • ELECTRIC BIKES

Directory

Condor Ferries
Condor House
New Harbour Road
South Hamworthy
Poole
Dorset BH15 4AJ
Tel: 0845 345 2000

France Canterbury
29/30 Palace Street
Canterbury
Kent CT1 2D2
Tel: 01227 454508

Ferries to France
The Courtyard
2 Woodland Park
Colwyn Bay
North Wales LL29 7DS
Tel: 0870 011 2499

Ferry Savers
International Life
Leisure Ltd
Kerry House
Kerry Street
Horsforth
Leeds
Tel: 0870 990 8492

Hoverspeed Ltd
International Hoverport
Dover
Kent
CT17 9TG
Tel: 0870 524 0241

Irish Ferries
11 rue de la Ferronnerie
75001 Paris
Tel: +33 1 44 88 54 50

Norfolkline
Redwood Park Estate
Stallingborough
North East Lincolnshire
DN41 8TH
Tel: 01469 570900

P&O Portsmouth
Peninsular House
Wharf Road
Portsmouth
Hampshire PO2 8TA
Tel: 0870 242 4999

P&O Stena Line
Channel House
Channel View Road
Dover
Kent CT17 9TJ
Tel: 01304 863000

Seafrance
Units 8-14 Honeywood Close
White Cliffs Business Park
Whitfield
Dover
Kent CT16 3PX
Tel: 01304 828300

WEB HOSTING

Financial Systems Limited
www.frenchpropertylinks.com
dfs@financialsystems.co.uk

Stickland Web Studio
www.sticklandweb.co.uk
mist@globalnet.co.uk
Tel: 01797 225807

LET YOUR PROPERTY
FROM ONLY £8 PER WEEK

Ensure that your property is fully booked for 2003 by advertising through French Magazine. With widespread, national distribution from only £425* for one year, we offer:

- Availability throughout the year in all major newsagents.
- Six new issues per year, allowing copy changes at any time.
- Free inclusion on www.holidays2france.com

french
magazine
THE NO 1 CHOICE FOR LETTING

Call now to advertise your property
01225 786840
email: sales@frenchmagazine.co.uk

*price based on a 1/6 page private advertisement for one year

INDEX TO ADVERTISERS

A4 Architects Associates	371	Herman De Graaf Immobilier	281
Action Habitat	299	Hexagone France Ltd	159
Adrian Barrett	371	Holiday Villas magazine	9
Agence Centre Croisette	343	Hoverspeed Ltd	387
Agence Immo Girma Mouly	303	Iain Stewart Architects	371
Agence L'Union	303	Immobilier St Michel	135
Agence Transimmo	197	J W Green Swimming Pools	379
Aims International	135	John Siddall Financial Services	4
Alioth Properties	113	Josselin Immobilier	113
Allez Français	197	KBM Consultancy	113
Andrew Bishop French Properties	277	La Foncière Charentaise	233
Andrew Copeland Group	374	La Meridienne Internationale	321
Aude Immo Futur	321	L'Affaire Française	233, 279
Beaches International Property	269, 341	L'Agence Bleue	341
Burgundy 4 U	217	Latitudes	194
Burgundy Property Specialists	225	Le Bonheur	303
Burrows Hutchinson	381	Le Moulin de La Mer	321
Cabinet Chaumette	171	Leggett Immobilier	235, 279
Cathers & Castles	299	Liliane Levasseur Hills	380
Charente Property Services	233	LRP Associates Ltd	197
Charles Loftie Immobilier	281, 299	Mediterranean Property Search	341
Conseil Patrimoine	171, 341	Muret Immobilier	235
Cotswold Carriers	379	Normandy La Manche Immobilier	135
DFX Interactive France	3	Pangon Immobilier	269
EasyJet	318	PKF (Guernsey) Ltd	370
Equinoxe immobilier	271	Podium Habitat	235
Era Acpi Immobilier	269	Profosse	378
Eurostar	274	Properties in France	197
Eymet Immobilier	279	Robert Lyell Architects	371
Fine Property France	233	Salut France	115
Finninger & Helbach	382	Sharlyn Interiors	376
Foncia	171	Sifex	6
French Discoveries	115, 135, 235	Simply Travel	357
French Language & Cooking	376	Solent Services Ltd	373
French Magazine	132, 179, 327, 338	Souillac Country Club	159
The French Property Shop	281	Success Immobilier	159
French Ways	110	Templeton Associates	372
George V Normandie	137	VEF	14
Grandchamp Immobilier	281	Vialex International	299
Greens Removals Of Suffolk	379	Vive La France	266
Halewood International		Waterside Properties International	277
Foreign Exchange	11	Welby	372
Harrison Stone	321	Woodstock Fires Ltd	375

Notes

Notes